# Advanced Economies
# and Emerging Markets

# Advanced Economies and Emerging Markets

## Prospects for Globalization

Marcus Goncalves, José Alves, Carlos Frota, Harry Xia, and Rajabahadur V. Arcot

**BEP** BUSINESS EXPERT PRESS

First published in 2014 by
Business Expert Press, LLC
222 East 46th Street, New York, NY 10017
www.businessexpertpress.com

ISBN-13: 978-1-63157-000-1 (hardback)
ISBN-13: 978-1-60649-829-3 (e-book)

Business Expert Press Economics Collection

Collection ISSN: 2163-761X (print)
Collection ISSN: 2163-7628 (electronic)

Cover and interior design by Exeter Premedia Services Private Ltd.,
Chennai, India

First edition: 2014

10 9 8 7 6 5 4 3 2 1

Printed in the United States of America.

*To my forever-beautiful wife, Carla, and my son Samir, both living here on earth, and to my children Andrea and Joshua, who are now living in Heaven. I also would like to express my gratitude to my father, Mario M. Goncalves, for planting the seeds of research in me while a child, and to my father-in-law, Don Fernando Davalos, for the many insightful discussions on foreign affairs.*

*To God be the glory!*

—Marcus Goncalves
Summer 2014

*To my loving parents Venkataraman V. Arcot and Tarabai V. Arcot, now living in Heaven*

—Rajabahadur V. Arcot

# Abstract

There is intense competition among emerging markets to capture their share of the global economy. This book addresses questions that are germane to accomplishing this goal. Most important to this end is the study and practice of international business and foreign trade. Undertaking such a study raises many questions such as: Why are emerging markets and the firms doing business in them internationalizing so aggressively? Why in the past decade has the pace of internationalization accelerated so rapidly? What competitive advantages do these emerging economies enjoy in comparison to advanced economies, such as the G20, and what are the origins of those advantages? Through what strategies are emerging market blocks such as the BRICS (Brazil, Russia, India, China, and South Africa) and the CIVETS (Colombia, Indonesia, Vietnam, Egypt, Turkey, and South Africa) building their global presence and expanding their market reach? How are emerging markets rivaling advanced economies and how are they affecting the already established rivalries among those economies? This book will answer these and other questions. In doing so, it will attempt to address the larger issue of what it all means for mainstream international business theory and its actual practice.

# Keywords

ASEAN, BRICS, CIVETS, emerging markets, FCPA, frontier markets, global corruption, global economic outlook, global economy, global microeconomics, international business, MENA, state capitalism

# Contents

# Preface

A significant transformation of the global economy is under way, one only dimly recognized by most Americans and the Western nations. As macroeconomics and trade now loom larger than nuclear stockpiles or Cold War creed, those countries with the fastest growing economies have begun to redraft the rules of power and influence throughout the world. These nations include the large emerging and frontier markets, which most of us, particularly the West, have failed to recognize their importance for far too long. No longer we can afford to ignore these economies and how these emerging market are impacting advanced economies. The G-20 group of countries has eclipsed the G-7 group of richest nations in the world.

*Advanced Economies and Emerging Markets: Prospects for Globalization* is the essential guide to better understanding the leading emerging and frontier markets in the world, and the interlocking dynamics they have with the advanced economies. This book not only provides a coverage of the BRICS, the CIVETS, the MENA, and the ASEAN emerging markets, but also the main frontier markets and the so called EAGLE economies. Five researchers and international business consultants, from five different countries spanning from the West to the East, explain who these countries are, why they have burst onto the world scene, and how they will reshape the world in the 21st century, challenging the status quo of advanced economies along the way.

Furthermore, this book also explains how the macroeconomic experience of emerging and frontier economies has tended to be quite different from that of advanced economies. Compared to advanced economies, emerging markets and even more so frontier economies have tended to be much more unstable, with more severe boom/bust cycles, episodes of high inflation, and a variety of financial crises. This book discusses how the standard macroeconomic models that are used in advanced economies can be modified to help understand this experience, and how institutional and policy reforms in emerging and frontier markets may affect their future macroeconomic performance.

This book has been, therefore, broken down into 15 chapters, each addressing an important aspect of this global balance shift taking place among advanced economies and emerging markets. It provides historical data, assessments and our opinions, when appropriate, as well as reflections from our own experience, as researchers, international business consultants, and global citizens. The following is a brief breakdown of each chapter of this book:

Chapter 1: The Influence of G-7 Advanced Economies and G-20 Group, provides an overview of who the G-7 and the G-20 group of countries are, their role on today's economic policy development and geopolitics. This chapter also discusses the challenges and current trends resulting from the inter-dynamics of these two important country group.

Chapter 2: The Counter-Influence of Emerging Markets across the Globe, describes the most recent developments of the G-20 group as they strive to be heard, not only by the G-7, but also by all international policy-setting organizations, such as the United Nations, the World Bank, and the World Trade Organization. This chapter discusses the latest trends and policies coming out of the G-20 and how it is shaping international businesses.

Chapter 3: Advanced versus Emerging Markets: Global Economic Prospects, provides an overview of the global economic prospects for these regions, not only with regards to the well known North-South trade routes, but also the strengthening South-South new trade relations.

Chapter 4: Coping with Emerging and Advanced Market Risks, provides an overview of the current risks at play on advanced economies, mostly associated with indebtness, but also monetary crises. This chapter also discusses the many challenges being dealt with by emerging and frontier markets and the risks international business professionals are exposed to on both major markets.

Chapter 5: Global Economies at War, discusses the struggle for power and influenced being fought across the globe among advanced economies and emerging markets, we the former attempts to hold on to global leadership and hegemony while the later continues to challenge the status quo with strength and at time, much wit.

Chapter 6: The Rebalance of Global Trade, continues the discussions introduced in Chapter 5, where here we see how a global trade rebalance is at play, prompting us, investors and consumers alike, to also reposition ourselves so we can take advantage of new opportunities, and career path never before presented.

Chapter 7: The IMF is Being Hit by BRICS, discuss the latest development among this leading emerging market bloc, as these nations organize to implement the first development bank to challenge the International Monetary Fund. This chapter offers analysis of the potential repercussions of this bank formation not only to the IMF and advanced economies, but also the new opportunities that it opens up to frontier markets that never had access to the infrastructure loans via IMF.

Chapter 8: CIVETS: A New Strong and Fast Emerging Market, examines the emerging economies that form the CIVETS, their strength and weaknesses, as well as there opportunities and threats.

Chapter 9: The Strength of ASEAN Economies, much as in Chapter 8, provides an overview of the ASEAN country bloc, and how they are positioning themselves amidst the global rebalance of trade.

Chapter 10: Can MENA's Rise be Powered by BRICS?, provides an overview of the MENA countries and the influence of the BRICS economies on their rise and continues and evolving bilateral trade.

Chapter 11: Entering an Emerging Market, provides lessons learned and best practices for entering an emerging market, as well as doing business in those countries, from developing a country profile to international marketing strategies, as well as dealing with local risks.

Chapter 12: The Importance of Market Research and Business Intelligence, emphasizes the need for a thorough investigation and understanding of a given emerging market before making a decision to enter it. It provides best-case scenarios and analysis for researching a new international market.

Chapter 13: Coping with Political and Economic Risks, provides valuable information in dealing with political and economic risks as multinationals and international business professionals conduct business abroad.

Chapter 14: FCPA: Dealing with Corruption and Crime, provides an introduction to the U.S. Foreign Corrupt Practice Act, the need to understand it and comply with its regulations when conducting business abroad, covering both the individual and corporate aspects of it, as well as some criticism to it.

Chapter 15: Coping and the Global and Emerging Market Crisis, discuss the current global market crisis the world is experiencing, from advanced economies to emerging markets, and how this crisis adversely impacts each of these markets in different ways, with a distinctive set of challenges, and how one should position to cope with it, and if at all possible, take advantage of it.

We are certainly living in a very interesting time, historical times we must say. This book provides breath and depth for international business professionals to cope with the challenging macroeconomic storms taking place at advanced economies, and navigate the newly presented uncharted waters of emerging and frontier markets with a string prospects of huge financial, professional, cultural, and personal gains.

Marcus Goncalves, Summer 2014.

# Acknowledgments

There were many people who helped us during the process of writing this book. It would be impossible to keep track of them all. Therefore, to all that we have forgotten to list, please don't hold it against us!

We would like to thank Dr. Patrick Barron, professor at the Graduate School of Banking at the University of Wisconsin, Madison, and of Austrian economics at the University of Iowa, in Iowa City for his contributions on the issue of currency wars in Chapter 5. Many thanks also to ambassador M. K. Bhadrakumar, former diplomat in the Indian Foreign Service with assignments in the Soviet Union, South Korea, Sri Lanka, Germany, Afghanistan, Pakistan, Uzbekistan, Kuwait, and Turkey for his valuable insights and contributions to foreign policy issues in the MENA region.

Many thanks also to Mr. Bo-Young Lin, from the Graduate Institute of International and Development Studies in Switzerland, and United Nations Conference on Trade and Development (UNCTAD) for his support and insights.

Last but not least, we'd like to express our gratitude to Nora Luquer for her invaluable contribution in editing our research work so that all of us, of many nationalities and based in different parts of the word, would have a *one voice* throughout this book.

# CHAPTER 1

# The Influence of the G-7 Advanced Economies and G-20 Group

## Overview

When we think of the G-20 countries, whose summit took place in St. Petersburg, Russia, on September 5–6, 2013, we should think about the group of 20 finance ministers and central bankers from the 20 major economies around the world. In essence, the G-20 is comprised of 19 countries plus the European Union (EU), represented by the president of the European Council and by the European Central Bank (ECB). We begin this book discussing the importance and influence of the G-20 because, not only does this group comprise some of the most advancing economies in the world, but also because collectively these 20 economies account for approximately 80 percent of the gross world product (GWP), 80 percent of the world's trade, which includes EUs intra-trade, and about two-thirds of the world's population.* These proportions are not expected to change radically for many decades to come.

The G-20, proposed by the former Canadian Prime Minister Paul Martin,[1] acts as a forum for cooperation and consultation on matters pertaining to the international financial system. Since its inception in September of 1999 the group has been studying, reviewing, and promoting high-level discussions of policy issues concerning the promotion of international financial stability. The group has replaced the G-8 group as the main economic council of wealthy nations.[2] Although not popular with many political activists and intellectuals, the group exercises major influence on economic and financial policies around the world.

---

* G-20 Membership from the Official G-20 website at www.g20.org

| G20 Countries | |
|---|---|
| Argentina | Japan |
| Australia | Mexico |
| Brazil | Russia |
| Canada | Saudia Arabia |
| China | South Africa |
| France | South Korea |
| Germany | Turkey |
| India | United Kingdom |
| Indonesia | United States |
| Italy | European Union |

*Figure 1.1  G-20 country list*

The G-20 Summit was created as a response both to the financial crisis of 2007–2010 and to a growing recognition that key emerging countries (and markets) were not adequately included in the core of global economic discussion and governance. The G-20 country members are listed in Figure 1.1.

It is important to note that the G-20 members do not necessarily reflect the 20 largest economies of the world in any given year. According to the group, as defined in its FAQs, there are "no formal criteria for G-20 membership, and the composition of the group has remained unchanged since it was established. In view of the objectives of the G-20, it was considered important that countries and regions of systemic significance of the international financial system be included. Aspects such as geographical balance and population representation also played a major part."[3] All 19-member nations, however, are among the top 30 economies as measured in gross domestic product (GDP) at nominal prices according to a list published by the International Monetary Fund (IMF)[4] in April 2013. That being said, the G-20 list does *not* include some of the top 30 economies in the world as ranked by the World Bank[5] and depicted in Figure 1.2, such as Switzerland (19th), Thailand (30th), Norway (24rd), and Taiwan (29th), despite the fact these economies rank higher than some of the G-20 members. In the EU, the largest economies are Spain (13th),

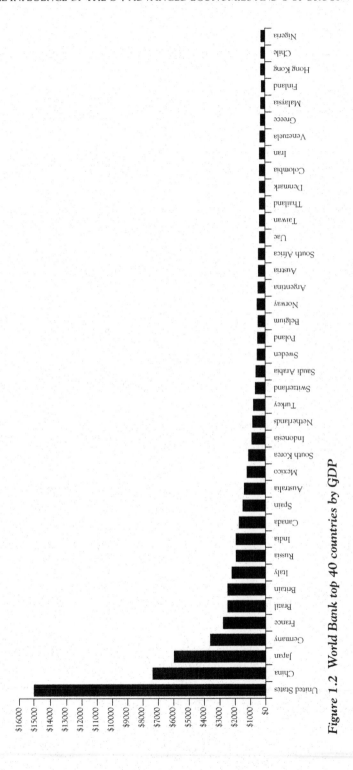

*Figure 1.2  World Bank top 40 countries by GDP*

the Netherlands (18th), Sweden (22nd), Poland (24th), Belgium (25th), and Austria (28th). These economies are ranked as part of the EU though, and not independently.

Asian economies, such as China (2nd) and India (10th), are expected to play an important role in global economic governance, according to the Asian Development Bank (ADB), as the rise of emerging market economies are heralding a new world order. The G-20 would likely become the global economic steering committee. Furthermore, not only have Asian countries been leading the global recovery following the *great recession*, but key indicators also suggest the region will have a greater presence on the global stage, especially considering the latest advances in GDP for countries such as Thailand and the Philippines. These trends are shaping the G-20 agenda for balanced and sustainable growth through strengthening intraregional trade and stimulating domestic demand.[6]

## The G-7 and G-20 Group Influence in the Global Economy

Prior to the G-20 enjoying the influence it has today in global economic policy making, the group of advanced economies, the G-8 group, consisting of the United States (U.S.), Canada, France, the United Kingdom (UK), Italy, Germany, Japan, and Russia, was a leading global economic policy forum. Figure 1.3 illustrates the breakdown of the G-8 countries by population. The U.S. population is about 300 million people, which is roughly a third of the population of all of the G-8 countries combined—equal to Japan and Russia combined, and to Germany, France, Italy, Canada, and the UK combined. Russia has been removed from the G-8 group which now is referred to as the G-7.

As the world economy continues to be increasingly integrated, the need for a global hub where the world economy issues and challenges could converge is a major necessity. In the absence of a complete overhaul of the United Nations (UN) and international financial institutions such as the IMF and the World Bank, the G-20 is the only viable venue to mitigate the interests of these leading nations. Since the G-20 group has overshadowed the G-7, it has become a major forum for global decision-making, central to designing a pathway out of the worst global financial crisis in almost a century. It did so by effectively coordinating

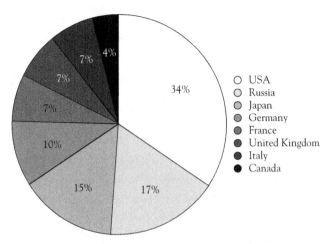

**Figure 1.3  List of G-8 Countries by power of influence**

*Source*: CIA World Factbook

the many individual policies adopted by its members and thus establishing its importance in terms of crisis management and coordination during an emergency.

The G-20 has failed, thus far, to live up to expectations as a viable alternative to the G-7, although it continues to be at the heart of global power shifts, particularly to emerging markets. Efforts to reform the international financial system have produced limited results. It has struggled to deliver on its 2010 summit promises on fiscal consolidation and banking capital, while the world watches the global finance lobbyists repeatedly demonstrate their ability to thwart every G-20's attempt to regulate financial flows, despite the volatility associated with the movement of large amounts of short-term funds. Larger economies, such as Germany and Spain have been concerned with the lack of effective regulation of financial flows. Emerging markets such as the BRIC (Brazil, Russia, India, and China) countries and the CIVETS (Colombia, Indonesia, Vietnam, Egypt, Turkey, and South Africa*) countries are scrambling to deflect the exportation of inflation from these advanced G-7 economies into their domestic economies. Countries such as Iceland, the UK, and Ireland,

---

* It is important to note that although South Africa is grouped with the CIVETS bloc, it also has been aggregated to the BRIC bloc, where it is more likely to belong.

whose banking systems had to undergo painful recapitalization, national-ization and restructuring to return to profitability after the financial crisis broke, also share these concerns.

In the words of Ian Bremmer,* in his book titled *Every Nation for Itself: Winners and Losers in a G-Zero World*,[7] when reflecting on the then newly created G-20 group, "I found myself imagining an enormous poker table where each player guards his stack of chips, watches the nineteen others, and waits for an opportunity to play the hand he has been dealt. This is not a global order, but every nation for itself. *And if the G-7 no longer matters and the G-20 doesn't work, then what is this world we now live in?*"†

According to Bremmer, we now are living in a time where the world has no global leadership since, he argues, the United States can no longer provide such leadership to the world due to its "endless par-tisan combat and mounting federal debt."[8] He also argues that Europe can't provide any leadership either as debt crisis is crippling confidence in the region, its institutions, and its future. In his view, the same goes for Japan, which is still recovering from a devastating earthquake, tsunami, and nuclear meltdown, in addition to the more than two decades of political and economic malaise. Institutions like the UN Security Council, the IMF, and the World Bank are unlikely to provide real leadership because they no longer reflect the world's true balance of political and economic power. The fact is, a generation ago the G-7 were the world's powerhouses, the group of free-market democracies that powered the global economy. Today, they struggle just to find their footing.

In Bremmer's view, "The G-Zero phenomenon and resulting lack of global leadership have only intensified—and analysts from conserva-tive political scientist Francis Fukuyama to liberal Nobel Prize winning economist Joseph Stiglitz have since written of the G-Zero as a fact of international life."[9] "The G-Zero," Bremmer continues, "won't last for-ever, but over the next decade and perhaps longer, a world without lead-ers will undermine our ability to keep the peace, to expand opportunity,

---

* Bremmer is the president of the Eurasia Group, the world's leading global political risk research and consulting firm.

† Emphasis is ours.

to reverse the impact of climate change, and to feed growing populations. The effects will be felt in every nation of the word—and even in
cyberspace."[10]

## Coping with Shifting Power Dynamics
## and a Multipolar World

In the past decade, the emerging markets have been growing at a much
faster pace than the advanced economies. Consequently, participation in
the global GDP, global trade, and foreign direct investment (FDI), particularly in the global financial markets, has significantly increased as well.
Such trends, according to a study conducted by the Banco de Espana's
analysts Orgaz, Molina, and Carrasco,[11] are expected to continue for the
next few years. The global economic crises has fostered relevant changes
to the governance of the global economy, particularly with the substitu-
tion of the G-7 with the G-20 group as a leading international forum in
the development of global economic policies.

The G-20's failure to effectively regulate global financial flows has
led to efforts to reclaim national sovereignty through so-called host or
home-country financial regulations, as national legislative bodies seek
control over financial flows. The impetus for both can be found in the
changing global order as it moves toward greater global balance.

For many decades various other groups, such as the G-7, the Non-
aligned Movement, India, Brazil, South Africa (IBSA), and the BRICS,
to name the main ones, have been applying some informal pressure,
largely reflecting the continued north-south or (advanced versus emerging markets) divide into global geopolitics and wealth. Although financial
analysts and policy makers in the advanced economies tend to view the
G-20 as a venue to build and extend the outreach of global consensus
on their policies, such expectations have been changing due to the establishment of a loose coalition with a distinctly contrarian view on many
global issues. This is particularly true in regard to the role of the state in
development and on finance.

This loose coalition, which has become more prominent since the
global financial crises of 2008, is spearheaded by the BRICS (the "S" is for
South Africa), led by China. While Chapter 7 provides a more in-depth

discussion on the role of the BRICS in this process, for now it is important to note how the BRICS countries are able to apply pressure on the G-20 group, particularly to advanced economies.

The BRICS cohort countries within the G-20 have a combined GDP three times smaller than that of the G-7. Nonetheless, the gap between the two decreases every year and is expected to disappear within the next two decades, if not sooner. Even more importantly, most of the economic growth within the G-20 is coming from the BRICS (and other emerging and so called "frontier" markets) rather than from the advanced economies (the G-7). Hence, while there are many other geopolitical dynamics playing out within the G-20, we believe the most important play at the moment and in the next two decades is a battle for strategic positioning by the advanced economies versus the emerging markets, who are led by the BRICS. Even more important is to watch as the BRICS jockey for support from other G-20 members such as Indonesia, Mexico, Saudi Arabia, and Turkey. While some allegiances may appear obvious, economic and political benefits often pull in opposite directions, leaving policy makers with difficult choices to make.

In order for the G-20 countries to continue to build on their collective success in the management of the global financial crisis, it is imperative for them to place more emphasis on global trade and financial reform. These elements are at the core of global trade and economic governance. Unfortunately, advanced economies, particularly in North America and Europe, are heading in a different direction than the emerging ones, particularly the BRICS, as a result of the shifting power dynamics in an increasingly multipolar world. In the past decade China prominently has exercised this shift.

Such shifting of power dynamics, or the fight to control it, is perhaps most evident in the efforts toward exclusive trade agreements in the Atlantic and Pacific oceans, such as the Transatlantic Trade and Investment Partnership (TTIP), where discussions began in July of 2013 between the United States and Europe. Similarly, the Trans-Pacific Partnership (TPP) also discussed collaborating with eleven other countries, including Japan.

TTIP's main objective is to drive growth and create jobs by removing trade barriers in a wide range of economic sectors, making it easier to buy and sell goods and services between the EU and the United States.

A research study conducted by the Centre for Economic Policy Research, in London-UK, titled *Reducing Trans-Atlantic Barriers to Trade and Investment: An Economic Assessment*,[12] suggests that TTIP could boost the EU's economy by €120 billion euros (US$197 billion), while also boosting the U.S. economy by €90 billion euros (US$147.75 billion) and the rest of the world by €100 billion euros (US$164.16 billion).

The success of TTIP and TPP could undermine the future viability of the World Trade Organization (WTO) as a global trade forum, such as the Doha Round. Although not isolated, China is party to neither group. The unspoken concern is that the two agreements are aimed at ensuring continued Western control of the global economy by building a strong relationship between the euro and the dollar while constraining and containing a growing and increasingly assertive China.

The TPP, on the other hand, suffers from a severe lack of transparency, as U.S. negotiators are pushing for the adoption of copyright measures far more constraining than currently required by international treaties, including the polemic Anti-Counterfeiting Trade Agreement (ACTA). The treaty, while also attempting to rewrite global rules on intellectual property enforcement is nonetheless, a free trade agreement. At the time of this writing (fall of 2013), the ACTA is being negotiated by twelve countries. As depicted in Figure 1.4, these countries include the United States, Japan, Australia, Peru, Malaysia, Vietnam, New Zealand, Chile, Singapore, Canada, Mexico, and Brunei Darussalam.

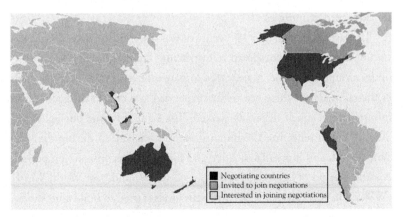

*Figure 1.4 The Trans-Pacific Partnership eleven member countries*

## The Impact of Indebtedness of the Advanced Economies on Emerging Markets

In September of 2013 Canadian Prime Minister Stephen Harper vehemently urged G-20 leaders not to lose sight of the vital importance of reining in debt across the group after several years of deficit-fueled stimulus spending. He stuck to the common refrain in the face of weak recoveries among member countries, including Canada. Specifically referring to the risk of accumulating public debt points, Mr. Harper also acknowledged that recoveries from the financial crisis, that started five years ago, have been disappointing because many of the advanced economies continue to grapple with high unemployment, weak growth, and rising income inequality.

Since the economic crisis of 2008, the United States and its financial analysts and politicians have been very vocal with ideas of *fiscal cliffs*, debt ceiling, and defaults. To some extent, the situation is not much different among the EU block. Debt to GDP ratios and deficit figures have been touted as omens of financial failure and public debt has been heralded as the harbinger of an apocalypse. The truth of the matter is that many countries around the world, especially in the emerging markets during the 1970's and 1980's, had experienced large amounts of debt, often in excess of 100 percent of GDP, as advanced economies are experiencing right now. Nonetheless, what is different this time is that while emerging markets had most of their debt in external markets and denominated in foreign currencies, they also had differing structures and institutions than the advanced economies.

The last quarter of the 19$^{th}$ century was a period of large accumulation of debt due to widespread infrastructure building in advanced economies around the globe, mainly due to new innovations at the time, such as the railroads. As these economies expanded and continued to invest in infrastructure, much debt was created. The same was true during World War I (WWI) reflecting the military spending taken on during the wartime period, and immediately after that during the reconstruction period. Another period of large debt was amassed during and post World War II (WWII). In this case, some of these debt levels started to build a bit earlier, as a result of the great recession, but most were the result of WWII. Finally, we have the period where most governments and policymakers of advanced economies struggled to move from the old economic systems to the current one. During these four different periods, most advanced economies experienced 100 percent or more debt to GDP ratios at least one or more times. The dynamics of debt to GDP ratios are in fact very diverse; their effects are widely varied and based on a variety of factors. Take for example the case of the UK in 1918, the United States in 1946, Belgium in 1983, Italy in 1992, Canada in 1995, and Japan in 1997. All of these countries went through a process of indebtedness, each with a full range of outcomes.

In the case of UK, policymakers tried to return to the gold standard at pre-WWI levels to restore trade, prosperity and prestige, and to pay off as much debt, as quickly as possible to preserve the image of British good credit. They sought to achieve these goals through policies that included thrift saving. Their efforts did not have the intended effects. The dual pursuit of going back to a strengthened currency from a devalued one, along with the pursuit of fiscal austerity seemed to be a deciding factor in the failure. Trying to go back to the gold standard made British exports less attractive than those of surrounding countries who had not chosen this path. Consequently, exports were low, and to combat this, British banks kept interest rates high. Those high interest rates meant that the debt the country was trying to pay off increased in value and the country's slow growth and austerity did not give them the economic power to pay off the debts as they wanted. In an effort to maintain integrity and the image of "Old Faithful Britain," the policymakers ruined their chances for a swift recovery.

In the United States, policymakers chose not to control inflation, and kept a floor on government bonds. Over time, these ideas changed and bond protection measures were lifted. In turn, the government's ability to intervene in inflation situations changed. The United States experienced rapid growth during this time, partially due to high levels of monetary inflation, but that inflation, even though it would "burst" at the start of the Korean War, allowed the United States to pay off much of its debt. This, coupled with the floor on U.S. bonds, created a favorable post high debt level scenario.

Japan's initial response to its debt situation was the cutting of inflation rates and the introduction of fiscal stimulus programs. This response did not have the intended effect, as currency appreciated. The underlying issues that had helped to cause the high debt to GDP ratios were still present, and would be until 2001 when the government committed to boosting the country's economy through policy and structure changes. Japan still has a very high debt to GDP ratio, but the weaknesses in the banking sector have been fixed and the country seems to be on a path to recovery.

Italy's attempts at fiscal reform included changes to many social programs, including large cuts to pension spending. The reforms, though, were not implemented quickly enough and did not address enough of the demographic issues to make a large impact. It wasn't until later that further fiscal consolidation was achieved. It is important to note that Italy's GDP growth did not help reduce debt during this period, and thus remained very weak.

Belgium used similar kinds of fiscal consolidation plans to those of Italy, but those plans were more widespread and implemented at a more rapid pace. The relative success of these initial fiscal consolidations helped to further growth and reduction of the debt to GDP ratio. These plans also fueled another round of successful consolidation when the country needed it to enter the EU.

Canada's initial reaction included fiscal changes such as tax hikes and spending cuts; a plan of austerity. The plan failed and deepened the country's debt. The second wave of fiscal consolidation was aimed at fixing some of the structural imbalances that had caused the debt levels in the first place. It worked, helped along by the strengthening of economic conditions in surrounding countries, mainly the United States. The Canadian example shows that external conditions are just as important for success as the policies or missions taken on within the country.

From all of these examples, we have an idea of the impact that advanced economies have on each other as well as on emerging markets. In an intertwined global economy, imbalances in one country's economy impact virtually every other country in the world. The extent of the impact and mitigation will always vary depending on internal and external market conditions, as well as policy development. Similarly solutions, like U.S. inflation adjustments, may not work today or in another country. For instance, if we take the global financial crises that started in 2008, allowing inflation levels to rise could pose risks to financial institutions, and could lead to a globally less-integrated financial system.

The most pertinent example would appear to be the kind of fiscal policies used in Canada, Belgium, and Italy. All three countries attempted to achieve low inflation, but their other policy reforms varied in success. More permanent fiscal changes tend to create more prominent and lasting reductions to debt levels. Even then, a country must be exposed to an increase in external demands if the country's recovery is to mirror the successful cases cited earlier. Consolidation needs to be implemented alongside measures to support growth and changes that address structural issues. The final factor to note is that even with a successful plan, the effects of the plan take time. Debt level reductions will not be quick in today's global and interwoven economies.

## The Crisis Isn't Over Yet

Advanced economies, specifically in the EU and the United States are still dealing with the global financial crises that started in 2008. Despite the positive rhetoric of policy makers and governments, on both sides of the Atlantic, Harvard economist Carmen Reinhart feels that the crisis is not yet over. She alleges that both the U.S. Federal Reserve and the European Central Bank (ECB) are keeping interest rates low to help governments out of their debt crises. In the past and as shown in the historial examples cited earlier, central banks are bending over backwards to help governments of advanced economies to finance their deficits.

As was mentioned earlier in this chapter, after WWII, all countries that had a big debt overhang relied on financial repression to avoid an explicit default, and governments imposed interest rate ceilings for government bonds. Liberal capital-market regulations and international capital mobility at the time reached their peak prior to WWI under the gold standard. But, the Great Depression followed by WWII, put the final nail in the coffin of laissez-faire banking.* It was in this environment that the Bretton Woods arrangement, of fixed exchange rates

---

* An economic theory from the 18th century that is strongly opposed to any government intervention in business affairs.

and tightly controlled domestic and international capital markets, was conceived. The result was a combination of very low interest rates and inflationary spurts of varying degrees across the advanced economies. The obvious results were real interest rates—whether on treasury bills, central bank discount rates, deposits or loans—that were markedly negative during 1945 and 1946. For the next 35 years, real interest rates in both advanced and emerging economies would remain consistently lower than during the eras of free capital mobility, including before and after the financial repression era. Ostensibly, real interest rates were, on average, negative. The frequency distributions of real rates for the period of financial repression (1945–1980) and the years following financial liberalization highlight the universality of lower real interest rates prior to the 1980s and the high incidence of negative real interest rates in the advanced economies. (See Figure 1.5.) Reinhart and Sbrancia[13] (2011) demonstrate a comparable pattern for the emerging markets.

Nowadays, however, monetary policy is doing the job, but unlike many policy makers would like us to believe, these economies are seldom able to break out of debt. Money to pay for these debts must come

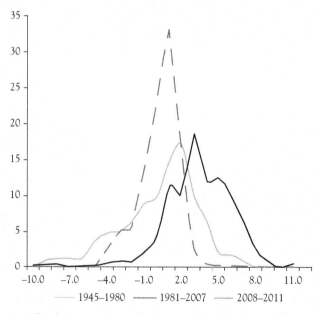

Figure 1.5 *Real interest rates frequency distributions: Advanced economies, 1945–2011*

from somewhere. Reinhart (2011)* believes those advanced economies in debt today must adopt a combination of austerity to restrain the trend of adding to the stack of debt and higher inflation. This is effectively a subtle form of taxation and consequently will cause a depreciation of the currency and erosion of people's savings.

We do not advocate for or against current central bank policies in these economies; this is not the premise of this book. Advanced economies, however, *do* need to deal with their debt as these high debt levels prevent growth and freeze the financial system and the credit process. As long as emerging markets continue to depend heavily on the exports of these advanced economies, they too will be negatively impacted. We believe, however, that the debt of the United States and the EU, in particular, affects the global economy significantly. The current central bank policies are not effective; money is being transferred from responsible savers to borrowers via negative interest rates.

In essence, when the inflation rate is higher than the interest rates paid on the markets, the debts shrink as if by magic. As dubbed by Ronald McKinnon[14] (1973), the term *financial repression* describes various policies that allow governments to *capture* and *under-pay* domestic savers. Such policies include forced lending to governments by pension funds and other domestic financial institutions, interest-rate caps, capital controls, and many more. Typically, governments use a mixture of these policies to bring down debt levels, but inflation and financial repression usually only work for domestically held debt. The eurozone is a special hybrid case. The financial repression implemented by advanced economies is designed to avoid an explicit default on the debt. Unfortunately, this is not only ineffective in the long run, but also unjust to responsible taxpayers. Eventually public revolts may develop, such as the ones already witnessed in Greece and Spain. Governments could write off part of the debt, but evidently no politician would be willing to spearhead such write-offs. After all, most citizens do not realize their savings are being eroded and that there is a major transfer of wealth taking place. Undeniably, advanced economies around the world have a problem with debt. In the past, several tactics, including financial repression, have dealt with such problems, and now it seems, debt is resurging again in the wake of the global and eurozone crises.

---

* Ibidem.

Financial repression, coupled with a steady dose of inflation, cuts debt burdens from two directions. First off, the introduction of low nominal interest rates reduces debt-servicing costs. Secondly, negative real interest rates erode the debt-to-GDP ratio. In other words, this is a tax on savers. Financial repression also has some noteworthy political-economic properties. Unlike other taxes, the "repression" tax rate is determined by financial regulations and inflation performance, which are obscure to the highly politicized realm of fiscal measures. Given that deficit reduction usually involves highly unpopular expenditure reductions and/or tax increases of one form or another, the relatively *stealthier* financial repression tax may be a more politically palatable alternative for authorities faced with the need to reduce outstanding debts. In such an environment, inflation, by historic standards, does not need to be very high or take market participants entirely by surprise.

Unlike the United States, which is resorting to financial repression, Europe is focusing more on austerity measures; despite the fact inflation is still at a low level. Notwithstanding, debt restructuring, inflation, and financial repression, are not a substitute for austerity. All these measures reduce a country's existing stock of debt, and as argued by Reinhart,[15] policy makers need a combination of both to bring down debt to a sustainable level. Although the United States is highly indebted, an advantage it has against all other advanced economies is that foreign central banks are the ones holding most of its debts. The Bank of China and the Bank of Brazil, two leading BRICS emerging economies, are not likely to be repaid. It does not mean the United States will default. We don't know that, no one does. It actually doesn't have to explicitly default since if you have negative real interest rates, a transfer from China and Brazil, the effect on the creditors is the same, as well as other creditors to the United States.

The real risk here for the United States, EU, and other advanced economies is that creditors may decide not to play along anymore, which would cause interest rates on American government bonds to climb. This act would be similar to the major debt crisis of Greece and Iceland, and what was happening in Spain until the ECB intervened. We believe the U.S. Federal Reserve Bank, and likely the ECB, is prepared to continue buying record levels of debt for as long as it takes to jump-start the economy. To counter the debasement of the dollar, China's central bank is likely to continue to buy U.S. treasury bonds in a constant attempt to stop the export of inflation from the United States into its economy and by preventing the renminbi from appreciating. In an attempt to save their economies from indebtedness, advanced economies are raging what Jim Rickards calls a *currency war*[16] against the emerging markets and the rest of the world.

We believe the combination of high public and private debts in the advanced economies and the perceived dangers of currency misalignments and overvaluation in emerging markets facing surges of capital inflows, are causing pressures toward currency intervention and capital controls, interacting to produce a home-bias in finance, and a resurgence of financial repression. At present, we find that emerging markets, especially the BRICS, are being forced to adopt similar policies as the advanced economies—hence the *currency wars*—but not as a financial repression, but more in the context of *macro-prudential* regulations.

Advanced economies are developing financial regulatory measures to keep international capital out of emerging economies, and in advanced economies. Such economic controls are intended to counter loose monetary policy in the advanced economies and discourage the so-called *hot money*,* while regulatory changes in advanced economies are meant to create a captive audience for domestic debt. This offers advanced and emerging market economies common ground on tighter restrictions on international financial flows, which borderlines protectionism policies. More broadly, the world is witnessing a return to a more tightly regulated domestic financial environment, i.e. financial repression.

We believe advanced economies are imposing a major strain on global financial markets, in particular emerging economies, by exporting inflation to those countries. Because governments are incapable of reducing their debts, central banks are pressured to get involved in an attempt to resolve the crisis. Reinhart argues that such a policy does not come cheap, and those responsible citizens and everyday savers, will be the ones feeling the consequences of such policies the most. While no central bank will admit it is purposely keeping interest rates low to help governments out

---

* Capital that is frequently transferred between financial institutions in an attempt to maximize interest or capital gain.

of their debt crises, banks are doing whatever they can to help these economies finance their deficits.

The major danger of such a central bank policy, which can be at first very detrimental to emerging markets that are still largely dependent on consumer demands from advanced economies, is that it can lead to high inflation. As inflation rises among advanced economies, it is also exported to emerging market economies. In other words, as the U.S. dollar and the euro debases and loses buying power, emerging markets experience an artificial strengthening of their currency, courtesy of the U.S. Federal Reserve and the ECB. In turn, this causes the prices of goods and services to also increase and hurts exports in the process.

Figure 1.5 strikingly shows that real export interest rates (shown for treasury bills) for the advanced economies have, once again, turned increasingly negative since the outbreak of the crisis in 2008. Real rates have been negative for about one half of the observations, and below one percent for about 82 percent of the observations. This turn to lower real interest rates has materialized despite the fact that several sovereigns have been teetering on the verge of default or restructuring. Indeed, in recent months negative yields in most advanced economies, the G-7 countries, have moved much further outside the yield curve, as depicted in Figure 1.6.

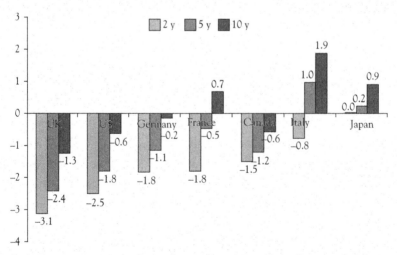

*Figure 1.6 G-7 real government bond yields, February 2012*

No doubt, a critical factor explaining the high incidence of negative real interest rates in the wake of the crisis is the aggressive expansive stance of monetary policy, particularly the official central bank interventions in many advanced and emerging economies during this period.

At the time of this writing, in the fall of 2013, the level of public debt in many advanced economies is at their highest levels, with some economies facing the prospect of debt restructuring. Moreover, public and private external debts, which we should not ignore, are typically a volatile source of funding, are at historic highs. The persistent levels of unemployment in many advanced economies also are still high. These negative trends offer further motivation for central banks and policy makers to keep interest rates low, posing a renewed taste for financial repression. Hence, we believe the final crisis isn't over yet. The impact that advanced economies are imposing on emerging markets, and its own economies, is only the tip of a very large iceberg.

# CHAPTER 2

# The Counter-Influence of Emerging Markets across the Globe

## Overview

The emerging markets have been the source of global economic growth for quite some time now, with far-reaching effects to the rest of the world, in particular to advanced economies. It is not news that emerging markets have become the sweethearts of the financial press and a favorite talking point of governments, foreign trade advisors, and corporations world-wide. Although these markets were best known in the past as a commodity paradise, or the place to go for natural resources, cheap labor, or low manufacturing costs, emerging markets today are positioned for growth. Rapid population development, growing middle-class, and sustained economic development are making many international investors and corporations look to emerging markets with new lenses.

Economic theorists' corroborate this point by arguing that free FDI across national borders is beneficial to all countries, as it leads to an efficient allocation of resources that raises productivity and economic growth everywhere. Although in principle this is often the case, at this time, for emerging markets, the situation is a bit different. It is much more apparent now when we look at country indicators from sources such as the IMF or World Bank, that large capital inflows can create substantial challenges for policymakers in those market economies. After the global financial crisis of 2008–2009, net private capital flows to emerging markets surged and have been volatile since then. This raises a number of concerns in those recipient economies. As advanced economies issued robust monetary stimuli to revive their sluggish economies, emerging markets faced an overabundance of foreign investments amid strong recoveries. Hence, policy tensions rapidly ensued between these two groups of economies. As strong FDI, mainly private net capital, was injected into emerging markets economies, both in pre- and post-global financial crisis periods, policymakers in those emerging economies reacted by actually reversing the flow of capital back into advanced market economies. This often resulted in an effort to control local currency appreciation, and fend off the exporting of inflation from advanced economies into these markets.

Therefore, we are all witnessing a rapid development in the global trade landscape, one that hitherto was dominated by advanced economies, with trading policies developed typically by members of the G-7 group of nations. Some members of the G-7 group though are beginning to lose their influence to emerging economies, as a result of profound changes the global markets are undergoing. One of the most important changes, henceforth the consequences of which still remain to be understood fully, is the growing role of the G-20 countries as new policymakers for international trade and fast developing emerging markets.

These groups of emerging economies, however, are not easy to define. While the World Bank coined the term *emerging countries* more than a quarter of a century ago, it only started to become a household term in the mid-1990s.* After the debt crises of the 1980s, several of these rapidly developing economies gained access to international financial markets, while at the same time they had liberalized their financial systems, at least far enough to enable foreign investors broad access into their markets.[1] From a small group of nations in East Asia, these groups of emerging economies have gradually grown to include several countries in Latin America, Central and Eastern Europe, the Middle East, as well as a few countries in Africa. The leading groups today are the Association of South East Asian Nations (ASEAN), the BRICS, the CIVETS, the Middle East and North Africa (MENA), in addition to what Jim O'Neil calls the N-11, or next-11 emerging economies, a focus of much discussion in this book.

---

* The term was coined in 1981 by Antoine W. van Agtmael of the International Finance Corporation of the World Bank, http://www.investopedia.com/articles/03/073003.asp, last accessed on October 29, 2013.

When studying emerging markets today, it is important to understand how the global economy is changing, what the world will look like tomorrow, five years from now, a decade from now, and how it will impact each of us. The weight of the emerging markets is already significant and being felt throughout the advanced economies and it is likely to expand further. The implications of the rise of the emerging markets on the world economy, some of which is already evident and will be discussed later in this chapter, cannot be disregarded by governance of the global economy organizations.

## The Influence of Emerging Markets across the Globe

The impact and influence of emerging markets on advanced economies and global trade is impressive. Today, these countries constitute over half of the world's population, with China and India accounting for over one third of it. As a result of intense economic transformations many of these emerging economies are facing rapid urbanization and industrialization. As of 2013 nine of the ten largest metropolitan areas in the world are located in emerging markets. (See Figure 2.1.)

By 2050, the world's population is expected to grow by 2.3 billion people, reaching about 9.1 billion. By then most of the world's new middle class will be living in the emerging economies of the world, and most of them in cities. Many of these cities have not yet been built, unless you count the plethora of ghost cities in China; cities built with the entire

| Top 10 largest cities in the World 2013 Emerging — Advanced | Population |
|---|---|
| 10. Cairo, Egypt | 19.6m |
| 9. Sao Paulo, Brazil | 19.8m |
| 8. Shanghai, China | 20.8m |
| 7. Mexico City, Mexico | 21.2m |
| 6. Manila, Philippines | 21.9m |
| 5. New Delhi, India | 22.2m |
| 4. Seoul, South Korea | 25.2m |
| 3. Jakarta, Indonesia | 28.0m |
| 2. Chongqing, China | 28.8m |
| 1. Tokyo, Japan | 35.1m |

*Figure 2.1  Top 10 largest cities in the world, 2013*

Source: IMF World Outlook, 2013

necessary infrastructure. Physical infrastructure, such as water supply, sanitation, and electricity systems, and soft infrastructure, such as recruitment agencies and intermediaries to deal with customer credit checks, will need to be built or upgraded to cope with the growing urban middle class.

As far as purchasing power, by 2030 the combined purchasing power of the global middle classes is estimated to more than double to $59 trillion. Most impressive, over 80 percent of this demand will come from Asia alone. That will come at a price though, as it will require an estimated $7.9 trillion in investments by 2020. Meeting these needs will likely entail public-private partnerships, new approaches to equity funding, and the development of capital markets.

Also impressive is the increasing size of these economies. The growth of economic strength of the BRICS countries alone is leading to greater power to influence world economic policy. Just recently, in October of 2010 emerging economies gained a greater voice under a breakthrough agreement that gave six percent of voting shares in the IMF to dynamic emerging countries such as China. As a result China became the IMF's third largest member. According to the IMF, and as depicted in Figure 2.2, by 2014 emerging markets are poised to overtake advanced economies in terms of share of global GDP.

As of 2013, as Figure 2.2 shows, emerging markets already account for about 50 percent of world's GDP and going forward, its contribution

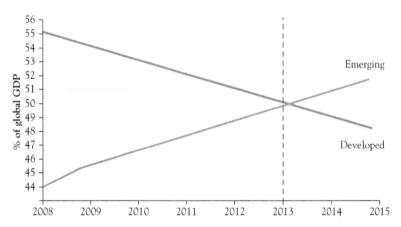

**Figure 2.2 Advanced economies and emerging markets share of global GDP**

Source: World Economic Outlook Database, International Monetary Found, October 2010

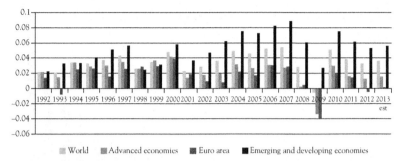

*Figure 2.3 Emerging markets are driven global GDP growth for more than a decade (2000)*

*Source:* IMF

is expected to be higher than advanced economies. Not only are these economies enormous, but they are growing exponentially. As Figure 2.2 illustrates the divergence between the economic growth of emerging markets and advanced economies is projected to continue in the years to come. Figure 2.3 shows that since 2000, emerging markets have driven global GDP growth.

The data indicates that emerging markets are now one of the main engines of world growth. As a result, emerging countries' citizens have reaped the benefits of such rapid development with higher standards of living, fostering the growth of a huge middle-class, with discretionary income to spend in goods and services, and thus impacting advanced economies in a very positive way.

These billions of new middle class consumers in the emerging markets represent new markets for advanced economies' exports and multinational corporations based in developed countries. Ford Motor Company, for example, draws almost 47 percent of its revenues from foreign markets, mainly from emerging markets. Also, strong growth in emerging markets increases the demand for those goods and tradable services where the advanced economies have comparative advantages.

According to the Economist Intelligence Unit, as of 2011, the change in real GDP per capita in emerging markets has significantly surpassed that of advanced economies. Figure 2.4 shows a striking contrast. As of 2011 per capita GDP, has risen substantially faster in many emerging market countries as compared to advanced economies. The top 10 are

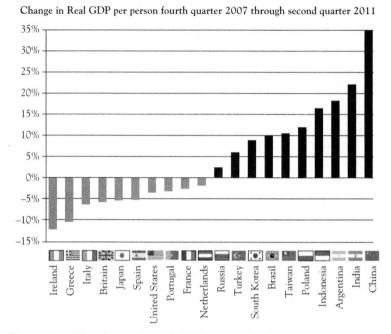

Figure 2.4 *The change in real GDP per capita in emerging markets has surpassed advanced economies by far*

Source: Economist intelligence Unit, Analytics, IMF; JPMorgan; The Economist

all emerging markets in Asia, South America, and Eastern Europe. China topped the world with nearly a 35 percent change in real GDP per person, followed by India, which had a rate change of more than 20 percent. Argentina and Brazil also grew significantly, as did Poland, Turkey, and Russia. Advanced economies, however, are debt-burdened and have detracted. Ireland and Greece have declined more than 10 percent. During the same period, the United States had the seventh worst change in real GDP per capita.

These are known macroeconomic facts. Perhaps even more striking is the microeconomic evidence of the economic success of emerging markets in the last decade and beyond. For instance, according to Forbes' Global 2000 ranking, four out of the 20 largest companies in the world, in terms of market value, are from emerging markets.[2] From these four companies, two oil and gas firms, one Russian (Gazprom), and one

Chinese (PetroChina) rank among the top 10. Also according to Forbes,[3] seven of the 24 richest individuals in the world are from the emerging markets, including Carlos Slim Helu (3rd) from Mexico; Li Ka-shing (9th) from Hong Kong; Prince Alwaleed Bin Talal Alsaud (13th) from Saudi Arabia; Mukesh Ambani (14th) from India; Anil Ambani (18th) from India; Azim Premji (21st) from India; and Lee Shau Kee (22nd) from Hong Kong.

If the present looks promising for emerging market economies, their potential future seems even brighter. According to available projections for long-term growth, based on demographic trends and models of capital accumulation and productivity, emerging markets are likely to become even more prominent in the world economy. Of course, political instabilities need to be accounted for, especially in the short term for some of these countries facing political turmoil. Nonetheless, a number of studies offer startling data regarding the growth prospects of emerging markets. According a study by Wilson & Purushothaman[4] (2003), by 2025 the BRIC countries could account for over half the size of today's six largest economies; in less than 40 years, they could be even larger. Other studies, such as Hawksworth[5] and Poncet[6] convey similar messages, notwithstanding some nominal differences.

Emerging market leaders are expected to become a disruptive force in the global competitive landscape. As emerging market countries gain in stature, new multinational companies (MNCs) will continue to take center stage in global markets. The rise of these emerging MNCs as market leaders will constitute one of the fastest-growing global trends of this decade and beyond. These MNCs will continue to be critical competitors in their home markets while increasingly making outbound investments into other emerging and advanced economies.

Many emerging market leaders have grown up in markets with *institutional voids*, where support systems such as retail distribution channels, reliable transportation and telecommunications systems, and adequate water supply simply don't exist. Physical infrastructure, such as water supply, sanitation and electricity systems, and soft infrastructure, such as recruitment agencies and intermediaries to deal with customer credit checks, are still being developed, if they exist at all, in order to cope with the growing urban middle class.

Addressing such concerns will require several trillions of dollars in investments by 2020, which could be very good news for advanced economies and professionals with an eye on, and expertise with, international businesses. Meeting these needs will likely entail public-private partnerships, new approaches to equity funding and the development of capital markets.

Having learned to overcome the challenges of serving customers of limited means in their own domestic markets, these emerging MNC market leaders are already developing and producing innovative designs, while reducing manufacturing costs, and often disrupting entire industries around the world. As a result, these companies possess a more innovative, entrepreneurial culture and have developed greater flexibility to meet the demands of their local and *bottom-of-the-pyramid* customers.

Therefore, the developments we observe today, with the rapid rising of emerging markets outpacing advanced economies, are likely to be the precursor of a profound rebalancing in the distribution of world output in the very near future. Of course, it cannot be excluded that this process might well be "non-linear," with episodes of discontinuity, perhaps also including financial crises somewhere down the line.

## The Influences of the ASEAN Bloc

Many emerging market countries that previously posed no competitive threat to advanced economies now do. The financial crisis that started in mid-1997 in Southeast Asia, and resulted in massive currency depreciations in a number of emerging markets in that region, spilled over to many other emerging nations as far as Latin America and Africa. But such crisis since then has subsided, as these same regions were the first to recover from the latest crisis of 2008. The intense currency depreciation in Asia during the late 1990's has positioned the region for a more competitive landscape across global markets.

According to an Organization for Economic Cooperation and Development (OECD) report[7] and as depicted in Figure 2.5,[8] although these emerging market economies in Asia have experienced massive exchange rate depreciations, they also have reinforced their absolute cost advantages given the increasing importance of these economies in world trade.

| Percent | | | |
|---|---|---|---|
| | vis-à-vis<br>U.S. Dollar | vis-à-vis<br>Japanese Yen | vis-à-vis<br>Deutsche Mark |
| China | 0 | 13 | 5 |
| Chinese Taipei | 15 | −3 | 10 |
| Hong Kong, China | 0 | 13 | 5 |
| Indonesia | −76 | −73 | −75 |
| Korea | −40 | −32 | −37 |
| Malaysia | −32 | −22 | −28 |
| Philippines | −32 | −24 | −29 |
| Singapore | 11 | 1 | 7 |
| Thailand | −40 | −32 | −37 |

*Figure 2.5 Changes in Asian emerging market economies exchange rates since mid-1997*

Note: Changes between 1 July 1997 and 18 March 1998.

Countries such as Thailand, Indonesia, and South Korea, which were impacted the most during the 1990's are now emerging market leaders, representing a major shift in the global competitive landscape. We believe this is a trend that will only continue to strengthen as these countries grow in size, establish dominance, and seek new opportunities beyond their traditional domestic and near-shore markets.

Meanwhile, advanced economies in the G-7 group are still struggling with indebtedness. The United States continues to deal with debt ceiling adjustments to cope with its ever-increasing government debt while the eurozone is far from solving its own economic problems. Conversely, despite inevitable risks and uncertainties, Southeast Asia registered solid economic growth in 2012 and continues to be on an upward trajectory for the foreseeable future, as China's economy stabilizes and higher levels of foreign direct investment (FDI) are pouring in.

The ASEAN is an organization of countries located in the Southeast Asian region that aims to accelerate economic growth, social progress, and cultural development among its members and to promote regional peace. The region has undergone a period of substantial resurgence after the 1997–1998 Asian financial crises, and has been playing second fiddle to more industrialized economies in Asia-Pacific, which manage to attract the majority of capital inflows. What we've seen since the financial crisis,

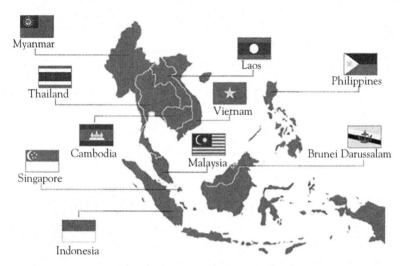

**Figure 2.6  List of ASEAN member countries as of 2012**[9]

*Source*: ASEAN

however, is that ASEAN has been showcasing its ability to recover and advance its position within global markets.

As of 2012, the ASEAN bloc is comprised of ten member states including Brunei Darussalam, Cambodia, Indonesia, Laos PDR, Malaysia, Myanmar, Philippines, Singapore, Thailand, and Vietnam. (See Figure 2.6.)

Studies carried out by the Asian Development Bank Institute (ADBI)[10] suggest that the emergence of international production networks in East Asia results from market-driven forces such as vertical specialization and higher production costs in the home countries, and institutional-led initiatives, such as free trade agreements. For instance, the region has experienced significant growth in the trade of parts and components since the 1990s, especially with China, who is one of the important major assembly bases. In addition, the decline in the share of parts and components trade in several members of the ASEAN bloc, such as Indonesia and Thailand, indicates the increasing importance of the bloc countries as assembly bases for advanced economies such as Japan, and its multinational enterprises (MNEs). China and Thailand are becoming important auto parts assembly bases for Japan and other advanced economies, attracting foreign investments into those countries, raising their GDP, and contributing more to the emergence of international production networks than just free trade agreements. Figure 2.7 provides a list of

| Rank ⬥ | Country ⬥ | Population in millions ⬥ | | GDP Nominal millions of USD ⬥ | | GDP Nominal per capita ⬥ | | GDP (PPP) millions of USD ⬥ | | GDP (PPP) per capita ⬥ | |
|---|---|---|---|---|---|---|---|---|---|---|---|
| — | *World* | *7,013.42* | | *71,707,302* | | *10,200* | | *83,140,055* | | *11,850* | |
| — | European Union | 502.56 | | 16,584,007 | | 32,518 | | 16,092,525 | | 32,021 | |
| — | United States | 314.18 | | 15,684,750 | | 49,922 | | 15,684,750 | | 49,922 | |
| — | China | 1,354.04 | | 8,227,037 | | 6,076 | | 12,405,670 | | 9,162 | |
| — | Japan | 127.61 | | 5,963,969 | | 46,736 | | 4,627,891 | | 36,266 | |
| — | *ASEAN* | *615.60* | *100.0* | *2,305,542* | *100.0* | *3,745* | *100.0* | *3,605,602* | *100.0* | *5,857* | *100.0* |
| — | South Korea | 50.01 | | 1,155,872 | | 23,113 | | 1,613,921 | | 32,272 | |
| 1 | Indonesia | 244.47 | 39.7 | 878,198 | 38.1 | 3,592 | 95.9 | 1,216,738 | 33.7 | 4,977 | 85.0 |
| 2 | Thailand | 64.38 | 10.5 | 365,564 | 15.9 | 5,678 | 151.6 | 651,856 | 18.1 | 10,126 | 172.9 |
| 3 | Malaysia | 29.46 | 4.8 | 303,527 | 13.2 | 10,304 | 275.1 | 498,477 | 13.8 | 16,922 | 288.9 |
| 4 | Singapore | 5.41 | 0.9 | 276,520 | 12.0 | 51,162 | 1,366.1 | 326,506 | 9.1 | 60,410 | 1,031.4 |
| 5 | Philippines | 95.80 | 15.6 | 250,436 | 10.9 | 2,614 | 69.8 | 424,355 | 11.8 | 4,430 | 75.6 |
| 6 | Vietnam | 90.39 | 14.7 | 138,071 | 6.0 | 1,528 | 40.8 | 320,677 | 8.9 | 3,548 | 60.6 |
| 7 | Myanmar | 63.67 | 10.3 | 53,140 | 2.3 | 835 | 22.3 | 89,461 | 2.5 | 1,405 | 24.0 |
| 8 | Brunei | 0.40 | 0.1 | 16,628 | 0.7 | 41,703 | 1,113.5 | 21,687 | 0.6 | 54,389 | 928.6 |
| 9 | Cambodia | 15.25 | 2.5 | 14,241 | 0.6 | 934 | 24.9 | 36,645 | 1.0 | 2,402 | 41.0 |
| 10 | Laos | 6.38 | 1.0 | 9,217 | 0.4 | 1,446 | 38.6 | 19,200 | 0.5 | 3,011 | 51.4 |

*Figure 2.7  List of ASEAN countries GDP*

Source: IMF Global Outlook 2012 estimates

ASEAN members and their respective GDP, as well as a comparison with major G-7 member states, with exception to China.

Of course, the ASEAN region has had its fair share of risks and challenges, which unfortunately are not going away. ASEAN politicians, like politicians everywhere, occasionally cave in to populist measures. Since the crises of 2008 these populist measures have been present in both the advanced economies and emerging markets, with only the level of intensity as the single variant. But ASEAN's deep commitment to macroeconomic stability, open trade, business-friendly policies, and regional cooperation has created the foundation for steady growth in those regions.

This is also true for many emerging market nations around the globe and in particular the BRICS. Nonetheless, the ASEAN region remains among the most attractive destination for foreign investors who are running out of options in other emerging markets. Its relative political and macroeconomic stability, low levels of debt, integration in East Asian production networks, and open trade and investment policies are giving the region a distinct advantage over other emerging markets around the world. As depicted in Figure 2.8, these countries have been growing at

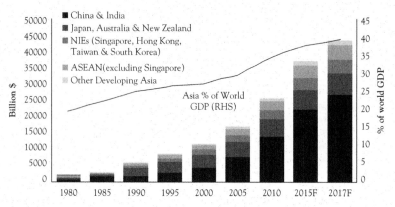

*Figure 2.8 Asian Economic GDP growth based on purchasing power parity (Current International Dollar Billion)\**

*An International dollar has the same purchasing power over GDP as the U.S. dollar has in the United States.
Source: International Monetary Found, World Economic Outlook, October 2012; Austrade

an average rate above six percent (in 2012) a year, with Indonesia and the Philippines exceeding GDP forecasts. Thailand, hit with devastating floods in 2011, has now recovered and is in full swing to achieve higher than expected GDP growth. The same goes for Malaysia, which has enjoyed the benefits of an expansionary election budget.

According to Arno Maierbrugger from Investvine,[11] the ASEAN economy will more than double by 2020, with the nominal GDP of the regional bloc increasing from $2 trillion in 2012 to $4.7 trillion. The global research firm IHS[12] argues that Vietnam and Myanmar are expected to reach a nominal GDP of $290 billion and $103 billion, respectively, by 2020, while Indonesia is expected to reach a projected nominal GDP of about $1.9 trillion. The report also says that overall emerging markets in Asia are expected to be the fastest growing in the world and will continue to expand. It estimated that GDP growth of emerging markets would exceed that of developed countries in 2020, continuing to expand thereafter.

Internal macroeconomic policies and structural reforms in the ASEAN region will continue to drive growth in the foreseeable future. The Philippines and Myanmar should see higher GDP growth as a result of earnest government efforts to improve economic governance. Myanmar, after 50 years of self-imposed isolation, fear, and poverty, has rejoined the international community, attracting fresh foreign investments, which should yield significant growth dividends.

In 2013, two parallel efforts toward trade integration, the ASEAN-driven Regional Comprehensive Economic Partnership (RCEP), and the U.S.-driven TPP, began vying for traction beyond the ASEAN bloc. Currently, the TPP is more advanced but faces important challenges before it can come to closure. Discussions on the RCEP have only just begun and also face significant obstacles, but progress could accelerate if an agreement on the basic parameters is reached soon. Although both of these trade agreements should be able to coexist, they not only include a set of advanced economies, which can be very beneficial to those countries, but also represent different philosophies as to how economic integration should be achieved.

The risk to emerging markets in the ASEAN bloc and the advanced economies partnership in trade, as in TTP, are the mounting tensions in the South China Sea, with China facing off against Vietnam and the Philippines. ASEAN's diplomatic attempts to defuse the conflict have only succeeded in raising them even further. It is important now that under a new chair in Brunei, ASEAN countries find ways to settle their internal differences, agree quickly on a code of conduct for the South China Sea, and engage China early in the process so that it becomes an important stakeholder in its implementation and international trade.

Despite geopolitical risks in the region, one of the major catalysts for ASEAN's accelerated growth is its relative low specialized labor costs. While estimates of cost levels in the manufacturing sector are not fully available, data from OECD and the IMF suggest that over the 1975 to 1996 period, China (including Taipei) and South Korea in particular, were able to maintain significantly lower levels of specialized labor costs than any other industrialized countries for which data exist. Important to note, as argued by Durant et al[13] (1998), is the fact that while in the past these potential competitive advantages deriving from nominal exchange rate depreciations often tended to be eroded by rising inflation, there is a widespread sentiment that recent global economic and in-country financial policy developments might have reinforced the absolute cost advantage that emerging markets might have already compared to OECD countries, which makes these markets even more competitive internationally.

Such arguments are reinforced by the fact that in principle, competitiveness is normally correlated with companies, which can gain and lose market shares, and eventually even go out of business. The same cannot be said for countries. As P. Krugman (1996) argues[14] countries cannot go out of business and therefore we should not care about competing countries. Nonetheless, in our opinion, countries still need to be concerned with shifts in market shares, since such shifts may indicate changes in the composition of country output and in the living standards of that nation. Hence, it is likely that labor cost levels in most other emerging market economies in the ASEAN bloc are also *much* lower, than in other nations, particularly advanced economies, as depicted in Figure 2.9.

We believe leading emerging markets will continue to drive global growth. Estimates show that 70 percent of world growth over the next

| | USA = 100 | | |
|---|---|---|---|
| | **1985** | **1990** | **1996** |
| United States | 100 | 100 | 100 |
| Japan | 74 | 116 | 169 |
| Germany[a] | 71 | 144 | 166 |
| France | 96 | 154 | 163 |
| Italy | 60 | 114 | 101 |
| United Kingdom | 100 | 158 | 148 |
| Canada | 84 | 118 | 102 |
| Australia | 98 | 118 | 145 |
| Belgium | 75 | 135 | 156 |
| Denmark | 97 | 205 | 218 |
| Korea | 29 | 51 | 58 |
| Netherlands | 65 | 122 | 120 |
| Spain | 49 | 108 | 100 |
| Sweden | 82 | 158 | 160 |
| Chinese Taipei | 41 | 70 | 70 |

[a] West Germany.

*Figure 2.9  Relative levels of unit labor costs in manufacturing*

Source: OECD calculations based on 1990 PPPs. For details on the methodological aspects, see OECD (1993)

decade, well into 2020 and beyond, will come from emerging markets, with China and India accounting for 40 percent of that growth. Such growth is even more significant if we look at it from the purchasing power parity (PPP) perspective, which, adjusted for variation, the IMF forecasts that the total GDP of emerging markets could overtake that of advanced economies as early as 2014. Such forecasts also suggest that FDI will continue to find its way into emerging markets, particularly the ASEAN bloc, but also to the fast-developing MENA bloc, as well as Africa as a whole, followed by the BRIC and CIVETS. In all, however, the emerging markets already attract almost 50 percent of FDI global inflows and account for 25 percent of FDI outflows.

As noted earlier, between now and 2050, the world's population is expected to grow by 2.3 billion people, eventually reaching 9.1 billion. The combined purchasing power of the global middle classes is estimated to more than double by 2030 to US$56 trillion. Over 80 percent of this demand will come from Asia. Most of the world's new middle class will live in the emerging world, and almost all will live in cities, often in smaller cities not yet built. This surge of urbanization will stimulate business but put huge strains on infrastructure.

## The Influences of the BRICS Bloc

The original BRIC countries included Brazil, Russia, India, and China. Jim O'Neill, a retired former asset manager at Goldman and Sachs, coined the acronym in 2001 in his paper entitled *Building Better Global Economic BRICs*.[15] The acronym came into widespread use as a symbol of the apparent shift in global economic power away from the developed G-7 economies toward the emerging markets. When we look at the size of its economies in GDP terms, however, the order of the letters in the acronym changes, with China leading the way (second in the world), followed by Brazil (sixth), India (ninth), and Russia (tenth).* In 2010, despite the lack of support from leading economists participating at the Reuters 2011 Investment Outlook Summit,[16] South Africa (28th) joined the BRIC bloc, forming a new acronym dubbed BRICS.[17]

---

* According to United Nations 2011 ranking.

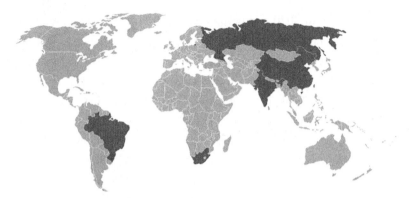

*Figure 2.10 The BRICS countries: Brazil, Russia, India, China, and South Africa*

It has been difficult to project future influences of the BRICS on the global economy. While some research suggests this bloc might overtake the G-7 economies by 2027,[18] other more modest forecasts argue that while the BRICS are developing rapidly, their combined economies could eclipse the combined economies of the current richest countries of the world by 2050.[19] In his recent book titled *The Growth Map: Economic Opportunity in the BRICs and Beyond*,[20] O'Neil corrects his earlier forecast by arguing the BRICS may overtake the G-7 by 2035. Such forecast represents an amazing accomplishment considering how disparate some of these countries are from each other geographically and the differences in their culture, political and religious systems. Figure 2.10 illustrates the BRICS geographical locations on the globe.

Notwithstanding these uncertain economic forecasts, researchers seem to agree that the BRICS have a major impact on their regional trading partners, more distant resource-rich countries, and in particular advanced economies. The ascent of these formerly impoverished countries is gaining momentum, and their confidence is evident. Former Chinese Premier, Wen Jiabao, stated in 2009 that China had "loaned huge amounts of money," to the United States, warning the United States and others to "honor its word" and "ensure the safety of Chinese assets." The former Prime Minister of India, Manmohan Singh, has blamed the "massive failure" of the global financial system in 2008 on authorities in "developed societies." His peers all name the United States specifically.

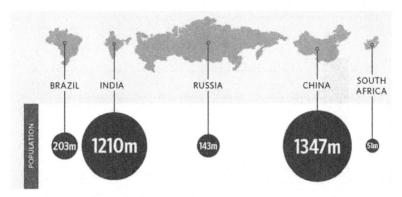

*Figure 2.11* **BRICS account for almost 50 percent of world population**

*Source*: Population Reference Bureau

Vladimir Putin, as the fourth president of Russia scorns "the irresponsibility of the system that claims leadership," while Luiz Inácio Lula da Silva, former president of Brazil, in an interview with *Newsweek* magazine during the G-20 Summit in London, said the United States bears the brunt of responsibility for the crisis, and for fixing it.[21]

No doubt, there is a lot of global macroeconomics synergy behind the BRICS, and the performance indicators are backing it up. As of 2012, these countries accounted for over a quarter of the world's land mass and more than 46 percent of the world's population,[22] although still only account for 25 percent of the world GDP.[23] (See Figure 2.11.) Nonetheless, by 2020, this bloc of countries is expected to account for nearly 50 percent of all global GDP growth.

Since its formation, it is clear the BRICS have been seeking to form a *political club*. According to a Reuter's article, the BRIC bloc has strong interest in converting "their growing economic power into greater geopolitical clout."[24] Granted, the BRICS bloc does not represent a political coalition currently capable of playing a leading geopolitical role on the global stage. That being said, over the last decade the BRICS has come to symbolize the growing power of the world's largest emerging economies and their potential impact on the global economic and, increasingly, political order. All BRICS countries are current members of the United Nations Security Council. Russia and China are permanent members with veto power, while Brazil, India, and South Africa are nonpermanent members

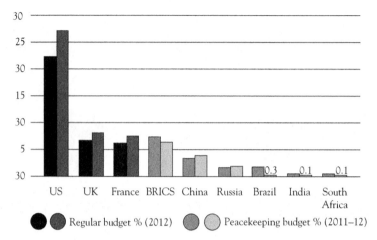

*Figure 2.12  BRICS have increased their participation and contribution to UN budgets*

currently serving on the Council. Furthermore, the combined BRICS hold less than 15 percent of voting rights in both the World Bank and the IMF, yet their economies are predicted to surpass the G-7 economies in size by 2032. This can only strengthen their position at the UN, IMF, and the World Bank.

As depicted in Figure 2.12, BRICS have stepped up their participation in the United Nations by donating large sums of money to its regular and peacekeeping budgets. Russia has led the bloc by holding the firm BRICS summit back in June of 2009 in Yekaterinburg, issuing a declaration calling for the establishment of an equitable, democratic and multipolar world order.[25] Since then, according to the Times,[26] the BRICS have met in Brasília, Brazil (2010), Sanya, China (2011), and New Delhi, India (2012).

In recent years, the BRIC have received increasing scholarly attention. Brazilian political economist Marcos Troyjo and French investment banker Christian Déséglise founded the BRICLab at Columbia University, a forum examining the strategic, political and economic consequences of the rise of BRIC countries, especially by analyzing their projects for power, prosperity and prestige through graduate courses, special sessions with guest speakers, Executive Education programs, and annual conferences for policymakers, business and academic leaders, and students.[27]

## The Challenge of Global Influence

The BRICS' continuing growing economic strength is advancing toward greater power to influence world economic policy. In October 2010, for example, emerging economies gained a greater voice under a landmark agreement that gave six percent of IMF voting shares to dynamic emerging countries such as China. Under this agreement, China will become the IMF's third-largest member.

The differences between the BRIC bloc, in terms of values, economics, political structure, and geopolitical interests, far outweigh the commonalities. There are, however, fundamental commonalities, particularly with regard to mild anti-Americanism, and the overall internal and domestic challenges these countries face, including institutional stability, social inequality, and demographic pressures. The BRICS bloc is important for members in terms of the symbolism of creating for themselves an important role on the global stage, with a desire to wield greater influence over the rules governing international commerce, and economic policy.

Castro Neves, a founding partner at CAC Political Consultancy, and also contributing editor at *The Brazilian Economy* magazine, argues that Brazil's "foreign policy priority is to consolidate its economic gains at the national level by building international influence and partners, and the BRICS group represents an important opportunity to realize that vision."[28] Fyodor Lukyanov, Editor of Global Affairs in Moscow, Russia, believes the bloc, although "unable to take a concerted stand on the new head of the IMF," has an opportunity "to have a more influential, if not major, global role in the future."*

We believe the absence of shared values between all BRICS members limits the global potential for the bloc. The inclusion of South Africa to the group may have been a good strategy, but the pull toward expanding the group to new members would dilute any cohesiveness it currently possesses.

# The Influences of the CIVETS Bloc

The CIVETS acronym, which includes Colombia, Indonesia, Vietnam, Egypt, Turkey, and South Africa countries, as illustrated in Figure 2.13, was coined by Robert Ward, Global Director of the Global Forecasting Team

---

* Ibidem.

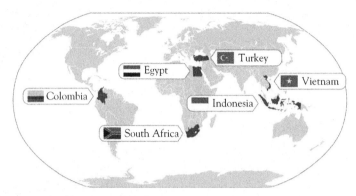

*Figure 2.13  The CIVETS Bloc*

of the Economist Intelligence Unit (EIU) in late 2009.[29] It was further circulated by Michael Geoghegan, President of the Anglo-Chinese HSBC bank, in a speech to the Hong Kong Chamber of Commerce in April 2010. These groups of countries are predicted to be among the next emerging markets to quickly rise in economic prominence over the coming decades for their relative political stability, young populations that focus on education, and overall growing economic trends. Geoghegan compared these countries to the civet, a carnivorous mammal that eats and partially digests coffee cherries, passing a transformed coffee bean that fetches high prices.

The CIVETS bloc is about 10 years younger than the BRICS with similar characteristics. All of these bloc countries are growing very quickly and have relatively diverse economies. They offer a greater advantage over the BRICS, as they don't depend as heavily on foreign demands. They also have reasonably sophisticated financial systems, controlled inflation, and soaring young populations with fast-rising domestic consumption.[30]

Geoghegan argued in 2010 that emerging markets would grow three times as fast as developed countries that year, suggesting that the center of gravity of the world growth and economic development was moving toward Asia and Latin America.* All the CIVETS countries except Colombia and South Africa also are part of O'Neil's *Next Eleven* (N-11) countries. As depicted in Figure 2.14, this includes: Bangladesh, Egypt, Indonesia, Iran, Mexico, Nigeria, Pakistan, Philippines, Turkey, South Korea, and Vietnam. These countries are believed to have a high chance

---

* Ibidem.

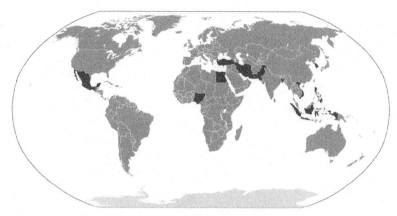

*Figure 2.14  The Next-Eleven (N-11) Countries*

of becoming, along with the BRICS, the world's largest economies in the 21st century.[31]

Some critics argue that the CIVETS countries have nothing in common beyond their youth populations. What does Egypt have in common with Vietnam? Data also suggest that on the negative side, liquidity and corporate governance are patchy, while political risks remain a factor, as seen with Egypt in the past few years.

## The Influences of the MENA Countries

According to the World Bank,[32] the bloc, commonly known as MENA covers an extensive region, extending from Morocco to Iran and including the majority of both the Middle Eastern and Maghreb countries. The World Bank argues that due to the geographic ambiguity and Eurocentric nature of the term *Middle East*, people often prefer to use the term WANA (West Asia and North Africa)[33] or the less common NAWA (North Africa-West Asia).[34] As depicted in Figure 2.15, MENA countries include Algeria, Bahrain, Djibouti, Egypt, Iran, Iraq, Israel, Jordan, Kuwait, Lebanon, Libya, Malta, Morocco, Oman, Qatar, Saudi Arabia, North and South Sudan, Syria, Tunisia, United Arab Emirates (UAE), Yemen, West Bank, and Gaza.

The MENA bloc, regardless if known as WANA or NAWA (we'll be using MENA throughout this book), is an economically diverse region that includes both the oil-rich economies in the Gulf, and countries that

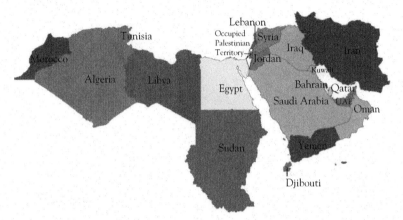

*Figure 2.15 The MENA countries (dark shade) and other countries often considered as part of the bloc (lighter shade)*

Source: GreenProfit

are resource-scarce in relation to population, such as Egypt, Morocco, and Yemen. According to the Middle East Strategy at Harvard (MESH) project at the John Olin Institute for Strategic Study at Harvard University, the population of the MENA region, as depicted in Figure 2.16, at its least extent is roughly 381 million people, about six percent of the total world population. At its greatest extent, its population is roughly 523 million.

Two years after the *Arab Spring* commenced, many nations in the MENA region are still undergoing complex political, social, and economic transitions. Economic performance indicators were mixed in 2012, while most of the oil-exporting countries grew at healthy rates; the same is not true for oil importing ones, which have been growing at a sluggish pace. However, due to the scaling-back of hydrocarbon production among oil exporters and a mild economic recovery among oil importers, the differences narrowed in 2013. In all, many of these countries are confronted with the immediate challenge of re-establishing or sustaining macroeconomic stability amid political uncertainty and social unrest, but the region must not lose sight of the medium-term challenge of diversifying its economies, creating jobs, and generating more inclusive growth.

| Population Size and Growth in the Countries of the Middle East and North Africa: 1950, 2007, and 2050 | | | | | |
|---|---|---|---|---|---|
| | Population in thousands | | | Ratio of population | |
| Country and region | 1950 | 2007 | 2050* | 2007/ 1950 | 2050/ 2007 |
| Middle East and North Africa (MENA) | 103,886 | 431,578 | 692,299 | 4.2 | 1.6 |
| MENA-Western Asia | 51,452 | 215,976 | 332,081 | 4.2 | 1.5 |
| Iran | 16,913 | 71,208 | 100,174 | 4.2 | 1.4 |
| Iraq | 5,340 | 28,993 | 61,942 | 5.4 | 2.1 |
| Israel | 1,258 | 6,928 | 10,527 | 5.5 | 1.5 |
| Jordan | 472 | 5,924 | 10,121 | 12.5 | 1.7 |
| Lebanon | 1,443 | 4,099 | 5,221 | 2.8 | 1.3 |
| Palestinian Territory | 1,005 | 4,017 | 10,265 | 4.0 | 2.6 |
| Syria | 3,536 | 19,929 | 34,887 | 5.6 | 1.8 |
| Turkey | 21,484 | 74,877 | 98,946 | 3.5 | 1.3 |
| Arabian Peninsula | 8,336 | 58,544 | 123,946 | 7.0 | 2.1 |
| Bahrain | 116 | 753 | 1,173 | 6.5 | 1.6 |
| Kuwait | 152 | 2,851 | 5,240 | 18.7 | 1.8 |
| Oman | 456 | 2,595 | 4,639 | 5.7 | 1.8 |
| Qatar | 25 | 841 | 1,333 | 33.6 | 1.6 |
| Saudi Arabia | 3,201 | 24,735 | 45,030 | 7.7 | 1.8 |
| United Arab Emirates | 70 | 4,380 | 8,521 | 62.9 | 1.9 |
| Yemen | 4,316 | 22,389 | 58,009 | 5.2 | 2.6 |
| Northern Africa | 44,099 | 157,068 | 236,272 | 3.6 | 1.5 |
| Algeria | 8,753 | 33,858 | 49,610 | 3.9 | 1.5 |
| Egypt | 21,834 | 75,498 | 121,219 | 3.5 | 1.6 |
| Morocco | 8,953 | 31,224 | 42,583 | 3.5 | 1.4 |
| Libya | 1,029 | 6,160 | 9,683 | 6.0 | 1.6 |
| Tunisia | 3,530 | 10,327 | 13,178 | 2.9 | 1.3 |

*Projected

*Figure 2.16 MENA's population size and growth*

Source: MESH & UN Population Division. World Population Prospects: The 2006 Revision (2007; http://esa.un.org/, accessed April 10, 2007): table A.2

The region's economic wealth over much of the past quarter century has been heavily influenced by two factors: the price of oil and the legacy of economic policies and structures that had emphasized a leading role for the state. With about 23 percent of the 300 million people in the Middle East and North Africa living on less than two dollars a day, however, empowering poor people constitutes an important strategy for fighting poverty.

Modest growth is anticipated, however, across the region. According to the IMF,[35] subdued growth in MENA oil importers is expected to improve in 2013, although such growth is not expected to be sufficient to even begin making sizable inroads into the region's large unemployment problem. The external environment continues to exert pressure on international reserves in many oil-importing countries among the MENA bloc and remains a challenge. In addition, sluggish economic activity with trading partners, mostly advanced economies, in particular the eurozone area, is holding back a quicker recovery of exports. Elevated commodity prices continue to weigh on external balances in countries that depend on food and energy imports. Tourist arrivals, which have decreased significantly since the terrorist attacks on the United States in 2001, are gradually rebounding, but remain well below pre-2011 levels and before the global recession set in.

According to a new study reported in the Dubai-based Khaleej Times,[36] the sunny region and its associated countries could solar power the world three times over. If such projections ever become reality, poverty may have a chance to be eradicated in the region. Countries that move fast, the study suggests, could have the competitive advantage. MENA countries, especially ones located on the Arabian Peninsula, as well as others like Jordan, Lebanon, and Israel are well positioned to take the lead in this industry. These countries are no strangers to the notion of solar energy. As the Khaleej Times article points out the countries in the MENA region have the "greatest potential for solar regeneration" supplying 45 percent of the world's energy sources possible through renewable energy. Renewable energy sources of interest in this region include Abu Dhabi's Masdar City, as well as its hosting of the World Renewable Energy Agency headquarters.

Funding for these projects may pose an issue. Foreign direct investment, according to the IMF,[37] is expected to remain restrained and lower than in other emerging markets and advanced economies. Moreover, growing regional economic and social spillovers from the conflict in Syria is expected to add to the complexity of MENA's economic environment. While oil-exporting countries, mainly in the Gulf Cooperation Council (GCC), face a more positive outlook, there is still the risk of a worsening of the global economic outlook, particularly with advanced economies, which are major consumers of oil. Should this occur, oil exporting nations within MENA will likely face serious economic pressures. A prolonged decline in oil prices, rooted in persistently low global economic activity, for instance, could run down reserve buffers and result in fiscal deficits for the region.

The latest IMF's World Economic Outlook[38] projections suggest that economic performance in the MENA bloc will remain mixed. According to Qatar National Bank Group (QNB Group),[39] this dual speed development should continue over the next few years, with the GCC countries as the driving force for growth in the MENA region and the main source of investment and financing. As shown in Figure 2.17, the Group forecasts MENA's economy to grow 2.1 percent in 2013 and 3.8 percent in 2014. Note in Figure 2.17 that the overall forecast disguises a significant difference in performance between oil exporters, including the GCC countries, and oil importers. The 2012 restrained growth of 2.7 percent in MENA oil importers is expected to fall to 1.6 percent in 2013 and recover to 3.2 percent in 2014, which will not create enough jobs to reduce these

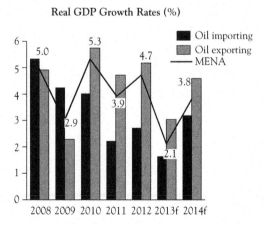

**Real GDP Growth Rates (%)**

*Figure 2.17 MENA's real GDP growth rates*

countries' large unemployment rates. Meanwhile, oil exporters' healthy growth rates are projected to moderate this year to three percent as they scale back increases in oil production amidst modest global energy demand. Continued large infrastructure investment is expected to lead to a rise in economic growth to 4.5 percent in 2014.

In addition, the MENA countries in transition continue to face political uncertainty with the challenge of delivering on the expectations for jobs and fostering economic cohesion, which also deters growth. In particular, the Syrian crisis has had a strong negative impact on growth in the Mashreq region: the region of Arab countries to the east of Egypt and north of the Arabian Peninsula, such as Iraq, Palestine/Israel, Jordan, Kuwait, Lebanon, and Syria. Syria has a large amount of refugees straining the fiscal resources of countries like Iraq, Jordan, Lebanon, and, to a lesser extent, Turkey. A notable example is the more than 800,000 Syrian refugees who have already entered Lebanon, about 19 percent of the population, and have had a substantial impact on the already weak fiscal position of the Lebanese budget. Equally damaging have been the setbacks of the political transitions as well as the escalation of violence in Libya, Egypt and Tunisia, which have further deterred FDI and much needed economic reforms.

Looking ahead, MENA countries will continue on their path of economic transition owing primarily to the benign GCC outlook, which will continue to act as the locomotive for regional growth. That said, caution must be given to the external environment in volatile oil importing countries with spillovers from the Syria conflict. Finally, as important as it is now to focus on maintaining economic stability, it is critical for MENA governments not to lose sight of the fundamental medium-term challenge of modernizing and diversifying the region's economies, creating more jobs, and providing fair and equitable opportunities for all.

# CHAPTER 3

# Advanced versus Emerging Markets

## Global Economic Prospects

### Overview

Advanced economies and emerging markets find themselves in different economic and political cycles, which are causing the global recovery to ascend at two different speeds. In 2011, the IMF estimated the global economy was growing at 4.4 percent, while advanced economies were growing at 2.4 percent and emerging markets at 6.5 percent. The global economic growth trend is changing significantly. Emerging markets were responsible for roughly 70 percent of the total growth of 2012, while most advanced economies are still with slow growth challenges, high unemployment, and very uncertain financial markets.

Furthermore, the average fiscal deficit for advanced economies is about seven percent of its GDP, almost two percent more than those of emerging markets, and it is likely this trend will continue for the next few years due to the high risk of fiscal sustainability. In our opinion, advanced economies should strive to balance their fiscal consolidation objectives and strengthen their economic growth.

Conversely, some emerging markets are reaching the point where their economies are beginning to overheat, which generates inflationary challenges and makes it harder to control capital flows. Such inflationary pressure in these markets is a sensitive issue. As food and basic product prices, which are included in the consumer price index (CPI) of many of these nations, such as India, Russia, and China, increase, even more inflationary pressures are created. Notwithstanding, China has continued to register robust economic performance, creating many job opportunities,

improving the standard of leaving of its people, and acting as an important generator of growth in the global economy.

As for advanced economies, the challenges these countries face, in
particular the United States and the EU are enormous. In early November
2013, the figures on growth, according to the U.S. federal government,
continued to show signs of underlying economic weakness as EU's
European Central Bank (ECB) unexpectedly cut interest rates to a record
low, reflecting the threat of deflation.

## Advanced Economies Prospects

According to a New York Times article[1] by Jack Ewing, the economy
in the United States would experience a 2.8 percent annualized growth
for the third quarter, which turned out to be too optimistic, despite the
fact that it was the fastest quarterly increase in output, well above the two
percent economists expected. Nearly a full point of that jump was caused
by a buildup in inventory, which can sap expansion. In reality, the annual
rate of growth in consumer spending slowed sharply to 1.5 percent; the
weakest quarterly increase in more than two years, while spending by the
federal government fell 1.7 percent.

Olivier Blanchard, chief economist at the IMF, argued in October
2013 that advanced economies were strengthening, while emerging market economies were weakening.[2] Blanchard maintained that while fiscal
risks in the United States, as worrisome as they are, should not lead investors to lose sight of the bigger picture. As the world economy has entered
yet another transition, advanced economies are slowly strengthening.
Simultaneously he contends, emerging market economies have slowed
down, more so than the IMF had in July 2013.*

According to Blanchard, advanced economies' growth should be
around 1.2 percent in 2013, and two percent in 2014, while growth in
emerging markets should be around 3.3 percent in 2013, and 3.1 percent
in 2014, representing a slightly positive growth for advanced economies
and slightly negative growth for emerging markets.

While the United States and the EU share many problems, it is clear
that the situation on much of the continent is worse. Many economies

---

* Ibidem.

in the EU are now stabilizing after six quarters of renewed recession, and unemployment across the 17 nations that share the euro currency stands at roughly 12 percent. In especially hard-hit countries like Greece and Spain, the unemployment rate is more than twice that number. As of September 2013, the latest data on unemployment in the U.S. stood at 7.2 percent. Amid the discouraging economic trends in the U.S., the consistently overly optimistic European Commission cut its growth forecast for 2014 to 1.1 percent from 1.2 percent.

Clearly, more than any other time in history, the United States and the EU's central banks are working together as much as possible, trying to prevent further deflation of their economies. The growth prospects in the United States were further compromised by a sudden drop in the eurozone inflation to an annual rate of 0.7 percent in October 2013, well below the ECB's official target of about two percent. The decline raised the threat of deflation, a sustained fall in prices that could destroy the confidence of consumers and the profits of companies, along with the jobs they provide.

While austerity rhetoric has taken root in both the United States and many European capitals, crimping fiscal policy, the course charted by central bankers in these two major advanced economies, in terms of monetary policy are beginning to go in different directions. Unlike the ECB, the United States has moved aggressively to stimulate the economy, not only cutting short-term interest rates to near zero, but embarking on three rounds of asset purchases aimed at lowering borrowing rates and augmenting the growth rate.

Looking ahead, the picture for growth remains cloudy for most advanced economies, particularly for the United States and the EU. We believe there are several economic and fiscal forces affecting the world today. The high indebtedness of advanced economies as a whole imposes major challenges for sustainable growth. In addition, emerging markets are still dependent on their exports to those nations, although these economies have begun diversifying their export market trading among each other with more frequency. The following is a brief overview of major global economic prospects for the main advanced economies and emerging markets, and how they are intertwined and impact one another.

# The United States

The U.S. economy, despite being the largest economy in the world, has not recovered fully from the 2008 financial crisis and ensuing recession. The federal system of government, designed to reserve significant powers to the state and local levels, has been strained by the national government's rapid expansion. Spending at the national level rose to over 25 percent of GDP in 2010, and gross public debt surpassed 100 percent of GDP in 2011. Obamacare, a 2010 health care bill, greatly expanded the central government's regulatory role, and the Dodd–Frank financial overhaul bill roiled credit markets. In the same year, the election of a Republican Party majority in the House of Representatives helped slow government spending down, but it divided the government, leaving economic policies in flux, which continued to endure well past the reelection of President Obama in 2012.

Economic freedom also is plummeting in the United States. According to the Heritage's 2013 Index of Economic freedom,*† the U.S has registered a loss of economic freedom for the fifth consecutive year, recording in 2013 its lowest Index score since 2000. Furthermore, our government has become increasingly more bloated, with trends toward cronyism that erodes the rule of law, thus stifling dynamic entrepreneurial growth. More than three years after the end of recession in June 2009, the United States continued to suffer from policy choices that have led to the slowest recovery in 70 years. Overall, businesses remain in a holding pattern, except for some sectors, such as the military and biotech. Unemployment is close to 7.5 percent. Prospects for greater fiscal freedom are uncertain due to the scheduled expiration of previous cuts in income and payroll taxes, and the imposition of new taxes associated with the 2010 health care law.

---

* http://www.heritage.org/index/country/unitedstates

† The concept of *economic freedom*, or economic liberty, denotes the ability of members of a society to undertake economic direction and actions. This is a term used in economic and policy debates as well as a politico economic philosophy. One major approach to economic freedom comes from classical liberal and libertarian traditions emphasizing free markets, free trade and private property under free enterprise, while another extends the welfare economics study of individual choice, with greater economic freedom coming from a "larger" set of possible choices.

As of fall 2013, Blanchard* contended that the private demand in the United States continued to be strong and that economic recovery should strengthen, assuming no fiscal accidents. We can't be sure of what he meant, but in our opinion, it seems logical that quantitative easing in the United States would need to continue for some time. Blanchard believes that, while the immediate concern for the United States is with the government shutdown that happened in the fall of 2013, and making sure it doesn't recur, the debt ceiling issue and, the sequester policies implemented should lead to fiscal consolidation into 2014, which is both too large and too arbitrary.

Blanchard also argues that failure to lift the U.S. debt ceiling would, however, be a game changer. If prolonged it would lead to extreme fiscal consolidation, and surely derail the U.S. recovery. He continues, "The effects of any failure to repay the debt would be felt right away, leading to potentially major disruptions in financial markets, both in the United States and abroad. We [the IMF] see this as a tail risk, with low probability, but, were it to happen, it would have major consequences."† He recommended U.S. policymakers "to make plans for exit from both quantitative easing and zero policy rates—although not time to implement them yet."‡

At the time of this writing, in fall 2013, the debt ceiling discussion continues with the fiscal deal passed by Congress. The good news is that the government was able to reopen and was able to attain the nearly $16.4 trillion limit on borrowing. The bad news is that there is no actual debt ceiling right now, as the deal just temporarily suspended enforcement of it. For those intellectuals and economists who advocate the abolition of a debt ceiling all together, the current state of affairs is actually great news. That is, the sky is the limit when comes to U.S. government spending until February 7, 2014.

The fact that there is no dollar amount set for how much debt the government can accumulate through February 2014 is now tired-strategy, as it was first deployed earlier this year during previous fiscal battles in Congress, much to the dismay of many anti-government waste groups.

Is it responsible governance, for an advanced economy such as the United States, the largest economy in the world, to suspend a debt ceiling

---

* Ibidem.
† Ibidem.
‡ Ibidem.

without a dollar amount? After all, common sense tells us that a real dollar figure in any budget, for a responsible individual or corporation, is a constant reminder of where we are in our personal or corporate finances. A dollar figure in a government's budget portrays how much it can spend, and the overall health of the country's finances.

It seems that a dollar figure in the U.S. federal budget may not be a good idea, especially when the country has credit agencies, such as Moody, Fitch, and Standards and Poor's (S&P) (although there may never be another downgrade of the U.S. economy by these agencies since the U.S. government sued S&P for its downgrade), watching the United States and suggesting to taxpayers, Congress, and foreign investors, that the United States may be broke.

In our research for this book, we spoke with many business executives from multinational companies, academic researchers, and professionals from around the world. Most of the professionals and executives we spoke to wondered aloud if the fiscal strategies now in place are designed to hide the true state of U.S. debt from its taxpayers, large foreign investors, and creditors on which the country depend. So, if we were to assume that there is some veracity in the IMF assertions, such as the above, it must be taken with a grain of salt. After all, we should not expect the IMF, so dependent on U.S political support and funds, to be wholly unbiased.

Such strategies and polices undermine any informed investor, those capable of seeing through smokescreens. Any foreign investor and nation buying U.S. treasury bills will recognize a bad deal when they see it. Once these investors realize these Treasury bills are the equivalent of junk, regardless of the official rating, the buying will dry up and disastrous consequences will ensue in the financial markets and the U.S. economy as a whole.

As a disclaimer, the authors of this book do not claim to be economists. The proposition of this book to be written by non-economists was by design. We are researchers and observers of what the data and the global trading dynamics tell us, especially between advanced economies and emerging markets. But it doesn't help to have a different opinion about the U.S economy, a less sanguine view. When the conservative Heritage Foundation[3] criticizes Washington's federal budget handling as a "smokescreen," alleging that the suspension of the debt ceiling is becoming increasingly less transparent to the American people, and that the

U.S. government spending exceeds federal revenues by more than one trillion dollars, it is difficult not to have a gloomy outlook.

As shown in Figure 3.1, since 1965, spending has been rising steadily. While federal revenues are recovering from the recent recession, spending is growing sharply, resulting in four consecutive years of deficits exceeding one trillion. Nonetheless, the U.S. Congress is still ignoring the proverbial elephant in the room, no matter how big and wide it gets as days go by, only so they can avoid debate on the specific dollar amount increase on the debt limit, thus making their political vote much easier to cast. It is much easier to vote on *when* we'll deal with a trillion dollar problem than to actually deal with the problem.

It took the U.S. government debt 200 years to reach $1 trillion in 1980, but just 20 years to reach $5 trillion in 2000, and only 13 years to reach about $17 trillion this year. The trend leaves no ambiguity. Despite the talks in Washington, logic indicates the deficit will continue to rise, with more power than in the past 10 years due to the increased interest rates, and the undeniable fact that more Americans are retiring. The debt, as it stands, will continue to increase. By how much will it increase? One, two, or perhaps $3 trillion if the United States engages in other wars in the interim.

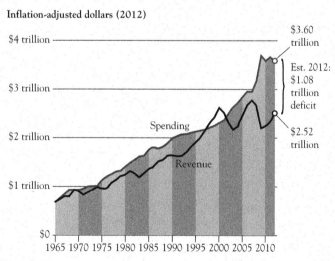

**Figure 3.1 Federal spending exceeds federal revenue by more than $1 Trillion**

Source: U.S. Office of Management and Budget

Huge swaths of the global financial system, including in advanced and in emerging economies, is structured around the understanding that United States. Treasuries are the safest asset in the world. What would happen if that assumption were ever called into question? We believe global financial havoc would ensue, which is precisely why Moody's thinks that a default on U.S. debt is unlikely, even if we smash into the debt ceiling.

Furthermore, if the U.S. Treasury wants to conserve enough cash to keep servicing the debt, then it will have to miss or delay a several other important payments in the near future. If the U.S. Treasury pays the required six billion dollar interest payment by the end of October 2013, and another $29 billion dollars in interest payment by November 15, 2013, the United States may have no choice but to delay social security checks, Medicare payments or military pay, unless it borrows more from China, or simply prints more money.

Restoring the United States to a place among the world's *free* economies will require significant policy reforms, particularly in reducing the size of government, overhauling the tax system, transforming costly entitlement programs, and streamlining regulations. Paraphrasing Mark Twain, history may not repeat itself and only rhymes. But we do believe wholeheartedly in Ayn Rand's assertion* that every one of us builds our own world in our own image. We have the power to choose, but no power to escape the necessity of choice.

# Japan

After 55 years of Liberal Democratic Party rule, the Democratic Party of Japan captured both houses of parliament in 2009 and installed Yukio Hatoyama as prime minister. Hatoyama resigned abruptly in June 2010 and was succeeded by Finance Minister Naoto Kan, who was replaced in September 2011 by Yoshihiko Noda. The March 2011 earthquake and tsunami further strained the beleaguered economy, which has been struggling for nearly two decades with slow growth and stagnation. Prime Minister Noda strived to include Japan in the TPP to stimulate the economy but faces strong resistance at home. Successive prime ministers have been unable or unwilling to

---

* In Atlas Shrugged's John Galt's manifesto.

implement necessary fiscal reforms. As a result of this long and persistent economic crisis, Japan's economy is still about the same size as it was in 1992. In essence, Japan has lost more than two decades of growth.[4] The 2008 global financial crisis and the 2011 Great East Japan Earthquake only aggravated the situation, imposing two severe and consecutive shocks to the Japanese economy. The earthquake alone, the worst disaster in Japan's post-war history, killed nearly 20,000 people and caused enormous physical damage.

According to the OECD,[5] prior to the global economic and financial crisis (as shown in Figure 3.2), Japan's initial strong recovery from the earthquake and tsunami stalled in mid-2012, leaving output 2.5 percent below the peak recorded in 2008. The earthquake and tsunami only compounded Japan's distressed economy. The country has experienced three recessions in less than five years.

Consequently, the major challenge for Japan's economy is to find a way to achieve sustained growth and fiscal sustainability following these two major disasters; the country suffered a 0.7 percent loss in real GDP in 2008 followed by a severe 5.2 percent loss in 2009. Exports from Japan also shrunk from $746.5 billion dollars to $545.3 billion dollars from 2008 to 2009, a 27 percent reduction.* Japan certainly is as handcuffed by its own rigidities as any other country. What is worrisome is that while some export-oriented industries have remained competitive, the Japanese domestic economy appears to be held hostage by bureaucracy, tradition, and overregulation.

---

* Ibidem.

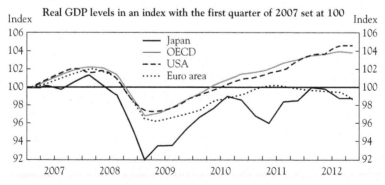

**Figure 3.2 Japan has faced two major economic shocks since 2008**

Source: OECD Economic Outlook Database

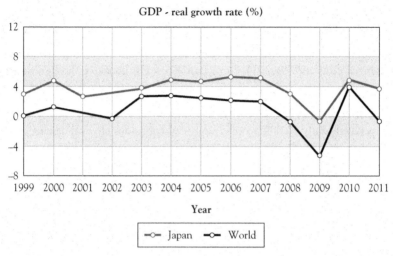

**GDP - real growth rate (%)**

*Figure 3.3 Japan's economy has fallen below global growth*

Other countries would do well to take note of this conundrum as the same concerns Japanese businesses face, certainly would affect businesses globally. It is the authors' suggestion that both advanced and emerging economies should take on these challenges, even the stalwart ones of old Europe: Spain, Italy and France. These all tend to be myopic toward a focus on domestic consumption instead of savings and investments. Often, insufficient attention is given to the unattractive, frequently politically toxic load of smaller policy challenges that can be critical to restarting a faltering economy. For the purpose of reference, in 2011, global real GDP growth was up a 3.9 percent,[6] as depicted in Figure 3.3, while Japan had fallen below global growth at –0.7 percent.

Furthermore, Japan's public debt ratio, as shown in Figure 3.4, has risen steadily for two decades, exceeding 200 percent of GDP. The country must, therefore, promote strong and protracted consolidation to mitigate fiscal sustainability. This is by far Japan's major policy challenge; as such policy will decelerate nominal GDP growth, making fiscal adjustments still more difficult. Hence, ending deflation and boosting Japan's growth potential is imperative in addressing the fiscal predicament in which it finds itself. Consequently, Japan's new government's determination to revitalize the economy through a three-leg strategy combining bold monetary policy, flexible fiscal policy, and a growth strategy is not only necessary, but admirable.

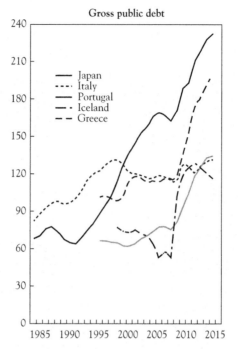

**Figure 3.4** *Japan's gross public debt as percentage of the GDP*

*Source:* OECD Economic Outlook, No 92, and revised OECD estimates and projections for Japan for 2012–14

One immediate way the country is responding to the crisis, according to Kathy Matsui,[7] chief Japan equity strategist for Global Investment Research with Goldman Sachs, is by Japanese companies buying companies overseas, more so than we have seen to date. But whether the recovery in Japan continues, it can only be sustained by Abenomics* policies in meeting two major challenges. The first, reflected in the debate about an increase in the consumption tax, is the right pace of fiscal consolidation as it should not be either too slow and compromise credibility, or too fast and stymie growth. The second is a credible set of structural reforms to transform a cyclical recovery into sustained growth.

---

* The term *Abenomics* is a portmanteau of "Abe" and "economics," which refers to the economic policies advocated by Shinzō Abe, the current Prime Minister of Japan.

Hopefully the Tokyo stock market will continue to rally. The Japanese yen and its stock market have benefited from Abenomics expansionary policies. Having lost as much as 18 percent by mid-May 2013, the yen currently is down around 12 percent on the year, which is a windfall for a currency-sensitive exporter, such as Japan. In the fall of 2012 the economy surged 65 percent, while in the second quarter of 2013 the economy expanded by 3.8 percent, faster than any other advanced economy. Prices are edging upward, which is a good thing for Japan's fight on deflation. Yet, the disposition in Tokyo among businessmen and economists remains perilously balanced between enthusiasm for the monetary and fiscal stimulus unleashed by Abenomics, and concern that promised structural reforms might not be implemented.

## The European Union

As of fall 2013, the EU has shown some signs of recovery. This is not due, however, to major policy changes, as in Japan, but partly to a change in mood, which could be a self-fulfilling prophecy. Southern periphery countries such as Spain, Greece, Italy, Portugal, still struggle as definite progress on competitiveness and exports are not yet strong enough to offset depressed internal demand. Hence, there is still much uncertainty in the EU, the largest economy in the world as a bloc. Bank balance sheets remain an issue, but should be reduced according to the promised *asset quality review* recommended by European Banking Authority (EBA). Such close scrutiny of EU's banks may turn up unexpected shortfalls though. Like Japan, larger structural reforms are needed urgently to increase the anemic potential growth rates of the EU.

### The Uncertain Fate of the Olive Growing Countries and the Euro

The debt crisis continues to overwhelm Europe, and the prospects for countries most entrenched in debt, including Portugal, Italy, Greece, Spain, and Ireland, are dismal. Worse, regardless of whether these countries voluntarily leave or are coerced to leave, it is conceivable that Germany may opt to go solo. The not-so-popular George Soros argues that the euro crisis is far worse than earlier estimations, suggesting that it could eventually end up dissolving the EU.

In a Berlin speech in late April 2012, Soros indicated that the EU crisis casts a shadow on the global economy, a consequence of its own political evolution. He argues that the Maastricht Treaty,*† which led to the creation of the euro, and created what was commonly referred to as the pillar structure of the European Union, was fundamentally flawed, as it established a monetary union without a political one. In essence, the euro was launched without any real democratic consultation or approval, intended by world leaders as political glue in the march toward pan-European sovereignty.

Whereas global analysts and the mainstream media seem to overlook much of this threat to the world's second largest reserve currency, the more immediate concern is the possibility that Germany will abdicate from the EU, causing the euro to plummet, which could subsequently trigger a major international monetary crisis. The EU may survive with a few less olive growers such as Portugal and Greece, but certainly not without the solid backing of Germany.

While the world watches with hopeful expectations for the first time in history, the synchronicity of the central banks of Europe, UK, China, India, Japan, and the United States printing fresh money and increasing the base supplies of their respective countries, we tend to forget important historic facts about Germany and the eurozone. Namely, Germany was never sanguine about the euro from the onset. In fact, most Europeans were not. We view it more as a quid pro quo case, whereby Germans accepted the euro in exchange for France's support of Germany's post-Cold War reunification. Trading the Deutsche mark for the euro, in and of itself, did not equate logically.

---

\* The Maastricht Treaty (formally, the Treaty on European Union or TEU) was signed on 7 February 1992 by the members of the European Community in Maastricht, Netherlands. On 9–10, December 1991, the same city hosted the European Council which drafted the treaty. Upon its entry into force on 1 November, 1993 during the Delors Commission, it created the European Union and led to the creation of the single European currency, the euro.
† 1990–1999. The history of the European Union—1990–1999. Europa. Last accessed on September 11, 2011.

EU's dire situation provides Germany with an opportunity to augment its political influence in the region, and a return on its investment of the euro, by way of financial rescue packages to olive growers. However, if such efforts fail, as is likely the case, Germany will have no compelling reason to remain with the EU, since Europeans are already becoming resentful of Germany and the EU. History has shown us time and again that austerity breed's political disgust, particularly when imposed by outside powers. A pro-German government in Holland has already fallen in local elections, and President Sarkozy lost ground in his reelection campaign, eventually losing the elections, precisely due to his perceived support of German policy. Then there are the German people who resist the idea of seeing their hard earned money squandered on people who refuse to tighten their belts.

The central bank's printing of money and Germany's financial packages are not ameliorating the situation. On the contrary, the olive growers are not alone. Many other countries are already in recession, including Slovenia, Italy, the Czech Republic, Ireland, Denmark, Netherlands, Belgium, and the UK. Whether the euro endures, Europe, especially the olive growing countries, is facing a long period of economic stagnation. We witnessed Latin American countries suffer a similar fate in the early 80s, and Japan, which has been in stagnation for almost a quarter century. While they have survived, the eurozone situation is graver, as the EU is not a single country but rather a union of many; the lingering deflationary debt trap threatens to destroy a still nascent political union.

We believe that only when a friendlier monetary policy and a milder fiscal austerity is proposed will the euro remain strong. This will weaken the eurozone's exports' competitiveness, and drag the recession to even lower levels, which in turn will force more eurozone countries to restructure their debts and may cause some to ultimately exit the euro.

## EU's Economic Prospects

The Economist magazine expects GDP will stagnate across the 28 largest economies within the EU in 2013, after falling by 0.5 percent in 2012, and expand by 1.4 percent in 2014. This is according to forecasts from the European Commission in early November 2013, as this chapter is written. Across the 17 largest countries in the EU, however, a weak recovery has begun, following a double-dip recession lasting 18 months. For 2013 GDP in the EU, as a whole, will fall by 0.4 percent, after falling by 0.6 percent in 2012. In 2014 GDP is expected to rise by 1.1 percent. Figure 3.5 provides information on GDP growth by country for those in the EU, those pegged to the euro, and those countries floating their currency as of the first quarter of 2013.

As was the case in 2013, growth in 2014 will be strongest (4.1 percent) in Latvia, which is poised to join the euro area in January. Indeed the three Baltic countries, including Lithuania outside the eurozone and Estonia already in it, will be the three fastest-growing economies in the EU. But the main impetus behind the euro area's recovery will be a combination of German growth of 1.7 percent coupled with a more modest return to growth in Italy and Spain, the region's third and fourth biggest economies. Outside the eurozone, Sweden and Britain are expected to do well in 2014, with growth of 2.8 percent and 2.2 percent respectively.

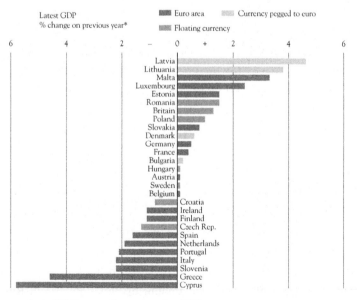

**Figure 3.5 GDP growth across the EU countries**

Source: Eurostat

The worse performers for 2014 are two countries also in the eurozone, who will experience a decrease on GDP: Cyprus and Slovenia. Cyprus's distresses will continue, with a further contraction, of 3.9 percent, while Slovenia's GDP also will slide again, by one percent. Nonetheless, such prospects should be considered positive; GDP is expected to fall in eight countries in the eurozone and 10 in the EU. Lastly, the minor recovery in 2014 should not bring much joy for the jobless, as unemployment in the eurozone still is expected to stay at 12.2 percent in 2014. This statistic is much higher with olive grower countries; Spain is registering 32 percent youth unemployment as of fall 2014.

We believe the euro area has the potential to take advantage of the global opportunities, especially emerging markets. The euro area is more open to trade than many other advanced economies. The EU's exports and imports of goods and services account for around one fifth of GDP, more than in the United States or Japan. The EU has been open to the idea of emerging markets. Its trade relations with emerging markets such as Asia, Turkey and Russia, for instance, as well as with central and eastern European countries, have strengthened noticeably over the past decade. Taken together, the share of emerging markets in the euro area trade has grown from about 33 percent, when the euro was introduced in 1999, to more than 40 percent as of 2013.[8]

One aspect less well known about the eurozone is that it is financially very flexible and open. The international balance sheet of the eurozone, its assets and liabilities vis-à-vis nonresidents account, is over 120 percent and 130 percent of euro area GDP, respectively. This is more than in many other advanced economies such as the United States, where the corresponding figures are 90 percent and 110 percent of GDP. In addition, according to Trading Economics,[9] the EU is becoming increasingly open. Since the euro was created, the size of the eurozone area's external assets and liabilities has grown by about 40 percent. Hence, if we were to focus on emerging markets alone, one of the most interesting developments in recent years is the fact that the eurozone has become an attractive destination for FDI from the largest of these economies. For instance, during 1999–2005, the amount of FDI from Brazil, Russia, India, and China in the eurozone tripled, to about €12 billion euros (US$16.2 billion).

# Emerging Markets

The long-term fundamentals for emerging market growth, we believe, are directly linked to the potential for emerging market companies to tap into the favorable long-term economic growth prospects for all the emerging economies. As pointed out in earlier chapters, those growth prospects are based on two main factors: positive demographic trends (with some exceptions) and balance sheets that are not reliant on and burdened by debt, as seen across advanced economies. Combined, these are potent and sustainable benefits for emerging markets.

The rising population numbers that many emerging nations are experiencing help to ensure that aggregate demand will grow faster while the strong and underleveraged balance sheets—of both consumers and sovereigns—help to assure investors the pace of investments and consumption can be kept in balance. This is in contrast to the deleveraging process—both at the government and consumer level—that will take years to run its course in many developed markets. Such deleveraging will continue to exert strong deflationary pressures on these developed economies. While there is a great deal of uncertainty as to how developed-market central banks will counter these pressures, any expansion of global liquidity should favor assets with better growth prospects, such as the ones found in emerging market economies.

We believe, however, that emerging markets need to exercise some caution (driven by the prospects for liquidity withdrawal), should the U.S Federal reserve and the ECB, as well as other advanced economies' central banks, begin to shutter their quantitative easing programs. Relatedly, we see signs that currency and interest rates in many emerging markets need to adjust to more sustainable equilibriums. For instance, in the BRICS bloc, currencies need to depreciate and real interest rates need to rise. While this may be tough to enact, it is necessitated by the deterioration of the aggregate current account balance of the emerging market universe since 2007, which has been caused by the weak demand from advanced economies, weakening commodity prices, and the *stimulating* domestic demand policies that have prevailed in many emerging markets since the global financial crisis.

A correction already has started as many emerging market currencies have been depreciating against the U.S. dollar and the euro for nearly a year. These downward trends have been distinctly unfavorable since the rebound at the end of the crisis. We also are starting to see some upward ticks in interest rates in certain countries. As part of this adjustment, there is a possibility that we will see lower economic growth, which could be negative for earnings-growth expectations. The market has already started to discount this notion, as seen through the lower valuations of emerging versus advanced economies.

The causes for such trends vary in opinion. There is a belief that emerging markets may be in a cyclical slowdown. Another belief is that emerging markets are now experiencing a decrease in growth potential. We believe, based on our own research that both are true. Extraordinarily favorable world conditions, be it strong commodity prices or global financial conditions, led to higher potential growth in the 2000s, with, in a number of countries, a cyclical component on top. As commodity prices began to stabilize and financial conditions tightened, potential growth is lowered and, in some cases, compounded by a sharp cyclical adjustment. Faced with these conditions, governments in emerging markets are now faced with two challenges: adjust to lower potential growth, and, where needed, deal with the cyclical adjustment.

Considering a potential slow down on these economies, at least when compared to the 2000 rates, structural reforms will not only be necessary, but urgent. Such structural reforms may include rebalancing toward consumption in China, or removing barriers to investment in India or Brazil. Regarding cyclical adjustments, the typical standard advice from macroeconomics applies, such as the consolidation of debt in countries with large fiscal deficits. Countries with inflation running persistently above government targets, such as in Vietnam and Indonesia, a tighter and, even more importantly, more credible monetary policy framework must be implemented.

When assessing the prospects for advanced economies, the architecture of the financial system is still evolving, and its future shape and soundness are still unclear. Unemployment remains too high, which will continue to be a major challenge for several years to come. As for emerging markets, and the implications of its rise in the world economy, the impact is multifaceted, and is already being felt around the globe. It encompasses two areas of immediate concern for central bankers in those countries and around the world, namely global inflation and global capital flows.

## The Impact of Emerging Markets Rise on the Global Economy

The integration into the global economy of a massive pool of low-cost, skilled workers from emerging markets has tended to exert downward pressure on import prices of manufactured goods and wages in advanced economies.[10] Emerging markets have significantly contributed to the increase of the labor force and the reduction of labor costs around the world. The available labor force in the global economy has actually doubled from 1.5 to 3 billion, mainly as a reflection of the opening up of China, India and Russia's economies.[11] The price of a wide range of manufactured goods has declined over the years. Furthermore, through numerous channels, this process of wage restrains and reduced inflationary pressure in the manufacturing sector also has affected wage dynamics and distribution in the services sector, mainly due to outsourcing. Consequently, these effects have contributed to the dampening of inflationary pressures.

Conversely, there are opposing dynamics to be considered between advanced economies and emerging markets. Some resources, such as energy and food, have become relatively scarce over time due to the increased demand from emerging economies, such as China and India. We believe this may have been a source of increased inflationary pressure over the past few years, although we acknowledge that it is difficult to make an exact assessment of this contribution, since commodity prices also are affected by supply conditions and geopolitical factors. Nonetheless, according to Pain, Koske, and Sollie's study,[12] the rapid growth in emerging countries and their increasing share in world trade and GDP may have contributed to an increase in oil prices by as much as 40 percent, and real metal prices by as much as 10 percent in the first five years of the new millennium.

All in all, it is difficult to measure accurately the total impact of emerging markets on inflation. For instance, the IMF has estimated that globalization, through its direct effects on non-oil import prices, has reduced inflation on average by 0.25 percent per year in advanced economies.[13] The overall impact, however, is more difficult to estimate and extricate from other factors that could reduce inflation. For example, the increases in productivity growth and the stronger credibility of monetary policy are two impending factors.

A New Form of Capitalism

Recently, Dr. Goncalves returned from China, and during his return flight, he came to the realization that although he teaches on the subject of China in his international business program at Nichols College, he had missed the point when it came to that country's profile. He kept thinking about how Taipei, a democracy in Taiwan, with all of its tall gray buildings seemed more like a communist country than China. In contrast, Hong Kong's Time Square, the World Trade Centre, Causeway Bay, and its SOHO seemed more like Manhattan on steroids. Despite the plethora of books and articles he's read on the subject, he came to realize that Chinese communism today isn't anything like his antiquated vision of it, which was formed by living in the United States and shaped by the Soviet Union (now Russia).

The communism he witnessed in Hong Kong and Macau, although we must note these two countries are China's Special Administration Regions (SARs), are true examples of capitalism at its core. In contrast to the West and most advanced economies today, unemployment rates in Hong Kong and Macau are only four and two percent respectively. Hong Kong hosts the most skyscrapers in the world, with New York City a distant second, with only half the amount. Hong Kong also holds the most Rolls Royce's in the world. Macau's per capita income is $68 thousand, in contrast to $48 thousand in the United States.

What impacted him the most during his 21 days there was the optimism of it's people. This is in contrast to the cynicism heard constantly in the West, where people seem to have lost their excitement about the future. There, young and old, people yearn and strive for more than what they have. He agrees with Goldman Sachs' Jim O'Neill, who coined the "BRIC countries" back in 2000, in his assertion that "China is the greatest story of our generation."[14] China's general macroeconomics is very promising. It scores well for its stable inflation, external financial position, government debt, investment levels, and openness to foreign trade. At the micro level it falls just below average on corruption and use of technology. But, the latter is changing rapidly.

There simply is no overstating China's importance to us all, particularly the West, notwithstanding the 1.3 billion Chinese. Like it or not, we must realize that the entire planet, all 6.5 billion, is and must be invested in China's success. Doubts? In 1995, China's economy was worth roughly $500 billion. In just sixteen years it has grown more than tenfold. By 2001, its GDP was $1.5 trillion, at the time it was smaller than the United Kingdom and France. Today, China is the second largest economy in the world.

Undeniably, it will be a hard road for China to maintain its consistent 9–10 percent annual growth moving forward. Their growth rates will most certainly decelerate. The question is by how much and how smoothly. In March 2014, the government announced a 7.5 percent growth target for its 35-year plan. This is best for its economy and people so that policy makers can better focus on the quality of the growth, instead of sheer quantity. After all, no country can sustain growth by building ghost cities as China has been doing. The good news is that China does not have to maintain the 10 percent GDP growth pace in order to continue to grow, and actually surpass the United States to become the largest economy in the world. For now, China is still only about one third of the U.S. economy (in comparable dollar terms).

It appears that China's Communist Party, with 80 million members, is not just the world's largest political party but also its biggest chamber of commerce. That can be worrisome, as China's influence and impact on all advanced and emerging markets around the world looms large. The eurozone crises have many of us in the United States concerned. As it deteriorates, it will definitely impact Wall Street and the U.S. economy. However, anything that happens in China is far more important and impactful to the fate of the world economy than the eurozone crises.

## China's Challenges

As Brazil, Russia, India, and China, the BRIC countries, advance full-steam ahead, Jim O'Neil's decade-old prediction for this group of only four countries remains prescient. BRIC is growing an economy that will surpass the combined size of the great G-7 economies by 2035.* Very little is said, however, about China's shattering stories of the hordes of small business owners committing suicide, leaving China, or flat out emigrating to the West. It makes me wonder how much vested interest Goldman Sachs has in such predictions.

---

* Ibidem, pg.201.

Don't get us wrong. We are avid proponents of the rise and formidable influence the BRIC countries are having on the global economy. In my (Dr. Goncalves) Advanced Economies and Emerging Market classes, my students are exposed to detailed characteristics of the engine propelling the BRICs, its impact on the G-7, and how to position themselves professionally to capitalize on it. But, we cannot ignore the public outcry of Chinese entrepreneurs facing the deterioration of business conditions in that country.

The somewhat positive step taken by the People's Bank of China (PBOC) in December 2012, to alleviate China's alleged liquidity crisis, should cause us to reassess the sustainability of its economy at current rates. China is far from a liquidity crisis, however, possessing an M2* that has surpassed the United States, reaching nearly US$11.55 trillion. This was due, in part, by reducing the reserve requirement ratio[†], (RRR), to 21 percent from its record high of 21.5 percent.

It is not clear to us whether China is on a sustainable economic path, at least until it slows down its equity investments and begins to pay more attention to and empower its middle class. The Chinese people won't be willing to spend if they don't have a decent health or retirement system, which impels them to save, on average, 30 percent of their income. China's obsession with extreme growth, sustained now for over a decade, has become the huge white elephant for global markets. Unless the Chinese government begins to deal diligently with this issue, it may not be able to prevent an epic hard landing of its economy.

---

* A category within the money supply that includes M1 in addition to all time-related deposits, savings deposits, and non-institutional money-market funds. M2 is a broader classification of money than M1. Economists use M2 when looking to quantify the amount of money in circulation and trying to explain different economic monetary conditions. SOURCE: Investopedia, http://www.investopedia.com/terms/m/m2.asp.

[†] The portion (expressed as a percent) of depositors' balances banks must have on hand as cash. This is a requirement determined by the country's central bank, which in the United States is the Federal Reserve. The reserve ratio affects the money supply in a country. This is also referred to as the "cash reserve ratio" (CRR). SOURCE: Investopedia, http://www.investopedia.com/terms/r/reserveratio.asp.

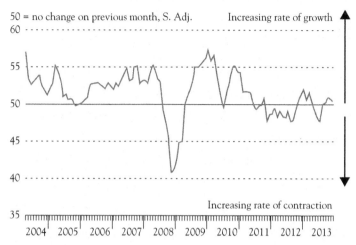

50 = no change on previous month, S. Adj.          Increasing rate of growth

Increasing rate of contraction

**Figure 3.6  China manufacturing PMI as of December 2013**[15]

*Source:* Markit Economics, HSBC

Much like Western economies, China blames the tightening of monetary policy as the feeder of its ever-growing white elephant. Again, much like the West, it looks more like a systemic issue, since its main markets, the United States and Europe, are both battling a probable imminent double recession, which is squeezing their buying power. In addition, ahead of the West, inflation is rising. Wage inflation especially is causing the hungry elephant to erode China's main competitive advantage in the manufacturing industry. The tightening of monetary policy is anathema to this, but the transformative systemic change in the Chinese economy isn't. Just look at the Purchasing Manager Index* (PMI), which dropped to 49 in December, much lower than market expectations, to realize that the manufacturing sector is bleeding. In early 2013 the PMI climbed to 53, but manufacturing goods in China have been declining. As depicted in Figure 3.6, in October 2013, China's PMI fell to 52.6, and even further, to 50.2 in February 2014.

---

* A monthly index of manufacturing, considered one of the most reliable leading indicators available to assess the near-term direction of an economy. An index reading above 50 percent indicates that the manufacturing sector is generally expanding, while a reading below 50 percent indicates contraction. The further the index is away from 50 percent, the greater the rate of change.

Such declines in PMI produce a ripple effect of stocks piling up, thereby driving the cost of doing business higher. So much so that it has become cheaper for China to transfer its manufacturing to the United States, primarily to South Carolina. Certainly, labor costs, even in the south of the United States, are higher than in China. But the cost of energy is a lot cheaper, as is the cost of real estate, infrastructure, and shipping across the Pacific.

What makes China's white elephant so pale is that small and medium businesses (SMBs), the driving force of China's manufacturing, do not have easy access to credit. China's four major banks, Bank of China, the China Construction Bank, the Industrial and Commercial Bank of China and the Agricultural Bank of China, control more than 70 percent of China's banking market. These are state-owned banks which favor state-owned companies, and, rarely, some fortunate private corporations. This resource misallocation is feeding the pallid pachyderm at the expense of SMBs, left with their only option of costly business financing.

We do not profess to be economists, but looking at the sheer size of China's white elephant, it is clear to us that monetary policy alone cannot fix the systemic insufficiencies of China's economy. As long as the economy remains vastly dependent on the United States and European consumerism, countries currently dealing with their own herd of white elephants, and unable to consume as before, China's exports will remain massively strained. Consequently, the country is being burdened with a severe excess capacity problem, pushing down the marginal returns of investment and GDP, while fostering an uptick of inflation, unemployment, and possibly more bubbles.

As the United States and Europe deal with their own economic crisis, they are being forced to place their deficit-fueled consumption economies on a stringent diet. To deal with their own white elephant they will have to shop and consume less, to give room for increasing saving rates, chronically low at the moment, and higher productivity. Such an unavoidable consumer diet could be disastrous for China, as data from the Economist Intelligence Unit and the U.S. Department of Commerce's (DOC) Bureau of Economic Analysis suggests that China will remain dependent on an export-led economy until at least late 2030. If true, China must find new markets and reduce its dependence on the West's economies.

Could the BRIC countries be the ace under China's sleeves? After all, as O'Neil predicted, in the next two decades, these four countries alone will account for half of the population of the entire world (i.e., huge middle-class), and their economies will be larger than the G-7 countries combined. Europe today has 35 cities with a population over one million, but by 2030, India alone will have 68 cities with over one million and China will have over one billion consumers living in it's cities. This staggering fact alone could mark the slow death of China's white elephant, by letting go of its dependence on the West, and the return of a progressive flame-throwing dragon, ready to sizzle its middle-class economy and the BRIC's with sales aplenty of manufactured goods.

The question remains, which will have more weight: the shortsighted state-capitalist elephant or the farsighted free-market driven dragon?

## Brazil: An Economy of Extremes

Dr. Goncalves recently returned from Brazil, and while observing the hustle and bustle of Rio's international airport, busier than ever, it dawned on him that Brazil has much to be proud of. He is Brazilian, and therefore, admits to being a tad biased, but the fact remains that a decade of accelerated growth and progressive social policies have brought the country prosperity that is ever more widely shared. The unemployment rate as of September 2013 was 5.4 percent, up from 5.3 percent in August of 2013.* Credit is flourishing, however, particularly to the swelling number of people who have moved out of poverty status and into the ranks of the middle class. Income inequality, though still high, has fallen sharply.

For most Brazilians life has never been as hopeful, and to some extent we see plenty of paradigm shifts. Women's salaries are growing twice as fast as those of men, even though they only occupy a mere 21.4 percent of executive positions and despite the fact they hold most of the doctoral degrees in the country (51.5 percent) and dominate the area of research (58.6 percent). Women also own more companies in the Latin American

---

* From 2001 until 2013, Brazil's unemployment rate averaged 8.8 percent reaching an all time high of 13.1 percent in April of 2004 and a record low of 4.6 percent in December of 2012.

region (11 percent) than any other emerging country. The new shifts in the Brazilian economy also benefit the black communities, which have seen their salaries increase four times faster than their white counterparts, bringing the population of the middle class blacks from 39.3 percent to 50.9 percent. According to research conducted by the Federal University of Rio de Janeiro, of 20.6 million people who entered the workplace, only 7.7 million were white. Overall, the country is enjoying the boom brought by commodities, in particular oil and gas, despite the global economic slowdown. Are advanced economies entrepreneurs taking advantage of this?

If not, they should, but with a caveat. We believe what worked for the Brazilian economy ten even twenty years ago, such as a focus on commodities, low labor costs, and excessive focus on exports, won't work moving forward. Today, Brazil is a new country, with new habits and customs, and believe it or not, a population that possesses an extremely elevated self-esteem. Meaning, the fledgling and rapidly growing Brazilian middle class, 52 percent of the population since 2008, is in love with itself and ready to spend. According to Goldman Sachs, more than two billion people around the world will belong to the middle-class by 2030, but the majority of Brazilians are already there.

In 2010, the United Nations Development Program's (UNDP) report, ranked Brazil among the ten worst countries in the world in terms of income inequality, with a Gini* Index of 0.56 (one being ideal and zero being the worst), tied with Ecuador and only better than Bolivia and Haiti. Brazil is home to 31 percent of all Latin American millionaires, about five thousand people with a net worth superior of $30 million. More than 100 thousand Brazilians own financial investments of at least one million reais, or about $500 thousand. But what this report fails to include is that in 2008 the Gini index was far worse: 0.515. Since then, 2010 data indicates unemployment fell from 12.3 percent to 6.7 percent and, as mentioned earlier, it is now at 4.9 percent. In 2003 there were 49 million Brazilians living in poverty. Six years later that number

---

* The Gini index is a measure of statistical dispersion intended to represent the income distribution of a nation's residents. It was developed by the Italian statistician and sociologist Corrado Gini.

plummeted to 29 million as a result of government sponsored social programs.

Brazil's primary challenge is in regard to education. In our view, the global economy has essentially become a knowledge economy. However, Brazil has not adequately invested in education, despite the commodities boon. Recently, the federal government launched several promising educational programs, such as "science without barriers," a program that finances and sends several thousand higher education students abroad in the STEM (science, technology, engineering, and math) disciplines. Sadly though, the reality today is that approximately 80 percent of all corporate professionals in Brazil do not have a college degree—one of the lowest rates in the world.

According to a United Nations Educational, Scientific and Cultural Organization (UNESCO) report, only 35 percent of Brazilians between the ages of 25 and 34 have high school diplomas, which is three times higher than those between the ages of 55 and 64 years of age. The new generation of professionals is not being educated quickly enough. Compare this data to South Korea, which planned for its economic growth by increasing the number of high school graduates from 35 to 97 percent. As of March 2013, the U.S. number was 75 percent. Still, in the past five years, there have never been as many Brazilians studying. In the past 10 years, 435 vocational schools were opened, and the number of universities jumped from 1800 to almost 3,000 institutions, while the number of college students jumped 46 percent, reaching 6.5 million. By comparison, the United States has 4,495 Title IV-eligible institutions, and about 20.3 million college students. As we look toward the future, despite all its shortcomings, we are looking at a much more educated workforce in Brazil.

Until now, Brazilians did not believe in their country's potential and suffered from a certain inferiority complex. Now, they have several reasons to take pride in being Brazilian: the impressive economic boom of late, greater access to education and to information (Brazil is fifth in the world in Internet access, behind only China, United States, India, and Japan), a democratization of the culture, and the recognition of Brazil as an emerging country abroad.

While there are a variety of different methodologies being used to study the relatively new field of *Happiness Economics*, or the efficiency with which countries convert the earth's finite resources into happiness or well-being measures. The think tank company Global Finance has ranked 151 countries across the globe on the basis of how many long, happy and sustainable lives they provide for the people who live in them per unit of environmental output. The Global Happy Planet Index[16] (HPI) incorporates three separate indicators, including ecological footprint, or the amount of land needed to provide for all their resource requirements plus the amount of vegetated land needed to absorb all their $CO_2$ emissions and the $CO_2$ emissions embodied in the products they consume; life satisfaction, or health as well as "subjective well-being" components, such as a sense of individual vitality, opportunities to undertake meaningful, engaging activities, inner resources that help one cope when things go wrong, close relationships with friends and family, or belonging to a wider community; and life expectancy. According to the report results, Brazil ranks 21, while the United States is 105. (Costa Rica leads the way and Vietnam is second.) Need we say more?

# CHAPTER 4

# Coping with Emerging and Advanced Market Risks

## Overview

For the past six years or so, advanced economies have been exposing international investors to a lot of risk, from the U.S. economy trembling over its fiscal cliff and the EU struggling to control the eurozone crisis, to Japan seemingly sunk into permanent stagnation. Hence, it would be easy to conclude that the biggest global risks, as of now, would come from these advanced economies.

Yet, that's not what Eurasia, a political risk consultancy group, argues. In its predictions for 2013,[1] the group puts emerging markets at the top of their risk rankings. That's because, they argued, the advanced economies have proved in recent years that they can manage crises. Conversely, there are several risks suggesting emerging markets will likely struggle to cope with the world's growing political pressures. Eurasia argues that, "But...with an absence of global leadership and geopolitics very much "in play," everyone will face more volatility. That's going to prove a much bigger problem for emerging markets than the developed world. In 2013, the first true post financial crisis year, we'll start to see that more clearly."

People tend to think of emerging markets, including the so-called BRIC nations, as immature states in which political factors matter at least as much as economic fundamentals for the performance of markets.*

It was even before the recent global financial crisis that growth of emerging markets had shaken the foundations of faith in free markets, which appeared to have fully and finally established the dominance of the liberal economic model tested by the past success of advanced economies. The model's fundamental components being private wealth, private

---

* Ibidem.

**(a) Unprecedented**

Emerging-market share of world GDP*

% point change on previous year                    % of total

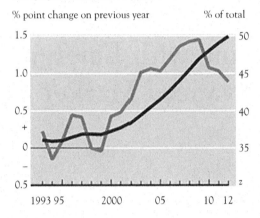

**(b)    The BRIC build-up**

GDP†, % change on previous year

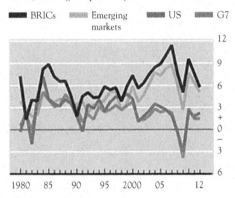

*At purchasing power parity
†Weighted by share of GDP at atpurchasing power parity

*Figure 4.1  Emerging markets led by BRIC have demonstrated stronger growth than the advanced economies*[2]

*Source*: IMF

investment, and private enterprise. Figure 4.1 illustrates the significant growth these regions have experienced in the past decade or so.

To combat the economic and social challenges surfaced from the global financial recession, both advanced and emerging economies have injected politics and political motivations, on a scale we haven't seen in decades, into the performance of global markets. Massive state interventions, including currency rate manipulation, inflation targeting, state capitalism, and economic nationalism in certain areas, have been accelerated in markets as world-wide governments and central banks try to stimulate growth and rescue vulnerable domestic industries and companies.

However, such a shift doesn't guarantee a panacea for all economic problems. Along with its own risks and intensified confrontation, emerging markets' most tumultuous growth model seems to have more or less reached a turning point. Growth rates in all the BRICs have dropped while the United States and EU are facing possible secular stagnation; stagnation that calls for a more thorough search for better measures and solutions.

## Currency Rate

*Currency war*, also known as competitive devaluation of currency, is a term raised as the alarm by Brazil's Finance Minister Guido Mantega to describe the 2010 effort by the United States and China to have the lowest value of their currencies.[3]

The rationale behind a currency war is really quite simple. By devaluing one's currency it makes exports more competitive, giving that individual country an edge in capturing a greater share of global trade, therefore, boosting its economy. Greater exports mean employing more workers and therefore helping improve economic growth rates, even at the eventual cost of inflation and unrest.

The United States allows its currency, the dollar, to devalue by expansionary fiscal and monetary policies. It's doing this through increasing spending, thereby increasing the debt, and by keeping the Federal funds rate at virtually zero, subsequently increasing credit and the money supply. More importantly, through "quantitative easing" (QE), it has been printing money to buy bonds, with its peak at $85 billion a month.

China tries to keep its currency low by pegging it to the dollar, along with a basket of other currencies. It keeps the peg by buying U.S. Treasuries, which limits the supply of dollars, thereby strengthening it. This keeps Chinese yuan low by comparison. Obviously, both United States and China benefitted from currency rate manipulation to secure their leading positions in international trade.

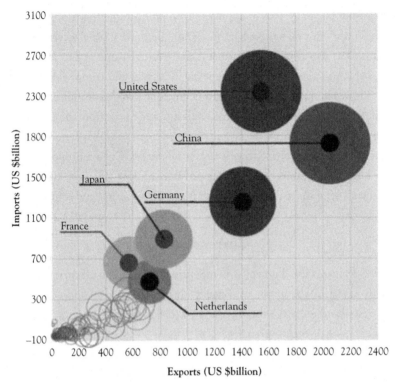

*Figure 4.2  Leading export and import traders of 2012*

*Sources*: International Trade Statistics 2013 (WTO)

According to the WTO International Trade Statistics 2013, and as depicted in Figure 4.2, the United States is still the world's biggest trader in merchandise, with imports and exports totaling US$3,881 billion in 2012. Its trade deficit amounts to US$790 billion, or 4.9 percent of its GDP. China follows closely behind the United States, with merchandise trade totaling US$3,867 billion in 2012. China's trade surplus was US$230 billion, or 2.8 percent of its GDP.

Through manipulation of currency rate, devaluation is also used to cut real debt levels by reducing the purchasing power of a nation's debt held by foreign investors, which works especially well for the United States. But such currency rate manipulation has invited destructive retaliation in the form of a quid pro quo currency war among the world's largest economies.

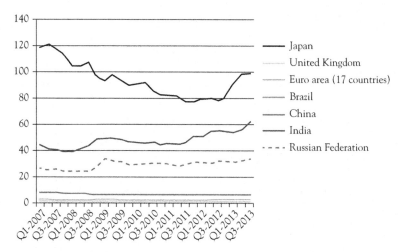

**Figure 4.3  Currency exchange rates, National units per US-Dollar (quarterly average)**

*Sources*: OECD Main Economic Indicators (MEI) database

A joint statement issued by the government and the Bank of Japan (BOJ) in January 2013 stated that the central bank would adopt a two percent inflation target. Later Haruhiko Kuroda, the BOJ's governor, announced the BOJ's boldest attempt, so far, to stimulate Japan's economy and end years of deflation. The bank intends to double the amount of money in circulation by buying about ¥13 trillion yens in financial assets, including some ¥2 trillion yens in government bonds, every month as long as necessary. BOJ's effort, together with the months of anticipation that preceded it, has knocked the yen down sharply against the dollar and other major currencies (as shown in Figure 4.3) and sparked a rally in Japanese shares. It also has further reignited fears of currency tensions around the globe.

The EU made its move in 2013 to boost its exports and fight deflation. The ECB, after cutting its policy rate to 0.5 percent in May, lowered its rate further to 0.25 percent on November 7, 2013. This immediately drove down the euro-to-dollar conversion rate to $1.37.

Brazil and other emerging market countries are concerned because the currency wars are driving their currencies higher, by comparison. This raises the price of commodities, such as oil, copper, and iron, that is, their primary exports. This makes emerging market countries less competitive and slows their economic growth.

In fact, India's new central bank governor, Raghuram Rajan, has criticized the United States and others involved in currency wars that they are exporting their inflation to the emerging market economies.

However, condemning the currency war and the United States, BRICS, except for China, had their currencies devaluated against the U.S. dollar after the financial crisis. (See Figure 4.3.)

In currency wars, exchange rate manipulation can be accomplished in several ways:

- Direct Intervention—Adopted by the PBOC and BOJ, in which a country can sell its own currency in order to buy foreign currencies, resulting in a direct devaluation of its currency on a relative basis.
- Quantitative Easing—Taken by U.S. Federal Reserve, in which a country can use its own currency to buy its own sovereign debt, or effectively foreign debt, and ultimately depreciate its currency.
- Interest Rates—Exercised by BOJ, Federal Reserve, and ECB in which a country can lower its interest rates and thereby create downward pressure on its currency, since it becomes cheaper to borrow against others.
- Threats of Devaluation—Used by the United States toward China, in which a country can threaten to take any of the above actions along with other measures and occasionally achieve the desired devaluation in the open market.

An important episode of currency war occurred in the 1930s. As countries abandoned the Gold Standard during the Great Depression, they used currency devaluations to stimulate their economies. Since this effectively pushes unemployment overseas, trading partners quickly retaliated with their own devaluations. The period is considered to have been an adverse situation for all concerned, as unpredictable changes in exchange rates reduced overall international trade.

## Control the Currency Rate and Capital Flows

To avoid a repeat of such painful history and damage to international trade caused by ongoing currency wars, Pascal Lamy, former Director-General of the WTO, pointed out in the opening to the WTO Seminar on Exchange Rates and Trade in March 2012 that "the international community needs to make headway on the issue of reform of the international monetary system. Unilateral attempts to change or retain the status quo will not work."

The key challenge to the rest of the world is the U.S. policy of renewed quantitative easing, which gives both potential benefits and increasing pressure to other countries. Among the benefits would be to help push back the risk of deflation that has been observed in much of the advanced world. Avoiding stagnation or renewed recession in advanced economies, in turn, would be a major benefit for emerging markets in world trade, whose economic cycles remain closely correlated with those in the developed world.[4] Another major plus would be to greatly reduce the threat of protectionism, particularly in the United States. The most plausible scenario for advanced country protectionism would be a long period of deflation and economic stagnation, as seen in the 1930s.[5]

Based on our observations, the adjustment issue has been relatively easier in other advanced economies (especially countries within the EU) that also are experiencing high unemployment and are threatened by deflation. In this situation, there could be a rationale not so much for a currency war as for a coordinated monetary easing across developed countries to help fend off deflation while also reducing the risk of big exchange rate realignments among the major developed economies.[6]

In contrast, it is more complicated for most emerging markets, such as China, that experience relatively stronger growth and higher inflationary rather than deflationary pressures. In this situation, the United States easing poses more challenging policy choices by creating added stimulus for capital flows to emerging markets, flows that have already been surging since 2010, and attracted both by high short-term interest rate spreads and the stronger long-term growth prospects of emerging economies.

To put currency rate and capital flows under reasonable control with the increasing pressure from U.S. monetary easing, there are three approaches suggested by the World Bank experts.[7]

First is to maintain a fixed exchange rate peg and an open capital account while giving up control of monetary policy as an independent policy instrument. This approach tends to suit smaller economies, such as Hong Kong, that are highly integrated both economically and institutionally with the larger economy to whose exchange rate they are pegged. It is less appropriate for larger developing countries, such as China, whose domestic cycles may not be at the same pace as the economy (in this case, the United States) to which they are pegged. Importing loose U.S. monetary policy will tend to stimulate excessive domestic money growth, inflation in the goods market, and speculative bubbles in asset markets. By taking this approach, China's adjustment will occur through high inflation, the highest among all major economies in Figure 4.4, and appreciation of the real exchange rate. Countries may attempt to avert some of these consequences by issuing domestic bonds to offset the balance of payments inflows. But this course also has disadvantages, for example, fiscal costs and a tendency to attract yet more capital inflows by pushing up local bond yields.

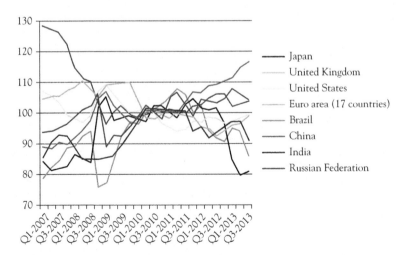

*Figure 4.4 Relative consumer price indices, 2010 = 100*

Sources: OECD Main Economic Indicators (MEI) database

Second is to pursue independent monetary policies that target their own inflation and activity levels, combined with relatively flexible exchange rates and open capital accounts, which a growing number of emerging economies have been moving toward in the aftermath of the financial crises of the late 1990s. Given rising inflation pressures, the appropriate monetary policy in many emerging markets at present would likely be to tighten, which will, however, attract even more capital inflows and further appreciate exchange rates. Sustained appreciation raises concerns about loss of export competitiveness and could lead to contentious structural adjustments in the real economy. So countries may also fear that large appreciations will undercut their long-term growth potential.[8] A standard recommendation for countries in this position is to tighten fiscal policy (increasing the rate of taxation and/or cutting government spending) as a way of reducing upward pressure on local interest rates and the exchange rate.

Third is to combine an independent monetary policy with a fixed exchange rate by closing the capital account through capital controls. Such controls may sometimes be a useful temporary expedient, but they are not unproblematic, especially in the longer term.

Figure 4.5 lists some of the main types of capital controls and some evidence of their varying effectiveness. Foreign exchange taxes can be effective in reducing the volume of flows in the short term, and can alter the composition of flows toward longer-term maturities. Unremunerated reserve requirements also can be effective in lengthening the maturity structure of inflows, but their effectiveness diminishes over time. There is some evidence that prudential measures that include some form of capital control (such as a limit on bank external borrowing) may be effective in reducing the volume of capital inflows.

In practice, most emerging economies combine the three in varying proportions, achieving, for example, a certain degree of monetary autonomy combined with a "managed" flexible exchange rate.

It is interesting to observe two major emerging economies as points on this continuum. Brazil is an example of flexible exchange rates, independent monetary policy, and high international financial integration, which is now experiencing a surge in its exchange rate and adding pressure to its competitiveness. In addition, a rising current account deficit

| Types of capital controls | Volume of inflows | Composition of inflows |
|---|---|---|
| Foreign exchange tax | Can somewhat reduce the volume in the short term. | Can alter the composition of inflows toward longer-term maturities. |
| Unremunerated Reserve Requirements (URRs): Typically accompanied by other measures | | Have been effectively applied in reducing short-term inflows in overall inflows, but their effect diminishes overtime. |
| Prudential measures with an element of capital control | Some evidence that prudential type controls can be effective in reducing capital inflows. | |
| Administrative controls: These are sometimes used in conjunction with URRs | Effectiveness depends largely on existence of other controls in the country. | |

*Figure 4.5 Effectiveness of capital control measures*[9]

is raising concerns about the risk of a future crisis. Under such circumstances, it is plausible for the policy makers to turn to a combination of exchange market intervention and capital flow controls to try to temper or smooth the pace of its currency appreciation. More importantly, Brazil may need to tighten fiscal policy to reduce incentives for capital inflows. Strengthening macro-prudential and financial regulation as well as developing capital markets can help reduce the risk of a build-up in financial fragility and improve the efficiency of capital allocation, along with better safety nets to reduce the costs of transitional unemployment. Many of these reforms will take time to implement.

China, another member of BRIC, represents a different point with limited exchange rate flexibility, backed by heavy exchange market intervention, and some capital controls. China also is experiencing the high inflation pressures in goods and asset markets predicted by the first approach offered by WTO. Chinese policy makers may understand and appreciate the potential macro-management benefits of greater exchange rate flexibility and more monetary autonomy. But the macroeconomic management has become intertwined with deep structural imbalances— high investment relative to consumption, industry relative to services, corporate profits relative to wages—each bolstered by vested interests and a complex political economy.

Authorities also are concerned about the size and duration of transitional unemployment caused by a downsizing of the tradable goods and export sectors, which may become a threat to the social stability ranking high on their priority list. Thus the move toward macroeconomic policy reform and more exchange rate flexibility in China, though inevitable, is likely to be prolonged.[10]

To echo what Lamy said at the WTO seminar, reform of the international monetary system to cease currency war and put capital flow under control takes time. Joint efforts, from advanced and emerging economies, are needed in global platforms such as the G-20 and the World Bank to coordinate advanced country macro-prudential and financial sector regulatory reform that can help reduce the risk and improve the quality of capital flows to emerging markets. Such process would not necessarily lead to radical accomplishment, but rather incremental action, backed by sound commitment to momentous progress over the medium term.

## Inflation Targeting

Inflation, a rise in the overall level of prices, erodes savings, lowers purchasing power, discourages investment, inhibits growth, fuels capital outflow, and, in extreme cases, provokes social and political unrest. People view it negatively and governments consequently have tried to battle inflation by adopting conservative and sustainable fiscal and monetary policies.

Because interest rates and inflation rates tend to move in opposite directions, central bankers have adopted "inflation targeting" to control the general rise in the price level based on such understanding of the links from the monetary policy instruments of interest rates to inflation. By applying inflation targeting, a central bank estimates, and makes public, a projected or "target" inflation rate and then attempts to use interest rate changes to steer actual inflation toward that target. Through such "transmission mechanism," the likely actions a central bank will take to raise or lower interest rates become more transparent, which leads to an increase in economic stability.

Inflation targeting, as a monetary-policy strategy, was introduced in New Zealand in 1990. It has been very successful in stabilizing both inflation and the real economy. As of 2010, as shown in Figure 4.6, it has been adopted by almost 30 advanced and emerging economies.

Inflation targeting is characterized by (1) an announced numerical inflation target, (2) an implementation of monetary policy that gives a major role to an inflation forecast and has been called forecast targeting, and (3) a high degree of transparency and accountability.[11]

A major advantage of inflation targeting is that it combines elements of both "rules" and "discretion" in monetary policy. This "constrained discretion" framework combines two distinct elements: a precise numerical target for inflation in the medium term and a response to economic shocks in the short term.[12]

### Inflation Targeting with Advanced Economies

There are a number of central banks in more advanced economies, including the ECB, the U.S. Federal Reserve (Fed), the BOJ, and the Swiss National Bank, that have adopted many of the main elements of inflation targeting. Several others are moving toward it. Although these central banks are committed to achieving low inflation, they do not announce explicit numerical targets or other objectives, such as promoting maximum employment and moderate long-term interest rates, in addition to stablizing prices.

In popular perception, and in their own minds, central bankers were satisfied with inflation targeting as an effective tool to squeeze high inflation out of their economies. Their credibility is based on keeping inflation down and therefore they always must be on guard in case prices start to soar.

This view is dangerously outdated after the financial recession. The biggest challenge facing the advanced economies' central banks today is that inflation is too low! After rebounding during the first two years of the recovery, due to U.S. quantitative easing and loosening monetary policy of other advanced economies, inflation in developed markets has drifted lower since mid-2011 and generally stands below central bank targets, as depicted in Figure 4.7. Given considerable slack in developed economies, however, inflation may drop further.

## Targeting Inflation

| Country | Inflation targeting adoption date | Inflation rate at adoption date (percent) | 2010 end-of-year inflation (percent) | Target inflation rate (percent) |
|---|---|---|---|---|
| New Zealand | 1990 | 3.30 | 4.03 | 1 – 3 |
| Canada | 1991 | 6.90 | 2.23 | 2 ± 1 |
| United Kingdom | 1992 | 4.00 | 3.39 | 2 |
| Australia | 1993 | 2.00 | 2.65 | 2 – 3 |
| Sweden | 1993 | 1.80 | 2.10 | 2 |
| Czech Republic | 1997 | 6.80 | 2.00 | 3 ± 1 |
| Israel | 1997 | 8.10 | 2.62 | 2 ± 1 |
| Poland | 1998 | 10.60 | 3.10 | 2.5 ± 1 |
| Brazil | 1999 | 3.30 | 5.91 | 4.5 ± 1 |
| Chile | 1999 | 3.20 | 2.97 | 3 ± 1 |
| Colombia | 1999 | 9.30 | 3.17 | 2 – 4 |
| South Africa | 2000 | 2.60 | 3.50 | 3 – 6 |
| Thailand | 2000 | 0.80 | 3.05 | 0.5 – 3 |
| Hungary | 2001 | 10.80 | 4.20 | 3 ± 1 |
| Mexico | 2001 | 9.00 | 4.40 | 3 ± 1 |
| Iceland | 2001 | 4.10 | 2.37 | 2.5 ± 1.5 |
| Korea, Republic of | 2001 | 2.90 | 3.51 | 3 ± 1 |
| Norway | 2001 | 3.60 | 2.76 | 2.5 ± 1 |
| Peru | 2002 | –0.10 | 2.08 | 2 ± 1 |
| Philippines | 2002 | 4.50 | 3.00 | 4 ± 1 |
| Guatemala | 2005 | 9.20 | 5.39 | 5 ± 1 |
| Indonesia | 2005 | 7.40 | 6.96 | 5 ± 1 |
| Romania | 2005 | 9.30 | 8.00 | 3 ± 1 |
| Serbia | 2006 | 10.80 | 10.29 | 4 – 8 |
| Turkey | 2006 | 7.70 | 6.40 | 5.5 ± 2 |
| Armenia | 2006 | 5.20 | 9.35 | 4.5 ± 1.5 |
| Ghana | 2007 | 10.50 | 8.58 | 8.5 ± 2 |
| Albania | 2009 | 3.70 | 3.40 | 3 ± 1 |

*Figure 4.6 Summary of Central Banks using inflation targeting to control inflation*

Sources: Hammond, 2011; Roger, 2010; and IMF staff calculations

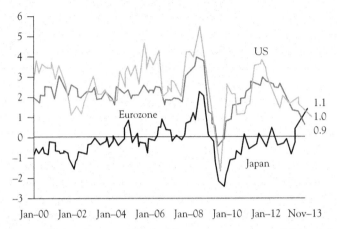

*Figure 4.7* **CPI Inflation of United States, eurozone and Japan from January 2000 to November 2013 (percent, year-on-year)**

Sources: Bloomberg & QNB Group Forecasts

The most obvious danger of such low inflation is the risk of slipping into outright deflation, in which prices persistently fall. As Japan's experience in the past two decades shows, deflation is both deeply damaging and hard to escape in weak economies with high debts. Since loans are fixed in nominal terms, falling wages and prices increase the burden of paying them. Once people expect prices to keep falling, they put off buying things, weakening the economy further.[13]

This is particularly severe in the eurozone, where growth averaged −0.7 percent in the first three quarters of 2013 and annual CPI inflation fell from 2.2 percent at the end of 2012 to 0.9 percent in the year to November 2013 (see Figure 4.7). At the same time the euro has appreciated 8.2 percent this year against a weighted basket of currencies, which is likely to be holding back inflation and growth. The ECB already cut its main policy rate from 0.5 percent to 0.25 percent in November, leaving little room for further interest rate cuts.

Meanwhile, inflation in the United States has fallen to around one percent, the lowest levels since 2009 when the global recession and collapsing commodity markets dragged down prices. These low inflation rates raise the risk that the United States together with the eurozone could be entering their own deflation trap with lost decades of low growth and deflation ahead.

Interestingly enough, Japan sets a deviant example in inflation targeting, in which its central bank wants to reversely boost inflation to a set target of two percent. Since the 1990s, the Japanese economy has languished in a weak state of feeble growth and deflation that has persisted into this century. From January 2000 to May 2013, annual inflation of the CPI was negative (averaging −0.3 percent), while real GDP growth was less than one percent over the same period.

The Prime Minister Shinzo Abe, who came to power at the end of 2012, introduced a raft of expansionary economic policies known as Abenomics (see Chapter 3), which included a 2 percent inflation target and buying about ¥13 trillion in financial assets (some ¥2 trillion in government bonds) every month as long as necessary. Together with heavy spending on public infrastructure and an active policy the Japanese yen was weakened.

Japan's economy has turned. Growth has averaged 3.1 percent so far in 2013 and inflation rose from −0.3 percent in the year in May to 1.1 percent in the year in October. This puts it above inflation in both the United States and eurozone for the first time this century. Rising Japanese inflation is a direct consequence of expansionary economic policies introduced in 2013, which could help the country escape from the lost decades of low growth and deflation from the real estate crash of 1989 until today. Abenomics including a surge of inflation is likely to have contributed significantly to Japan's improving economic performance.

The current situation in United States and eurozone calls for a continuation and possibly acceleration of unconventional monetary policy to offset the dangers that deflation could pose on an already weak recovery. The experience of Japan provides a useful historical precedent. It is likely that the ECB will engage in unconventional monetary policies to provide stimulus by extending its long-term refinancing operations (LTROs), which provide unlimited liquidity to EU banks in exchange for collateral at low interest rates. The ECB also must also stress that its target is an inflation rate close to two percent for the eurozone as a whole, even if that means higher inflation in Germany.

The United States which is still buying $85 billion worth of bonds a month is already likely to postpone tapering QE until early 2014. If inflation continues to slow, QE tapering could take even longer to be implemented. Meanwhile, the Fed also can change its forward guidance as it just did to reduce the threshold below which unemployment must fall even further from six-and-a-half percent to six percent or below, before interest rates are raised.[14]

## Inflation Targeting with Emerging Economies

In emerging markets the inflation picture looks quite different. With unemployment rates hovering around long-term averages, these economies appear to be operating near their full potential. Correspondingly, emerging-markets consumer price inflation has been low since 2012 and has edged higher in recent months. In the aggregate, consumer price weighted emerging markets inflation ticked up to 4.2 percent year-over-year in September 2013, compared with 4.1 percent in August and four percent at the end of 2012 (see Figure 4.8). The sequential trend inflation rate (three months over three months, seasonally-adjusted annual rate) has risen more sharply since midyear, reaching 5.5 percent in September 2013.[15]

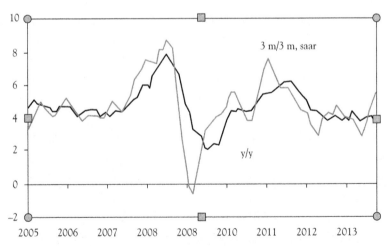

**Figure 4.8 Emerging markets consumer price (percent)**

Source: J.P. Morgan Asset Management, data through September 2013

The concern for emerging-market economies is high inflation together with potential slower growth. Inflation has started to pick-up in emerging markets during 2013, even as growth has fallen short of expectations. Growth looks particularly disappointing when compared with figures from before the 2008 financial crisis. A poorer growth-inflation trade-off suggests that economic potential in emerging markets has slowed considerably. This observation is a particular worry in the largest emerging markets, including China, India, and Brazil. All have been growing at poor rates compared with previous years, but inflation hasn't fallen significantly during the past year.

Inflation targeting has been successfully practiced in a growing number of countries over the past 20 years, and many more countries are moving toward this framework. Although inflation targeting has proven to be a flexible framework that has been resilient in changing circumstances including during the recent global financial crisis, emerging markets must assess their economies to determine whether inflation targeting is appropriate for them or if it can be tailored to suit their needs. Facing the unique challenge of high inflation with slow growth, emerging economies may include currency rate and other alternatives, along with interest rates, to play a more pivotal role in stabilizing inflation.

## State Capitalism

The spread of a new sort of state capitalism in the emerging world is causing increasing attention and problems. As a symbol of state owned enterprises (SOEs), over the past two decades striking corporate headquarters have transformed the great cities of the emerging markets. China Central Television's building resembles a giant alien marching across Beijing's skyline; the gleaming office of VTB, a banking powerhouse, sits at the heart of Moscow's new financial district; the 88-story PETRONAS Towers, home to Malaysia's oil company, soars above Kuala Lumpur. These are all monuments to the rise of a new kind of *Hybrid Corporation*, backed by the state but behaving like a private-sector multinational.[16]

State capitalism is usually described as an economic system in which commercial and economic activity is undertaken by the state, with management and organization of the means of production in a capitalist manner, including the system of wage labor, and centralized management.[17]

State capitalism can also refer to an economic system where the means of production are owned privately but the state has considerable control over the allocation of credit and investment, as in the case of France during the period of dirigisme. Alternatively, state capitalism may be used similar to state monopoly capitalism to describe a system where the state intervenes in the economy to protect and advance the interests of large-scale businesses. This practice is often claimed to be in contrast with the ideals of both socialism and laissez-faire capitalism. In 2008, the term was used by U.S. National Intelligence Council in "Global Trends 2025: A World Transformed" to describe the development of Russia, India, and China.

Marxist literature defines state capitalism[18] as a social system combining capitalism, in which a wage system of producing and appropriating surplus value, with ownership or control by a state. Through such combination, a state capitalist country is one where the government controls the economy and essentially acts like a single huge corporation, extracting the surplus value from the workforce in order to invest it in further production.

State-directed capitalism is not a new idea. It's remote roots can be traced back to the East India Company. After Russia's October Revolution in 1917, using Vladimir Lenin's idea that Czarism was taking a "Prussian path" to capitalism, Nikolai Bukharin identified a new stage in the development of capitalism, in which all sectors of national production and all important social institutions had become managed by the state. He officially named this new stage as "state capitalism."[19]

Rising powers have always used the state to drive initial growth, for example Japan and South Korea in the 1950s, Germany in the 1870s, or even the United States after the war of independence. But these countries eventually found the limits of such a system and subsequently moved away from it.

Singapore's economic model, under Lee Kuan Yew's government, is another form of state capitalism, where the state lets in foreign firms and embraces Western management ideas while owning controlling shares in government-linked companies and directs investments through sovereign wealth funds, mainly Temasek.

Within the EU, state capitalism refers to a system where high coordination between the state, large companies and labor unions ensure economic growth and development in a quasi-corporatist model. Vivien Schmidt cites France and, to a lesser extent, Italy as prime examples of modern European State capitalism.[20]

The leading practitioners of state capitalism nowadays are among emerging markets represented by China and Russia, after Boris Yeltsin's reform. The tight connection between government and business is so obvious, whether in major industries or major markets. The world's ten biggest oil-and-gas firms, measured by reserves, are all state-owned, and state-backed companies account for 80 percent of the value of China's stock market and 62 percent of Russia's. Meanwhile, Brazil has pioneered the use of the state as a minority shareholder together with indirect government ownership through the Brazilian National Development Bank (BNDES) and its investment subsidiary (BNDESPar).[21]

State capitalists like to use China's recent successes against the United States and EU's troubles in the financial crises. They argue that state owned enterprises have the best of both worlds: the ability to plan for the future, but also to respond to fast-changing consumer tastes. State capitalism has been successful at producing national champions that can compete globally. Two-thirds of emerging-market companies on the Fortune 500 list are state-owned, and most of the rest enjoy state support of one sort or another. Chinese companies are building roads and railways in Africa, power plants and bridges in South-Asia, and schools and bridges in the United States. In the most recent list of the world's biggest global contractors, compiled by an industry newsletter, Chinese companies held four of the top five positions. China State Construction Engineering Corporation has undertaken more than 5,000 projects in about 100 different countries and earned $22.4 billion in revenue in 2009. China's Sinohydro controls more than half the world's market for building hydropower stations.[22]

In 2009, just two Chinese state-owned companies, namely China Mobile and China National Petroleum Corporation, made more profits ($33 billion) than China's 500 most profitable private companies combined. In 2010, the top 129 Chinese SOEs made estimated net profits of $151 billion, 50 percent more than the year before (in many cases helped by near-monopolies). In the first six months of 2010 China's four biggest state commercial banks made average profits of $211 million a day.

Under state capitalism, governments can provide SOEs and companies under their indirect control with the resources that they need to reach global markets. One way is by listing them on foreign exchanges, which introduces them to the world's sharpest bankers and analysts. Meanwhile, they can also acquire foreign companies with rare expertise that produces global giants. Shanghai Electric Group enhanced its engineering knowledge by buying Goss International for $1.5 billion and forming joint ventures with Siemens and Mitsubishi. China's Geely International gained access to some of the world's most advanced car-making skills through its acquisition of Volvo for $1.8 billion.*

Governments embrace state capitalism because it serves political as well as economic purposes. Especially, during the recent recession, it puts vast financial resources within the control of state officials, allowing them access to cash that helps safeguard their domestic political capital and, in many cases, increases their leverage on the international stage.

### Risks Associate with State Capitalism

Dizzied by the strength of state capitalism demonstrated through the recent financial crisis, it is easy for outside investors to become blind to the risks posed by the excessive power of the state. Companies are ultimately responsible not to their private shareholders but to the government, which not only owns the majority of the shares but also controls the regulatory and legal system. Such inequality creates lots of risks for investors.

There is striking evidence that state-owned companies are less productive than their private competitors. An OECD paper in 2005 noted that the total factor productivity of private companies is twice that of state companies. A study by the McKinsey Global Institute in the same year found that companies in which the state holds a minority stake are 70 percent more productive than wholly state-owned ones.

Studies also show that SOEs use capital less efficiently than private ones, and grow more slowly. The Beijing-based Unirule Institute of Economics argues that, allowing for all the hidden subsidies such as free land, the average real return on equity for state-owned companies between

---

* Ibidem.

2001 and 2009 was 1.47 percent.* SOEs typically have poorer cost controls than regular companies. When the government favors SOEs, the others suffer. State giants soak up capital and talent that might have been used more efficiently by private companies.

SOEs also suffer from "principal-agent problem," which indicates the tendency of managers, as agents who run companies, to put their own interests prior to the interests of the owners who are the principals. This problem is getting more severe under state capitalism. Politicians who can control or influence the nomination of SOE executives may have their own agenda while being too distracted by other things to exercise proper oversight. Boards are weak, disorganized, and full of insiders.

For example, the Chinese party state exercises power through two institutions: the State-Owned Assets Supervision and Administration Commission (SASAC) and the Communist Party's Organization Department. They appoint all the senior managers in China Inc. Therefore, even the most prestigious top executives of China's SOEs are cadres first and company men second, who naturally care more about pleasing their party bosses than about the market and customers. Ironically, China's SOEs even have successfully attempted to make them pay more dividends to their major shareholder, that is, the state.

Politicians under state capitalism have far more power than they do under liberal capitalism, which creates opportunities for rent seeking and corruption on the part of the SOE elite. State capitalism suffers from the misfortune that it has taken root in countries with problematic states. It often reinforces corruption because it increases the size and range of prizes for the victors. The ruling parties of SOEs have not only the government apparatus but also huge corporate resources at their disposal.

In China where its long history combines with a culture of *guanxi* (relationships) and corruption, the PBOC, China's central bank, estimates that between the mid-1990s and 2008, some 16,000–18,000 Chinese officials and SOE executives made off with a total of $123 billion. Russia has the nepotism and corruption among a group of "bureaugarchs," often-former KGB officials, who dominate both the Kremlin and business. Other BRIC countries suffer from similar problems. Transparency International, a campaigning group, ranks Brazil 72nd in its corruption

---

* Ibidem.

index for 2013, with China 80th, India 94th, and Russia an appalling 127th. In contrast, as Figure 4.9 shows, advance economies favoring a free market model score much better than their emerging market counterparts under state capitalism.

State capitalism also stems the rise of various degrees of globalization as it shackles the flow of money, goods, ideas, information, people, and services within countries and across international borders. Ensuring that trade is fair is harder when companies enjoy the direct or indirect support of a national government. Western politicians are beginning to lose patience with state-capitalist powers that rig the system in favor of their own companies.

More worrying is the potential for capriciousness. State-capitalist governments can be unpredictable with scant regard for other shareholders. Politicians can suddenly step in and replace the senior management or order SOEs to pursue social rather than business goals. In 2004, China's SASAC and the Communist Party's Organization Department rotated the executives of the three biggest telecoms companies. In 2009, they

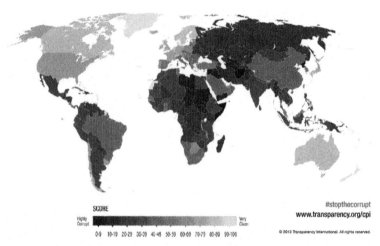

*Figure 4.9 Corruption Perceptions Index 2013*

Source: Transparency International Transparency International*

---

* More detailed information available at http://cpi.transparency.org/cpi2013/results/

reshuffled the bosses of the three leading airlines. In 2010, they did the same to the heads of the three largest state oil companies, each of which is a Fortune 500 company.

### Response to State Capitalism

Will state capitalism completely reverse globalization's progress? Ian Bremmer, the founder and president of the Eurasia Group, indicated that it is highly unlikely. Despite the relatively high growth of emerging markets after the global financial crisis, it has not proven that government engineered growth can outstrip the expansion of well-regulated free markets over the long run. States like China and Russia will face tremendous pressures as internal issues contradict their development. Recently, we witnessed the terrible environmental price China continues to pay for its growth. And Russia's vulnerable reliance on Vladimir Putin, at the expense of credible governing institutions, put their economic resilience to the test. A free market does not depend on the wisdom of political officials for its dynamism; that's the primary reason it will almost certainly withstand the state capitalist challenge.

However, the financial crisis and advanced countries' apparent responsibility for it may ensure the growth of state capitalism over the next several years. The future of this path will depend on a range of factors, including any wavering of Western faith in the power of free markets, the U.S. administration's capacity to kick-start its economic growth, the ability of the Russian government's dependence on oil exports to withstand the pain inflicted by prices drop, the Chinese Communist Party's ability to create jobs and maintain tight control of its own people, and dozens of other variables. In the meantime, corporate leaders and investors must recognize that free market capitalism is no longer the unchallenged international economic paradigm and that politics will have a profound impact on the performance of markets for many years to come.[23]

Increasingly, multinational companies and international traders are operating in an environment where they have to pay much more attention to politics, and they can't invest purely on the basis of where the markets may be attractive.

## Economic Nationalism

In the good old days, growth in trade and cross-border investment brought prosperity and development. Globalization appeared to deliver rising living standards for all, and there was no conflict. Leaders of nations could simultaneously support the architecture of globalization while taking the plaudits for prosperity at home. That's all changed. As English statesman Lord Palmerston noted: "nations have no permanent friends or allies, they only have permanent interests."

Nations led by politicians, who are primarily interested in strengthening their political capitals by serving and protecting their most powerful constituents (the local voters, political benefactors, or powerful industries and interest parties), naturally try to help boost their domestic economies rather than making choices with the global economy in mind. In the aftermath of the global financial crisis, these interests dictated a body of policies that emphasized domestic control of the economy, labor, and capital formation, even if this required the reversal of the trend to greater global integration and a return to economic nationalism.[24]

The financial crisis inevitably revealed that integration reduces the effectiveness of a nation's economic policies, unless other nations take

|  | Discretionary fiscal stimulus | Financial assistance (excluding guarantees) | Total crisis fighting |
|---|---|---|---|
| UK | 1.6 | 32.1 | 33.7 |
| Japan | 4.2 | 26.5 | 30.6 |
| China | 5.8 | 21.3 | 27.1 |
| US | 3.8 | 21.4 | 25.2 |
| Russia | 5.4 | 16.7 | 22.1 |
| Brazil | 12 | 13.3 | 13.5 |
| India | 12 | 9.6 | 10.8 |
| Germany | 3.6 | 4.2 | 7.8 |
| France | 1.5 | 2.7 | 4.2 |
| Italy | 0.3 | 0.7 | 1.0 |

Figure 4.10  2009–2010 fiscal stimulus and financial bailouts, percentage GDP (Select G-20 countries)

Source: IMF, 2009b

coordinated action. Governments' initial reaction to the global financial crisis was to pour large amounts of government spending in a competitive rather than cooperative way to bailout its own economy first, as shown in Figure 4.10.

As it became clear that the recession would last longer than originally anticipated, governments started to throw up barriers to trade and investment meant to keep local workers employed through the next election. Economic nationalism leads to the imposition of tariffs and other restrictions on the movement of labor, goods, and capital. The United States tacked a 127 percent tariff on to Chinese paper clips; Japan put a 778 percent tariff on rice. Protection is worse in the emerging world, as shown in Figure 4.11. Brazil's tariffs are, on average, four times higher than in the United States', and China is three times higher.

Besides tariffs, big emerging markets like Brazil, Russia, India, and China have displayed a more interventionist approach to globalization that relies on industrial policy and government-directed lending to give domestic sellers more advantages. Industrial policy enjoys more respectability than tariffs and quotas, but it raises costs for consumers and puts more efficient foreign firms at a disadvantage. The Peterson Institute estimates local-content requirements cost the world $93 billion in lost trade in 2010.[25]

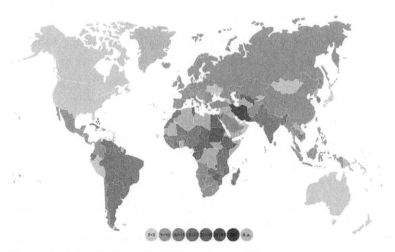

**Figure 4.11 2012 Year of MFN applied tariff**

Source: © World Trade Organization 2013

For advanced economies, government procurement policies also favor national suppliers. "Buy American" campaigns as seen in the recent U.S. presidential election and preferential policies are used to direct demand. Safety and environmental standards are used to prevent foreign products penetrating national markets. According to Global Trade Alert, a monitoring service, at least 400 new protectionist measures have been put in place each year since 2009, and the trend is on the increase.

Another obvious move in economic nationalism is through capital markets. Nations facing financial difficulties with high levels of government debt seek to limit capital outflows. These would prevent depositors and investors withdrawing funds to avoid potential losses from sovereign defaults. In Europe, there was a tendency for a breakdown in the common currency and redenomination of investments into a domestic currency.

In Cyprus, explicit capital controls designed to prevent capital flight were implemented. On the other hand, low interest rates and weak currencies in developed economies have led to volatile and destabilizing capital inflows into emerging nations with higher rates and stronger growth prospects. Brazil, South Korea, and Switzerland have implemented controls on capital inflows.

As a result, global capital flows fell from $11 trillion in 2007 to a third of that in 2012. The decline happened partly for cyclical reasons, but also because regulators of nations who saw banks' foreign adventures end in disaster have sought to gate their financial systems.

Political tension and national security can make existing economic nationalism more complicated and intensified. Mr. Snowden first revealed the existence of the clandestine data-mining program of U.S. National Security Agency (NSA) in June 2013. The NSA involves U.S. firms in the IT and telecoms space. Basically, it ensures U.S. firms operate under certain kinds of rules in connection with the U.S. government and the military industrial complex. Snowden's revelations provoked a storm in the Chinese media and added urgency to Beijing's efforts to use its market power to create indigenous software and hardware.

As a consequence, U.S. technology companies including Cisco Systems immediately face new challenges in selling their goods and services in China, as fallout from the U.S. spying scandal starts to take a toll. Snowden's revelations of the U.S. spying on several countries provoked a storm in the Chinese media and added urgency to Beijing's efforts to use its market power to create indigenous software and hardware. Cisco Systems warned its revenue would dive as much as 10 percent in the fourth quarter of 2013, and keep dipping until after the middle of 2014, in part due to a backlash in China after Snowden's revelations about U.S. government surveillance programs. Beijing may be targeting Cisco in particular as retaliation for Washington's refusal to buy goods from China's Huawei Technologies Co., a telecommunications equipment maker that the United States claims is a threat to national security because of links to the Chinese military.

### Response to Economic Nationalism

Economic nationalism may offer near-term pain relief but, as a political response to economic failure, it only risks locking in that economic failure for the long term. The world learned from the Great Depression that protectionism makes a bad situation worse.

Trade encourages specialization, which brings prosperity. Economic cooperation encourages confidence and enhances security. Global capital markets, for all their problems, allocate money more efficiently than local ones.

In December 2013, the WTO sealed its first global trade deal after almost 160 ministers gathered on the Indonesian island of Bali and agreed to reforms to boost world commerce. Tense negotiations followed 20 years of bitter disputes. At the heart of the agreement were measures to ease barriers to trade by reducing import duties, simplify customs procedures, and make the procedures more transparent and thus end years of corruption at ports and border controls.

"For the first time in our history, the WTO has truly delivered," WTO chief Roberto Azevedo told exhausted ministers after the long talks. "This time the entire membership came together. We have put the 'world' back in World Trade organization," he said. "We're back in business … Bali is just the beginning."

China, a key member of BRICS, also started to respond to the challenge in the right way. On December 2nd of 2013, the PBOC issued a set of guidelines on how financial reform will proceed inside the new Shanghai

Free Trade Zone (SFTZ). This 29 sq. km (about 18 sq. miles) enclave, created three months earlier, has been trumpeted by Li Keqiang, the country's prime minister, as a driver of economic reform under his new administration.

To boost cross-border investment and trade, the PBOC wants to allow firms and individuals to open special accounts that will enable them to trade freely with foreign accounts in any currency. Selected foreign institutional investors may be allowed to invest directly in the Shanghai stock market. Interest rates may be liberalized for certain accounts at designated firms inside the SFTZ, which would open a new window of globalization and free capital market in China.

## Conclusion

As mentioned at the beginning of this chapter, the BRICS economies are contributing less to global growth. In 2008 they accounted for two-thirds

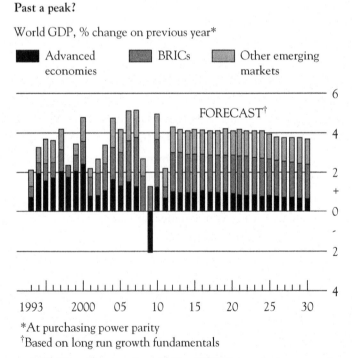

**Past a peak?**

World GDP, % change on previous year*

*At purchasing power parity
†Based on long run growth fundamentals

*Figure 4.12 Emerging markets led by BRIC have demonstrated stronger growth than the advanced economies*

Source: Goldman Sachs

of world GDP growth. In 2011 they accounted for half of it, in 2012 a bit less than that. The IMF sees growth staying at about that level for the next five years. Goldman Sachs predicts that, based on an analysis of fundamentals, the BRICs share will decline further over the long term.

Other emerging markets will pick up some of the slack including the "Next 11" that includes Bangladesh, Indonesia, Mexico, Nigeria, and Turkey. Although there are various reasons to think the N-11 cannot have an impact on the same scale as that of the BRICs, emerging markets other than BRIC will play a vital role in the future. Advanced economies will continue to lose their share which will contribute to a general easing of the pace of world growth,[26] as shown in Figure 4.12.

Internationally, lower growth could focus leaders on increased cooperation and a new push for liberalization, which will mitigate (as discussed) the risks of currency war, inflation targeting, state capitalism, and economic nationalism. A predicted slowdown could bring new consensus to global trade talks as witnessed in Bali in December 2013. More deals that address nontariff trade barriers, and especially those on trade-in services, could yield bigger benefits down the road.

# CHAPTER 5

# Global Economies at War

## Overview

More than half a decade has passed since the financial crisis hit, traversing the global economy very rapidly, confirming just how interconnected the world has become as ideas, information, capital, and new technologies have streamed across borders with increasing ease. Nevertheless, the lack of sustained financial crisis response has made it clear just how fractured the international political landscape has become, as advanced and emerging economies' diverging interests make global coordination ever more difficult. Hence, despite sustained globalization, and in some cases because of it, we are seeing a growing vacuum of global leadership, as well as traditional geopolitical risks, which consequently are on the rise.

This chapter attempts to address key global issues for tomorrow that demand our attention today. It provides an overview of many of the most volatile, significant, and misunderstood developments reshaping the global geopolitical landscape, from the growing global vulnerability of public and private institutions to the increasing impact of public opinion and protest.

As James Rickards argues[1] the world is amidst a full-blown currency war, and assuming this is true, there are several undercurrents between advanced economies and emerging markets to which we need to be attentive, beginning with the United States-China dynamics, the relations between China and the Russian Federation, and more broadly the rest of Asia. We also attempt to address the significant shifts in the Middle East, and the unconventional energy revolution in North America that is primed to reshape global energy markets and the world's balance of power. The central focus of this chapter, aside from developing awareness that global economies are at war, is the fact that the world, more than ever before, is constantly and rapidly changing, and international business professionals must seek guidance on how to understand the key players in the evolving global landscape.

Such trends have gained momentum in shaping global trade, especially among advanced economies and emerging markets, leading to a host of new challenges to policymakers worldwide, as well as international traders and multinational corporations. In a world where the international agenda is coming undone, local and shorter-term challenges take precedence for policymakers and international business leaders. That itself is an issue, as longer-term risks go unaddressed and loom larger. Furthermore, we have seen an increased vulnerability of elites, as a host of new voices, whether from the voting booth in advanced economies, populist parties, growing middle classes in emerging markets, or through new technologies, have put added strain on leaders who are increasingly *takers* rather than *makers* of policy.

## Economies at War

Since 2010, government officials from the G-7 economies have been very concerned with the potential escalation of a global economic war. Not a conventional war with fighter jets, bullets, and bombs, but rather, a "currency war." Finance ministers and central bankers from advanced economies worry that their peers in the G-20, which also includes several emerging economies, may devalue their currencies to boost exports and grow their own economies at their neighbors' expense.

Brazil led the charge, being the first emerging economy to accuse the United States of instigating a currency war in 2010, when the U.S. Federal Reserve bought piles of bonds with newly created money. From a Chinese perspective, with the world's largest holdings of U.S. dollar reserves, a U.S. lead currency war based on dollar debasement is an American act of default to its foreign creditors. So far the Chinese have been more diplomatic, but their patience is waning.

These two countries are not alone, as depicted in Figure 5.1. Several other emerging markets, such as Saudi Arabia, Korea, Russia, Turkey, and Taiwan also have been impacted by a weak dollar. Quantitative easing (QE) made investors flood emerging markets with hot money in search of better returns, which consequently lifted their exchange rates. But Brazil

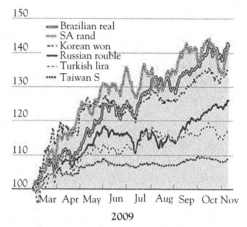

*Figure 5.1  Emerging market currencies inflated by weak dollar*

*Source*: Thompson Reuters Datastream

was not alone, as Japan's prime minister, Shinzo Abe, also has reacted to the QEs in the United States and pledged bold monetary stimulus to restart growth and vanquish deflation in the country.

As advanced economies, like the three largest world economies— United States, China and Japan respectively—try to kick-start their sluggish economies with ultra low interest rates and sprees of money printing, they are putting downward pressure on their currencies. The loose monetary policies are primarily aimed at stimulating domestic demand, but their effects spill over into the global currency world.

Japan faces charges that it is trying to lower the value of its currency, the yen, to stimulate its economy and get an edge over other countries. The new Japanese government is trying to get Japan, which has been in recession, moving again after a two-decade bout of stagnant growth and deflation. Hence, it embarked on an economic course it hopes will finally jump-start the economy. The government coerced the Bank of Japan to accept a higher inflation target, which triggered speculation that the bank will create more money. The prospect of more yen in circulation has been the main reason behind the yen's recent falls to a 21-month low against the dollar and a near three-year record against the euro.

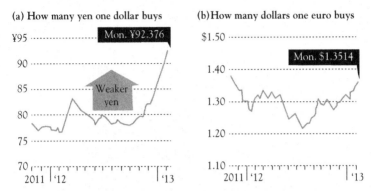

*Figure 5.2  Central banks in the United States and Japan has flooded their economies with liquidity*

Source: WSJ Market Data Group

Since Abe called for a weaker yen to bolster exports, the currency has fallen by 16 percent against the dollar and 19 percent against the euro. As the yen falls, its exports become cheaper, and also those of its neighbors, such as of Asian neighbors South Korea and Taiwan. At the same time, the exports for those countries further afield in Europe, become relatively more expensive. As depicted in Figure 5.2, central banks in the United States and Japan have flooded their economies with liquidity since mid-2012 and into 2013, causing the both the yen and the dollar to weaken against other major currencies.

In our opinion, common sense could prevail, putting an end to the dangerous game of beggar (and blame) thy neighbor. After all, the IMF was created to prevent such races, and should try to broker a truce among foreign exchange competitors. The critical issues in the United States, as well as China and Japan, stem from ineffective public policy, but also a failed and destructive economic policy. These policy errors are directly responsible for the opening salvos of the currency war clouds now looming overhead.*

---

* Our opinion expressed here is from the point of you of international trade and currency exchange as far as it affects international trade, and not from the geopolitical and economic aspects of the issue. We approach the issue of currency wars not from the theoretical, or even simulation models undertaken from behind a desk in an office, but from the point of view of practitioners engaged in international business and foreign trade, on the ground, in four different countries.

So far, Europe has felt the most impact of the falling yen. At the height of the eurozone's financial crisis in 2012, the euro was worth US$1.21, which was potentially benefitting big exporters like BMW, AUDI, Mercedes, or Airbus. However, at the time of this writing in December 2013, the euro is at US$1.38 even though the eurozone is still the laggard of the world economy.

Across the 17-strong euro area a recovery has been underway following a double-dip recession lasting 18 months, but it is a feeble one. For 2013 as a whole, GDP still will continue to fall by 0.4 percent (after declining by 0.6 percent in 2012), but it is expected to rise by 1.1 percent in 2014.[2] A rise in the value of the euro has to do with the diminishing threat of a collapse of the currency, will do little to help companies in the eurozone—and barely help it regrow.

Chinese policymakers reject the conventional thinking proposed by advanced economies. How about the yen's extraordinary rise over the last 40 years, from JPY360 against the dollar at the beginning of the 1970s to about JPY102 today?* Not to mention that despite this huge appreciation, Japan's current account surplus has only gotten bigger, not smaller. They also could argue that the United States' prescription for China's economic rebalancing, a stronger currency, and a boost to domestic demand was precisely the policy followed by the Japanese in the late-1980s, leading to the biggest financial bubble in living memory and the 20-year hangover that followed.

Furthermore, the demand by the United States, which is backed by the G-7 to revalue the renminbi, in our view, is a policy of United States default. During the Asian crisis in 1997–98, advanced economies, under the auspices of the IMF, insisted that Asian nations, having borrowed so much, should now tighten their belts. Shouldn't advance economies be doing the same? In addition Chinese manufacturing margins are so slim that significant change in exchange rates could wipe them out and force layoffs of millions of Chinese. As it is, labor rates are already climbing in China, further squeezing margins. Lastly, a revaluation of the yuan would only push manufacturing to other cheaper emerging markets, such

---

* As of December 2013

as Vietnam, Cambodia, Thailand, Bangladesh, and other lower paying nations without improving the advanced economies trade deficits.

Some G-7 policymakers believe these criticisms grumbles are overdone; arguing that the rest of the world should praise the United States and Japan for such monetary policies, suggesting the eurozone should do the same. The war rhetoric implies that the United States and Japan are directly suppressing their currencies to boost exports and suppress imports, which in our view is a zero-sum game, which could degenerate into protectionism and a collapse in trade.

These countries, however, do not believe such a currency devaluation strategy will threaten trade. Rather, their belief seems to be that as central banks continue to lower their short-term interest rate to near zero, exhausting their conventional monetary methods in the process, they must employ unconventional methods, such as QE, or try to convince consumers that inflation will arise. The goal is to lower real (inflation-adjusted) interest rates. If so, inflation should be rising in the United States and in Japan, which according to Figure 5.3, it is.

Over the past decade, Japan has seen the consumer price index (CPI) for most periods hover just below the zero-percent inflation line. (See Figure 5.3.) The notable exceptions were in 2008, when inflation rose as high as two percent, and in late 2009, when prices fell at close to a two percent rate. The rise in inflation coincided with a crash in capital spending. The worst period of deflation preceded an upturn. Of course,

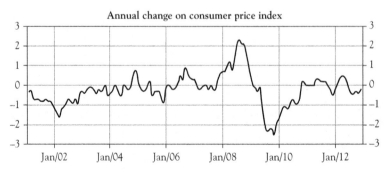

**Figure 5.3 Japan's inflation rate has been climbing since 2010 as a result of economic stimulus**

Source: Trading Economics,[3] Japan's Ministry of Internal Affairs & Communications

the graph does not provide enough data to conclude causal effects, but it seems, however, that the relationship between growth and Japan's mild deflation may be more complicated than the Great Depression-inspired deflationary spiral narrative suggests. The principal goal of this policy was to stimulate domestic spending and investment, but lower real rates usually weaken the currency as well, and that in turn tends to depress imports. Nevertheless, if the policy is successful in reviving domestic demand, it will eventually lead to higher imports.

At least that's the idea behind the argument. The IMF concluded that the United States' first rounds of QE boosted its trading partners' output by as much as 0.3 percent. The dollar did weaken, but that became a motivation for Japan's stepped-up assault on deflation. The combined monetary boost on opposite sides of the Pacific has been a powerful elixir for global investor confidence, if anything, to move hot-money emerging markets where the interests were much higher than in advanced economies.

The reality is that most advanced economies have overconsumed in recent years. It has too much debt. Rather than dealing with the debt—living a life of austerity, accepting a period of relative stagnation—these economies want to shift the burden of adjustment onto its creditors, even when those creditors are relatively poor nations with low per capita incomes. This is true not only for China but also for many other countries in Asia and in other parts of the emerging world. During the Asian crisis in 1997–98, Western nations, under the auspices of the IMF, insisted that Asian nations, having borrowed too much, should tighten their belts. However, the United States doesn't seem to think it should abide by the same rules. Better to use the exchange rate to pass the burden onto someone else than to swallow the bitter pill of austerity.

Meanwhile, European policymakers, fearful that their countries' exports are caught in this currency war crossfire, have entertained unwise ideas such as directly managing the value of the euro. While the option of generating money out of thin air may not be available to emerging markets, where inflation tends to remain problematic, limited capital controls may be a sensible short-term defense against destabilizing inflows of hot money. Figure 5.4 illustrates how the inflows of hot-money leaving advanced economies in search of better returns on investments in

**Figure 5.4** *In 2009 emerging markets significantly outperformed advanced (developed) economies*

Source: FTSE All-World Indices

emerging markets have caused these markets to significantly outperform advanced (developed) markets.

## Currency War May Cause Damage to Global Economy

As more countries try to weaken their currencies for economic gain, there may come a point where the fragile global economic recovery could be derailed and the international financial system thrown into chaos. That's the reason financial representatives from the world's leading 20 industrial and developing nations spent most of their time during the G-20 summit in Moscow in September 2013.

In September 2011, Switzerland took action to arrest the rise of its currency, the Swiss franc, when investors, looking for somewhere safe to store their cash from the debt crisis afflicting the 17-country eurozone, saw in the Swiss franc the traditional instrument to fulfill that role. The Swiss intervention was viewed as an attempt to protect the country's exporters.

In our view, policymakers are focusing on the wrong issue. Rather than focus on currency manipulation, all sides would be better served to hone in on structural reforms. The effects of that would be far more beneficial in the long run than unilateral United States, China, or Japan currency action, and more sustainable. The G-20 should focus on a comprehensive package centered on structural reforms in all countries, both advanced economies and emerging markets. Undeniably, exchange rates should be an important part of that package. For instance, to reduce the U.S. current-account deficits, Americans must save more. To continue to simply devalue the dollar will not be sufficient for that purpose. Likewise, China's current-account surpluses were caused by a broad set of domestic economic distortions, from state-allocated credit to artificially low interest rates. Correcting China's external imbalances requires eliminating these distortions as well.

As long as policymakers continue to focus on currency exchange issues, the volatility in the currency markets will continue to escalate. Indeed, it has become so worrisome that the G-7 advanced economies have warned that volatile movements in exchange rates could adversely hit the global economy. Figure 5.5 provides a broad view (rebased at 100 percent on August 1st, 2008) of main exchange rates against the dollar.

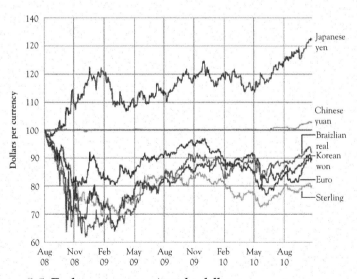

*Figure 5.5 Exchange rates against the dollar*

Source: Bloomberg

When it became clear that Shinzo Abe with his agenda of growth-at-all-costs would win Japan's elections, the yen lost more than 10 percent against the dollar and some 15 percent against the euro. In turn, the dollar dropped to its lowest level against the euro in nearly 15 months. These monetary debasement strategies are adversely impacting and angering export-driven countries such as Brazil, and many of the BRICS, ASEAN, CIVETS, and MENA blocs. But these strategies also are stirring the pot in Europe. The eurozone has largely remained quiet regarding monetary stimulus and now finds itself in the invidious position of having a contracting economy and a rising currency.

These currency moves have shocked BRICS countries as well as other emerging-market economies, including Thailand. The G-20 is clearly divided between the advanced economies, including the UK, United States, Japan, France, Canada, Italy, and Germany, and emerging countries such as Russia, China, South Korea, India, Brazil, Argentina, and Indonesia. Top leaders of Russia, South Korea, Germany, Brazil, and China have expressed their concern over the currency moves, which drive up the value of their currencies and undermine the competitiveness of their exports. If they decide to enter the playing field, like Venezuela, which has devalued its currency by 32 percent, the world would plunge into competitive devaluations. Competitive devaluations would lead to run-away inflation or hyperinflation. Nobody will win with these types of currency wars.

James Rickards, author of "Currency Wars: The Making of the Next Global Crisis," expects the international monetary system to destabilize and collapse. In his views, "there will be so much money-printing by so many central banks that people's confidence in paper money will wane, and inflation will rise sharply."[4]

If policymakers truly want to ward off this currency war, then it is a matter of doing what was done in 1985 with the Plaza Accord.* This

---

* The Plaza Accord was an agreement between the governments of France, West Germany, Japan, the United States, and the United Kingdom, to depreciate the U.S. dollar in relation to the Japanese yen and German Deutsche Mark by intervening in currency markets. The five governments signed the accord on September 22, 1985 at the Plaza Hotel in New York City.

time, however, we will need a different version, as it will not be about the United States and the then G-5 in 1985. It will have to be an *Asian Plaza Accord* under the support and auspices of the G-20. It should be about the Asian export led and mercantilist leadership agreeing among them. The chances of this happening, of advanced economies seeing the necessity of it, or these economies relinquishing its powers in any meaningful way, are not possible under current political strategies.

## Currency War Means Currency Suicide

Special contribution by Patrick Barron*

What the media calls a "currency war," whereby nations engage in competitive currency devaluations in order to increase exports, is really "currency suicide." National governments persist in the fallacious belief that weakening one's own currency will improve domestically produced products' competitiveness in world markets and lead to an export driven recovery. As it intervenes to give more of its own currency in exchange for the currency of foreign buyers, a country expects that its export industries will benefit with increased sales, which will stimulate the rest of the economy. So we often read that a country is trying to "export its way to prosperity."

Mainstream economists everywhere believe that this tactic also exports unemployment to its trading partners by showering them with cheap goods and destroying domestic production and jobs. Therefore, they call for their own countries to engage in reciprocal measures. Recently Martin Wolfe in the Financial Times of London and Paul Krugman of the New York Times both accused their countries' trading partners of engaging in this "beggar-thy-neighbor" policy and recommended that England and the United States respectively enter this so-called "currency war" with full monetary ammunition to further weaken the pound and the dollar.

---

* Patrick Barron is a private consultant in the banking industry. He teaches in the Graduate School of Banking at the University of Wisconsin, Madison, and teaches Austrian economics at the University of Iowa, in Iowa City, where he lives with his wife of 40 years. We recommend you to visit his blog at http://patrick-barron.blogspot.com/ or contact him at PatrickBarron@msn.com.

I, Patrick, am struck by the similarity of this currency-war argument in favor of monetary inflation to that of the need for reciprocal trade agreements. This argument supposes that trade barriers against foreign goods are a boon to a country's domestic manufacturers at the expense of foreign manufacturers.

Therefore, reciprocal trade barrier reductions need to be negotiated, otherwise the country that refuses to lower them will benefit. It will increase exports to countries that do lower their trade barriers without accepting an increase in imports that could threaten domestic industries and jobs. This fallacious mercantilist theory never dies because there are always industries and workers who seek special favors from government at the expense of the rest of society. Economists call this "rent seeking."

### A Transfer of Wealth and a Subsidy to Foreigners

As I, Patrick, explained in my article *"Value in Devaluation?"*[5] inflating one's currency simply transfers wealth within the country from non-export related sectors to export related sectors and gives subsidies to foreign purchasers.

It is impossible to make foreigners pay against their will for the economic recovery of another nation. On the contrary, devaluing one's currency gives a windfall to foreigners who buy goods cheaper. Foreigners will get more of their trading partner's money in exchange for their own currency, making previously expensive goods a real bargain, at least until prices rise.

Over time the nation which weakens its own currency will find that it has "imported inflation" rather than exported unemployment, the beggar-thy-neighbor claim of Wolfe and Krugman. At the inception of monetary debasement the export sector will be able to purchase factors of production at existing prices, so expect its members to favor cheapening the currency. Eventually the increase in currency will work its way through the economy and cause prices to rise. At that point, the export sector will be forced to raise its prices. Expect it to call for another round of monetary intervention in foreign currency markets to drive money to another new low against that of its trading partners.

Of course, if one country can intervene to lower its currency's value, other countries can do the same. So the ECB wants to drive the euro's value lower against the dollar, since the U.S. Federal Reserve has engaged in multiple programs of quantitative easing. The self-reliant Swiss succumbed to the monetary debasement Kool-Aid last summer when its sound currency was in great demand, driving its value higher, and making exports more expensive. Lately the head of the Australian central bank hinted that the country's mining sector needs a cheaper Aussie dollar to boost exports. Welcome to the modern version of currency wars, AKA currency suicide.

There is one country that is speaking out against this madness: Germany. But Germany does not have control of its own currency. It gave up its beloved Deutsche Mark for the euro, supposedly a condition demanded by the French to gain their approval for German reunification after the fall of the Berlin Wall. German concerns over the consequences of inflation are well justified. Germany's great hyperinflation in the early 1920's destroyed the middle class and is seen as a major contributor to the rise of fascism.

As a sovereign country Germany has every right to leave the European Monetary Union (EMU) and reinstate the Deutsche Mark (DM). I, Patrick, would prefer that it go one step further and tie the new DM to its very substantial gold reserves. Should it do so, the monetary world would change very rapidly for the better. Other EMU countries would likely adopt the Deutsche Mark as legal tender, rather than reinstating their own currencies, thus increasing the DM's appeal as a reserve currency.

As demand for the Deutsche Mark increased, demand for the dollar and the euro as reserve currencies would decrease. The U.S. Federal Reserve and the ECB would be forced to abandon their inflationist policies in order to prevent massive repatriation of the dollar and the euro, which would cause unacceptable price increases.

In other words, a sound Deutsche Mark would start a cascade of virtuous actions by all currency producers. This Golden Opportunity should not be squandered. It may be the only non-coercive means to prevent the total collapse of the world's major currencies through competitive debasements called a currency war, but which is better and more accurately named currency suicide.

### Value in Devaluation?

The euro is in trouble. That is not news. What is news is that people with deep pockets are willing to pay for economists to provide a solution. Lord Wolfson,[6] the chief executive of Next, UK, has offered a £250,000 prize for the best way a country can exit the EMU. Five finalists for the prize were announced in March 2013, but none of the five finalists— Neil Record, Jens Nordvig, Jonathan Tepper, Catherine Dobbs, and Roger Bootle—advocates a return to sound money; all assume that new, national fiat currencies will float; and all assume that unproductive countries will benefit from devalued new currencies.

The theory is that a devalued currency will spur export-driven economic growth. Furthermore, they have little confidence that economic reforms—which they all, by the way, do recommend—will be achieved in the near term and see devaluation as a quicker alternative. But will this work? First a word about devaluation itself.

Devaluing against Gold

Historically, devaluation of a currency referred to its relationship to gold. Gold could not be expanded in any appreciable amounts very quickly. It had to be dug up, minted, and placed into circulation at some expense over a long period of time. Coin clipping and substituting a base metal for some percentage of the gold in coins were early means of money debasement. Later, paper currencies could be expanded as quickly and as cheaply as the mint could run paper through its presses, but even this pales in comparison to these electronic times in which money can be expanded to any amount desired at the click of a mouse.

Devaluations occurred, of course, even when governments admitted that gold was money. Notable examples are the Swiss devaluation in 1936, detailed so succinctly by Mises in Human Action, and America's shocking 69 percent devaluation in 1934. Both of these, and others like them, were considered shameful and self-serving acts. Devaluation was tantamount to an admission of fraud. The country's central bank had printed and circulated more units of currency than it could redeem at the currency-to-gold price it had promised its trading partners. This, of course, had disastrous effects on everyone who held contractual promises to be paid in gold.

## Devaluing against Other Fiat Currencies

The devaluation advocated by many economists today is quite different in one regard. There is no commodity reserve—gold or silver, for example—against which the nation's currency is to be devalued. Modern devaluation advocates refer to the currency's value, or exchange ratio, in relation to all other fiat currencies. The exchange value between currencies is governed by purchasing-power parity, which is the simple comparison of the price levels of two countries as expressed in local currency. Nevertheless, the mechanism for devaluing is still the same as that which occurred under gold: inflation of the fiat-money supply.

For example, the central bank could give foreign buyers more local currency with which to buy local goods. This increased supply of local currency eventually works its way through the economy, raising all prices. Economists refer to this process as "importing inflation." The devaluation advocates attempt to convince their countrymen that what was once a shameful act is now a positive good. For example, the Swiss are trying to lower the value of their currency in relation to all others.

What of the proposition that taking positive steps to devalue one's own currency against all others, if it can be achieved, will actually help a country become more competitive? What have others said on this subject?

## Insights from Immanuel Kant, Frederic Bastiat, and Henry Hazlitt

A policy of currency devaluation can be judged by whether or not it satisfies Immanuel Kant's "categorical imperative," which asks whether the action will benefit all men, at all places, and at all times. Certainly devaluation will benefit exporters, who can expect to make more sales. Their foreign customers get more local currency in exchange for their own. Exports increase. The exporter's position is one that is best examined by considering Frederic Bastiat's brilliant essay "That Which Is Seen, and That Which Is Not Seen" and "The Lesson" found in Henry Hazlitt's *Economics in One Lesson.*

At the instance of exchanging his money for more local currency, the foreign buyer will indeed be inclined to purchase more of the goods from the country that devalued. This we can see, and most pundits consider it a good thing. The exporter's increased sales can be measured. This is seen. But what about the importer's lost sales? Importers can expect the opposite. The local currency will buy less, and they can expect sales to fall due to the necessity of raising prices to reflect the reduced purchasing power of their local currency. How can someone measure sales that never happened? This is Bastiat's unseen.

Hazlitt would tell us to look at the longer-term effects of Bastiat's insight. What is seen is that exporters get first use of the newly created money and buy replacement factors of production at current prices. The increased profits from the higher sales enrich them, because they are the early receivers of the money. But how about those who get the money much later, such as wholesalers, or not at all, such as retirees?

Over time the new money causes all prices to rise, even the exporter's factors of production. The benefits to the exporter of the monetary intervention have slowly evaporated. The costs of his factors of production have risen. His sales start to fall back to pre-intervention levels. What can he do except lobby the government for another shot of monetary expansion to give his customers even more local currency with which to buy his products?

## Monetary Expansion Creates the Boom-Bust Cycle

Even this increase in overall prices and their redistributive effects is not the entire story. The increase in the nation's money supply will cause the boom-bust business cycle. The Wolfson Prize finalists, who see historical evidence in the beneficial effects of devaluation, have misinterpreted the boom phase. For example, Jonathan Tepper writes "in August 1998, Russia defaulted on its sovereign debt and devalued its currency. The expected catastrophe didn't happen." Later he writes, "Argentina was forced to default and devalue in late 2001 and early 2002. Despite dire predictions, the economy did extraordinarily well." But these are merely the expected and temporary appearances of the boom phase caused by monetary expansion. Not only does the bankrupt nation shed itself of its debt and get to keep its ill-gotten gains; its expansionist monetary policy touches off a speculative boom. Neither Russia nor Argentina has built sustainable, capitalist economies.

## The Exporter as Wealth-Transfer Agent

It should be clear that there is no net benefit to the country that drives down the purchasing power of its currency through monetary expansion. The only reason the exporter makes more sales is that the buyer of the exporter's goods gets a lower price. This lower price was not the result of manufacturing efficiencies, but of a subsidy—a transfer of wealth—from some in the exporting country to the foreign purchaser of the goods. With each successive monetary expansion, wealth is funneled to the exporter, his employees, and others who get the money early in the expansion phase. All others are harmed. In effect, his fellow citizens who are the late receivers of the new money have subsidized the exporter's sales. The exporter is the unseen means by which the transfer is affected. The nation as a whole is worse off; it is not more competitive.

## Delaying Real Reform in a Fruitless "Race to the Bottom"

Politicians and their professional economist supporters are doing their fellow citizens an injustice by pursuing devaluation as a quick and easy means to improve national competitiveness. The source of real competitive advantage is through liberal reform of economic policies that reward industriousness in a people, to protect their property and even that of foreigners from confiscatory taxation, and encourage savings. Over time the country's capital base, in relation to its population, will increase; an increase in capital per capita, as economists say, thus raising real prosperity through increased worker productivity. Instead of forthrightly pursuing economic reform, which one must admit will be difficult, politicians and their professional-economist supporters are fomenting a "race to the bottom," by which each country tries to boost exports via competitive devaluations against all others. The nation's capital base will slowly dwindle through the backdoor export subsidy made possible through monetary debasement.

## The Moral Hazard of the Welfare State

There is nothing preventing any member of the EMU from becoming more competitive right now. All that is required is willingness to lower prices. As the common medium of exchange, the euro reveals uncompetitive economic structures. So why do those countries wish to become more competitive, but refrain from lowering prices? The answer is the welfare state. In an unhampered market economy, there is no structural unemployment. All who wish to work can do so, because there is never a dearth of work to be done. But the welfare state removes the cost of pricing one's labor or one's goods and services too high. One might say that the welfare state underpins structural rigidities in an economy, such as labor laws, licensing, and so on, by removing the cost of market interventions. Devaluation does not address this underlying problem; therefore, devaluation will not cure a country's lack of competitiveness.

# Conclusion

Devaluation means monetary expansion. The new money must enter the economy somewhere , for example, payments to exporters. The ensuing bubble is misinterpreted as a sign of the success of devaluation, but the well-known deleterious effects of a rising price level, income redistribution, and malinvestment accompany the bubble. As the prices for exporters' factors of production rise and the benefits of devaluation fade away, there will be calls for more money expansion. If more than one country pursues this policy, there ensues a disastrous race to the bottom.

The solution is sound money. Sound money reveals bad economic policy and forces each country to live within its means. Governments will come under pressure to liberalize their economies and shed themselves of the parasitic destroyers of wealth. Devaluation retards this process.

# CHAPTER 6

# The Rebalance of Global Trade

## Overview

That global trade imbalance matter has been made abundantly clear by the ongoing global economic malaise. The likely path to more sustainable levels of trade deficits, nevertheless, remains far less clear. Consider the potential global impact of populist cries for protectionist trade policies ostensibly aimed at easing the difficult transition to more sustainable trade and debt balances. In the event of a trade war, which we discussed in Chapter 5 and is already happening, we will all lose. Perhaps even more unsettling, however, is how these consequences would most likely manifest across nations. The evidence presented in this chapter suggests that countries like China, which depend heavily on total trade in relation to their overall economy, could suffer most severely. This evidence further suggests that instead of pursuing short-term quick fixes that would exacerbate the malady, global policymakers must work together to establish a long-term path to more sustainable trade and debt balances.

Many take as fact that the current pattern of global imbalances, or the large and persistent trade deficits and surpluses across different parts of the world, ultimately unsustainable, is due to China and ASEAN consuming too little and saving too much. Since the global economy is a closed trading system, trade deficits and surpluses across all national economies must always sum exactly zero. Therefore, because one part of the world saves too much and runs trade surpluses means other parts of the world, particularly the United States, must run trade deficits.

However, just because deficits and surpluses are tightly inter-connected it does not mean that trade surpluses in China or ASEAN, for instance, have been responsible for United States and EU trade deficits.

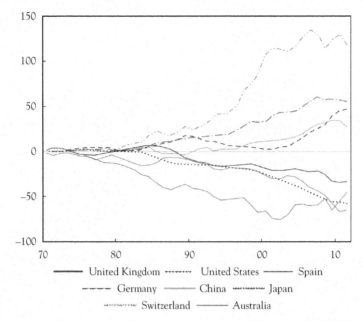

**Figure 6.1  Cumulative Current Accounts as a Percentage of GDP, 1970–2010**

*Source:* CFA Institute[1]

In addition, China's high level of savings might be dynamically welfare optimizing for its citizens. Note also that private enterprise in China might find self-accumulation the only way to generate investment funds.

The fact remains that countries with a current account surplus, as depicted in Figure 6.1, must also be those with exports in excess of imports, as shown in Figure 6.2. The range of imbalances among these nations has widened dramatically in recent decades, leading to a very unsustainable path. Notice in Figure 6.1 that Switzerland, Germany, and China currently enjoy the largest net trade surpluses, while the United States, the United Kingdom, and Spain have the largest net deficits.

The magnitude of trade deficits matters because a country with an ongoing trade deficit is, by definition, reducing its foreign assets or borrowing. Not as well understood is that global trade patterns are financed by gross asset flows, not net asset flows. Hence, a country must have sufficient gross foreign assets to finance any trade imbalance on an ongoing

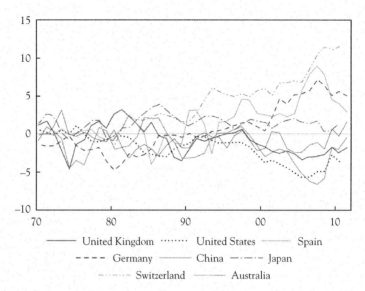

**Figure 6.2  Net Exports as a Percentage of GDP, 1970–2010**

*Source:* CFA Institute*

basis. Undeniably, these gross asset financial flows grease the skids of global trade. Practically speaking, trade deficits must be paid for by either selling down gross assets or increasing gross liabilities by selling debt.

Despite the many theories and conjectures offered, the global economy continues to struggle as it attempts to recover, slowly and painfully, from the financial crisis it entered in 2007. According to the IMF's July 2012 report, for example, world output growth—expressed at market exchange rates—will be roughly 2.5 percent in 2013 and about 0.5 percent faster in 2014. These rates of growth are concerning, and are far slower than those that preceded the crisis, although they are still positive. Meanwhile, China's economic growth continues to sputter, even if at a lower rate. The euro is still under threat, and the United States is still combating serious trade disadvantages.

In our view, the EU's underlying problem is not budget deficits or even unsustainable debt; these are mainly symptoms. The main problem with the EU is the huge divergence in costs between the core and the periphery. In the past decade costs between Germany and some of the peripheral countries have diverged by anywhere from 20 percent to

* Ibidem.

40 percent. This divergence has made the latter uncompetitive and has resulted in the massive trade imbalances within Europe.

Trade imbalances, of course, are the obverse of capital imbalances, and the surge in debt in peripheral Europe, which is debt owed ultimately to Germany and the other core countries, was the inevitable consequence of those capital flow imbalances. While EU's policymakers alternatively worry over fiscal deficits, surging government debt, and collapsing banks, there is almost no prospect of their resolving the European crisis until they address the divergence in costs. Of course if they don't resolve this problem, the problem will be resolved for them in the form of a break-up of the euro.

There is no doubt that trade deficits and surpluses narrowed significantly during this so-called *great recession*.* The economic activity in the advanced economies, mainly the G-7 nations, fell by five percent, while the number of unemployed people around the world surged by more than 30 million.[2] The global economy contracted by 0.8 percent in 2009, but it rebounded strongly in the next two years as central banks around the world, led by the U.S. Federal Reserve, embarked on massive monetary stimulus programs.[†]

As depicted in Figure 6.3, the situation was so dire that in November of 2010, at the G-20 meeting in Seoul, the United States and other G-7 member countries running high external deficits challenged those countries that maintain surpluses: China, Germany, and Japan, along with other smaller emerging countries, to pick up the slack in global demand. Predictably, this effort brought no tangible results.

Although we believe a global rebalance is to some extent necessary to reduce trade deficits and surpluses, we argue that too much emphasis on that may not be healthy for the global economy. Focusing too much on rebalancing the global economy can actually be ill advised. Mind you, this is not a book on international economics; none of the authors are economists. But from the point of view of international trade and foreign

---

* The great recession refers to the global contraction from December 2007 to June 2009 that resulted in the world economy shrinking for the first time since 1945. The Great Recession was so-called because its severity and depth made comparisons with the Great Depression of the 1930s inevitable.

† Ibidem.

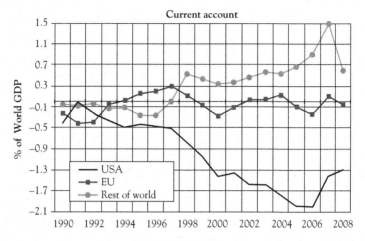

*Figure 6.3  The imbalance of the global economy as a result of the great recession*

Source: IMF[3]

affairs, global rebalance should be viewed as an idea, an overall goal, and not as a task, or a mission.

For starters, emerging markets remain heavily dependent on consumer demand in the United States and Western Europe. If this consumer demand grows more slowly in the future, due to the unwinding of household debts, the influence of higher risk premium on investment, and the effect of rising national debt on government expenditures, would the export-led emerging market economies continue to grow? The answer to this question is critical, as it directly impacts strategies that will need to be in place to stimulate domestic demand for the four billion people in the emerging markets.

In the same way, assuming a rebalancing of the global trade is a realistic strategy, what would be the impact of such rebalancing trade flows across the different emerging markets, such as the ASEAN, CIVETS, MENA, and BRICS? Who is more likely to gain, or lose, from such rebalancing, and what should the policy response, according to these countries' different economic structures, degrees of openness, and socio-political institutions look like?

Furthermore, assuming global trade and capital flows were rebalanced sustainably, what implications would this have for the future of reserve currencies around the world? Can the U.S. dollar retain its reserve currency status while enabling global financial capital to flow to the most profitable investment opportunities and global trade to flow where it is needed most? Lastly, what reserve currency regime is required for sustainable trade and capital flows? These questions are not easily answered.

While Michael Pettis[4] argues that the global economy is already undergoing a critical rebalancing, he points out that that the severe trade imbalances impelled on the recent financial crisis was the result of unsuccessful policies that distorted the savings and consumption patterns of some nations, mainly G-7.* Pettis cautions about the yet to be seen consequences of these destabilizing policies, predicting severe economic dislocations in the upcoming years. He warns of a lost decade for China, the breaking of the Euro, and a continuing decline of the U.S. dollar, all with long-lasting effects.

In Pettis' views, there are myriad causes for his dismal global outlook and economic prospect. He points to China's maintenance of massive investment growth by artificially lowering the cost of capital, which he warns to be unsustainable. He worries that Germany is endangering the euro by favoring its own development at the expense of its neighbors' states. He also argues that the U.S. dollar's role as the world's reserve currency burdens the American economy. Pettis suggests that while many of these various imbalances may seem unrelated, including the U.S. consumption splurge, the surging debt in Europe, China's investment debauch, Japan's long stagnation, and the commodity boom in Latin America, they are all closely tied together, making any attempt to rebalance the global economy impossible, unless each of the domestic issues (for both G-7 and G-20) are resolved. Moreover, he argues that it will be impossible to resolve any issue without forcing a resolution for all.

In our opinion, policymakers around the world, mainly between the G-7, are focusing too much effort on global rebalancing, which, in our view, only encourages currency tensions, such as the current one between China and the United States and, ominously, contributes to mounting protectionist sentiment and tensions. Such efforts also divert attention from most importantly, the needs for reforms at home. We argue that, rather than focusing on global rebalancing, the G-7 nations, and to some

---

\* Ibidem.

extent the G-20, should concentrate more on repairing their domestic problems and expanding their domestic demand at the maximum sustainable rate.

We are of the position that a major rebalancing of global demand, or more explicitly, a decrease of aggregate demand in deficit countries relative to that of surplus countries must occur, to foster smaller trade deficits and surpluses, which has already occurred during the great recession. Global demand has already undergone a major rebalancing during 2008–2009 as a consequence of the global credit crunch.

As depicted in Figure 6.4, countries with large current account deficits, such as the United States and Spain, also experienced the biggest housing bubbles and have the most indebted consumers, forcing government authorities to cut much more spending than surplus countries did. Hence, for all the reasons aforementioned, we argue that a long-term trend toward rebalancing, as promoted by G-7 nations, is very unlikely to happen.

The idea may be popular among the G-7 group, but we don't believe it will gain traction among the G-20. As advanced economies, without much success so far, continue to pressure emerging markets to engage in rebalancing, the G-7, particularly the United States, may be forced to

| | US$, bn | As a percent of GDP | | |
|---|---|---|---|---|
| | 2009 | 2006–2008 | 2009 | 2010 |
| United States | −378.0 | −5.3 | −2.9 | −3.2 |
| Spain | −74.1 | −9.5 | −5.4 | −4.9 |
| Italy | −713 | −2.8 | −3.4 | −2.8 |
| Australia | −40.9 | −5.2 | −4.1 | −3.5 |
| United Kingdom | −28.8 | −2.5 | −1.3 | −1.7 |
| Saudi Arabia | 20.5 | 26.6 | 5.5 | 9.1 |
| Russia | 49.0 | 7.2 | 4.0 | 4.5 |
| Japan | 141.8 | 4.0 | 2.8 | 3.1 |
| Germany | 160.6 | 6.9 | 4.8 | 5.5 |
| China | 297.1 | 10.0 | 6.0 | 5.0 |

*Figure 6.4 Nations with largest current Account surpluses and deficits*

Source: IMF, Carnegie Endowment[5]

take a stand: either tackle the profound domestic vulnerabilities that have been exposed, or put at risk the open, rules-based trading system that has bolstered significant postwar prosperity.

Despite the challenges of rebalancing the global economy, we identify three great challenges confronting the global recovery. The first one is the exiting stimulus policies in the United States. The first phase of the stimulus exit, widely known as the large fiscal contraction, or "fiscal cliff," appears to have survived without significant damage to consumers and investment demands. The second phase of this stimulus exit still lies ahead in the future, when the U.S. Federal Reserve Bank begins to reduce its bond purchases. Judging by the near panic in the financial markets following a speech by Chairman Bernanke in the fall of 2013 announcing its imminence, this second phase may prove to be problematic. Yet, the U.S. Federal Reserve Bank remains sensitive to the fact that unemployment remains high, as such is determined to ensure that monetary tightening will only occur in response to clear signs that the economy is strengthening.

The second challenge is to avoid the sharp slowdown in emerging markets in the past couple years (2012–2013), particularly in China, from collapsing. Growth has slowed precipitously in the BRICS and ASEAN, among others. Yet, even with this slowdown, we believe emerging markets as a group will continue to benefit from technological advancements, high savings rates, significant investments in education, and favorable demographics, including an ever increasing middle-class. Despite the global crisis, emerging markets are still growing at an average rate of five percent. China suffers from overly large and misallocated credit-fueled investments as well as inadequate demand by households. As its huge reservoir of surplus labor depletes, China's wages are now rising fast, pointing to a country less competitive in international markets and more inclined to consume. China is unlikely to return to the fiery 9–W10 percent growth of the last three decades, but its solid fiscal position, robust household balance sheets, and huge reserves suggest it will find a way to sustain a more moderate pace and continue to support the global recovery.

The third and greatest challenge is to complete the extremely painful adjustment of the EU's periphery. Countries such as Greece, Spain, and Italy need to regain international competitiveness and reorient the economy away from domestic activity, such as construction and public services, and more toward exports and import-substitutes, such as manufacturing and tourism. This is now happening at a steady if unspectacular pace and is reflected in sharply lower current account deficits. For instance, in 2012 and 2013, exports in Italy and Spain grew in line with world trade*, while imports fell about three times faster than GDP.

In sum, how should global trade imbalances rebalance? The inexorably deleveraging of current large trade deficits has been damaging and requires global cooperation to put into place a credible fiscal plan to bring down deficits deliberately. Such alternative solutions as monetary policy alone will continue to prove insufficient, and seeking a solution by waging a trade war should be fiercely resisted. Following such quick-fix paths could produce severe consequences for the global economy, and heavily trade-dependent countries would feel the impact even more harshly.

---

* Around 2.5/3 percent.

# CHAPTER 7

# The IMF Is Being Hit by BRICS

## Overview

As mentioned earlier, BRICS is the acronym for a bloc of five major emerging economies including Brazil, Russia, India, China, and South Africa. The bloc was originally known as "BRIC" before the inclusion of South Africa in 2010. Jim O'Neill coined the acronym in a 2001 paper entitled "Building Better Global Economic BRICs."[1] The acronym has come into widespread use as a symbol of the apparent shift in global economic power away from the developed G-7 economies toward the developing world. The BRICS members are all emerging economies, either at a developing or newly industrialized stage, but distinguished by their large, fast-growing economies[2] and significant influence on regional and global affairs. All five countries are members of the G-20.

As of 2013, these five BRICS countries represent almost three billion people, with a combined nominal GDP of US$16.039 trillion dollars,[3] and an estimated US$4 trillion dollars in combined foreign reserves.[4] From advanced economies such as the EU, the BRICS are viewed as less interested in shared ideas of a multilateral world, and more inclined toward a nationalistic, multipolar world that emphasizes their own newly found strengths and interests. The result is fading authority and consensus on the world stage. The cold war *spheres of influence* between two powers are long gone. The new world order of U.S. dominance is diminishing. But no clear leadership or rules have yet replaced this. New struggles of trends such as human rights and democracy—and sovereignty—still have to be decided.

Recent developments, such as the danger of a property bubble in China, a decline in world trade, and volatile capital flows in emerging markets, could derail the global economic recovery and have a lasting impact. Arguably, in our view, 2013's economic deceleration to a large extent reflects the inability of global leaders to address the many challenges that were already present from 2001 to 2012.

Policymakers around the world remain concerned about high unemployment and the social conditions in their countries. The political brinkmanship in the United States continues to affect the outlook for the world's largest economy, while the sovereign debt crises and the danger of a banking system meltdown in peripheral eurozone countries, remain unresolved. The high levels of public debt coupled with low growth, insufficient competitiveness, and political gridlock in some European countries are still stirring financial markets' concerns about sovereign default and the viability of the euro.

Given the complexity and the urgency of the situation, advanced economies around the world, in particular the United States and European countries are facing difficult economic management decisions with challenging political and social ramifications. Although European leaders do not agree on how to address the immediate challenges, there is recognition that, in the longer term, stabilizing the euro and putting Europe on a higher and more sustainable growth path will necessitate improvements to the competitiveness of the weaker member states.

Meanwhile, emerging markets are coping with the consequence of advanced economies' debt. In our view, given the expected slowdown in economic growth in China, India, and other emerging markets, reinforced by a potential decline in global trade and volatile capital flows in the next five to eight years, it is not clear which regions of the world can drive growth and employment creation in the short to medium term, but we believe the BRICS will play a major role in this process. Africa too, as well as the whole MENA bloc, should see high growth levels in the next decade as discussed in more detail throughout this book.

When we look at advanced economies as compared to emerging markets, the IMF[5] accurately estimated that, in 2012, the eurozone would have contracted by 0.3 percent, while the United States would have continued to experience a weak recovery with an uncertain future. Large emerging economies such as the BRICS are growing somewhat less than they did in 2011, but still growing at around 4–5 percent annually. Meanwhile, other emerging markets such as ASEAN also continue to show robust growth rates, around 5–7 percent, while the MENA, as well as sub-Saharan African countries, continues to gain momentum.

According to John Hawksworth and Dan Chan at PWC,[6] the world economy is projected to grow at an average rate of just over three percent per annum from 2011 to 2050, doubling in size by 2032 and nearly doubling again by 2050. Meanwhile, China is projected to overtake the United States as the largest economy by 2017 in purchasing power parity (PPP) terms and by 2027 in market exchange rate terms. India should become the third "global economic giant" by 2050, well ahead of Brazil, who is expected to become the fourth largest economy, ahead of Japan. Hawksworth and Chan also argue that Russia may overtake Germany to become the largest European economy before 2020 in PPP terms and by around 2035 at market exchange rates. Emerging economies such as Mexico and Indonesia could be larger than the UK and France by 2050, and Turkey larger than Italy.

The American or EU citizen who has traveled to India knows that his money stretches further than it does at home. To be precise, one can buy 2.8 times as much in India with a dollar's worth of rupees than one can with a dollar in the United States, according to the IMF.[7] This is because India's prices are only about 35 percent of America's, when converted into a common currency at market exchange rates. This magic is not unique to India of course. It applies across most developing countries. This is not true, however, when Americans visit countries like Switzerland, where prices are 175 percent of America's level, Denmark with 153 percent, or Australia at 149 percent.

In the biggest emerging economies, however, this magic is fading. Ten years ago, Brazil's price level was only 40 percent of America's, but as of July of 2013, it was 90 percent. China's also has risen from 39 percent to 67 percent over the same period, while Russia's has soared from 31 percent to almost 83 percent. Taken together the BRICs have become notably more expensive over the past decade. Their combined price level rose rapidly toward advanced economies levels from 2003 to 2011, before plateauing in the past two years.

This dramatic convergence of price levels is an underrated economic force. It is one telling reason why the BRICS' dollar GDP is now worth exceedingly more than anyone expected back in 2003, when O'Neill released the first of his long-range projections of the BRICS' economic fate over the next half-century. At the time, the projections raised eyebrows. Now that the BRIC economies have faltered, O'Neill's whole thesis has been sneered at. But, looking back at his attempt to look forward, O'Neill was, if anything, too conservative about his forecast. The BRICS combined dollar GDP will be 70 percent bigger in 2013 than O'Neill/Goldman Sachs had projected ten years ago.

Some of that over performance is due to the fact the BRICs have grown faster over the past decade than Goldman Sachs expected. China, for instance, is still growing faster than envisioned, despite its slowdown from double-digits growth rates. The same is not true for the other three countries, although a big part of the overrun is due to the fact the BRICS became pricier faster than Goldman Sachs foresaw. The following is a short profile of the BRICS, their strengths and weaknesses as of 2013.

### Brazil

Following more than three centuries under Portuguese rule, Brazil gained its independence in 1822, maintaining a monarchical system of government until the abolition of slavery in 1888 and the subsequent proclamation of a republic by the military in 1889. Brazilian coffee exporters politically dominated the country until populist leader Getulio Vargas rose to power in 1930. Brazil is by far the largest and most populous country in South America. The country underwent more than a half-century of populist and military government until 1985, when the military regime peacefully ceded power to civilian rulers.

Brazil continues to pursue industrial and agricultural growth and development of its interior. Exploiting vast natural resources and a large labor pool, it is today South America's leading economic power and a regional leader, one of the first in the area to begin an economic recovery since 2008. Highly unequal income distribution and crime remain pressing problems. Characterized by large and well-developed agricultural, mining, manufacturing, and service sectors, Brazil's economy outweighs that of all other South American countries, and Brazil is expanding its presence in world markets. Since 2003, Brazil has steadily improved its macroeconomic stability, building up foreign reserves, and reducing its debt profile by shifting its debt burden toward real denominated and domestically held instruments.

In 2008, Brazil became a net external creditor and two ratings agencies awarded investment grade status to its debt. After strong growth in 2007 and 2008, the onset of the global financial crisis hit the country in 2008. Brazil experienced two quarters of recession, as global demand for Brazil's commodity-based exports declined and external credit dried up. However, Brazil was one of the first emerging markets to begin a recovery. In 2010, consumer and investor confidence revived and GDP growth reached 7.5 percent, the highest growth rate in the past 25 years. But rising inflation led the government to take measures to cool the economy; these actions and the deteriorating international economic situation slowed growth to 2.7 percent in 2011, and 1.3 percent in 2012. Unemployment is at historic lows and Brazil's traditionally high level of income inequality has declined for each of the last 14 years.

Brazil's historically high interest rates have also made it an attractive destination for foreign investors. Large capital inflows over the past several years have contributed to the appreciation of the currency, hurting the competitiveness of Brazilian manufacturing and leading the government to intervene in foreign exchange markets and raise taxes on some foreign capital inflows. President Dilma Rousseff has retained the previous administration's commitment to inflation targeting by the central bank, a floating exchange rate, and fiscal restraint. In an effort to boost growth, in 2012 the administration implemented a somewhat more expansionary monetary policy that has failed to stimulate much growth.

According to Professor Klaus Schwab's Global Competitiveness Report[8] at the World Economic Forum, Brazil has made significant improvement in its macroeconomic condition, despite its still-high inflation rate of nearly seven percent. Schwab argues that, overall, Brazil's fairly sophisticated business community enjoys the benefits of one of the world's largest internal markets (seventh in the world), which allows for important economies of scale and continues to have fairly easy access to financing for its investment projects.

Notwithstanding these strengths, the country also faces important challenges, beginning with the lack of trust in its politicians, which remains low, as well as government efficiency, which is also low, due to excessive government regulation and wasteful spending. The quality of transport infrastructure, which was the cause of recent riots in Brazil during the fall of 2013, remains an unaddressed long-standing challenge. The quality of education is another challenge for the government, affecting Brazil's ability to compete abroad, unable to match the increasing need for a skilled labor force. Moreover, despite the red tape, government bureaucracies, and increasing efforts to facilitate entrepreneurship, especially for small companies, the time needed to start a business remains among the highest in Schwab's countries sample (130th and 139th, respectively). Taxation still is perceived to be too high and to have distortionary effects to the economy.*

With regards to social sustainability, Brazil's overall good performance masks a number of environmental concerns, such as the deforestation of the Amazon; the country possesses one of the highest rates of deforestation in the world. In general, outside of Brazil, the other four BRICS (Russia, India, China, and South Africa) all reveal significant weaknesses in both dimensions of sustainable competitiveness.

## Russia

Founded in the 12th century, the Principality of Muscovy was able to emerge from over 200 years of Mongol domination (13th–15th centuries) and to gradually conquer and absorb surrounding principalities. In the early 17th century, a new Romanov Dynasty continued this policy of expansion across Siberia to the Pacific. Under Peter I (ruled 1682–1725), hegemony was extended to the Baltic Sea and the country was renamed the Russian Empire. During the 19th century, more territorial acquisitions were made in Europe and Asia.

Defeat in the Russo-Japanese War of 1904–05 contributed to the Revolution of 1905, which resulted in the formation of a parliament and other reforms. Repeated devastating defeats of the Russian army in World War I led to widespread rioting in the major cities of the Russian Empire and to the overthrow in 1917 of the imperial household. The communists under Vladimir Lenin seized power soon after and formed the Union of Soviet Socialist Republics (USSR). The brutal rule of Iosif

---

* Ibidem.

Stalin (1928–53) strengthened communist rule and Russian dominance of the Soviet Union at a cost of tens of millions of lives.

The Soviet economy and society stagnated in the following decades until General Secretary Mikhail Gorbachev (1985–91) introduced *glasnost* (openness) and *perestroika* (restructuring) in an attempt to modernize communism, but his initiatives inadvertently released forces that by December 1991 splintered the USSR into Russia and 14 other independent republics. Subsequently, Russia has shifted its post-Soviet democratic ambitions in favor of a centralized semi-authoritarian state in which the leadership seeks to legitimize its rule through managed national elections, populist appeals by President Putin, and continued economic growth. Russia has severely disabled a Chechen rebel movement, although violence still occurs throughout the North Caucasus.

Russia has undergone significant changes since the collapse of the Soviet Union, moving from a globally isolated, centrally planned economy to a more market-based and globally integrated economy. Economic reforms in the 1990s privatized most industries, with notable exceptions in energy and defense-related sectors. The protection of property rights is still weak and the private sector remains subject to heavy state interference.

In 2011, Russia became the world's leading oil producer,[9] surpassing Saudi Arabia. Russia is also the second-largest producer of natural gas, holding the world's largest natural gas reserves, the second-largest coal reserves, and the eighth-largest crude oil reserves. Russia is also a top exporter of metals such as steel and primary aluminum. Notwithstanding, Russia's reliance on commodity exports, as in Brazil's, makes it vulnerable to boom and bust cycles that follow the volatile swings in global prices. Hence, the government, since 2007, embarked on an ambitious program to reduce this dependency and build up the country's high technology sectors, but with few visible results so far.*

The economy had averaged seven percent growth in the decade following the 1998 Russian financial crisis, resulting in a doubling of real disposable incomes and the emergence of a middle class. The Russian economy, however, was one of the hardest hit by the 2008–09 global economic crisis as oil prices plummeted and the foreign credits that Russian banks and firms relied on dried up.

---

* Ibidem.

According to the World Bank[10] the government's anti-crisis package in 2008–09 amounted to roughly 6.7 percent of GDP. The economic decline bottomed out in mid-2009 and the economy began to grow again in the third quarter of 2009. High oil prices maintained Russian growth in 2011–12 and helped Russia reduce the budget deficit inherited from 2008–09, which helped Russia reducing unemployment to record lows and lower inflation.

Russia joined the WTO in 2012, which will reduce trade barriers in Russia for foreign goods and services and help open foreign markets to Russian goods and services. At the same time, Russia has sought to cement economic ties with countries in the former Soviet space through a Customs Union with Belarus and Kazakhstan, and, in the next several years, through the creation of a new Russia-led economic bloc called the Eurasian Economic Union (EEU).

Nonetheless, Russia is experiencing several challenges. The country has had difficulty attracting foreign direct investment and has experienced large capital outflows in the past several years, leading to official programs to improve Russia's international rankings for its investment climate. Russia's adoption of a new oil-price-based fiscal rule in 2012 and a more flexible exchange rate policy have improved its ability to deal with external shocks, including volatile oil prices. Russia's long-term challenges also include a shrinking workforce, rampant corruption, and underinvestment in infrastructure.

Nevertheless, according to Klaus Schwab[11] at the World Economic Forum, Russia has sharply improved its macroeconomic environment due to low government debt and a government budget that has moved into surplus, although the country still hasn't managed to address its weak public institutions or the capacity for innovation. Hence, the country still suffers from inefficiencies in the goods, labor, and financial markets, where the situation is deteriorating for the second year in a row.

Russia's weak level of global competition, caused by inefficient anti-monopolistic policies and high restrictions on trade and foreign ownership, contributes to this inefficient allocation of Russia's vast resources, hampering higher levels of productivity in the economy.* Moreover, as the country moves toward a more advanced stage of economic development,

---

* Ibidem.

its lack of business sophistication and low rates of technological adoption will become increasingly important challenges for its sustained progress. On the other hand, its high level of education enrollment, especially at the tertiary level, its fairly good infrastructure, and its large domestic market represent areas that can be leveraged to improve Russia's competitiveness.

## India

The Indus Valley civilization, one of the world's oldest, flourished during the third and second millennia B.C. and extended into northwestern India. Aryan tribes from the northwest infiltrated the Indian subcontinent about 1500 B.C., and then merged with the earlier Dravidian inhabitants creating the classical Indian culture. The Maurya Empire of the 4th and 3rd centuries B.C., which reached its apex under Ashoka*, united much of South Asia. The Golden Age ushered in by the Gupta dynasty (fourth to sixth centuries A.D.) saw a flowering of Indian science, art, and culture. Islam spread across the subcontinent over a period of 700 years. In the 10th and 11th centuries, Turks and Afghans invaded India and established the Delhi Sultanate. In the early 16th century, the Emperor Babur established the Mughal Dynasty, which ruled India for more than three centuries.

European explorers began establishing footholds in India during the 16th century. By the 19th century, Great Britain had become the dominant political power on the subcontinent. The British Indian Army played a vital role in both World Wars. Years of nonviolent resistance to British rule, led by Mohandas Gandhi and Jawaharlal Nehru, eventually resulted in Indian independence, which was granted in 1947. Large-scale communal violence took place before and after the subcontinent partition into two separate states, India and Pakistan.

The neighboring nations have fought three wars since independence, the last of which was in 1971 and resulted in East Pakistan becoming the separate nation of Bangladesh. India's nuclear weapons tests in 1998 emboldened Pakistan to conduct its own tests that same year. In

---

* Ashoka Maurya (304–232 BCE) was an Indian emperor of the Maurya Dynasty who ruled almost the entire Indian subcontinent from 269 BCE to 232 BCE.

November 2008, terrorists originating from Pakistan conducted a series of coordinated attacks in Mumbai, India's financial capital. Despite pressing problems such as significant overpopulation, environmental degradation, extensive poverty, and widespread corruption, economic growth following the launch of economic reforms in 1991 and a massive youthful population are driving India's emergence as a regional and global power.

India is developing into an open-market economy, but there remain traces of its past autarkic policies. Economic liberalization measures, including industrial deregulation, privatization of state-owned enterprises, and reduced controls on foreign trade and investment, began in the early 1990s and have served to accelerate the country's growth; growth that has averaged fewer than seven percent per year since 1997.

India's diverse economy encompasses traditional village farming, modern agriculture, handicrafts, a wide range of modern industries, and a multitude of services. Slightly more than half of the work force is in agriculture, but services, particularly information technology and information systems (IT&IS) are the major source of economic growth, accounting for nearly two-thirds of India's output, with less than one-third of its labor force. India has capitalized on its large educated English-speaking population to become a major exporter of information technology services, business outsourcing services, and software workers.

In 2010, the Indian economy rebounded robustly from the global financial crisis, in large part due to strong domestic demand, and growth exceeded eight percent year-on-year in real terms. However, India's economic growth began slowing in 2011 due to a slowdown in government spending and a decline in investment, caused by investor pessimism about the government's commitment to further economic reforms. High international crude prices have also exacerbated the government's fuel subsidy expenditures, contributing to a higher fiscal deficit and a worsening current account deficit.

In late 2012, the Indian Government announced additional reforms and deficit reduction measures to reverse India's slowdown, including allowing higher levels of foreign participation in direct investment in the economy. The outlook for India's medium-term growth is positive due to a young population and corresponding low dependency ratio, healthy savings and investment rates, and increasing integration into the global economy.

India has many long-term challenges that it has yet to fully address, including poverty, corruption, violence and discrimination against women and girls, an inefficient power generation and distribution system, ineffective enforcement of intellectual property rights, decades-long civil litigation dockets, inadequate transport and agricultural infrastructure, accommodating rural-to-urban migration, limited non-agricultural employment opportunities, and inadequate availability of basic quality of life and higher education.

On the topic of education, in his New York Times bestseller *Imagining India: the Idea of a Renewed Nation*, the co-chairman of Infosys Technologies, Nandan Nilekani argues that "reforms that expand access are thus the most crucial for the disempowered. They are critical in bringing income mobility to the weakest and poorest groups. And this mobility is at the heart of the success of free markets: we tend to forget that a prerequisite to productivity and efficiency is a large pool of educated people, which requires in turn easy and widespread access to good schools and colleges."[12]

Nilekani argues that the government of India ignores such challenges of fairness and equality at their peril. He contends that if discontent is left to fester, it will trigger enormous backlashes against open market policies, which actually is happening with Wal-Mart's expansion in the country. In August 2013, an article in the Business Standard[13] discussed Wal-Mart's ongoing Enforcement Directorate (ED) investigation into its investment in the Bharti Group, a business conglomerate headquartered in New Delhi, India, where in 2010 the retailer giant made an investment in the form of compulsory convertible debentures (CCD). In addition, Wal-Mart was concerned with the political uncertainty in India, with the general election slated for 2014, along with the possibility of a statewide block to foreign direct investment (FDI) in retailing as a potential barrier for the company in that country.

Hence, as of 2013, India is the worst performer among the BRICS, with concerns in both areas of sustainability. Regarding social sustainability, India is not able to provide access to some basic services to many of its citizens; only 34 percent of the population has access to sanitation. The employment of much of the population is also vulnerable, which combined with weak official social safety nets, makes the country vulnerable to economic shocks. In addition, although no official data are reported for youth unemployment, numerous studies indicate that the percentage is very high.[14]

According to Amin,[15] India's economy was once ahead of Brazil and South Africa, but it now trails them by some 10 places, and lags behind China by a margin of 30 positions. The country continues to be penalized for its disappointing performance in areas considered basic factors of competitiveness. The country's supply of transport and energy infrastructure remains largely insufficient and ill adapted to the needs of the economy. Indeed, the Indian business community repeatedly cites infrastructure as the single biggest hindrance to doing business, well ahead of corruption and bureaucracy. It must be noted, however, that the situation has been slowly improving since 2006.*

The picture is even bleaker in the health and basic education sectors. According to the World Economic Forum's Global Competitiveness Report,[16] despite improvements across the board over the past few years, poor public health and education standards remain a primary cause of India's low productivity. Turning to the country's institutions, discontent within the business community remains high regarding lack of reforms and the perceived inability of the government to push them through. Indeed, public trust in politicians has been weakening for the past three years. Meanwhile, the macroeconomic environment continues to be characterized by large and repeated public deficits and the highest debt-to-GDP ratio among the BRICS. On a positive note, inflation returned to single-digit territory in 2011.

Despite these considerable challenges, India does possess a number of strengths in the more advanced and complex drivers of competitiveness. This reverse pattern of development is characteristic of India. It can rely on a fairly well developed and sophisticated financial market that can channel financial resources to good use, and it boasts reasonably sophisticated and innovative businesses environment. As argued by Vinay Rai and William Simon in their book titled *Think India*, [17] there is a "new India rising up, and it is going to change the world, from Bollywood to world financial markets, from IT to manufacturing, for service to design." "In the India of today," Rai and Simon continue, "activity in construction, in manufacturing, in innovation, abounds everywhere from large

---

* Ibidem.

cities to small towns and rural villages. Every sector of the economy, without exception, is growing. And not just growing, but at starling rates that reach fifty to a hundred percent annually."*

Rai and Simon argue that India is not Japan, Brazil, the EU, or even China, as India's people, with their diversity, openness, practicality, innovation, and service orientation, are the country's real strength. Indians creative energy, unleashed after hundreds of years of slavery and foreign rule, are driving modern India to new heights. Just imagine, by 2020, one-half of the world population of people under age of twenty-five will be in India! Mumbai has today some of the most expensive real estate in the world, with over 18 million clustered around the cresent-shaped bay, with a density more than triple of Tokyo. Electronic City, an industrial park that's home to over hundred electronics and software firms in Bangalore, India's Silicon Valley, is the dynamic epicenter of 21st century India.

The rising of consumerism class is impressive. Their new spending power will make India the biggest cash-drawer worldwide for consumer goods and services.† The Indian consumer, due to colonial prejudices toward moneylenders, had hitherto considered taboo the buying of a house or a car on credit. Now that attitude is being debunked as the enthusiasm of Indians to consume grows, as their disposable income continues to rise. Hence, their new enthusiasm to take out a loan to pay for everything from television sets to a trip overseas is making bankers from around the world levitate, although in our view, it may not necessarily be a good thing for Indian families to enter into debt.

More and more banks are investing in India, either by establishing presence there or buying stake in Indian banks. The list of foreign banks in India today is impressive, including global stalwarts such as Deutsche Bank, Citigroup, Goldman Sachs, and investment banks such as JM Morgan Stanley, Barclays, and Merrill Lynch.

Larry Summers, the former president of Harvard University, said in 2006 that Harvard had made a "fundamental error of judgment" in not recognizing India's potential and promise early enough. A mistake, according to Summers, that Harvard would correct by setting up a dedicated "India Center" with an initial funding of US$1 billion dollars.

---

\* Ibidem.

† Ibidem.

Back in 2006, the World Economic Forum's (WEF) Global Competitiveness Report[18] ranked India highest among all BRIC nations, the 43rd most competitive country in world—out of 148 countries surveyed—versus China's 54th at the time. Today (2013), India has dropped its ranking significantly, to 60th, versus China's even more significant rise to 29th. The rest of the BRICS countries, Brazil, Russia, and South Africa, by comparison, rank 56th, 64th, and 53rd respectively.[19] Stalled reforms, slowing growth, and a sliding rupee have singled India out as an underperformer on the world stage. India's ranking declined by three places to 59th position in the Global Competitiveness Index 2012–2013 of the WEF due to disappointing performance in the basic factors underpinning competitiveness.

The fact remains, however, that India has several advantages over China, according to the WEF Competitiveness report:*

- China has less chance for innovation in its relatively closed state-controlled market. India, the largest democracy in the world, has a free market and a free press, which empowers its people to be innovative and creative, even at the grassroots levels.
- India's growing workforce of people below the age of 25 is a major competitive weapon in its arsenal, the benefits of which will soon start trickling in. China's one-child policy, while reducing pressure of a population growing too fast and is under revision, is making the nation age faster as well.
- Many Indians speak fluent English while most Chinese don't.
- Both India and China (even more so than India), are known for manufacturing, but India has lured several Fortune 500 companies to set up high-end/high-tech research and development centers on their soil.
- Efficient capital markets, quality of public institutions, and a sound judicial system accounts for India besting its competitors.[20]

The Goldman Sachs analysis[21] that puts the United States in third place economically by 2050, behind India and China, while it seems so unlikely to many, seems more logical when you recognize that the brightest 25 percent of India population outnumber the entire population of

---

* http://www.weforum.org/pdf/Global_Competitiveness_Reports/Reports/ gcr_2007/gcr2007_rankings.pdf, last accessed on 02/02/2012..

the United States. Will the same still be true in 2050? If we do the math, the answer is a resounding yes.

## China

For centuries China stood as a leading civilization, outpacing the rest of the world in the arts and sciences, but in the 19th and early 20th centuries, the country was beset by civil unrest, major famines, military defeats, and foreign occupation. After World War II, the communists under Mao Zedong established an autocratic socialist system that, while ensuring China's sovereignty, imposed strict controls over everyday life and cost the lives of tens of millions of people.

After 1978, Mao's successor Deng Xiaoping and other leaders focused on market-oriented economic development and by 2000 output had quadrupled. For much of the population, living standards have improved dramatically and the room for personal choice has expanded, yet political controls remain tight. Since the early 1990s, China has increased its global outreach and participation in international organizations.

Since the late 1970s China has moved from a closed, centrally planned system to a more market-oriented one that plays a major global role, becoming in 2010, the world's largest exporter. Reforms began with the phasing out of collectivized agriculture, and expanded to include the gradual liberalization of prices, fiscal decentralization, increased autonomy for state enterprises, creation of a diversified banking system, development of stock markets, rapid growth of the private sector, and opening to foreign trade and investment.

China has implemented reforms in a gradualist fashion. In recent years, China has renewed its support for state-owned enterprises in sectors it considers important to economic security, explicitly looking to foster globally competitive national champions. After keeping its currency tightly linked to the U.S. dollar for years, in July 2005 China revalued its currency by 2.1 percent against the U.S. dollar and moved to an exchange rate system that references a basket of currencies. From mid-2005 to late 2008 cumulative appreciation of the renminbi against the U.S. dollar was more than 20 percent, but the exchange rate remained virtually pegged to the dollar from the onset of the global financial crisis until June 2010, when Beijing allowed resumption of a gradual appreciation.

The restructuring of the economy and resulting efficiency gains have contributed to a more than tenfold increase in GDP since 1978. Measured on a purchasing power parity (PPP) basis that adjusts for price differences, in 2012, China stood as the second-largest economy in the world after the United States, having surpassed Japan in 2001. The dollar values of China's agricultural and industrial output each exceed those of the United States. China is also second to the United States in the value of services it produces. Still, per capita income is below the world average.

According to U.S. CIA's World FactBook,[22] the Chinese government faces numerous economic challenges, including: (a) reducing its high domestic savings rate and correspondingly low domestic demand; (b) sustaining adequate job growth for tens of millions of migrants and new entrants to the work force; (c) reducing corruption and other economic crimes; and (d) containing environmental damage and social strife related to the economy's rapid transformation. Economic development has progressed further in coastal provinces than in the interior, and by 2011 more than 250 million migrant workers and their dependents had relocated to urban areas to find work.

One consequence of population control policy is that China is now one of the most rapidly aging countries in the world. Deterioration in the environment—notably air pollution, soil erosion, and the steady fall of the water table, especially in the North—is another long-term problem. China continues to lose arable land because of erosion and economic development. The Chinese government is seeking to add energy production capacity from sources other than coal and oil, focusing on nuclear and alternative energy development.

In 2010–11, China faced high inflation resulting largely from its credit-fueled stimulus program. Some tightening measures appear to have controlled inflation, but GDP growth consequently slowed to fewer than 8 percent for 2012. An economic slowdown in Europe contributed to China's, and is expected to further drag Chinese growth in 2013. In addition, debt overhangs from the stimulus program, particularly among local governments, and a property price bubble currently challenges policy makers. The government's 12th Five-Year Plan, adopted in March 2011, emphasizes continued economic reforms and the need to increase domestic consumption in order to make the economy less dependent on exports in the future. However, China has made only marginal progress toward these rebalancing goals.

Therefore, China's competitiveness performance notably has weakened in the past few years. Social sustainability is measured partially for China, as the country does not report data related to youth unemployment or vulnerable employment. However, the available indicators[23] show a somewhat negative picture, with rising social inequality and general access to basic services such as improved sanitation remaining low.

According to the Global Competitiveness Report,* after five years of incremental but steady progress, China has lost some competitive advantages. Without a doubt, the country continues to lead the BRICS economies by a wide margin, ahead of second-placed Brazil, China boasts US$8.2 billion dollars in nominal GDP versus Brazil's US$2.4 billion dollars. Although China's decline is small, its global competitiveness deterioration is more pronounced in those areas that have become critical for China's competitiveness, namely financial market development, technological readiness, and market efficiency.

For market efficiency, insufficient domestic and foreign competition is of particular concern, as the various barriers to entry appear to be more prevalent and more important than in previous years. On a more positive note, China's macroeconomic situation remains very favorable, despite a prolonged episode of high inflation. China runs a moderate budget deficit, boasting a low, albeit increasing, and government debt-to-GDP ratio of 26 percent, while its gross savings rate remains above 50 percent of GDP.

The rating of its sovereign debt is significantly better than that of the other BRICS and indeed of many advanced economies. Moreover, China receives relatively high marks when it comes to health and basic education, as enrollment figures for higher education continues to be on the rise, even though the quality of education, in particular the quality of management schools, and the disconnect between educational content and business needs in the country, remain important issues.

### South Africa

Dutch traders landed at the southern tip of modern day South Africa in 1652 and established a stopover point on the spice route between the Netherlands and the Far East, founding the city of Cape Town. After the

---

* Ibidem.

British seized the Cape of Good Hope area in 1806, many of the Dutch settlers traveled north to establish their own republics. The discovery of diamonds in 1867 and gold in 1886 stimulated wealth and immigration, while intensifying the subjugation of the native inhabitants. The Dutch traders resisted British invasions but were defeated in the Boer War in 1899–1902. The British and the Afrikaners, as the Dutch traders became known, ruled together beginning in 1910 under the Union of South Africa, which became a republic in 1961 after a whites-only referendum.[24]

In 1948, the National Party was voted into power and instituted a policy of apartheid, or the separate development of the races, which favored the white minority at the expense of the black majority. The African National Congress (ANC) led the opposition to apartheid and many top ANC leaders, such as Nelson Mandela, spent decades in South Africa's prisons. Internal protests and insurgency, as well as boycotts by some Western nations and institutions, led to the regime's eventual willingness to negotiate a peaceful transition to majority rule. The first multi-racial elections in 1994 brought an end to apartheid and ushered in majority rule under an ANC-led government.

Since then, South Africa has struggled to address apartheid-era imbalances in decent housing, education, and health care. ANC squabbling, which has grown in recent years, pinnacled in September 2008 when President Thabo Mbeki resigned, and Kgalema Motlanthe, the party's General-Secretary, succeeded him as interim president. Jacob Zuma became president after the ANC won general elections in April 2009.

South Africa is a middle-income, emerging market with an abundant supply of natural resources. It has a well-developed financial, legal, communications, energy, and transport sectors and a stock exchange that is the 15th largest in the world. Even though the country has modern infrastructure that support a relatively efficient distribution of goods to major urban centers throughout the region, some factors are delaying growth.

From 1993 until 2013, South Africa GDP growth rate averaged 3.2 percent reaching an all time high of 7.6 percent in March of 1996. The economy began to slowdown in the second half of 2007 due to an electricity crisis. State power supplier Eskom encountered problems with

aging plants and meeting electricity demand necessitating load-shedding*
cuts in 2007 and 2008 to residents and businesses in the major cities.
Since then Eskom has built two new power stations and installed new
power demand management programs to improve power grid reliability.
Subsequently, the global financial crisis reduced commodity prices and
world demand. Consequently, in 2009, South Africa's GDP fell nearly
two percent, to a record low of –6.3 percent in March of 2009, but it
has recovered since, at an annualized 0.70 percent in the third quarter of
2013 over the previous quarter.[25]

South Africa export-based economy is the largest and most developed
in Africa. The country is rich in natural resources and is a leading producer of platinum, gold, chromium, and iron. From 2002 to 2008, South
Africa grew at an average of 4.5 percent year-on-year, its fastest expansion
since the establishment of democracy in 1994. However, in recent years,
successive governments have failed to address structural problems such as
the widening income inequality gap between rich and poor, low-skilled
labor force, high unemployment rate at nearly 25 percent of the work
force, deteriorating infrastructure, high corruption and crime rates.

As a result, since the recession in 2008, South Africa growth has been
sluggish and below African average. South Africa's economic policy has
focused on controlling inflation, however, the country has had significant budget deficits that restrict its ability to deal with pressing economic
problems. The current government faces growing pressure from special
interest groups to use state-owned enterprises to deliver basic services to
low-income areas and to increase job growth.

Sub-Saharan Africa has grown impressively over the last 15 years, registering growth rates of over five percent in the past two years, while the
region continues to exceed the global average and to exhibit a favorable
economic outlook. Indeed, the region has bounced back rapidly from the
global economic crisis, when GDP growth dropped to two percent in 2009.

---

* A load shedding, also referred to as rolling blackout, is an intentionally engineered electrical power shutdown where electricity delivery is stopped for non-
overlapping periods of time over different parts of the distribution region. Load
shedding is a last-resort measure used by an electric utility company to avoid a
total blackout of the power system.

These developments highlight its simultaneous resilience and vulnerability to global economic developments, with regional variations. Although growth in sub-Saharan middle-income countries seems to have followed the global slowdown more closely, such as in South Africa, lower-income and oil-exporting countries in the region have been largely unaffected.

As mentioned earlier in this section, South Africa is ranked 52nd in 2013, the best economy in sub-Saharan Africa, and the third among the BRICS economies. The country benefits from the large size of its economy. Particularly impressive is the country's financial market development, indicating high confidence in South Africa's financial markets at a time when trust is returning only slowly in many other parts of the world. South Africa also does reasonably well in more complex areas such as business sophistication and innovation, benefitting from good scientific research institutions and strong collaboration between universities and the business sector in innovation.

According to WEF's 2013's Global Competitiveness report,[26] these combined attributes make South Africa the most competitive economy in the African region, but in order to further enhance its competitiveness, the country will need to address some weaknesses. Out of 148 countries surveyed by WEF, South Africa still rank 113th in labor market efficiency, a drop of 18 places from 2012 position, due to its rigid hiring and firing practices, a lack of flexibility in wage determination by companies, and significant tensions in labor-employer relations.

The educational sector is another challenge, as efforts must also be made to increase the university enrollment rate in order to better develop its innovation potential. Combined efforts in these areas will be critical in view of the country's high unemployment rate of 24.7 percent, although it has improved since 2012, at which time the rate was at 25.7 percent. In addition, South Africa's infrastructure, although good by sub-Sahara's standards, requires upgrading. The poor security situation remains another important obstacle to doing business in South Africa. The high business costs of crime and violence and the sense that the police are unable to provide sufficient protection from crime do not contribute to an environment that fosters competitiveness. Another major concern remains the health of the workforce, which WEF* ranked 132nd out of

---

* Ibidem.

148 economies, as a result of high rates of communicable diseases and poor health indicators.

## BRICS' Global Influential Ascend

The BRICS, as the biggest emerging markets, are uniting to tackle under-development and currency volatility, as well as pooling foreign-currency reserves to ward off balance of payments or currency crises. The plan calls for an implementation of an institution that encroaches on the roles of the World Bank and IMF. At the time of this writing, the leaders of the BRICS bloc were getting ready to approve the establishment of a new development bank during an annual summit in the eastern South African city of Durban.*

Meanwhile, the IMF seems to be fermenting over the BRICS. After years promoting and showcasing them, in November of 2013 it admitted the bloc had either "exhausted their catch-up growth models, or run into the time-honored problems of supply bottlenecks and bad government."[27] We believe, however, the IMF was caught off guard by the aggressiveness of the emerging market rout when the U.S. Federal Reserve began to reconsider its quantitative easing policies in May 2013, threatening to decrease the dollar liquidity that has fuelled the booms—and masked the woes—in Asia, Latin America, and Africa. This dependence on the dollar has disrupted growth in many regions of the world, especially those more dependent on the U.S. consumer marker and the dollar as a currency.

This issue is not new. In the last decade, a few Latin American countries—the most dollarized region in the world—began introducing measures to create incentives to internalize the risks of dollarization, the development of capital markets in local currencies, and de-dollarization of deposits. These all contributed to a decline in credit dollarization globally, but predominantly in Latin America and the BRICS countries. Bolivia, Paraguay, Peru, and Uruguay have been gradually declining in financial dollarization.

---

* There have been speculations that the location of this new BRICS' IMF-like bank will be based in Durban, South Africa.

## Coping with De-dollarization

For several decades, dollarization has greatly complicated the policy response in several crises and near-crisis episodes, especially for emerging economies. In some cases, it has been the primary source of financial vulnerability that triggered a crisis not only for BRICS countries, but also for other emerging countries such as the CIVETS and the MENA blocs. The urge to *de-dollarize*, or to withdraw from U.S. Treasury bills and the dollar, is a direct result of foreign countries' mistrust in the United States. government's ability to control its massive budget deficits. As depicted in Figure 7.1, according to the IMF,[28] the degree of dollarization has declined sharply in Latin America over the past decade.

The same trend holds true for other emerging markets around the world. A case in point is Iran. On March 20th back in 2012, as Iran was celebrating its greatest holiday of the year, New Year's Eve, it not only celebrated the beginning of a new year but also the end of the dollar as an acceptable currency for payment of its oil.

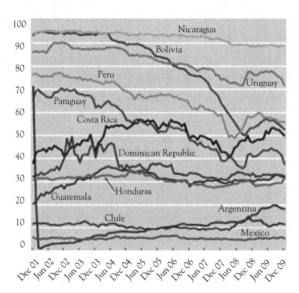

*Figure 7.1 Latin America de-dollarization has been high in the past decade (percent of foreign deposits of to total bank deposits)*

Source: IMF

Although the holiday, known as Nowruz, is typically commemorated by a symbolic purging of the home and spiritual representation of creation and fertility, in 2012, Iran celebrated it by changing its oil payment policy. Essentially, Iran made the decision to no longer accept the U.S. dollar as payment for oil, and instead, decided to accept other currencies and commodities.

Ever since President Obama signed one of the most severe sanction bills against Iran into law, (H.R. 2194), which prohibits any person or business from investing more than 20 million dollars in Iranian petroleum resources, Iran appears determined to phase out the dollar as a form of payment for its oil and derived products. However, if Iran continues to follow through with its decision to refuse dollars-for-oil, it may trigger an intense reaction from the U.S. government, especially for the dollar-reserve currency, mainly supported by the Saud family's determination to accept only dollars for oil, the so called petro-dollars.

The charter of the Iranian oil bourse, a commodity exchange which opened more than five years ago, calls for the commercialization of petroleum and other byproducts in various currencies other than the U.S. dollar, primarily the euro, the Iranian rial, and a basket of other major (non-U.S.) currencies. While there are three other major U.S. dollar-denominated oil markers in the world (North America's West Texas Intermediate crude, North Sea Brent Crude, and the UAE Dubai Crude), there are just two major oil bourses: the New York Mercantile Exchange (NYMEX) in New York City, and the Intercontinental Exchange (ICE) in London and Atlanta.

Iran sits on the largest oil and gas reserves in the world, as depicted in Figure 7.2. Consequently, the country has been developing a fourth oil market where U.S. dollars are not accepted for oil trade. In fact, Iran has proposed the creation of a Petrochemical Exporting Countries Forum (PECF), aimed at financial and technological cooperation among members, as well as product pricing and policy making in production issues— not unlike the Organization of the Petroleum Exporting Countries (OPEC). The British newspaper, The Guardian, cites Iran, Saudi Arabia, United Arab Emirates (UAE), Russia, Qatar, and Turkey as potential members of PECF.

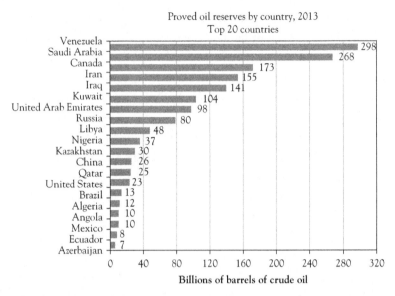

**Figure 7.2 Iran's oil reserves is the fourth in the World**

In the wake of such tensions, India is pondering whether to use gold or yen as payment for oil. India has expanded on this conundrum by proposing the setup of a multilateral nondollarized bank that would be funded exclusively by emerging nations to include the BRICS countries for the purpose of financing projects in those countries.

The policy debate about de-dollarization, notwithstanding the U.S. and Iran conflicts, has heated up around the world. Is de-dollarization a realistic goal for the world? If so, how might it be implemented? Can Iran, the BRICS, the CIVETS, ASEAN, and the MENA countries trigger a chain of events that may threaten to crumble the U.S. dollar as the world's premiere reserve currency? What would be the consequences to the United States, and the world economy, if the dollar were to no longer be the OPEC measure for oil prices? Certainly, the United States would no longer be able to enjoy the lowest price of gasoline as a non-oil producer nation. The price of fuel would likely skyrocket, increasing the price of all other commodities which ultimately would impact the micro-economics in advanced economies.

While dollarization is a sensible response of economic agents to political or economic uncertainties, its adverse effects often motivate countries, especially emerging economies, to reduce its level. Dollarization is also a rational reaction to interest rate arbitrage opportunities. It may have some benefits, and in extreme cases may be the only viable option available to a country. In such cases, dollarization can be the choice of policymakers or a result of private agents' decision to stop using the local currency. However, most countries seek to limit the extent of dollarization, owing to its potential adverse effects on macroeconomic policies and financial stability. These include a reduction or loss of control of monetary and exchange rate policy, a loss of seigniorage*, and increased foreign exchange risk in the financial and other sectors.

Often, key policies that encourage de-dollarization, especially among the emerging markets, focus on policymakers' intentions to gain greater control of monetary policy, often drawing on the experiences of past countries' successful de-dollarization experiences. We believe durable de-dollarization depends on a credible disinflation plan and targeted microeconomic measures. An effective de-dollarization policy makes the local currency more attractive to local consumers, more than foreign currency. De-dollarization, therefore, entails a mix of macroeconomic and microeconomic policies to enhance the attractiveness of the local currency in economic transactions and to raise awareness of the exchange-risk related costs of dollarization, thus providing incentives to economic agents to de-dollarize voluntarily. It may also include measures to force the use of the domestic currency in tandem with macroeconomic stabilization policies.

On May 16, 2008, Yekaterinburg, Russia hosted the official diplomatic meeting and in June 2009, the BRICS held their first summit in Yekaterinburg. The Yekaterinburg Summit discussions were dominated with negative criticism against the U.S. dollar, with President Putin, of Russia going so far as to publicly endorsing the yuan as a global reserve currency. The group later agreed to replace the U.S. dollar by the IMF's special drawing rights (SDR).

CitiGroup economists already have proposed the idea of the 3G (Global Growth Generators) countries, comprised of 11 countries'

---

* Seigniorage is the difference between the value of money and the cost to produce and distribute it.

economies identified as sources of growth potential and of profitable investment opportunities, in an attempt to effectively put an end to the BRICS bloc.[29] There is also a geostrategic move to pit India as a linchpin in the Pivot of Asia strategy announced in 2010, intended as a new direction for U.S. foreign and strategic policy in the Asia-Pacific region. It was a policy designed under the assumption that U.S. interventions in other regions were winding down. As Secretary of State, Hilary Clinton noted:

"In the last decade, our foreign policy has transitioned from dealing with the post-Cold War peace dividend to demanding commitments in Iraq and Afghanistan. As these wars wind down, we will need to accelerate efforts to pivot to new global realities... In the next 10 years, we need to be smart and systematic about where we invest time and energy, so that we put ourselves in the best position to sustain our interests, and advance our values. One of the most important tasks of American statecraft over the next decade will therefore be to lock in a substantially increased investment—diplomatic, economic, strategic, and otherwise—in the Asia-Pacific region.... U.S. commitment there is essential. It will help build that architecture and pay dividends for continued American leadership well into this century, just as our post-World War II commitment to building a comprehensive and lasting transatlantic network of institutions and relationships paid off many times over—and continues to do so. The time has come for the U.S. to make a similar investment as a Pacific power, a strategic course set by President Barack Obama from the outset of his administration and one the is already yielding benefits."[30]

The United States wants to ally with India, Japan, Thailand, South Korea, and the Philippines. Could it be that the United States wants to form a sort of *Pacific Rim-region* alliance, to effectively divide the two prominent BRICS nation, India and China, and effectively generate a global discourse to hedge China from becoming an attractor against American hegemony?

At the moment there is no clear answer. Even academicians have expressed concern about the potential demise of the dollar and the role it plays in global markets, as it guarantees the strength to American society and the military. Joshua Zoffer, staff writer of The Harvard International Review, sums up concerns of a strong BRICS IMF-like development bank and the weakening influence of the dollar in an essay titled *Future of Dollar Hegemony*:

"As the issuer of the international reserve currency, the U.S. has garnered two unique economic benefits from dollar hegemony. First, in order for other countries to be able to continually accumulate dollar reserves by purchasing dollar-denominated assets, capital has to flow out of the U.S. and goods must flow in. As a result, the value of the dollar must be kept higher than the value of other currencies in order to decrease the price of imported goods. While this arrangement has come at the cost of an ever-growing current account deficit, it has also subsidized U.S. consumption and fueled the growth of the U.S. economy.

The second benefit of this system is its effect on the market for U.S. government debt. The largest market in the world for a single financial asset is the multi-trillion dollar market for American bonds. This market, considered by many to be the most liquid in the world, allows any nation or large investor to park massive amounts of cash into a stable asset with a relatively desirable rate of return. While the depth and stability of U.S. financial markets as a whole were part of the original reason nations gravitated toward the dollar as a reserve currency, the explosive growth of U.S. government debt has made U.S. Treasury bonds the center of the foreign exchange market and the most widely held form of dollar reserves. The use of the U.S. Treasury securities in currency reserves has created an almost unlimited demand for U.S. debt; if the federal government wishes to issue debt, someone will buy it if only as a way to acquire dollar holdings. This artificially high demand means that the U.S. can issue debt at extremely low interest rates, especially relative to its national debt and overall economic profile. And while the U.S. has had to pay off its existing debt by issuing new securities, no nation wants to call in its debt for fear that it would devalue the rest of its dollar holdings. While precarious and arguably dangerous in the long term, *the reality is that as long as the dollar is the international reserve currency, the U.S. will have a blank check that no one wants to cash.**

Whether you agree with U.S. fiscal policy, it is indisputable that the ability to finance its debt has allowed the U.S. to provide its citizens with

---

* Emphasis added.

a high standard of living and fund its enormous military programs. *Essentially, dollar hegemony has served as the backbone of U.S. primacy.*\* Domestically, the ability to run effectively unlimited budget deficits has allowed the U.S. to fund its massive entitlement programs and, more recently, afford sweeping bailouts at the height of the recession. The U.S. has used its unlimited allowance, afforded by dollar hegemony, to finance its high standard of living and maintain the prosperity required of a hegemon. More importantly, the U.S. has used the demand for American debt to fund its military apparatus."[31]

The BRICS effort to create their own IMF-like bank seems, to address not only a viable alternative for loans aside from the IMF, but also a counter-strategy to fend off advanced economies' strategies such as 3G and Pivot of Asia, thus reducing their exposure to the dollar-pegged polices.

### BRICS Capitalization of an IMF-Like Development Bank

In early 2012, the BRICS countries, together representing 43 percent of the world's population and 18 percent of the world's GDP, met in New Delhi, India, for their fourth annual convention. In this meeting of five countries, now attracting more than half of total global financial capital, a plan was announced to establish a BRICS-focused development bank, to be funded solely by BRICS countries, no longer having to rely on the World Bank and the IMF, which, for nearly 70 years, have served as omniscient monetary levers for Western interests.

The BRICS countries officially announced the formation of the BRICS Bank in their 5th Summit at Durban, South Africa. This marks an important step to the potential institutionalization of a post-western global order, which is causing a lot of debate, mainly focusing on the viability of a bank. In our view, such an event can be compared only to the one in San Francisco, during the Summit of the Allies in 1945, when new institutions were being founded for the post-Second World War world order.

This IMF-like BRICS development bank, which will focus on funding infrastructure projects without the neo-liberal prescriptions imposed

---

\* Emphasis added.

by the World Bank, is being funded with an initial capital of US$100 billion. Since there is reticence from some of the members to contribute more than US$10 billion, China will be the major contributor. China is no stranger to money lending. In 2010 it helped create and fund the Chiang Mai Initiative (CMI), a multilateral currency swap arrangement among the ten members of the ASEAN, Japan, and South Korea, which draws from a foreign exchange reserves pool worth US$120 billion. That pool expanded to $240 billion in 2012.[32] It wouldn't be surprising if there was a sudden push for an *Asian Monetary Fund* to be developed.

Although the BRICS nations at the time of these writing in fall 2013, are still unable to settle the location or structure of the bank, its purpose will initially focus on infrastructure. During the G-20 Summit in St. Petersburg, Russia, in September of 2013, the BRICS nations decided to fund their development bank with $100 billion. Russia, Brazil, and India agreed to contribute $18 billion to the BRICS currency reserve pool, while China agreed to contribute $41 billion and South Africa $5 billion.[33] The reserves are aimed at financing joint development ventures, and are set to rival the dominance of the World Bank and the IMF. It is unclear if the amount of initial capitalization will exceed the planned seed-capital, as very different sums of money are being mentioned. Nonetheless, assuming the BRICS countries maintain current growth trends, we believe within the next eight years the bloc may have the ability to fund this bank, thus challenging the IMF and Western advanced economies.

In addition to crafting its own economic and monetary policies, another implication for a BRICS' "IMF-like" international bank is the possibility of an alternative global currency to the dollar. What would the world prefer: debased fiat money of the Anglo-American led debtor countries or a currency backed by nations whose citizens are enriched with savings and where economies are producing needed goods and services?

Looking back to Bretton Woods, one cannot ignore the massive debt incurred by the U.S. Treasury alone: $16.7 trillion at the time of this writing, and rising. Estimated U.S. population as of summer of 2013 was 316,669,430, so each citizen's share of this debt is about $52,881.59. The National Debt has continued to increase an average of $1.93 billion per day since September 30, 2012. Conversely, the BRICS have accumulated impressive cumulative reserves topping four trillion. In the short term, this plan is contingent on the extent to which it reconciles the competing agendas of the BRICS nations.

A bank such as this could become attractive for emerging markets, considering the track record of the IMF and World Bank austerity policies in the region, which are very mixed. There is little doubt that many nations would welcome an alternative to these institutions, which would make the BRICS development bank very influential, if we consider the fact that many policymakers believe that the current economic crisis has led to unwielded power of both the World Bank and the IMF, and that this power is uncontested.

There remains the issue of limited IMF and World Bank power. The aftermath of the Asian financial crisis saw a number of countries in Asia and Russia hoarding foreign exchange reserves precisely so they did not have to repay the IMF or World Bank again, or comply with the austerity plans not often prescribed to advanced economies and which resorts to monetization of the debt. The proposed BRICS development bank represents an important new development that potentially further circumscribes the influence of those institutions. At least in theory, the BRICS bank could erode the role and status of the IMF and the World Bank. Although it may take a few years before the bank is operational, in the long term this BRICS bank could have a significant impact on the IMF, the World Bank, and global development, as the bank would have access to a vast and growing emerging market. We caution though that the power struggle between nations could lead to difficulties.

At present, China holds vast foreign exchange reserves and is likely to play a major role in the BRICS bank. South Africa, with the weakest economy among the BRICS, due to increased reliance on minerals prone for eventual depletion, may have the most to gain from the establishment of the bank. Nevertheless, we believe the entire BRICS bloc could benefit from the international clout the new bank would wield.

Meanwhile, American politicians plan on increasing the U.S. debt even further by at least $1 trillion a year into the foreseeable future—the stock market rebounds every time the Federal Reserve Bank suggests the potential for more stimulus—the European sovereign debt crisis is an ongoing financial crisis that has made it nearly impossible for some countries in the eurozone to refinance their government debt. During the early summer of 2012, Spain's borrowing costs skyrocketed to seven percent yield on the 10-year bond after Moody's downgraded its bond rating. As of summer 2013, yield fell to five percent, as a result of ECB backstop, but we don't believe it to be sustainable. Spain's borrowings costs will likely continue to rise as a result of the United States' own challenges in jumpstarting its economy.

Also in summer of 2013, Italy, too, is struggling to sell its bonds, being forced to pay the most in nearly a year to sell three-year paper at auction. Italian debt has underperformed that of Spain due to political turmoil involving its former premier Silvio Berlusconi whose outcomes could bring down the Italian government.

A bias we could not avoid during the research of this book is that we are avid believer in a free-market system. Hence, we also believe government programs and monetary stimulus tend, all too often, to be a waste of money. Every policy, rule, and regulation sponsored by government and imposed onto its citizens—that is, printing of fiat money throughout most of the advanced economies—appears to be a type of price fixing; in this case, to promote currency debasement. In the long run such strategies simply aren't sustainable. It only degrades society's wealth and over time pools more and more of society's assets into the hands of unscrupulous leaders and financiers. Inevitably, the printing press creates an overabundance of money, which in turn makes people feel rich and overspend, creating yet another (false!) boom that will lead to another real bubble. Eventually the bubble bursts, turns to a bust, and the cycle repeats itself.

With that in mind, and with the two major world currencies and economies struggling to stabilize, global markets may begin to falter if the continued monetary dominance of an Anglo-American currency is still warranted, as it was in Bretton Woods' times. Even more worrisome is the lack of real compromise over the prospect of money and power among these major global markets: the United States and the EU. Meanwhile, the BRICS, led by China, seem to favor an alternative to the U.S. dollar, especially considering these countries are asked to rely on a monetary system with increasingly shaky economic fundamentals, and currently barred from trading with Iran, if they want to continue trade relations with the United States.

It is no surprise then that the BRICS are pushing for the rapid realignment of control for international funding. In all likelihood, struggling countries, mainly from Africa, East Europe, and Latin America, also may express their desire to align themselves with this new *BRICS Monetary Fund*. It is even possible that other resource rich nations, such as Chile, Bolivia, and Indonesia, may wish to engage as well.

We would not be surprised if the United States continues to overheat its monetary printing press, to the delight of Wall Street, to the point where some savings rich Western nations, such as Germany, Switzerland, and the Nordic Countries may also be tempted to join the BRICS in their quest for an international reserve standard based on sounder currency. We would argue for monetary competition in lieu of currency value fixing, as money has proven over the course of history to be whatever we decided it would be.

# CHAPTER 8

# CIVETS

# A New Strong and
# Fast Emerging Market

## Overview

Until recently, the best notorious work of Goldman Sach's economist Jim O'Neil was probably the development of the BRIC* acronym. Now, however, the new grouping of Colombia, Indonesia, Vietnam, Egypt, Turkey, and South Africa countries, dubbed CIVETS also is becoming well known. Although it is not certain who created the acronym – some assert HSBC's chief executive Michael Geoghegan while others claim the Economist Intelligence Unit—all parties believe this new bloc is becoming the next big strategy for growth, foreign investments, and global policy influence.

The authors believe the future of robust global growth and development are being concentrated in the emerging markets. These emerging economies don't have the debt problems with which advanced economies are dealing. We also believe most of the world's consumption will continue to grow with emphasis on emerging market as the merging middle class demands also continue to grow.

While advanced economies, including the UK, those in Europe and North America are deemed to be in a long period of stagnation, much like the BRICS and MENA, the CIVETS countries are home to large youth populations and a fast-growing middle class. These new emerging economies are becoming the perfect storm for Western capital investment seeking new opportunities.

---

* Later turned into BRICS, by the BRIC nations themselves with the inclusion of South Africa, although in this chapter we keep this country as part of CIVETS, as originally intended by those whom coined the term.

According to HSBC, in its Business Without Borders[1] newsletter, while the past decade was all about the BRICS countries the next will be focused on the CIVETS. The article goes as far as suggesting that CIVETS "rising middle class, young populations and rapid growth rates make the BRICs look dull in comparison."* In concept, we tend to agree with HSBC's assessment of the CIVETS and BRICS. Figures 8.1 and 8.2 provide some evidences. Although we believe in the strength and positive factors surrounding the BRICS in relation to advanced economies, we also acknowledge that there is little in the way of shared interests to unite the BRICS countries. Russia and China are authoritarian states, while Brazil and India are noisy democracies. Brazil and South Africa, both big agricultural and mineral resources exporters seeking freer trade, have little in common with India, which protects its farmers with high tariff barriers. Russia, whose economy is based largely on energy exports, has little in common with China, a net oil importer. China, with over 1.3 billion people, is more than 25 times bigger than South Africa's 50 million. But the BRICS are a model of solidarity when compared to the CIVETS.

The organization of the CIVETS into a cohesive coherent group could be analogous to herding cats; interesting enough, the word civet also is used to refer imprecisely to a number of catlike creatures of different genii and species. We also worry that some countries that should have been part of the bloc are not, such as Mexico, Myanmar, Nigeria, and Kenya.

---

\*    Ibidem.

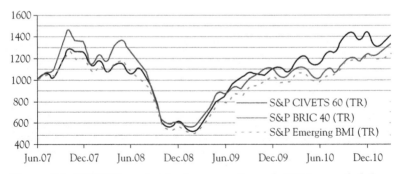

**Figure 8.1  CIVETS market performance through 2007 exceeded the BRIC**

Source: LesEchos[2]

| | **BRIC Countries** | **CIVETS Countries** |
|---|---|---|
| Countries | Brazil, Russia, India and China | Colombia, Indonesia, Vietnam, Egypt, Turkey and South Africa |
| | | |
| Name by | Goldman Sachs | Economist Intelligence Unit (EIU) |
| | | |
| Growth rate during next 20 yrs | 4.9% (prediction by EIU) | 4.5% (prediction by EIU) |
| | | |
| Population comparison | Brazil-201 mn; Russia-139 mn; India-1.2 bn and China-1.3 bn. | Colombia-44 mn; Indonesia-242.9 mn; Vietnam-89.5 mn; Egypt-80 mn; Turkey-77 mn; South Africa-49.9 mn |
| | | |
| International reach | Have own companies that are destined to be very important outside their own countries | Lack established multinational corporations (MNCs) |
| | | |
| Economic power | Already changing the rules of the game | Do not have the economic power to "reshape the global economic order." Combined GDP will only amount to one-fifth the size of the G7 nations' combined GDP by 2030 |

*Figure 8.2  A comparison between the BRIC and the CIVETS economies*

*Source:* WealthOpinion, Knowledge@Wharton[3]

For instance, Thailand, with a population of 69 million, an average age of 34, and a GDP growth forecast of more than six percent in 2012 is not part of the group. Egypt's poor economic performance of late can be considered temporary fallout from the Arab Spring upheavals, but what about South Africa, which in the nearly 18 years since the advent of majority rule has chalked up an average annual GDP growth of 3.3 percent? If compared to South Africa, Bangladesh could have been included, as it boasts a population of 150 million with a median age of 23, and GDP growth averaging six to eight percent. Let's not forget Nigeria, with a population of 140 million people, an average age of 19, and a GDP growth of 6.9 percent since 2005. Nonetheless, according to the HSBC, "the six countries in the group are posting growth rates higher than five percent, with the exception of Egypt and South Africa, and are trending upwards. Lacking the size and heft of the BRICs, these upstarts nevertheless offer a more dynamic population base, with the average age being 27, soaring domestic consumption and more diverse opportunities for businesses seeking international expansion."*

Governments in advanced economies are taking notice of such positive trends and making commitments to expand their presence in those emerging markets and assist their own multinational companies to access these markets in order to hit ambitious export-led growth targets. In England, for example, the Department for Business, Innovation and Skills is offering assistance to 50,000 small and medium size enterprises (SMEs) to expand their exports into these high-growth markets by 2015.[4] The government is offering financial and diplomatic levers to assist those businesses. As discussed in Chapter 7, the United States is pushing for a Pivot of Asia strategy, and in the EU, Martin Hutchinson, a noted commentator, author, and longtime international merchant banker, tells the European Business Review magazine that the next hot emerging-market economies is in fact the CIVETS, or the "new" BRICs.[5]

Despite the various opinions, including ours, on which countries should have been part of the CIVETS acronym, the bloc's economies are being considered the new strong and fast growth markets in the world. Reasons for that are easily illustrated by its economic figures. As depicted in Figure 8.1, CIVETS markets have been outperforming the BRICS since 2009. Half of Turkey's 72 million inhabitants are under the age of 28 and its economy is expected to be the second-fastest growing in the world by 2018. To date, there are more than 900 British companies already operating in Egypt, a country poised to expect a doubling of its population over the next 25 years. South Africa's infrastructure investment programs are providing a huge opportunity to companies that can contract expertise, goods, and services into them over a generation or more. Advanced economies are benefiting from this boom by way of bolstering their own growth.

Notwithstanding historic political upheaval in Egypt over the last year, large amounts of FDI are finding its way to that country. The UK remains the country's largest investor, with investments of about

---

\* Ibidem.

£13 billion pounds (US$20.8 billion). Egyptian's transition government has signaled a wish to speed up economic reform along with the formation of a new democracy in order to attract more outside investment, but already high inflation alongside political uncertainty tops the agenda for the immediate future. That said, thereafter it is expected that the Egyptian economy will grow at a rate of three percent annually.

Its highly mobile, well-educated youth is an important part of Egypt's business opportunity. But a second reason economies like those of Egypt or Turkey are appealing is that they provide a relatively hospitable back door into the emerging potential in neighboring, harder-to-access countries in the BRICS, ASEAN, and the MENA regions. We argue that these blocs are in many ways interdependent. Figure 8.2 provides a comparison between the BRICS and the CIVETS countries. Looking closely one can identify a multitude of ways in which these economies intertwine land resources and opportunities to each other, and open up nontraditional ways to many other emerging and advanced economies.

For instance, a British company, Faun Trackway, landed a contract to supply temporary helipads to the Colombian government's anti-narcotraffic forces, which provided them a gateway into the U.S. market because those forces are bankrolled by American state budgets. In South Africa, the British Prime Minister David Cameron, backed an African Union's idea to launch an African free trade area by 2017, which would in turn simplify and standardize trade tariffs and infrastructure among member states, allowing investors to benefit not only from the South African economy, but also many other leading economies in Africa, such as the MENA bloc.

The following is a breakdown of the CIVETS countries, their economies' threats, opportunities, and challenges.

### Colombia

Colombia is emerging as an attractive driving force in the South American region. The country boasts 44 million people and a GDP of $231 billion, which certainly positions itself for future growth. In a world in which resources prices are likely to tick upwards due to Chinese and Indian demand, Colombia's agricultural and natural-resources orientation is in high demand globally. In addition, should the U.S. Congress ever actually ratify the U.S.-Colombia Free Trade Agreement, which was signed back in November 2006, there should be a further boost to the Colombian market.

Colombia is the oldest democracy in Latin America,[6] but it has suffered several conflicts with guerrilla groups for more than 40 years, threatened its stability. This has changed dramatically, however, since the implementation of the policy *seguridad democrática*[7] (democratic security) implemented in 2003, which has improved significantly the reputation of the country around the world. Improved security measures have led to a 90 percent decline in kidnappings and a 46 percent drop in the murder rate over the past decade, which has helped per-capita GDP double since 2002. As of 2011 and depicted in Figure 8.3, Colombia's GDP growth has been larger than Latin America, the eurozone, and the United States, with only China surpassing it. Colombia's sovereign debt was promoted recently to investment grade by all three ratings agencies (Fitch, S&P, and Moody's). In addition, Colombia has substantial oil, coal, and natural gas deposits, and as of 2010, a total FDI of $6.8 billion in 2010, with the United States as its principal partner.

Colombia's economy is slowly returning to growth, over 3.5 percent on average for the past few years. Its unemployment rate, however, is among the highest in the region. Its currency, the peso, is rising on the country's commodities boom, and fiscal deficit remains a challenge. As of August 2010, Colombia had a budget deficit of 3.6 percent of its

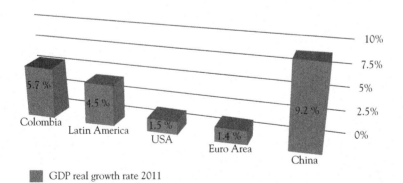

■  GDP real growth rate 2011

*Figure 8.3 Colombia GDP growth rate*

Source: IMF

GDP, which according to The Daily Market,[8] is still reasonable. Inflation rate in 2013 was 2.6 percent and external debt a modest 47 percent of GDP.

There has been a surge of new policies favoring entrepreneurism and creation of businesses, which allow foreigners to integrate into this market.[9] Foreign investment in Colombia has increased five-fold between 2002 and 2010,[10] increasing significantly its infrastructure. The oil boom since 2010[11] has provided a major boost to its economic recovery, and the country is being proactive in devising strategies to avoid the Dutch disease as billions of dollars in FDI are injected in the country's economy.

## Indonesia

Indonesia is a country with 243 million people and a GDP of $521 billion. The country boasts a substantive and well-diversified economy, with agriculture, natural resources, and substantial manufacturing. The level of corruption in the government and society, however, is very high, but still lower than in Russia. The country is situated strategically between China and India, meaning it should benefit as both those behemoths grow.

After emerging as the third-fastest-growing member of the G-20 in 2009, Indonesia has continued to display strong growth performance. For the past half-decade, Indonesia's annual GDP growth rate has averaged about six percent, the fastest in Southeast Asia, due in large part to a consumer-spending boom, which according to Moody's, the compound credit loan growth rate in the country has been over 22 percent for the past six years, while non-mortgage consumer credit nearly tripled in the last five years. During this time, credit card use has greatly proliferated, with the number of credit cards jumping by 60 percent, while the actual value of transactions almost tripled. This prompted the Bank of Indonesia, the country's central bank, fearing a consumer debt crisis, to limit the number of credit cards a single person is allowed to hold, while barring Indonesians who earn less than $330 dollars a month from being issued any credit cards.

In addition, the ultra-low interest rates in ailing advanced economies, combined with the United States Federal Reserve's multi-trillion dollar

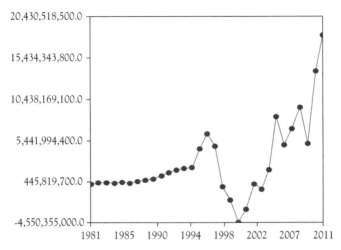

**Figure 8.4  Foreign direct investment in Indonesia more than tripled since 2008**

*Source:* IndexMundi.com

QE programs, that has led to a $4 trillion tsunami of *hot money** flowing into emerging market assets since 2008, and has enabled Indonesia to grow at a very fast pace, following the footsteps of China and India's fast economic growth. (See Figure 8.4.)

Multinational corporations from advanced economies have taken notice of Indonesia's consumer spending boom. Automakers including Nissan, Toyota, and General Motors have committed to spend up to $2 billion to expand their manufacturing operations in the country in the next few years. Cheap financing also has been fueling a surge in motorcycle sales, which grew 13.9 percent in August 2013 from a year earlier. Retail sales that have been growing at an annual rate of 10–15 percent in recent years have attracted numerous Western consumer brands like L'Oreal, Unilever, and Nestle that are seeking to cash in on Indonesia's consumer spending boom.[12]

---

* According to Investopedia, "Money that flows regularly between financial markets as investors attempt to ensure they get the highest short-term interest rates possible. Hot money will flow from low interest rate yielding countries into higher interest rates countries by investors looking to make the highest return. These financial transfers could affect the exchange rate if the sum is high enough and can therefore impact the balance of payments. http://www.investopedia.com/terms/h/hotmoney.asp.

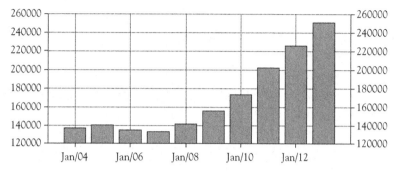

*Figure 8.5 Indonesia external debt has nearly doubled since 2008*

The huge inflows of hot money into the country have benefitted many foreign holders of Indonesian local currency government bonds, which rose from 14 percent to 34 percent, while the country's external debt nearly doubled, as depicted in Figure 8.5. These massive capital inflows into Indonesia, however, have contributed to a nearly 50 percent strengthening of the rupiah currency's exchange rate against the U.S. dollar. It also pushed the country's ten-year government bond yields down to record lows of five percent from its 10–15 percent before the 2008 global economic crisis range. This was bad for the local economy, which experienced a major rise in inflation rates, causing the Bank of Indonesia, to cut their benchmark interest rate from 12.75 percent to just 5.75 percent to stem export-harming currency appreciation.

Infrastructure spending and high commodity prices boosted most of the investment growth in 2009, but such record low interest rates have also fueled an increasing credit and consumption boom in Indonesia, with domestic consumer spending accounting for nearly 60 percent of the country's overall economy. In addition, the country has the lowest unit labor costs in the Asia-Pacific region, and a very ambitious government committed to attract even higher FDI into its economy, in an attempt to turn the nation into a manufacturing hub. But despite all the positive trends, corruption is still a major problem in the country.

## Vietnam

Vietnam, while new to global trade, only becoming a member of the WTO in 2007, has been one of the fastest-growing economies in the world for the past 20 years, with the World Bank projecting an average of 7.2 percent, annually in 2013 and the next few years. Its membership in the ASEAN, and its proximity to China may very well lead the country to become a new potential manufacturing hub as its labor costs are lower than those of China. Foreign investors rank Vietnam as an attractive destination for future investments. The country is one of the most popular destinations for expansion within the ASEAN region.[13] It has been hailed as the next China, and with good reason: Vietnam has a culture that's similar to the Red Dragon in that it's an ex-Communist, one-party state, and attracts FDI due to its cheap labor costs.

After the death of its leader Le Duan in 1986, Vietnam began making the transition from a planned economy to a socialist-oriented market economy after suffering an inflation rate of 700 percent and a stagnant economy.[14] The Communist Party launched a broad economic reform package called Doi Moi ("Renewal"), very similar to the Chinese model (economic openness mixed with communist politics), achieving similar results. Between 1990 and 1997 Vietnam's economy grew at 8 percent per annum, with similar results in the following years.

This rapid growth from the extreme poverty of 1986 has given rise to advanced economies—especially Westerns—consumerist habits, particularly among the new rich of Vietnam, causing a widening gap of social inequality and rise in inflation up to 12 percent. In light of stable increases in GDP per capital and average disposable incomes during recent years, the still high percentage of food in the CPI basket emphasizes the substantial, negative impact of high inflation on Vietnam's economy. The rise of food and fuel prices in the world market also imposes a burden on Vietnamese consumers. About 43 percent of disposable income is spent on food and eating activities, which means that the majority of people's consumption budget currently goes to the food sector, giving it substantial revenues as compared to other industries. As the wet markets serve as the main retail channel of most types of food, it is fair to say that nearly 40 percent of people spending will go to these wet markets for food purchases. Revenue of food "industry" will mostly be concentrated in the traditional markets, not on fast-food chains, restaurants, or retail chains as in the United States.

In Vietnam, the stronger integration with the world economy gives rise to sprawling of modern commercial centers, luxurious shopping complexes, and gigantic malls in big cities. The traditional consumption habits, however, still prevail and steer most people to traditional markets, sometimes called flea markets or wet market. These traditional markets are the major channel of retail dating back more than a thousand years ago since the very first urban areas arose and society formed an organized structure under the rule of dynasties. According to Vietnam Association of Retail,[15] there are now approximately 9000 traditional markets nationwide and up to 80 percent of all retail sales are conducted through these traditional channels. In all, as depicted in Figure 8.6, retail businesses in Vietnam continues to soar.

According to statistics from the Ministry of Industry and Finance, as of May 2012,[16] there are approximately 638 supermarkets and 117 malls across the nation. The number of newly established supermarkets and malls after five years of joining the WTO (2007–11) is 27 percent higher than in the five-year period prior to the WTO integration. Hence, the Communist Party leaders are very keen on maintaining the growth rate, so that within the next ten years the nation can attain the status of an industrialized country.* Whether the country will be able to achieve this status within such timeframe is yet to be seen, but Vietnam has unquestionably attained relatively stable macroeconomic conditions.

According to the World Bank,[17] as of 2013, the country has been able to maintain a moderate level of inflation at 6.7 percent, while also maintaining a stable exchange rate. The dong depreciated by 1.6 percent in the

---

* Ibidem.

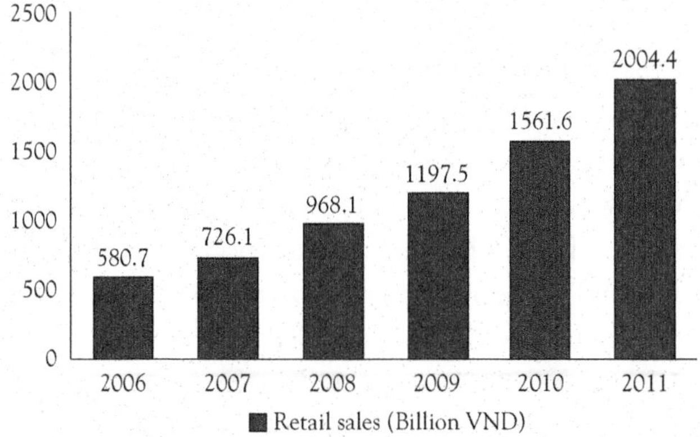

Figure 8.6 *Revenue from retail sales and services in Vietnam 2006–11*

past 12 months, based on average exchange rates by commercial banks. Simultaneously, the government has been able to significantly increase foreign reserves. It has grown from 2.2 months of import cover at the end of first quarter of 2012 to 2.8 months at the end of first quarter of 2013. This while reducing sovereign risks, with the country's credit default swap (CDS) about 250 basis points in June 2013 compared to about 350 in June 2012.

As a result of strong foreign investment, which accounted for 66 percent of Vietnam total exports, Vietnam's solid export growth has been significant. The total export value rose by 16 percent in the first half of 2013 compared to the same period last year, with a wider diversification of export composition although more concentrated on high-tech products, such as cell phones and parts, surpassing the country's traditional exports of crude oil, garment, and footwear. In fact, cell phones, electronics, and computers, combined now account for nearly a fifth of Vietnam total exports. Most significantly, in 2012, Vietnam achieved its first ever surplus in trade balance since 1992.

But there are some concerns looming over Vietnam's economic outlook. The total FDI ratio has recently declined from a record 11.8 percent in 2008 to about 7.7 percent in the first half of 2013, and other ASEAN countries, such as Indonesia and Thailand, are performing better, while new competitors, such as Myanmar, closing in. Vietnam's growth has slowed down since the onset of economic reforms in the late-1980s. Real GDP grew by 5.25 percent in 2012, which although impressive if compared to advanced economies, is the lowest level since 1998.

At this pace, the World Bank has predicted that the country's economy during 2010–13, for the first time in nearly two decades, would grow at a slower pace than Indonesia and the Philippines. The main cause for the slowdown is the decline in FDI and consequently, low Purchasing Managers Index (PMI), which has remained below 50 marks for most of 2012 and 2013; PMI below 50 signals contraction in production. There has also been a slowdown in retail sales and services, from 24 percent in 2011 to 16 percent in 2012, and to 11.9 percent in the first half 2013. Figure 8.7 provides a snapshot of Vietnam's economic achievements and challenges.

*Figure 8.7 Vietnam's economic achievement and challenges as of July 2013*

Source: The World Bank

### Egypt

Occupying the northeast corner of the African continent, Egypt is bisected by the highly fertile Nile valley, where most economic activity takes place. Egypt's economy was highly centralized during the rule of former President Gamal Abdel Nasser but opened up considerably under former Presidents Anwar El-Sadat and Mohamed Hosni Mubarak. Cairo, from 2004 to 2008, aggressively pursued economic reforms to attract FDI and facilitate GDP growth. Notwithstanding the relatively high levels of economic growth in recent years, living conditions for the average Egyptian remains poor, which has contributed to major public discontentment.

The first year after the fall of the Egyptian president, Hosni Mubarak, in February 2011 was very disruptive for Egypt's economy. After 30 years of dictatorship, elections brought to power the Muslim Brotherhood, who promised to be inclusive and tolerant. But since the Brotherhood Muhammad Morsi became president at the end of June of 2012, the political climate in the country has become even more chaotic. Egyptian society is ever more polarized, and protests frequently turned into violence. The security forces vacillates between support for the Islamists and deep-seated suspicion of them. All the while Egypt's economy has continued to slide toward major disarray, as most economic indicators point to challenging times.

Following the political unrest, the Egyptian government drastically increased social spending to address public dissatisfaction, but political uncertainty at the same time caused economic growth to slow significantly, reducing the government's revenues. Tourism, manufacturing, and construction were among the hardest hit sectors of the Egyptian economy. Subsequently, the government had to resort to the utilization of foreign exchange reserves to support the Egyptian pound. At the time of this writing, it is clear that Egypt will likely seek a loan from the IMF, or perhaps from the newly former BRICS development bank.

Since the revolution, according to YaLibnan, a leading specialized source of Lebanese news,[18] the Egyptian pound has slid about 10 percent, while unemployment hit 20 percent. As of fall 2013, FDI is withering, and total reserves have fallen from $35 billion to $10 billion in the past four years. Many of Egypt's most dynamic businessmen have fled the country, fearing they will be arraigned for complicity with Mr. Mubarak, while the government threatens to reverse a number of privatizations. Meanwhile, the price of food is soaring at a time when the average family spends nearly half of its income to feed itself, forcing a quarter of Egypt's 83 million people to live below the poverty line.

According to the Pew Center's Global Attitudes Project more than 70 percent of Egyptians are unhappy with the way the economy was moving, and 49 percent believe that a strong economy is more important than a good democracy. We believe the number of people disillusioned with the revolution is likely to increase as the economy weakens further. Hafez Ghanem, Senior Fellow, Global Economy and Development with the Brookings Institution,[19] argues that the Egyptian economy is unlikely to collapse suddenly, but in the absence of a serious macroeconomic stabilization program it will continue to deteriorate gradually.

The Egyptian economy is plagued with low growth, increasing unemployment and inflation, as shown in Figure 8.8, excluding corruption, as the country witnessed more than 6,000 corruption investigations and several high profile incriminations since February 2011. The future of Egypt's economy will depend on how well the transition to democracy will be. We must consider the fact that Egyptian politics is polarized and it is difficult to see how serious economic reforms would be implemented without first reaching compromise on some problematic political issues.

Ashraf El-Arabi, Planning and International Cooperation Minister, argues that Egypt's economic growth rate in the second quarter of

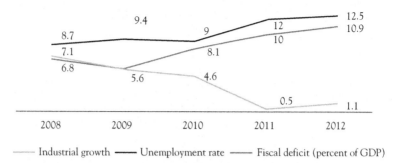

**Figure 8.8 Egypt's selected economic indicators**

*Source:* Brookings Institution.

2012/13 fiscal years would likely be 0.2 percent lower than the previous quarter, while in the first quarter the economy grew by 2.6 percent, with a forecasted growth for October–December 2012 period in the neighborhood of 2.4 percent. Although Egypt has opened its markets to global trade and investment, nontariff barriers continue to constrain trade freedom. The investment regime has been stable, but flows have slowed significantly due to the challenging economic and political situation, and the central bank has imposed controls on capital transfers. The state-dominated financial system has been stressed, with negative impacts from the global crisis exacerbated by domestic turbulence.

It's clear that Egypt is facing a major economic crisis, and needs to implement credible reforms to stabilize the economy, control corruption, and lay the foundation for inclusive growth. Such reforms would normally include a reduction in the fiscal deficit to bring the domestic debt under control and a further depreciation of the Egyptian pound to encourage exports and tourism.

The Egyptian government is negotiating with the IMF to obtain support for such a stabilization program. IMF support is desirable because it would open the doors for increased assistance from other bilateral and multilateral donors, and thus help ease the pain of stabilization. The revolution severely retrained economic growth in Egypt. Growth predictions by the World Bank[20] are to reach only one percent in 2013, compared with 5.2 percent prior to the revolution.

Analysts expected Egypt to regain its growth trajectory once political stability returned, which has not been the case so far, as the political

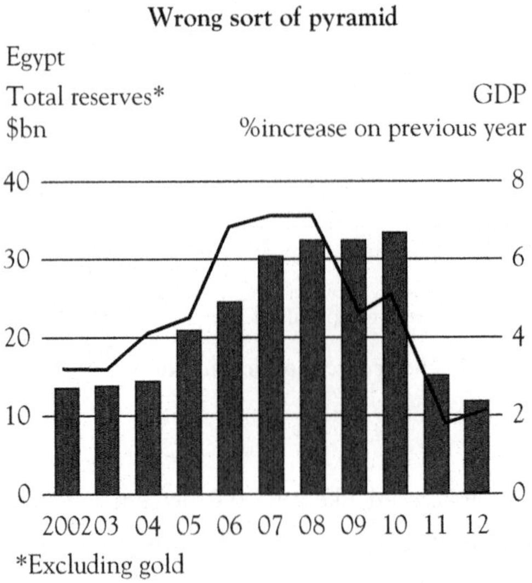

**Wrong sort of pyramid**

Figure 8.9 A snapshot of the severe downturn of Egypt's GDP growth since 2008

Source: IMF

instability persists. Egypt does possess many assets, including fast-growing ports on the Mediterranean and Red Sea linked by the Suez Canal, a growing tourism network, and vast untapped natural gas reserves. Nonetheless, as long as the political unrest endures, chances for an economic rebound are nominal. Hence, Egypt's economy is expected to grow 2.6 percent in 2014, well below the 3.5 percent projected by the government.[21] A Reuters poll also suggested growth would pick up to four percent only starting in 2015. Figure 8.9 provides a snapshot of the severe downturn of Egypt's GDP growth since 2008.

Given its challenges vis-à-vis politics and economics transition, Egypt has been experiencing an extended period of instability. Much-needed improvements in economic policy have been delayed, and the effectiveness of reforms that might have helped to open markets and improve productivity have been undercut by the tenuous rule of law and the legacy of Egypt's socialist past. Deeper institutional reforms critically are needed to spur lasting economic growth and development. Those reforms include strengthening the judicial system, better protection of property rights, and more effective action against growing corruption.

## Turkey

Located between Europe and major energy producers in the Middle East, Caspian Sea, and Russia, Turkey was founded in 1923 from the Anatolian remnants of the defeated Ottoman Empire. After a period of one-party rule, an experiment with multi-party politics led to the 1950 election victory of the opposition Democratic Party and the peaceful transfer of power. Since then, Turkey's political parties have multiplied and democracy has been disrupted by periods of instability and intermittent military coups in1960, 1971, and 1980, which in each case ultimately resulted in a return of political power to civilians.

Turkey has a dynamic economy that has trading links with the European Union but without the constraints of the eurozone or EU membership. The country joined the UN in 1945 and NATO in 1952. Subsequently, in 1964 Turkey became an associate member of the European Community. Over the past decade, it has undertaken many reforms to strengthen its democracy and economy, and began accession membership talks with the EU in 2005. The country is a founding member of the OECD (1961) and the G-20. Since December 31, 1995, the country is part of the EU Customs Union.

An aggressive privatization program has reduced state involvement in basic industry, banking, transport, and communication, and an emerging cadre of middle-class entrepreneurs is adding dynamism to the economy and expanding production beyond the traditional textiles and clothing sectors. According to a survey by Forbes magazine[22] in March 2013, Istanbul, Turkey's financial capital, boasted a total of 37 billionaires (up from 30 in 2012), ranking 5th in the world behind London and Hong Kong in 4th (43 billionaires), New York (62 billionaires), and Moscow (84 billionaires). Turkey's major cities and its Aegean coastline attract millions of visitors every year.

Its ostensibly free-market economy is increasingly driven by its industry and service sectors, although its traditional agriculture sector still accounts for about 25 percent of employment. Turkey has major natural-gas pipeline projects that make it an important energy corridor between Europe and Central Asia. The automotive, construction, and electronics industries are rising in importance and have surpassed textiles within Turkey's export mix. In 2006, oil began to flow through the Baku-Tbilisi-Ceyhan pipeline, marking a major milestone that will fetch up to one million barrels per day from the Caspian to market. Several gas pipeline projects also are moving forward to help transport Central Asian gas to Europe via Turkey, which over the long term will help address Turkey's dependence on imported oil and gas to meet 97 percent of its energy needs.

In 2011, the World Bank[23] placed Turkey as the world's 15th largest GDP-PPP and 18th largest Nominal GDP. After Turkey experienced a severe financial crisis in 2001, Ankara adopted financial and fiscal reforms as part of an IMF program. Then, according to data from the OECD,[24] following weak growth in 2012, the economy began to regain momentum as consumption and investment contracted and offset a surge in exports. Growth is projected to surpass to above three percent in 2013 and, as the global recovery gathers strength, to pick up to 4.5 percent in 2014. Inflation and current account deficit, however, remain above comfort levels.

According to the OECD,* a tight fiscal stance decided upon has been set for 2013 and 2014, but policymakers should allow the economy to stabilize and have flexibility to consider some temporary stimulus should conditions turn out much worse than projected. Internationally comparable general government accounts would help implement and assess the stance of fiscal policy. Monetary policy needs to reduce inflation without undermining the recovery and without pushing up the real exchange rate thus hurting competitiveness. Disinflation would limit the costs on this front. Structural reforms to accelerate formalization and productivity gains remain crucial for strong and sustainable growth.

As depicted in Figure 8.10, the reforms strengthened the country's economic fundamentals and ushered in an era of strong growth, averaging more than six percent annually until 2008, growing faster than any other OECD country. Global economic conditions and tighter fiscal policy, however, caused GDP to contract in 2009, but Turkey's well-regulated financial markets and banking system helped the country weather the global financial crisis. GDP rebounded strongly to 9.2 percent in 2010 and continued to grow, as exports returned to normal levels following the recession.

---

* Ibidem.

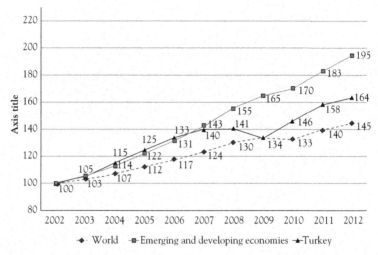

**Figure 8.10  Turkey's real GDP growth 2002–2012**

*Source*: Conference Board Database

Despite impressive growth over the past decade, as a group, Turkish performance lagged significantly behind emerging and developing economies, as well as advanced economies (see Figure 8.10), but starting in 2009 real GDP rose by 95 percent compared to Turkey's 64 percent. Real GDP in large emerging markets such as China, India, Bangladesh, and Indonesia all grew more rapidly than in Turkey, as it did in many smaller African and Latin American countries. Turkey's rank in global GDP improved marginally over the decade, as in purchasing-power adjusted terms, it went from 17th to 16th in global GDP rankings, surpassing Australia. Measured by current exchange rates, however, the country rose from 21st to 17th, surpassing Taiwan, Switzerland, Belgium, Netherlands, and Sweden, but falling behind Indonesia.* Notwithstanding, Turkey's performance, when leveraged against the emerging markets, is less distinguished, but it is significant when compared to advanced economies. The IMF is predicting Turkey's real GDP to be 3.8 percent in 2013, falling back to 3.5 percent in 2014.[25]

---

* Note that such comparisons of rankings over time using current dollars can be misleading due to movements in real exchange rates.

Growth dropped to approximately three percent in 2012. Turkey's public sector debt to GDP ratio fell to about 40 percent, and at least one rating agency has upgraded Turkey's debt to investment grade in 2012. Turkey remains dependent on often volatile, short-term investment to finance its large trade deficit. The stock value of FDI stood at $117 billion at year-end in 2012. Inflows have receded because of continued economic turmoil in Europe and the United States, the source of much of Turkey's FDI. Turkey's relatively high current account deficit, uncertainty related to monetary policy-making, and political turmoil within Turkey's region leave the economy vulnerable to destabilizing shifts in investor confidence.

### South Africa

South Africa is another resource-rich economy, with 49 million people and a GDP of $280 billion, which positions the country with a decent-sized economy. The IMF,[26] however, argues South Africa faces low growth, widespread unemployment, and a high reliance on foreign capital inflows.

Rising commodity prices, renewed demand in its automotive and chemical industries, and spending on the World Cup have helped South Africa; a diversified economy rich in resources such as gold and platinum, resume growth after it slipped into recession during the global economic downturn.

Despite considerable success on many economic and social policy fronts over the past 19 years, South Africa faces a number of long-standing economic problems that still reflect the long-lasting and harmful legacy of apartheid. Unemployment remains excessively high, and educational outcomes are poor on average and extremely uneven, which aggravates the excess supply of unskilled labor as well as worsening income inequality. In addition, the prospects for sustained improvements on the quality of life of its people are compromised by environmental challenges, notably climate change and water issues.

The OECD[27] argues that South Africa needs to achieve rapid, inclusive economic growth while at the same time making the transition to a low-carbon economy and effectively managing the country's scarce water resources. Tackling the key problems effectively will require continued and

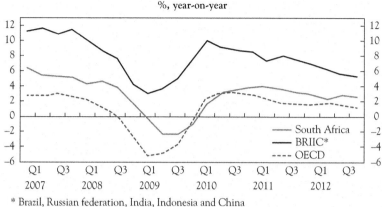

%, year-on-year

* Brazil, Russian federation, India, Indonesia and China

*Figure 8.11 South Africa GDP growth*

Source: OECD

skillful management of macroeconomic policies, but above all improved implementation of structural policies, with education being a particularly critical area. As shown in Figure 8.11, the global economic crisis that started in 2008, and the weak global economic outlook, is not helping the country.

South Africa has, however, posted major achievements since the transition to majority rule in 1994. Per capita GDP has increased by 40 percent in inflation-adjusted terms. The poverty rate has dropped by 10 percent, and schools and hospitals have been built in previously underserved areas, while government-financed houses have been made available to many in need, and social transfers now reach more than half of all households. In addition, the country has strong macroeconomic policy institutions. The government's medium-term fiscal policy framework has been a pillar for the country's prudent fiscal policy, while monetary policy has anchored inflation expectations.

Many see the nation as a gateway to investment into the rest of Africa, including HSBC, which sees long-term growth potential in mining, energy, and the chemical firm Sasol Ltd. Notwithstanding, South Africa, and the whole continent of Africa, is rich in minerals and oil. China has an economy that requires them in abundance. Since the mid-1990s the economy of sub-Saharan Africa has grown by an average of five percent a year. At the start of this period Africa's trade with China was negligible.

It is now worth roughly $200 billion a year. Most of Africa's exports are raw materials. China sends manufactured goods back in return.

Natural resources make up a quarter or more of export revenues for nearly half of the 45 countries in sub-Saharan Africa. Nine of them, including Nigeria and Angola, which have two of Africa's largest economies, benefit from exports of oil and gas. Yet mining and oil are far from the whole story in South Africa. The IMF[28] recently (2013) warned that South Africa is trailing other emerging markets and must quickly implement reforms if it wants to avoid a crisis, pointing to painfully high unemployment and a plethora of other economic troubles staking the country. The country's growth has underperformed and vulnerabilities have increased considerably, including continued sluggish growth of two percent in 2013 and 2.9 percent in 2014.

But while much of the world staggered in the wake of the global financial meltdown, South Africa has managed to stay on its feet—largely due to its prudent fiscal and monetary policies. The country is politically stable and has a well-capitalized banking system, abundant natural resources, well-developed regulatory systems, as well as research and development capabilities, and an established manufacturing base. The World Bank ranked South Africa as an "upper middle-income country." It is the largest economy in Africa. It was admitted to the BRIC group of countries of Brazil, Russia, India, and China (known as BRICS) in 2011.

With a world-class and progressive legal framework, South African legislation governing commerce, labor, and maritime issues is particularly strong, and laws on competition policy, copyright, patents, trademarks, and disputes conform to international norms and standards. The country's modern infrastructure supports the efficient distribution of goods throughout the southern African region.

The economy has a marked duality, with a sophisticated financial and industrial economy having grown alongside an underdeveloped informal economy. It is this "second economy" which presents both potential and a developmental challenge.

In its 2012–13 Global Competitiveness report,[29] the World Economic Forum ranked South Africa second in the world for the accountability of its private institutions, and third for its financial market development, "indicating high confidence in South Africa's financial markets at a time when trust is returning only slowly in many other parts of the world." The country's securities exchange, the JSE, is ranked among the top 20 in the world in terms of size.

South Africa's success in reforming its economic policies is probably best reflected by its GDP figures, which reflected an unprecedented 62 quarters of uninterrupted economic growth between 1993 and 2007, when GDP rose by 5.1 percent. With South Africa's increased integration into the global market, there was no escaping the impact of the 2008–09 global economic crises, and GDP contracted to 3.1 percent.

While the economy continues to grow - driven largely by domestic consumption—growth is at a slower rate than previously forecasted. It is projected to grow at 2.7 percent in 2013, 3.5 percent in 2014 and 3.8 percent in 2015. According to figures from the National Treasury, total government spending will reach R1.1 trillion rand in 2013. This represents a doubling in expenditure since 2002/3 in real terms.

To ensure that there is a similar improvement in service-delivery outcomes, the government is deploying measures to strengthen the efficiency of public spending and to root out corruption. Under its inflation-targeting policy, implemented by the South African Reserve Bank (SARB), prices have been fairly steady. In January 2013, the annual consumer inflation rate was 5.4 percent, dipping from December 2012's 5.7 percent. Stable and low inflation protect living standards, especially of working families and low-income households.

The country's outlook is affected both by national concerns, such as unrest in and pressure on the mining industry, as well as international sluggishness, with Europe as one of South Africa's chief export destinations. However, trade and industrial policies encourage local firms to explore new areas of growth based on improved competitiveness. China, India, and Brazil offer significant opportunities. Infrastructure, mining, finance, and retail developments across Africa are helping to fuel a growth trajectory in which South Africa can participate.

## The Problem of Corruption

According to Transparency International [30] (TI), many of the CIVETS, as well as the BRICS and the MENA, countries experience major challenges

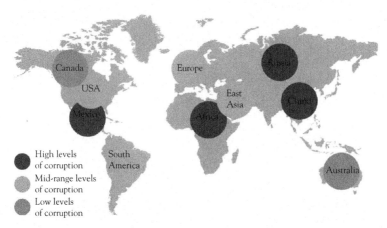

**Figure 8.12  2011 Global Corruption Index**

*Source*: LexisNexis

with corruption. Figure 8.12 provides a global picture of 2011 corruption scores according to LexixNexis'[31] RiskRadar*. When we look at the BRICS, for example, Chinese firms have the weakest overall performance among the bloc nations. In its report titled *Transparency in Corporate Reporting: Assessing Emerging Market Multinationals*[32] TI analyzed 100 of the fastest growing companies based in 16 emerging markets. Three quarters of the businesses scored less than five out of ten, where zero is the least transparent. Scores were based on publicly available information about anti-corruption measures, transparency in reporting, how the companies structure themselves and the amount of financial information they provide for each country in which they operate.

Chinese companies accounted for more than a third of the assessed businesses. According to TI China must take "immediate action"[†] to raise standards. Companies in India scored best out of the BRICS with a result of 5.4. The studies credit this to national laws obliging publication of key financial information on subsidiaries. Some 75 of the 100 companies in the report come from BRICS nations, which have contributed 50 percent

---

* The RiskRadar is a content platform for people who wish to keep abreast of the latest developments in AML and anti-bribery and corruption. The RiskRadar is powered by LexisNexis.

† Ibidem.

of world growth since the financial crisis. The study said about 60 percent of the firms evaluated does not disclose information about political contributions. TI called on companies in emerging markets to disclose to the public what they are doing in terms of prevent corruption as well as their relationship with their governments. It added legislation forcing companies to publish what they pay to governments in every country where they operate.

To continue to foster consistent growth, emerging markets must be partners in playing their part in the global fight against corruption. As emerging market companies expand their global influence they should seize the opportunity to become active participants in the role of stopping corruption internationally.

Government infrastructure contracts in the CIVETS bloc, as well as BRIC and MENA in general, might be hard to access without breaking the U.S. 1977 Foreign Corrupt Practice Act (FCPA) or the 2011 UK Bribery Act, making such companies exposed to DOD and SEC prosecutions. This is because requests for bribes are increasing in state procurement processes at both the provincial and local government levels. This could be a major problem for emerging market growth, not only the CIVETS. As defined by the U.S Department of Justice,[33]

> The FCPA of 1977 was enacted for the purpose of making it unlawful for certain classes of persons and entities to make payments to foreign government officials to assist in obtaining or retaining business. Specifically, the anti-bribery provisions of the FCPA prohibit the willful use of the mails or any means of instrumentality of interstate commerce corruptly in furtherance of any offer, payment, promise to pay, or authorization of the payment of money or anything of value to any person, while knowing that all or a portion of such money or thing of value will be offered, given or promised, directly or indirectly, to a foreign official to influence the foreign official in his or her official capacity, induce the foreign official to do or omit to do an act in violation of his or her lawful duty, or to secure any improper advantage in order to assist in obtaining or retaining business for or with, or directing business to, any person.

Fraud in the construction sector, according to Grant Thornton,[34] a global think-tank based in the UK, could be worth as much as $860 billion globally, which is about 10 percent of industry revenues, and it could hit $1.5 trillion by 2025.

It is important to note, however, corruption is not only a challenge in emerging markets. Advanced economies also are plagued by it, either as the proverbial "cost for doing business in emerging markets," for accepting bribes, or for being victims of extortion. Across Australia, Canada, India, the UK, and the United States it is evident that fraud in the development of infrastructure is commonplace and in some cases endemic.

In the UK, the three biggest areas of construction fraud are bid rigging or alterations to contracts and false misrepresentation, which spans use of illegal workers, falsifying reports, results or certificates, and noncompliance with regulations. Grant Thornton's report refers to *breakfast clubs*,* where contractors meet to decide who will win the latest contract. In New York, the think-tank calculated that five percent of construction projects' were awarded to five Mafia families alone (2011). The problem is that many companies are not aware of their increased level of liability or new legal risks that threaten their business. The drive for growth also is increasing corporate corruption risk as businesses expand into emerging markets where corruption tends to be more prevalent. In countries such as the UK, Canada and Australia, the propensity of bid rigging has been normalized to the extent that it might even be perceived as legal, according to Grant Thornton's report.

To prevent fraud, policymakers in emerging markets need to combat the practice by making the issue a priority in national agendas. They needs to devise processes to scrutinize in-country multinational firms and their own corporations—in particularly, they would be well serviced to not forget to extend this same scrutiny to government agencies. Policymakers must be able, and capable, to place aside reputational issues and prosecute fraudulence. The use of information systems and technology, in an effort to tap into big data to identify and predict fraud, also is paramount. Governments also must encourage whistle blowing, and provide full support and cooperation to these practices listed in this book.

---

* Ibidem.

# CHAPTER 9

# The Strength of ASEAN Economies

## Overview

The group of ten countries assembled in Association of Southeast Asian Nations (ASEAN), has a common ambition than merely consolidating their economies. Their goal is to become the center of gravity of the entire Asian region, in order to multiply channels of dialogue and diplomacy among the main international players, with the objective of promoting peace, stability, and security in the new geopolitical environment of rising regional powers. The East Asia Summits (EAS) are a good example of the regional architecture ASEAN is trying to build with its partners. The project of economic integration summarized below is then conceived as a tool to achieve wider strategic goals than merely promoting economic growth and development.

It's helpful to remind our readers of this wider perspective as we tapped into a trove of data and analysis from various international research institutions including but not limited to the World Bank, the IMF, the OECD economic data forecasts, the Asian Development Bank, the ASEAN secretariat, the CIA Facebook 2014, Goldman Sachs, the Aseanist Times, the International Business Times, and the Economy Watch.

## The ASEAN Economic Community

In January 2007, the ten Southeast Asian nations agreed to implement the ASEAN Economic Community (AEC) with four objectives: (a) a single market and production base; (b) a highly competitive economic region; (c) a region of equitable economic development; and (d) a region integrated into the global economy.

The AEC is a highly ambitious effort to enhance ASEAN's global competitiveness. Through the free flow of goods, services, and skilled labor, the project intends to establish an efficient *single market and production base* encompassing nearly 600 million people and $2 trillion in production. Business communities in the ASEAN hold that the regional economic integration would not disrupt their businesses, citing that it would give even more opportunities rather than threats.

The ASEAN Business Advisory Council (ASEAN BAC) conducted a survey of 502 executives from companies of various sizes operating in the ASEAN region. The results of the survey, entitled *2013 ASEAN-BAC Survey on ASEAN Competitiveness,*[1] suggest that the ASEAN economic integration will pose a low or very low threat, 2.49 out of 5 (1=very low to 5=very high) to their organizations.

The survey was conducted in 2010 by ASEAN-BAC in collaboration with fellow scholars from Lee Kuan Yew School of Public Policy at the National University of Singapore. The integration of the regional politics and the economy within the AEC, would take effect by the end of 2015, allowing free flow of economic activities and resources within the region. The survey showed that about 60 percent of the businesses in the region believed that AEC would provide high or very high opportunities for their organizations, as reflected by an average ratio of 3.59 out of 5 (1=very low to 5=very high).

The AEC areas of cooperation include human resources development and capacity building; recognition of professional qualifications; closer consultation on macroeconomic and financial policies; trade financing measures; enhanced infrastructure and communications connectivity; development of electronic transactions through e-ASEAN; integrating industries across the region to promote regional sourcing; and enhancing private sector involvement for the building of the AEC. In short, the AEC will transform ASEAN into a region with free movement of goods and services, investment, skilled labor, and freer flow of capital.

This agenda of economic convergence and interdependence has been viewed, since its outset, as one of the dimensions of the ASEAN Community, which member states decided to implement, to be effective by 2015. Economically speaking, with the implementation of the AEC, it is expected that ASEAN exports will expand by 42.6 percent, while imports will expand by 35.4 percent.

At the country level, the projections indicate a relatively low export increase of about 10.4–43.7 percent for the region's most export-oriented economies such as Brunei, Malaysia, Thailand, and Singapore, and relatively high increases of 55.4–101.1 percent for the CLMV (Cambodia, Laos, Myanmar, and Vietnam) Asian sub-group economies. Table 9.1 lists the forecasted effects on international trade for the region by 2015.

The result will be a small increase in the region's steady state trade surplus, attributed to the increased FDI inflows that the AEC is assumed

*Table 9.1 Effects on International Trade in the ASEAN region (2015)*[2]

| Change in exports, percent from baseline | | | | | |
|---|---|---|---|---|---|
| | **AFTA** | **AFTA+** | **AEC** | **AEC+** | **AEC++** |
| ASEAN | 6.5 | 31.2 | 42.6 | 70.9 | 88.9 |
| Cambodia | 37.0 | 70.3 | 77.6 | 86.8 | 113.9 |
| Indonesia | 6.5 | 22.5 | 53.6 | 84.0 | 109.5 |
| Laos | 41.0 | 85.0 | 101.1 | 103.6 | 110.3 |
| Myanmar | 8.7 | 43.9 | 65.8 | 100.7 | 163.2 |
| Malasia | 4.5 | 26.4 | 35.6 | 53.3 | 65.4 |
| Phillippines | 2.9 | 25.4 | 45.4 | 67.3 | 82.4 |
| Singapore | 4.5 | 39.7 | 43.7 | 61.1 | 64.9 |
| Thailland | 8.8 | 27.8 | 33.6 | 63.5 | 85.5 |
| Vietnam | 15.4 | 49.0 | 55.4 | 160.1 | 239.5 |
| Brunei | 2.1 | 9.8 | 10.4 | 8.6 | 13.7 |
| PARTNERS | | | | | |
| China | 0.0 | −0.7 | −0.8 | 7.5 | 6.9 |
| Japan | −0.1 | −0.6 | −0.5 | 8.4 | 7.6 |
| Korea | −0.2 | −1.1 | −1.5 | 7.1 | 6.6 |
| India | 0.1 | −0.1 | −0.3 | 57.4 | 57.0 |
| Australia | −0.1 | −0.5 | −1.0 | 5.3 | 4.4 |
| New Zealand | −0.3 | −0.5 | −0.6 | 6.1 | 5.1 |
| USA | 0.0 | −0.3 | −0.8 | −1.4 | 2.9 |
| Europe | −0.1 | −0.3 | −0.9 | −1.3 | 0.6 |
| World | 0.4 | 1.8 | 2.1 | 6.4 | 8.4 |

to generate. Those inflows will give rise to steady-state outflows of investment income (profits), which need to be covered by a larger trade surplus. Following is a brief highlight of each of the ASEAN country members as of fall 2013.

### Brunei Darussalam

Brunei is a country with a small, wealthy economy that is a mixture of foreign and domestic entrepreneurship, government regulation, welfare measures, and village tradition. The Sultanate of Brunei's influence peaked between the 15th and 17th centuries when its control extended over coastal areas of northwest Borneo and the southern Philippines. Brunei subsequently entered a period of decline brought on by internal strife over royal succession, colonial expansion of European powers, and piracy. In 1888, Brunei became a British protectorate, and independence only was achieved in 1984. Since then, the same family has ruled Brunei for over six centuries.

The country is almost wholly supported by exports of crude oil and natural gas, with revenues from the petroleum sector accounting for 60 percent of GDP and more than 90 percent of exports. Brunei is the third-largest oil producer in Southeast Asia, averaging about 180,000 barrels per day. It is also the fourth-largest producer of liquefied natural gas in the world. The government, however, understands the risks of having too much of the country's GDP relying on a single industry, and has demonstrated progress in its basic policy of diversifying the economy away from oil and gas.

Brunei's policymakers also are concerned that steadily increased integration into the world economy will undermine internal social cohesion, though it has taken steps to become a more prominent player by participating as an active player in the Asian Pacific Economic Cooperation (APEC) group.

According to Trading Economics,[3] Brunei's personal income tax rate is 0 percent (2013), while inflation rates are also extremely low at 0.30 percent (August 2013). The per capita GDP in Brunei is among the highest in Asia, and substantial income from overseas investment supplements income from domestic production. As Figure 9.1 shows,

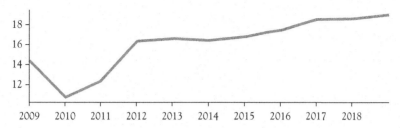

*Figure 9.1 Brunei's growing GDP*

Source: Quandl

the country's GDP in 2012 was $16.63 billion, with an estimated GDP growth of $18.8 billion by 2018.[4] The economy is projected to grow by an average of 2.4 percent from 2013 to 2017 as Southeast Asia recovers from a slowdown in 2011 and 2012, according to the OECD.[5] For Bruneian citizens the government provides for all medical services, subsidizes food and housing, and provides complimentary education through the university level. The government owns a 2,262 square mile cattle farm in Australia, larger than Brunei itself, which supplies most of the country's beef.[6] Eggs and chickens largely are produced locally, but most of Brunei's other foods are imported.

Agriculture and fisheries sectors are among the government's highest priorities in its efforts to diversify the economy, but while the country is best known for its substantial hydrocarbon reserves, the government also is starting to focus on green forms of energy, including solar. However, compared to some Southeast Asian neighbors, the Sultanate has set more modest goals and has been slower to develop alternatives to oil and gas.

The government actively encourages more FDI into the economy by offering new enterprises that meet certain criteria or a *pioneer status,* which exempts profits from income tax for up to five years, depending on the amount of capital invested. The normal corporate income tax rate is 30 percent, but as stated earlier, there is no personal income tax or capital gains tax. Hence, increased investment in research and development (R&D),[7] combined with targeting niche markets, are two cornerstones of a strategy being rolled out by the government aimed at encouraging economic diversification. Japanese Mitsubishi has committed $2 million investment in R&D, a figure that could expand multifold if results are satisfactory.

Brunei recorded a trade surplus of $719 million Brunei dollars (US$578 million) in July of 2013. From 2005 until 2013, Brunei's Balance of Trade averaged $1,307 million Brunei dollars (US$1,051 million) reaching an all-time high of $2,971 million Brunei dollars (US$2,390 million) in September of 2008. As an oil producer, Brunei has been able to run consistent trade surpluses despite having to import most of what it consumes. Oil and natural gas account for over 95 percent of Brunei's exports, in addition to clothing.

Brunei mainly imports machinery and transport equipment, manufactured goods, food, fuels and lubricants, chemical products, and beverages and tobacco. Brunei's main trading partners are Singapore, Malaysia, China, Japan, the United States, and Germany. Singapore, however, is the largest trading partner for imports, accounting for 25 percent of the country's total imports in 2012. Japan and Malaysia are the second-largest suppliers. As in many other countries, Japanese products dominate local markets for motor vehicles, construction equipment, electronic goods, and household appliances. As of 2012, the United States was the third-largest supplier of imports to Brunei as of 2012.[8]

### Cambodia

In 1995, the government transformed the country's economic system from a planned economy to its present market-driven system.[9] Hence, Cambodia currently follows an open market economy and has seen rapid economic progress in the last decade,[10] where growth was estimated at 7 percent while inflation dropped from 26 percent in 1994 to only 6 percent in 1995. Imports increased due to the influx of foreign aid, and exports, particularly from the country's garment industry.

In October 2004, King Norodom Sihanouk abdicated the throne and his son, Prince Norodom Sihamoni, was selected to succeed him. Local elections were held in Cambodia in April 2007, with little of the pre-election violence that preceded prior elections. National elections in July 2008 were relatively peaceful, as were commune council elections in June 2012.

Nonetheless, since 2004, amidst all Cambodia's political turmoil, garments, construction, agriculture, and tourism have driven Cambodia's

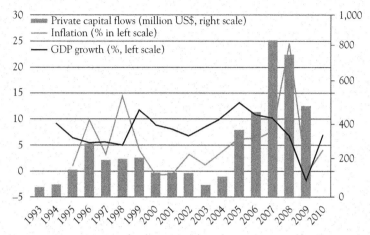

*Figure 9.2  Cambodia's economic performance 1993–2010*

Source: CamproPost

economic growth, as depicted in Figure 9.2.[11] GDP has climbed more than six percent per year between 2010 and 2012. In 2007, Cambodia's GDP grew by an estimated 18.6 percent.

In 2005, exploitable oil deposits were found beneath Cambodia's territorial waters, representing a potential revenue stream for the government, if commercial extraction becomes feasible.[12] Mining also is attracting some investor interest and the government has touted opportunities for mining bauxite, gold, iron, and gems. The tourism industry has continued to grow rapidly with foreign arrivals exceeding two million per year since 2007 and reaching over three million visitors in 2012. Cambodia, nevertheless, remains one of the poorest countries in Asia and long-term economic development remains a daunting challenge, due to endemic corruption, limited educational opportunities, high-income inequality, and poor job prospects.

As depicted in Figure 9.3, and according to the Council for the Development of Cambodia[13] (CDC), per capita GDP is still low compared with most neighboring countries in ASEAN, although rapidly increasing since 1998 when the Riel greatly depreciated against the dollar. In 2013, per capita GDP reached US$830, an increase of approximately 70 percent from US$487 in 2005. The CDC projected per capita GDP to reach US$984 in 2012 respectively.

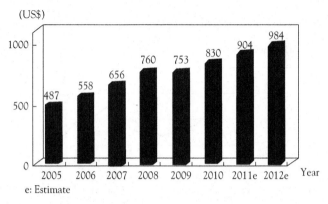

*Figure 9.3 Cambodia's GDP per capita (USD)*

Source: CDC

Cambodia's two largest industries are textiles and tourism, while agricultural activities remain the main source of income for many Cambodians living in rural areas.[14] The service sector is heavily concentrated on trading activities and catering-related services. About four million people live on less than $1.25 per day, and 37 percent of Cambodian children under the age of five suffer from chronic malnutrition. Over half of the population is under 25 years of age. This young population lacks education and productive skills. This is particularly true in the impoverished countryside, which also lacks basic infrastructure.

The major economic challenge for Cambodia over the next decade will be developing an economic environment in which the private sector can create enough jobs to handle Cambodia's demographic imbalance. The Cambodian government is working with bilateral and multilateral donors, including the Asian Development Bank, the World Bank, and IMF to address the country's many pressing needs, as more than 50 percent of the government budget is received by donor assistance. Presently, Cambodia's main foreign policy focuses on establishing friendly borders with its neighbors, particularly Thailand and Vietnam, as well as integrating itself into the regional ASEAN and global WTO trading system.

## Indonesia

Indonesia has the largest economy of the ASEAN. With the population exceeding 240 million, it is the four largest country in the world.

Indonesia has a land area of around two million sq. km (736,000 sq. miles) and a maritime area of 7.9 million sq. km. The Indonesian archipelago is the largest in the world and consists of over 16,000 islands and stretches 5,000 km from east to west.

Despite the political turmoil of the late 1990s, Indonesia is politically stable today. Stability has not come easily but the democratic process prevailed with two consecutive mandates (to be concluded in 2014) of the first elected president, Dr Susilo Bambang Yudhoyono.

The reforms of 1999 ended the formal involvement of the armed forces in the government. Like other members of ASEAN, Indonesia has a market-based economy in which the government has traditionally played a major role. It has been a WTO member since 1995 and is now a proud member of the Group of Twenty Finance Ministers and Central Bank Governors, also known as G-20. Its economy is ranked as the 15th and 16th largest by the World Bank and the IMF, respectively.

Under President Suharto's "New Era," which extended from 1967 to 1997, the Indonesian economy grew in excess of seven percent until the Asian financial crisis, which was the lowest point of the economy and resulted in political instability. Since then, the rupiah has strengthened with the return of political and economic stability.

The banking sector and capital markets have been restructured. GDP growth, as depicted in Figure 9.4, rose steadily at four percent to six

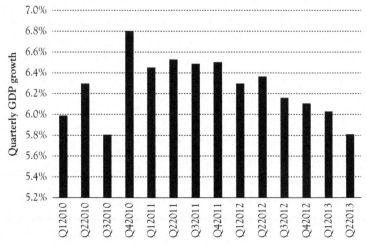

*Figure 9.4 Indonesia GDP growth has declined since Q4 2010*

Source: Badan Pusat Statisk

percent annually from 1998 to 2007. In 2008, there was a decline caused by a slump in exports and manufacturing and the global downturn that stunted its growth. During the second half of 2009, the growth rate did not gain new capital investment, which is attributed more to the lack of available credit and financing than any domestic economic issues. Indonesia recovered fairly quickly from the 2009 downturn and real GDP growth of six percent was reached in 2011. Subsequently, however, the country's economy has slowed and 5.8 percent will be the real GDP growth at the end of 2013.

Indonesia has been a net petroleum exporter and a member of OPEC, but left the organization in 2008 and has been importing oil since. This was mainly due to maturation of existing fields. In 2007, Indonesia ranked second (after Qatar) in world gas production. The oil and gas sector contributed over 31 percent to total government revenue in 2008 and maintains a positive trade balance. Indonesia had proven oil reserves of 3.99 billion or 0.29 percent of the world's reserves. In 2008, its natural gas consumption was 33.8 billion cu m and proven natural reserves of 3 trillion cu m. Indonesia is also rich in minerals and has been exploring and extracting bauxite, silver, tin, copper, nickel, gold, and coal. A mining law passed in 2008 has reopened the coal industry to foreign investment. Indonesia exported 140 million tons of coal in 2008. The country ranks fifth among the world's gold producers.

The government made economic advances under the first administration of President Yudhoyono (2004–09), introducing significant reforms in the financial sector, including tax and customs reforms, the use of Treasury bills, and capital market development and supervision. During the global financial crisis, Indonesia outperformed its regional neighbors and joined China and India as the only G-20 members posting growth in 2009.

The government has promoted fiscally conservative policies, resulting in a debt-to-GDP ratio of less than 25 percent, a fiscal deficit below three percent, and historically low rates of inflation. Fitch and Moody upgraded Indonesia's credit rating to investment grade in December 2011. Indonesia still struggles with poverty and unemployment, inadequate infrastructure, corruption, a complex regulatory environment, and unequal resource distribution among regions. In 2014, the government faces the ongoing challenge of improving Indonesia's insufficient infrastructure to remove impediments to economic growth, labor unrest over wages, and reducing its fuel subsidy program in the face of high oil prices.

## LAOS

In its foreign relations, Laos has slowly shifted from hostility to the West and a pro-Soviet stance to a more amenable and open policy with its neighbors in the region. Laos remains a one-party communist state and the political environment is stable. The LPR has been in power since 1975 and rules by decree.

Laos became a full-fledged member of ASEAN and joined the WTO in 2010. The country is a member of many international organizations such as United Nations, ASEAN Free Trade Area (AFTA), Asian Development Bank (ADB), Food and Agriculture Organization (FAO), World Bank's International Bank of Reconstruction and Development (IBRD), and IMF.

The Laos government started encouraging private enterprise in 1986 and now is transiting to a market economy but with continued governmental participation. Prices are generally determined by the market and import barriers have been eased and replaced with tariffs. The private sector now is allowed direct imports and farmers own land and sell their crops in the markets. From 1988 to 2009, the economy grew significantly, as shown in Figure 9.5, at an average 6–8 percent annually. Despite being rich in natural resources the country remains underdeveloped, however, and nearly 70 percent of the population lives off subsistence agriculture, which contributes to roughly 30 percent of the GDP.

Industry is a growing sector (11 percent) and contributes 33 percent of its GDP. The main activity is the extraction industry with mining of tin, gold, and gypsum. Other industries include timber, electric power, agricultural processing, construction, garments, cement, and tourism. The service sectors account for nearly 37 percent of GDP and four new banks have opened in the last two years. Laos operates a managed exchange rate and the Lao kip has been strengthening.

A new commercial banking law was introduced in 2006. Lending to the private sector more than doubled in 2008 to the equivalent of

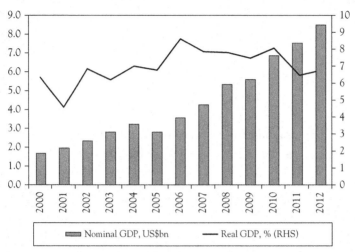

*Figure 9.5  Laos's economic growth in GDP terms*

Sources: Goldman Sachs; Forbes: Asian Development Bank

15 percent of GDP. The country's first stock market launched in 2010 with 10 companies listed. A special economic zone is being set up in Savannakhet to promote foreign and domestic investment. Tourism has become a major revenue earner and has provided employment to many.

Poverty has reduced substantially from 46 percent in 1992 to 26 percent in 2009. Exports in 2009 included copper, gold, clothing, hydropower, wood and wood products, and coffee and were sent mainly to Thailand (35 percent), Vietnam (16 percent), and China (nine percent). Imports were mostly comprised of machinery and equipment, vehicles, fuel, and consumer goods. The country is rich in hydropower generation, which provides almost 90 percent of electricity. There are no indigenous sources of oil and natural gas but PetroVietnam is exploring for oil and gas jointly with Laos. There are considerable untapped deposits of minerals and these are largely untapped. There are also ample sources of gemstones, especially high quality sapphires, agate, jade, opal, amber, amethyst, and pearls.

Numerous foreign mining companies are operating in Laos. In 2010, only China had mining projects here. The biggest source of income and investment continues to be hydropower and Laos hopes to become the "battery of Asia." It plans to increase exports of hydroelectricity to 20,000

MW per year by 2020. Thailand is its main customer and the two countries already have an electricity purchase contract for 5,000 MW scheduled for 2015. Investment in hydropower projects has been rising with accumulated investment in 2000–2009 standing at $2.65 billion with Thailand, $2.24 billion with China and $2.11 billion with Vietnam. Laos was previously a major source of opium but major steps were taken to quell production, which is now at its lowest level since 1975.

Infrastructure development, streamlining business regulations and improving finance have been identified as the main priorities for the government. Construction roads and buildings for the Southeast Asian Games in December 2012 and for the celebration of the 450th anniversary of Vientiane as the country's capital in 2010 have aided infrastructure development. A mini construction boom is being experienced around Vientiane. The manufacturing and tourism sectors are seen as the key sectors for private sector growth. The garment sector has created employment for over 20,000. There is still a vital a need to focus attention on ameliorating transportation and skill levels of workers.

Laos continues to remain dependent on external assistance to finance its public investment. In 2009, it launched an effort to increase tax collection and included value added tax (VAT), which has yet to be imposed. It also simplified investment procedures and expanded bank facilities for small farmers and entrepreneurs. Inflation is in check and has averaged five percent and the currency, the kip, has been rising steadily against the U.S. dollar. In practice, the Lao economy is highly dollarized. Laos' bill on imported oil remains large. The country's international reserves have been strengthened through investments in hydropower and mining. The government maintains controls of the price of gasoline and diesel. The economy is expected to grow by around seven to eight percent annually.

### Malaysia

Malaysia is one of ASEAN's more successful economies and has been declared a middle-income country. It boats a free market economy and is fully integrated into the global economy. It has benefited from the advantage of being located on the Straits of Malacca, one of the most important shipping lanes in the world that connect the trade route between the East and the West.

Stemming from agriculture and mining based economy in the 1970s, it has been able to transform (itself) into a high-tech industrialized nation. The country has a well-developed infrastructure and a vast array of natural resources. Over 59 percent of Malaysia is forested. It is a major producer of tin, palm oil, rubber, petroleum, copper, iron ore, natural gas, and bauxite. Services account for 48 percent GDP, industry accounts for 42 percent and agriculture 10 percent.

The manufacturing sector is productive in electronics, hard drives, and automobiles. The service sector has become increasingly important and this includes growth in real estate, transport, energy, telecommunications, distributive trade, hotel and tourism, financial services, information and computer services and health services. Malaysia has a well-diversified economy.

The economy has been growing at six percent to eight percent and GDP, as depicted in Figure 9.6, touched $381 billion in 2009. There was a decline, however, during the Asian financial crisis when the government fixed the exchange rate of its currency, the ringgit, to the U.S. dollar in order to leverage the decline.

Since 2006, the Malaysian ringgit has operated as a managed float. The country went through another steep decline during the global

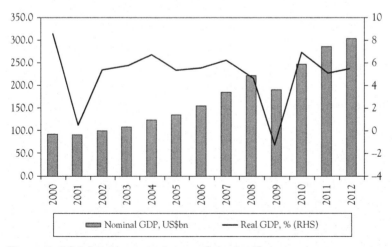

*Figure 9.6 Malaysia economic growth is significant*

economic stagnation of 2008–2009, but is slowly recovering. The government has injected the economy with a healthy stimulus package to jump-start growth. Inflation, unemployment, and poverty levels are low. The government has instituted banking and financial reforms. Local banks have consolidated and fiscal liberalization is being introduced gradually. Greater incentives are provided to invite foreign investment, especially in high-tech areas such as MSC Malaysia (MSC).[15]

The MSC Malaysia, formerly known as the Multimedia Super Corridor, is a Special Economic Zone (SEZ) in Malaysia, which was officially inaugurated by the fourth Malaysian Prime Minister Mahathir Mohamad on February 12, 1996. The establishment of the MSC program was crucial to accelerate the objectives of Vision 2020 and to transform Malaysia into a modern state by the year 2020, with the adoption of a knowledge-based society framework. Figure 9.7 provides an insight into Malaysia's growth outlook projections from 2013 through 2017 in various different sectors of the industry.

Exports remain the main driver of the economy, which totaled US$156 billion in 2009. Oil and gas exports provide 40 percent of government revenue. Other top exports are electronic equipment, semiconductors, wood and wood products, palm oil, rubber, textiles, and chemicals. The present government is working to catapult the economy further up the value-added production chain and reduce dependency on exports. It is

|  | | 2013 | 2014 | 2015 | 2016 | 2017 |
|---|---|---|---|---|---|---|
| Real GDP growth | 5.0 | 5.1 | 5.2 | 5.2 | 5.2 | |
| Domestic demand | 6.9 | 6.5 | 6.2 | 6.2 | 6.2 | |
| CPI inflation | 2.2 | 2.4 | 2.6 | 2.4 | 2.2 | |
| Gross domestic investment | 29.4 | 29.4 | 28.8 | 28.6 | 28.3 | |
| Gross national saving | 35.3 | 35.1 | 34.0 | 33.6 | 33.1 | |
| Federal government overall balance | –3.9 | –3.3 | –2.8 | –2.7 | –3.0 | |
| Revenue | 21.0 | 20.5 | 20.2 | 20.2 | 20.0 | |
| Expenditure and net lending | 24.9 | 23.8 | 23.1 | 23.0 | 23.0 | |
| Federal government debit | 53.1 | 52.3 | 50.8 | 49.5 | 48.8 | |
| Current account balance | 20.1 | 21.0 | 21.0 | 21.6 | 22.7 | |

*Figure 9.7 Malaysia's growth outlook projections 2013–2017*

Source: Trading economics, IMF Global Outlook Report

actively promoting investments in biotechnology, pharmaceuticals, manufacturing of automotive components, tourism, research and development, manpower development, and environment management. There are 13 free industrial zones (FIZ) and 12 free commercial zones (FCZ) where raw materials, products, and equipment may be imported with minimum customs formalities.

A unique feature of the Malaysian economy is the New Economic Policy (NEP) launched in 1971 to reduce the socioeconomic disparity between the Malay majority and the Chinese minority. It was primarily an affirmative action system with the end goal of transferring 30 percent of the country's wealth to the *bumiputera* (natives) Malays. The policy was implemented through programs that give preferential treatment to Malays through special rights in ownership of land and property, businesses, civil service jobs, education, politics, religion, and language. In 1991, this policy was renamed the National Development Policy (NDP); the modified NDP still espouses the original goals, income inequality had been reduced, and the main objectives had not transpired. Much debate over this has ensued and many have felt that this policy created a small and wealthy Malay elite, as it reduced the Chinese and Indian minorities to second-class citizens. Hence, April 2009, the government removed some of the controversial ethnic Malay affirmative action requirements.

Overall, the government is improving from its already favorable investment climate by allowing 100 percent ownership in the manufacturing industry, liberalizing the financial sector, and removing capital controls on overseas investments. Numerous infrastructure projects using state funding also have been initiated. Malaysia's purchasing power remains among the highest in ASEAN.

### Myanmar

Unlike most other ASEAN countries, Myanmar is not yet a fully free market economy. After it gained independence, as a reaction to years of colonization, the country adopted central planning, which resulted in a severe decline of the economy. From being one of the wealthiest export nations (rice, teak, mineral, and oil), it experienced severe inflation.

The subsequent military coup of 1962 saw further deterioration of the economy as Myanmar adopted the "Burmese Way of Socialism." Industries were nationalized and the state owned all sectors of the economy, leaving only agriculture to the masses. By 1987, Myanmar made the UN's list of least developed countries.

The country has suffered mismanagement of resources, low productivity, high inflation, large budget deficits and an overvalued currency, government control of financial institutions, poor infrastructure, and rampant corruption. In 1988 the government changed course and opened the economy to expansion of the private sector, encouraging foreign investment, and participation in some sectors. Progress has been slow but increased trade with regional neighbors, fellow ASEAN nations, India and China has resulted. There exists a large informal economy, which includes trade in currency and commodities.

Myanmar has immense natural resources but the economy remains essentially agro-based. Over 50 percent of its GDP is derived from rice and other crops such as sesame, groundnuts, sugarcane, livestock, fisheries, and forestry. Myanmar has one of the largest teak reserves in the world. It is also a net exporter of oil and natural gas and has substantial confirmed deposits. It has the 10th largest natural gas reserves in the world and the seventh largest in Asia. Precious stones are also abundant; 90 percent of the world's rubies come from Myanmar. It also produces large amounts of sapphires, pearls, and jade, which are exported mainly across the border to Thailand. A large illicit cross-border trade exists, as Western sanctions do not allow major jewelry companies to import gems from Myanmar. Manufacturing remains a small component of the economy, just over 10 percent in 2008. Food processing, mining (copper, tin, tungsten, and gems), cement, fertilizer, oil and natural gas production, and garments are its principal industries. The currency, the kyat, remains officially overvalued. A dual exchange rate exists and such inflation is a serious problem, which averaged 7 percent in 2009, down from 22 percent in 2008 and 33 percent in 2007.

Myanmar has not received any loans from the World Bank since 1987 or any assistance from the IMF despite its membership to both organizations. It has been a member of the ADB since 1973 but has received no

| Economic indicator | 2008 | 2009 | 2010 | 2011 | 2012 |
|---|---|---|---|---|---|
| Per capita GNI, Atlas method ($) | ... | ... | ... | ... | ... |
| GDP growth (% change per year) | 3.6 | 5.1 | 5.3 | 5.5 | 6.3 |
| CPI (% change per year) | 22.5 | 2.3 | 8.2 | 2.8 | 3.5 |
| Unemployment rate (%) | 4.0 | 4.0 | 4.0 | 4.0 | ... |
| Fiscal balance (% of GDP) | (2.5) | (5.2) | (5.4) | (3.9) | (5.4) |
| Export growth (% change per year) | 12.3 | (1.4) | 25.8 | 13.3 | 11.2 |
| Import growth (% change per year) | 25.6 | 1.9 | 15.8 | 24.4 | 22.0 |
| Current account balance (% of GDP) | (3.1) | (2.6) | (1.2) | (2.5) | (4.0) |
| External debt (% of GNI) | ... | ... | ... | ... | ... |

() = negative, . . . = data not available, CPI = consumer price index, GNI = gross domestic product, GDP = gross national income.

*Figure 9.8 Myanmar's economic indicators, 2008–2012*

Sources: ADB 2013, Asian Development Outlook

assistance in over 20 years. Its economic indicators, however, are positive, as depicted in Figure 9.8.

Liberalization of the economy is a work in progress. Production controls in agriculture have been removed. Privatization of state-owned enterprises is currently occurring. Over 100 state-owned companies were up for sale in 2010. The government reports that in 2009 it sold 260 state-owned buildings, factories, and land plots. With the opening of the economy, foreign investments from China, South Korea, India, and ASEAN countries, including Singapore, Malaysia, and Thailand have increased.

Tourism has grown and infrastructure is being developed with participation from foreign investors. New industrial zones are being developed. Myanmar is an active participant and member of the Greater Mekong Sub-region Economic Cooperation Program (the GMS Program) together with Cambodia, China, Laos, Thailand, and Vietnam as well as the Bay of Bengal Initiative for Multi-sectorial Technical and Economic Cooperation (BIMSTEC) with Bangladesh, Bhutan, India, Nepal, Sri Lanka, and Thailand. The Shwe Gas Project in the Bay of Bengal is a consortium of Kores Gas Corporation (KOGAS), which has a 51 percent stake; Oil and Natural Gas Corporation (ONGC), GAIL (India); and the Myanmar-state oil company. The government has signed a contract to sell production to China, which is building a pipeline connecting a gas field to China.

Myanmar has the highest potential for hydropower in Southeast Asia and the government has set the goal of generating all electricity from hydropower by 2030. There are over 36 hydropower plants under construction. China has invested $200 million of the total $600 million cost and helped in the construction of the largest hydropower project in Ye Village. Another large project under construction is the Ta Sang project, which involves the building of a dam on the Salween River in the northeast of the country. This is a joint venture with a Thai company MDX Group. The project should be completed by 2022, with the electricity produced being to Thailand. In return, Myanmar will receive a certain percentage of free power.

Myanmar's chief trading partners are Thailand, China, India, Singapore, Japan, Malaysia, and Indonesia. It has border trade agreements with China, India, Bangladesh, Thailand, and Laos. Several Memoranda of Understandings have been signed with these countries to expand bilateral trade. Myanmar remains isolated from much of the Western world and sanctions are still imposed by the United States, EU, Australia, and Canada. Trade with the United States and the EU were less than seven percent of total trade in 2007. Foreign currency reserves totaled $3.6 billion in 2009 mainly due to gas exports. GDP growth is estimated by the IMF to remain at around 5 percent for the next few years into 2015.

### The Philippines

The Philippines was hit in the fall of 2013 by a natural disaster of tremendous consequences and the level of damage caused by it will most likely slow down its economy for a while, as the effort of its people and government takes priority in creating a robust economy and better conditions for development.

The history of the Philippines economy goes back to the end of WWII. Then, there was strong economic expansion and the Philippines became one of the Asia's strongest economies. Sadly, the economy declined to become one of the poorest in the region due to years of economic mismanagement, political turmoil and misallocation of scarce resources. Oligopolies ruled a legacy of the U.S. colonial period, where farmland was concentrated in large estates.

As a policy, protectionism was used to prevent imports and restrictions were placed, preventing foreign ownership and other assets. This was exacerbated by rampant corruption, and tax revenue remained low at only 15 percent of the GDP. There was underinvestment in infrastructure and disproportionate economic development, with the region around Manila producing 36 percent of the output with only 12 percent of the population. The result was economic stagflation during the Marcos era, severe recession in the mid-1980s, and political instability during the Aquino years (1986–1992).

Crumbling infrastructure, trade and investment barriers, and a lack of competitiveness hampered long-term economic growth. More than half of GDP came from the service sector (53.5 percent); industry contributed 31.7 percent; and agriculture, forestry, and fishing accounted for the remaining 14.8 percent. Over 11 percent of the labor force was forced to go abroad to work and send remittances to their families. These remittances totaled $1.4 billion in 2007 and accounted for 10 percent of the GDP. A number of economic reforms were implemented during the Ramos presidency to help regain stability and the Philippine economy began to stabilize.

Macroeconomic stability has returned but long-term growth is doubtful due to poor infrastructure and education. GDP grew by 7.1 percent in 2007, the highest in 30 years. In 2008, GDP growth slowed to 3.7 percent. This was mainly the result of high inflation coupled with the worldwide downturn in export demand. Furthermore, the Philippines have suffered from a strong decrease in capital investment. Services grew by 3.1 percent in 2008 and 2.8 percent in 2009. Manufacturing had slightly better growth, despite drops in orders in the fourth quarter. Construction showed strong growth, while mining, metals, and agriculture displayed a sluggish performance.

The budget has shown a deficit every year since 1998, though trends in the last decade have been encouraging. The deficit is a direct result of overspending and poor collection of revenue. Attempts are being made to bring down debt ratios and raising new taxes has helped. Value added tax (VAT) was implemented in 2005 and raised from 10 percent to 12 percent and expanded its coverage. A law passed to increase revenue using a performance-based collection system. Though a deficit remains despite efforts to balance the budget for five consecutive years, deficit spending is considered necessary to cope with the economic crisis. A deficit of 0.9 percent of GDP was seen in 2008 and 3.2 percent in 2009.

Another source of revenue that needs improvement is the extractive industry. It is estimated that the Philippines possesses untapped mineral wealth of $840 billion. Mining has declined from 30 percent to only one percent of GDP but the country was a top mining producer in the 1970s and 1980s. In 2004, the Philippine Supreme Court ruled that foreign companies would be permitted to obtain mining and energy contracts with the Philippine government. Foreign companies now are permitted to own up to 100 percent equity and invest in large-scale exploration, development and utilization of minerals, oils, and gas. GDP grew at around 1.1 percent in 2009 and 3.5 percent in 2010.

The government has taken steps to jumpstart the economy by introducing a $7 billion stimulus package. This money will be used to expand welfare, improve infrastructure, and provide tax breaks for both private citizens and corporations. The country continues to have strong potential especially in the areas of mining, natural gas production, manufacturing, business process outsourcing (BPO), and tourism.

Inflation and unemployment remain major challenges. Infrastructure must be improved and greater reforms put in place to increase productivity and competitiveness. Tax revenues need to be increased further and reduction of poverty remains a top priority. We believe that trade liberalization to spur investment and increase competitiveness can help achieve greater growth. These reforms would lower cost of doing business and removing obstacles to growth.

Philippine GDP growth, as shown in Figure 9.9, which cooled from 7.6 percent in 2010 to 3.9 percent in 2011, expanded to 6.6 percent in 2012—meeting the government's targeted six percent to seven percent growth range. The 2012 expansion partly reflected a rebound from depressed 2011 exports and public sector spending levels. The economy has weathered global economic and financial downturns better than its regional peers due to minimal exposure to troubled international

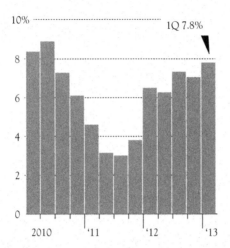

*Figure 9.9 Philippines economic growth 2010–2013*

Source: National Statistical Coordination Board, the Wall Street Journal

securities, lower dependence on exports, relatively resilient domestic consumption, large remittances from four- to five-million overseas Filipino
workers, and a rapidly expanding business process outsourcing industry.
The current account balance had recorded consecutive surpluses since
2003; international reserves are at record highs; the banking system is
stable; and the stock market was Asia's second best performer in 2012.

Efforts to improve tax administration and expenditure management
have helped ease the Philippines' tight fiscal situation and reduce high
debt levels. The Philippines received several credit rating upgrades on its
sovereign debt in 2012, and has had little difficulty tapping domestic and
international markets to finance its deficits. Achieving a higher growth
path nevertheless remains a pressing challenge.

Economic growth in the Philippines averaged 4.5 percent during the
Macapagal-Arroyo administration but poverty worsened during her term.
Growth has accelerated under the Aquino government, but with limited
progress thus far in improving the quality of jobs and bringing down
unemployment, which hovers around seven percent. Underemployment
is nearly 20 percent and more than 40 percent of the employed are estimated to be working in the informal economy sector. The Aquino administration has been working to boost the budgets for education, health,
cash transfers to the poor, and other social spending programs, and is

relying on the private sector to help fund major infrastructure projects under its Public-Private Partnership program. Long-term challenges include reforming governance and the judicial system, building infrastructure, and improving regulatory predictability.

### Singapore

Singapore has a highly developed and successful free-market economy. It enjoys a remarkably open and corruption-free environment, stable prices, and a per capita GDP higher than that of most developed countries. The economy depends heavily on exports, particularly in consumer electronics, information technology products, pharmaceuticals, and on a growing financial services sector. Real GDP growth averaged 8.6 percent between 2004 and 2007.

The economy contracted one percent in 2009, as shown in Figure 9.10, as a result of the global financial crisis, but rebounded 14.8 percent in 2010, on the strength of renewed exports, before slowing to 4.9 percent in 2011 and 2.1 percent in 2012. This was largely a result of soft demand for exports during the second European recession. Over the longer term, the government hopes to establish a new growth path that focuses on

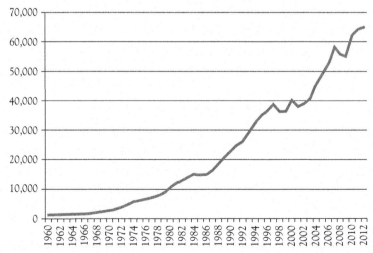

*Figure 9.10 Singapore's annual per capita GDP*

Source: Singapore Department of Statistics.

raising productivity, which has sunk to a compounded annual growth rate of just 1.8 percent in the last decade. Singapore has attracted major investments in pharmaceuticals and medical technology production and will continue efforts to establish itself as Southeast Asia's financial and high-tech hub.

Singapore is poised to undertake a plethora of reforms in order to be one of the hubs of the global economy. Political pressure is forcing Singapore to rethink the liberal immigration policy that was once part of its strategy to become a global city. Although creative foreign workers have contributed greatly to economic development, at the same time its liberal immigration policy creates many non-negligible issues, and ones in which society will need to cope. The government is tightening entry conditions for foreign workers, while at the same time encouraging foreign entrepreneurs. It is investing heavily in development of human capital of indigenous workers and encouraging businesses to upgrade their technology and production methods.

As part of that investment effort, the government has lent strong backing to small and medium-sized enterprises (SMEs). They account for over half of total enterprise value and employ nearly 70 percent of the workforce. Their rise, though, has been largely driven by government policy, which has funded them and boosted domestic market growth. This begs the question as to how sustainable this state's SME policy is in the long term. R&D is considered an important component of Singapore's policy of productivity-driven economic growth. In the last two years since 2013, the government has brought local SMEs into R&D with cash incentives to help them develop.

Combined public and private R&D expenditure have put Singapore among the most R&D-intensive countries. Nevertheless, it lags behind in private R&D spending. As a small city-state with no natural resources, Singapore has been careful in managing its human capital, regarding such management as an important source of competitiveness and strength for the economy. Over the years, public expenditure on education has consistently been the second highest, after defense, in the government's annual fiscal budget. In the 2012 budget, for example, expenditure on education claimed a 17.9 percent share, compared with 20.8 percent for defense. Such emphasis on education has helped contribute to Singapore's stronger record in human capital development than other countries in the region. Over the past decade, a major force shaping the human capital landscape in Singapore has been the increased presence of foreign workers.

As part of the overall strategy to transform Singapore into a global city, the government aggressively liberalized the foreign worker and immigration policy.[16] From 2000 to 2011, the number of nonresidents rose from 754,500 to 1,394,400, representing a jump from 18.7 percent to 26.9 percent of the total population. In contrast, the share of Singapore citizens (excluding permanent residents and nonresidents) in the population steadily declined from 74.1 percent in 2000 to 62.8 percent in 2011.[17] The aggressive pursuit of the global city vision has transformed not only the physical look of the city-state, but also its business environment and production coupled with these changes.

The composition of the labor force has also been significantly altered— both in terms of the local-foreign mix and the mix between workers in *old* and *new* industries. While the open-door labor policy brought in a large number of highly skilled, high wage foreign workers, it has also led to a huge influx of low-skilled, low-wage foreign workers. Whereas the former could potentially expand the economy's range of skill sets and raise its productivity level, the latter could substantially offset such positive effects. Indeed, with the readily available low-wage foreign workers, firms in Singapore might not find many incentives to upgrade their technologies and production structures, or to invest in training or upgrading workers' skills sets.

### Thailand

Recent political unrest in Bangkok and other cities, due to deep divisions in Thai society, has created uncertainty for the future of this vibrant economy. With a well-developed infrastructure, a free-enterprise economy, generally pro-investment policies, and strong export industries, Thailand has achieved steady growth largely due to industrial and agriculture exports— mostly electronics, agricultural commodities, and processed foods.

Bangkok is trying to maintain growth by encouraging domestic consumption and public investment. Unemployment, at less than one percent of the labor force, stands at one of the lowest levels in the world, which puts upward pressure on wages in some industries. Thailand also attracts nearly 2.5 million migrant workers from neighboring countries. Bangkok is implementing a nation-wide 300 baht per day minimum wage policy and deploying new tax reforms designed to lower rates on middle-income earners.

The Thai economy has both internal and external economic shocks in recent years. The global economic crisis severely cut Thailand's exports, with most sectors experiencing double-digit drops. In 2009, the economy contracted 2.3 percent. However, in 2010, Thailand's economy expanded 7.8 percent, its fastest pace since 1995, as exports rebounded. In late 2011 historic flooding in the industrial areas north of Bangkok, crippled the manufacturing sector and interrupted growth. Industry has recovered since the second quarter of 2012 and GDP expanded 5.8 percent in 2012. The government has invested in flood mitigation projects to prevent similar economic damage.

## Vietnam

Vietnam is one of the success stories of Asia's revival, a country marked by tragedy and despair because of the conflict that desecrated the former Indochina and ended three decades ago. The Vietnamese quickly learned the lessons from the changing international environment. Even before the dissolution of the former Soviet Union, this densely populated developing country has transitioned from the rigidities of a centrally planned economy since 1986. Vietnamese authorities have reaffirmed their commitment to economic modernization in recent years.

Agriculture's share of economic output has continued to shrink from about 25 percent in 2000 to less than 22 percent in 2012, while industry's share increased from 36 percent to nearly 41 percent in the same period. State-owned enterprises account for 40 percent of the GDP. Notwithstanding, in terms of nominal GDP, Vietnam's economy has grown consistently since 2000, as shown in Figure 9.11. Likewise, poverty has declined significantly, and Vietnam is working to create jobs to meet the challenge of a labor force that is growing by more than one million people every year.

Unfortunately, what is also depicted in Figure 9.11, the global recession hurt Vietnam's export-oriented economy, with real GDP in 2009–12

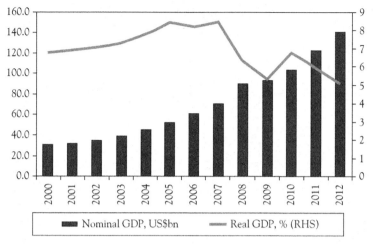

*Figure 9.11 In terms of nominal GDP, Vietnam's economy has grown consistently since 2000*

growing less than the seven percent per annum average achieved during the previous decade. In 2012, however, exports increased by more than 12 percent, year-on-year; several administrative actions brought the trade deficit back into balance. Between 2008 and 2011, Vietnam's managed currency, the dong, was devalued in excess of 20 percent, but its value remained stable in 2012.

Foreign direct investment inflows fell 4.5 percent to $10.5 billion in 2012. Foreign donors have pledged $6.5 billion in new development assistance for 2013. Hanoi has vacillated between promoting growth and emphasizing macroeconomic stability in recent years. In February 2011, the government shifted away from policies aimed at achieving a high rate of economic growth, which had fueled inflation, to those aimed at stabilizing the economy, through tighter monetary and fiscal control.

In early 2012 Vietnam unveiled a broad, *three-pillar* economic reform program, proposing the restructuring of public investment, state-owned enterprises, and the banking sector. Vietnam's economy continues to face challenges from an undercapitalized banking sector. Non-performing loans weigh heavily on banks and businesses. In September 2012, the official bad debt ratio climbed to 8.8 percent, though some financial analysts believe it could be as high as 15 percent.

# CHAPTER 10

# Can MENA's Rise Be Powered by BRICS?

## Overview of the MENA Region

This chapter provides an overview of the MENA (Middle East and North Africa) region followed by a review of recent trade and investment relations between MENA and BRICS countries. It also reviews and discusses challenges and opportunities for economic development arising from the complementarities and interactions between countries form both blocs.

The people of the MENA region have long played an integral, if somewhat volatile, role in the history of human civilization. MENA is one of the cradles of civilization and of urban culture. Three of the world's major religions originated in this region, including Judaism, Christianity, and Islam. Universities existed in this region long before they did in Europe. In today's world, MENA's politics, religion, and economics have been inextricably tied in ways that affect the world economy. The region's vast petroleum supply, which accounts for two-thirds of the world's known oil reserves, is a major reason for the world's interest, especially from advanced economies. MENA's influence, however, extends beyond its rich oil fields. It occupies a strategically important geographic position between Asia, Africa, and Europe. It has often been caught in a tug-of-war of land and influence that affects the entire world.

According to the World Bank[1] the diversity of countries in the MENA region, as depicted in Figure 10.1, is great, particularly in terms of population and resources, and can be segmented in three groups:

- Oil exporters—these countries are rich in resources and have large shares of foreign residents. It is comprised of the six Gulf Cooperation Council (GCC) members (Bahrain, Kuwait,

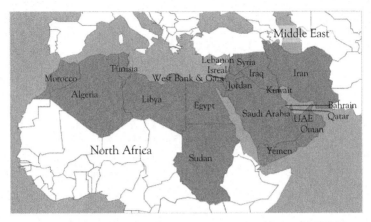

*Figure 10.1  Map of the Middle East and North Africa (MENA) Region*

Oman, Qatar, Saudi Arabia, and the United Arab Emirates) and Libya.

- Developing countries—these are countries rich in resources with large native populations and include Algeria, Iran, Iraq, Syria, and Yemen.
- Oil importing countries—these are countries poor in resources that are small producers or importers of oil and gas, and include Egypt, Morocco, Tunisia, Jordan, and Lebanon.

In terms of population, the MENA region has quadrupled from 1950 to 2007, and is expected to increase by 60 percent until 2050. MENA's rapid population growth exacerbates the challenges that this region of the world faces as it enters the third millennium. For hundreds of years, the population of MENA hovered around 30 million, but reached 60 million early in the 20th century. Only in the second half of the 20th century the population growth in the region gained momentum. The total population increased from 100 million in 1950 to 380 million in 2000, an extra 280 million people in only 50 years.

As depicted in Figure 10.2, during this period the population of the MENA region increased 3.7 times, more than any other major world region over the past century. MENA's annual population growth reached a peak of 3 percent around 1980, while the growth rate for world as a whole reached

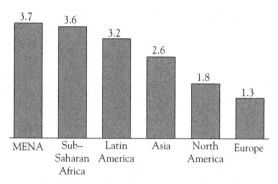

**Figure 10.2  Ratio of Population Size in 2000 to Population Size in 1950, by Major World Regions**

*Source*: United Nations, World Population Prospects: The 2000 Revision (New York: United Nations, 2001)

its peak of 2 percent annually more than a decade earlier.* Improvements in human survival, particularly during the second half of the 20th century, led to rapid population growth in MENA. The introduction of modern medical services and public health interventions, such as antibiotics, immunization, and sanitation, caused death rates to drop rapidly in the developing world after 1950, while the decline in birth rates lagged behind, resulting in high rates of natural increase (the surplus of births over deaths).[2]

On average, fertility in MENA declined from seven children per woman (1960) to 3.6 children (2001). The total fertility rate, the average number of births per woman, is less than three in Bahrain, Iran, Lebanon, Tunisia, and Turkey, and is more than five in Iraq, Oman, Palestinian Territory, Saudi Arabia, and Yemen. Even though the decline in fertility rates is expected to continue in the MENA region, the population will continue to grow rapidly for several decades. In a number of countries, each generation of young people enters childbearing years in greater numbers than the previous generation, so as a whole they will produce a larger number of births. The population of the region is increasing at two percent per year, the second highest rate in the world after sub-Saharan Africa. Nearly seven million people are added each year. As indicated in Figure 10.3, the population growth is most significant in the Western Asian countries encompassing Iran, Iraq, Israel, Jordan, Lebanon, Palestinian Territory, Syria, and Turkey.

---

* At a 3 percent rate of growth, a population doubles in size in 23 years.

| | Pop. mid-2001 (millions) | Births per 1,000 pop. | Deaths per 1,000 pop. | Rate of natural increase (%) | Projected pop. (millions) | | Projected pop. change 2001–2050 (%) | Percent urban | Percent of pop. age | |
|---|---|---|---|---|---|---|---|---|---|---|
| | | | | | 2025 | 2050 | | | <> | 65+ |
| Middle East and North Africa | 385.6 | 26 | 7 | 2 | 568.7 | 719.4 | 87 | 59 | 36 | 4 |
| Algeria | 31 | 25 | 6 | 1.9 | 43.2 | 51.5 | 66 | 49 | 39 | 4 |
| Bahrain | 0.7 | 21 | 3 | 1.9 | 1.7 | 2.9 | 300 | 88 | 31 | 2 |
| Egypt | 69.8 | 28 | 7 | 2.1 | 96.2 | 114.7 | 64 | 43 | 36 | 4 |
| Iran | 66.1 | 18 | 6 | 1.2 | 88.4 | 100.2 | 52 | 64 | 36 | 5 |
| Iraq | 23.6 | 37 | 10 | 2.7 | 40.3 | 53.6 | 127 | 68 | 42 | 3 |
| Israel | 6.4 | 22 | 6 | 1.6 | 8.9 | 10.6 | 64 | 91 | 29 | 10 |
| Jordan | 5.2 | 27 | 5 | 2.2 | 3.7 | 11.8 | 128 | 79 | 40 | 5 |
| Kuwait | 2.3 | 20 | 2 | 1.8 | 4.2 | 6.4 | 181 | 100 | 26 | 1 |
| Lebanon | 4.3 | 23 | 7 | 1.7 | 5.4 | 5.8 | 35 | 88 | 29 | 7 |
| Libya | 5.2 | 23 | 4 | 2.4 | 8.3 | 10.3 | 106 | 36 | 37 | 4 |
| Morocco | 29.2 | 26 | 6 | 2 | 40.5 | 48.4 | 66 | 55 | 33 | 5 |

| Oman | 2.4 | 39 | 4 | 3.5 | 4.9 | 7.6 | 218 | 72 | 41 | 2 |
| Palestine[4] | 3.3 | 42 | 5 | 3.7 | 7.4 | 11.2 | 239 | – | 47 | 4 |
| Qatar | 0.6 | 31 | 4 | 2.7 | 0.8 | 0.9 | 45 | 91 | 27 | 2 |
| Saudi Arabia | 21.1 | 35 | 6 | 2.9 | 40.9 | 60.3 | 185 | 83 | 43 | 2 |
| Syria | 17.1 | 31 | 6 | 2.6 | 27.1 | 35.2 | 106 | 50 | 41 | 3 |
| Tunisia | 9.7 | 19 | 6 | 1.3 | 12.5 | 14.2 | 46 | 62 | 31 | 6 |
| Turkey | 66.3 | 22 | 7 | 1.5 | 85.2 | 97.2 | 47 | 66 | 30 | 6 |
| United Arab Emirates | 3.3 | 18 | 4 | 1.4 | 4.5 | 5.1 | 54 | 84 | 26 | 1 |
| Yemen | 18 | 44 | 11 | 3.3 | 39.6 | 71.1 | 295 | 26 | 48 | 3 |

*Figure 10.3 Population Size and Growth of MENA Region*

Sources: Carl Haub and Diana Cornelius, 2001 World Population Data Sheet; UNICEF, The State of the World's Children 2001, Table 7

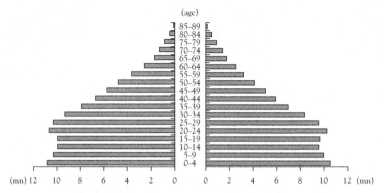

*Figure 10.4 MENA's population pyramid, 287 million, 2010*

MENA's demographics of a young population pose both strengths and weaknesses as shown in Figure 10.4.

When it comes to economic performance of MENA in terms of GDP, the region has essentially two distinct groups of countries: the Gulf countries that until 2011 have had a GDP per capita above US$10,000; and the North Africa and other Middle East countries, which have not exceeded US$5,000 per capita, as depicted in Figure 10.5. This variation in development levels indicates the superior performance of the resource-rich labor importing countries. However, as discussed later, the reasons for these outcomes are not solely related to resources but also with the historical and institutional development of the MENA's countries before, during, and post colonial times.[3]

According to IMF Survey Magazine,[4] the healthy growth rates of the region's oil exporters—Algeria, Bahrain, Iran, Iraq, Kuwait, Libya, Oman, Qatar, Saudi Arabia, the United Arab Emirates, and Yemen—are projected to moderate from an average of 5.7 percent in 2012 to 3.2 percent in 2013. This is mainly due to a scaling back of increases in oil production amid modest global demand. The average real GDP per capita from 1980 to 2010, however, lagged significantly behind other regions of the world, as depicted in Figure 10.6. Nevertheless, despite the recent turmoil in the MENA region, GDP is expected to be over five percent by 2016.

By contrast, the region's oil importers—Afghanistan, Djibouti, Egypt, Jordan, Lebanon, Mauritania, Morocco, Pakistan, Sudan, and Tunisia—face a difficult external environment. On average, this group of

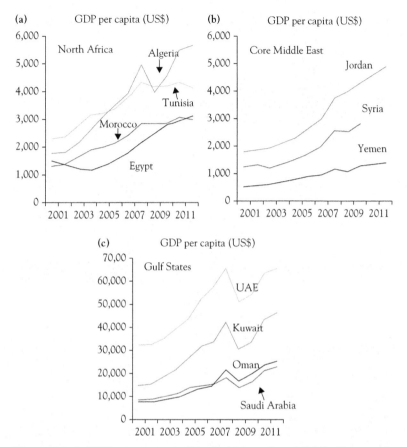

**Figure 10.5 GDP per capita in North Africa, Core Middle East, and Gulf Countries[5]**

countries is projected to post moderate growth of three percent in 2013. For the Arab countries in transition, continued political uncertainty is preventing growth. Hence, to assess to what extent the MENA region has benefited from globalization it is worthwhile to examine exports and FDI flows. In regards to exports we find that the percentage of non-oil exports in MENA region is significantly lower than in emerging countries in Asia and other low and middle income countries, as depicted in Figure 10.7, suggesting that the region is not as globally integrated as others.

Second, in terms of FDI inflows to the region, we find that in the period from 1995 to 2011 the FDI inflow to the MENA region was

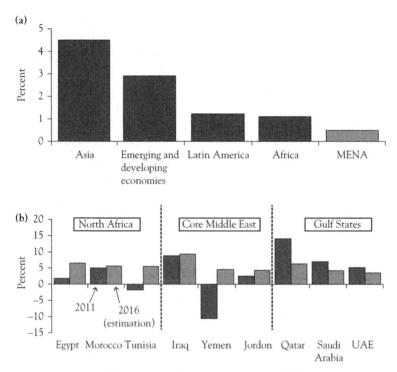

**Figure 10.6 Real GDP per capita and expected GDP growth in selected MENA countries**

*Source*: IMF

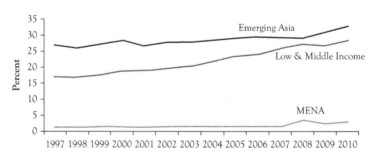

**Figure 10.7 Non-fuel exports (percentage of world non-oil exports)**

stagnant and lower than the world average. This was true again after the 2008 world crisis, as depicted in Figure 10.8.

With high fiscal deficits and reduced international reserve buffers, many oil importers have no time to waste embarking on difficult policy

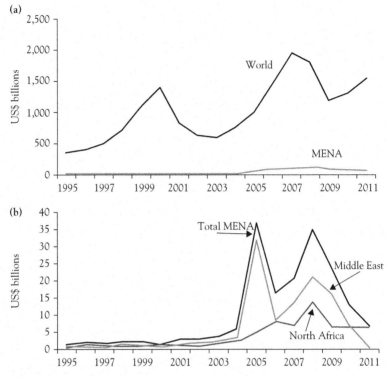

*Figure 10.8 FDI flows to the MENA region relative to the world and after 2008 world crisis*

choices—considerable fiscal consolidation, implemented in a growth-friendly and socially balanced way—and greater exchange rate flexibility. This should help maintain macroeconomic stability, instill confidence, preserve competitiveness, and mobilize external financing, thus putting in place important preconditions for a healthy economic recovery.*

Finally, it is important to understand the role of tourism as source of revenue in the MENA region. With its world-class combination of cultural and natural attractions, the MENA region, according to the World Bank,[6] has long held a powerful allure for tourists. It has made tourism an important source of revenue and growth. In 2011, the industry contributed an estimated US$107.3 dollars, representing 4.5 percent of the region's GDP, and accounted for 4.5 million jobs, almost seven percent of total employment. Figure 10.9 illustrates the percentage of tourism

---

* Ibidem.

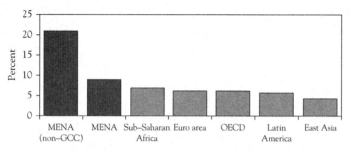

*Figure 10.9 International tourism receipts (percent total exports), 2010*

revenues for 2010 between the non-Gulf Cooperation Council (GCC) MENA countries, the MENA, and other regions of the world.

## Long-term Issues of the MENA Countries

According to O'Sullivan and Galvez[7] at the World Economic Forum (WEF), the Arab Spring has accentuated problems in the MENA region that already existed for some time. These issues include a high level of unemployment, which is more acute among youth, pervasive corruption combined with lack of transparency and accountability, a bloated public sector that hinders the development of private enterprises, limited levels of entrepreneurship, and inflation in resource-poor countries.* Therefore, the MENA bloc could substantially benefit from other blocs, particularly the BRICS.

To understand how MENA could be further connected with the BRICS countries it is important that we take a closer examination of each of these internal issues.

- **Unemployment**—Data from WEF[†] suggests that in the MENA region the Palestinian Authority has the highest unemployment rate (above 20 percent) followed by Yemen, Tunisia, Jordan, and Algeria (above 10 percent), whereas the GCC countries have the lowest rates, as depicted in Figure 10.10A. However, unemployment is particularly serious among young people (15–24 years old), as depicted in Figure 10.10B.

---

* Ibidem.
† Ibidem.

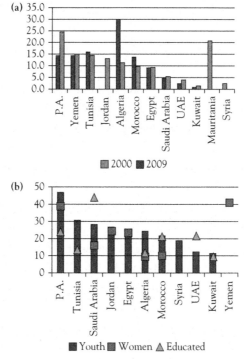

**Figure 10.10A and B  Unemployment rates in MENA**

*Source:* O'Sullivan, Rey, and Galvez, 2011, based on World Bank data

As O'Sullivan point out, every year there are about 2.8 million young workers who enter the labor market but they find it increasingly more difficult to procure viable employment. Moreover, few countries, such as Saudi Arabia, Palestine, Morocco, and UAE have a large percentage of unemployed who are educated due to a persistent mismatch between job market requirements and skills acquired at a university. Lastly, the gender gap in unemployment, meaning the very low participation of women in the labor force, indicates another missed opportunity for the optimization of resources for economic development.

- **Corruption, lack of transparency, and poor accountability—** The Arab Spring was motivated in large part for these three issues, the solution to which will invariably mean a change to the political structures in most of the MENA countries.

According to Transparency International only* two MENA
countries perform well in the corruption index: Qatar at 7.7,
and UAE at 6.3[†], with the average score for the MENA region
at 3.1. The reform processes in some MENA countries, such
as Egypt and Tunisia, however, promise to change the institutional frameworks, with transparency likely to increase.

- **Bloated public sector distorts labor markets**—Employment
  in the public sector ranges from 22 percent in Tunisia to
  about 33–35 percent in Syria, Jordan, and Egypt, but if we
  exclude the agricultural sector then the public sector employment reaches 42 percent in Jordan and 70 percent in Egypt.
  The public sector provides higher salaries, job security, and
  social status that the private sector cannot match, thus reducing the pool of qualified candidates for the private sector.
  Moreover, during periods of crisis many of the MENA's governments have responded by increasing salaries and creating
  more jobs to appease discontent and increase consumption.
  This has short and long term consequences. In the short term
  it offers relief and an economy with a stimulus; in the long
  term it has a negative impact on the public budget's sustainability, particularly in resource-poor countries, and inhibits
  the innovation and entrepreneurship in the private sector.

- **Low entrepreneurship levels**—The World Bank Group
  Entrepreneurship Survey[8] suggests that in high-income
  countries there are about four companies created per 1000
  working people, whereas in the MENA the average is only
  0.63 new firms. In the BRICS region the rates are 2.17 new
  firms in Brazil, 4.3 in Russia, 0.12 in India, and no available data for China or South Africa. Based on the OECD
  research O'Sullivan[9] mentioned, low business creation in
  MENA region is due to the high barriers for small firms doing
  business (e.g., corruption, licenses, rigid laws, taxes, unfair
  competition), lower social status attached to entrepreneurial

---

\* http://archive.transparency.org/regional_pages/africa_middle_east/middle_
east_and_north_africa_mena, last accessed 01/03/2014.

[†] Scale from low=1 to high=10.

activity as compared with public sector, and low participation of women in the workforce.

- **High inflation in resource-poor MENA countries**—The average inflation in the MENA countries from 1999 to 2005 was about three percent but it increased to 6.5 percent in the following five years (2006–2010). While the resource-rich countries found compensatory measures to cope with negative effects of inflation, the resource-poor countries did not. The reason for high inflation in resource-poor countries is mainly due to a spike in import prices of food and fuel. O'Sullivan et al* note that given the rising incomes of middle class in most emerging economies and the instability in MENA countries, the inflation is likely to continue here.

In addition to the factors described, the economic growth of the MENA region is also due to other economic and structural factors, namely low levels of competitiveness in manufacturing sectors, lack of export-market diversification, and low intra-regional integration.[†] These issues present opportunities for the BRIC countries, which can provide assistance and complementarities for furthering economic development in the MENA region. Thus, it is important that we review the recent economic developments in the MENA region.

## The Economic Impact of the Arab Spring

When comparing the economic performance of the MENA region to other regions, we find that MENA countries have been performing relatively well, on par with sub-Saharan Africa and Latin America, but below emerging Asian countries, yet above OECD and EU countries as depicted in Figure 10.11.

The impact of the Arab Spring has had varying effects in the MENA region depending on the extent of the turmoil and economic fundamentals. First, the political and social instability caused an immediate negative effect in the countries affected by the turmoil. However, as O'Sullivan et al[‡]12 noted, the countries with stronger economic fundamentals, such

---

* Ibidem.
† Ibidem.
‡ Ibidem.

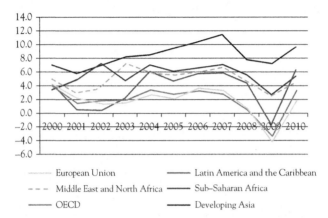

**Figure 10.11  GDP growth by region, percent change, constant prices**

Source: O'Sullivan et al, 2011, based on IMF and OECD data

as Egypt and Tunisia, are expected to recover faster if a successful political transition and economic reform continue to be implemented. In contrast, countries such as Morocco and Jordan did not experience significant tensions but their respective economies are more exposed to negative spillovers and likely to recover at a slower pace. Second, the turmoil caused a significant rise in oil prices, which indirectly benefited the resource-rich countries. Moreover, the weak economic performance of OECD countries is likely to have a negative impact in MENA countries as trade and investment originated at OECD is likely to remain slow.

## Trade Diversification and Intra-Regional Trade Are Low

In 2009 the trade of the MENA region was US$932 billion in exports and US$742 billion in imports, however it was not diversified. The major export category in MENA countries is oil, representing about 62 percent of total exports, while the imports are manufactured goods, 54 percent of the total imports, as depicted in Figure 10.12.

Regarding MENA's partners, as of 2011 the most significant was the EU followed by China and the United States, as depicted in Figure 10.13. Note however, that as a single country China is the most influential trading partner of MENA.

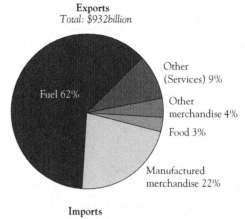

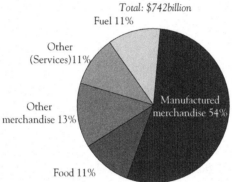

*Figure 10.12 MENA's Exports and Imports of Goods and Services with the World, by Commodity, or Type of Service, 2009*

Source: Akhtar, Bolle, & Nelson, 2013

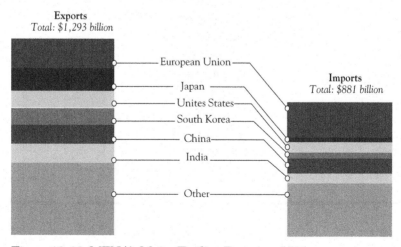

*Figure 10.13 MENA's Major Trading Partners, 2011*

Source: Akhtar, Bolle, & Nelson, 2013

MENA has failed, however, to increase its global market share in part because the region's exports flow mainly to Europe and are concentrated in traditional products. Europe has been the main destination for MENA exports, reflecting proximity, and long-standing linkages. Since the 1970s, the region's exports to Europe have accounted for close to 60 percent of total exports, while exports to Asia Pacific and Latin America, respectively, have accounted for 15 percent and one percent of total exports. Until the mid-1970s, the focus on European markets linked the region to an engine of global growth. But, more recently, this focus has implied that MENA has not been benefiting from the high growth rates achieved in emerging Asian and Latin American powerhouses, including Brazil, India, and China.

Notwithstanding, exports from the MENA region have increased significantly in the past years. When considering exports as a percentage of GDP, MENA's exports have increased from 35 percent in 1990, to 39.2 percent in 2000, up to 53 percent in 2009.* However, as O'Sullivan and his colleagues noted, a closer analysis reveals two noteworthy trends. First, the increase of exports is mainly due to increased value of oil exports from resource-rich countries, as depicted in Figure 10.14.

And second, the current account balance of resource-poor countries is worsening, as depicted in Figure 10.15. Looking ahead, there

---

* Ibidem.

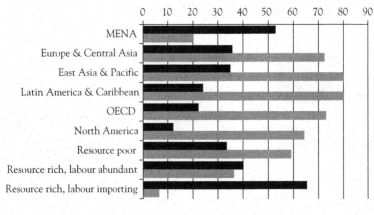

■ Exports (% of GDP)   ■ Manufactured exports (% of merchandise exports)

*Figure 10.14 Exports as a share of GDP are high in MENA, but manufactured exports are comparatively low*

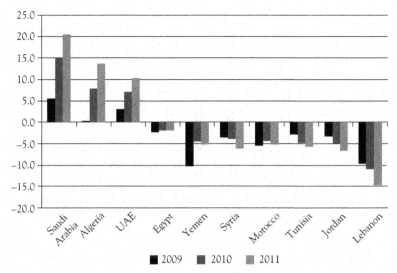

*Figure 10.15 Current account balance as percent of GDP*

are unknowns as to the timing of Europe's recovery. Moreover, there is a broad consensus that, over the medium term, growth in Europe will lag behind that of emerging Asia and Latin America. As such, it is even more important to redirect MENA's exports to these dynamic regions of the global economy, such as the BRICS and ASEAN, and to allow MENA to link more closely to the new growth engines and thus provide a foundation for high and sustained growth.

MENA exports, according to IMF's Masood Ahmed[10] have primarily concentrated on consumer goods, and less so in high value-added, high technology, intermediate and capital goods, which have seen the most growth in recent years. Consumer and primary goods currently account for 64 percent of total exports in this region, compared to 41 percent for Asian countries, 57 percent for Latin American countries, and 66 percent for African countries. Capital goods, on the other hand, account for only six percent of MENA exports, similar to the seven percent in low-income countries, while they account for 37 percent of Asian exports and 11 percent of Latin American exports. These export patterns hold back MENA's potential for trade and, indeed, MENA countries trade less with the rest of the world than could be expected. MENA's total exports in 2009 amounted to only 28 percent of GDP, compared to 30 percent

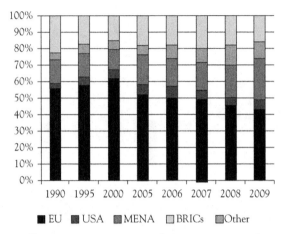

*Figure 10.16 Resource-poor countries' main export market is the EU, and BRIC markets is still modest*

for Asia Pacific, 56 percent when excluding the three largest economies, Japan, India, and China, given that large economies typically have lower export shares.

When examining the export markets for MENA countries we find that the resource-poor countries mostly export to the EU, and that intra-regional trade among MENA countries has increased, but compared with EU and other markets it is still modest, as shown in Figure 10.16. Moreover, in terms of trade with the BRICS countries the exports have increased, but are not yet significant, which suggests that there may be opportunities for further exports into the BRICS markets.

A country's export volumes are driven partly by characteristics such as proximity to markets, tariff rates, the establishment of free trade agreements, or cultural linkages with trading partners. However, these characteristics do not explain MENA's low export-to-GDP ratio—quite the opposite. Looking at the exports of the each MENA country, as depicted in Figure 10.17, we find other interesting patterns. First, Tunisia and Morocco have a large percentage of exports to EU. Second, Mauritania's exports are concentrated in the BRIC, particularly China, where it exports 40 percent of iron ore. Third, Lebanon, Djibouti, and Jordan send most of their exports to MENA countries. Lastly, Egypt is the country with the most balanced export markets.

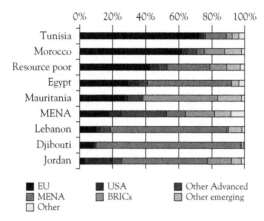

Figure 10.17 *Resource-poor countries' main export market is the EU, but to varying degrees*

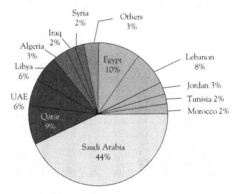

Figure 10.18 *FDI inflows to the MENA region, 2010*

Trade variations, as noted by O'Sullivan et al,[11] are due in part to varying supply and demand chains. In terms of demand, China imports oil, gas, natural resources, and EU manufactured goods.

### Foreign Direct Investment at MENA

As of 2010, foreign direct investment (FDI) in MENA countries amounted to US$64.5 billion, and nearly two thirds of which derives from resource-rich countries, namely in Saudi Arabia, which attracted over 44 percent of MENA's total FDI.* The resource-poor countries attracted about 25 percent of the FDI, as shown in Figure 10.18, with

---

* Ibidem.

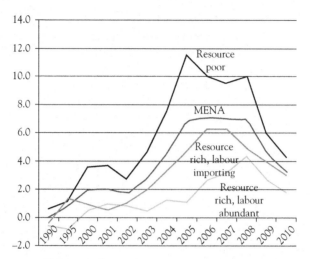

*Figure 10.19* **FDI as a share of GDP in the MENA region, 2010**

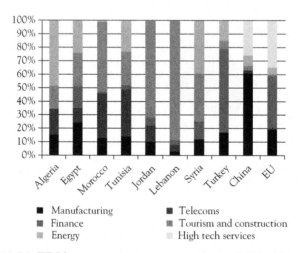

*Figure 10.20* **FDI by economic sector, cumulative 2000–07, percent of GDP**

Egypt and Lebanon as the main recipients. The remaining FDI was chan-
neled to resource-rich countries characterized by political instability.
Overall the data suggests that investments are attracted by opportunities
in resource-rich countries provided they offer a relatively stable context.

Interestingly, when considering FDI as a share of GDP (Figure 10.19),
we find that resource-poor countries are performing better than other
countries in the region, which points to increasing opportunities for

investment. The FDI inflow to resource-poor countries jumped from 0.6 percent of GDP in 1990 to 12 percent in the mid-2000s. Due to the financial crisis of 2008–09, there was a decline, but the relative performance of the resource-rich countries remained.

When looking at non-energy sectors that have attracted FDI to resource-poor countries we find that it is attributed mostly to service industries, namely telecommunications, tourism, and construction, while the manufacturing industries have received a low level of FDI, as depicted in Figure 10.20.

## Integration of BRICS with MENA

The economic integration of MENA's region with Brazil, Russia, India, China, and South Africa has increased recently with varying levels of integration. In general this trend brings visible benefits, but it is not without challenges. Benefits include increasing revenues through exports, higher quality consumer welfare by lowering prices on consumption, and lowering manufacturing input costs. Challenges consist mainly of increased competition for domestic companies in MENA, particularly, as World Bank's Pigato[12] noted, for unskilled and resource-intensive manufacturing and food items in labor abundant countries.

The prospect of furthering integration seems to combine a mix of economic optimist with political caution. A report by Ernst & Young and Oxford Economics[13] predicts that MENA's trade flows will grow fastest with Russia, India, and China over the period 2011–2020. Researchers of this study expect global trade to grow at about 9.4 percent per annum (p.a.), but MENA's trade flows will grow even faster, specifically trade with Russia will grow at 14.4 percent p.a., with India at 13.5 percent p.a. and with China at 12.5 percent p.a. On the other hand, annual trade with the United States, EU, and Japan will grow at slower pace, respectively: 8.4 percent, 7.7 percent and 7.3 percent.

Brazil and MENA's integration is based on a growing economic partnership catalyzed in 2003 when President Lula da Silva proposed the creation of the Summit South America and Arab Countries.[14] Since then the volume of trade between Brazil and MENA countries increased at a rate of 13 percent per annum, from US$4.9 billion in 2002 to US$26 billion in 2012.

Yet all this economic optimism may need to be tempered by political risks to MENA countries. A cursory glance of this issue, namely, the United States changing direction toward the Middle East, will be reviewed later on in this chapter. First, the next section examines the prospect of further economic integration of each BRIC country with MENA region.

## Brazil and MvENA

In 2010, Brazil's balance of trade with Arab countries was positive. The export volume was US$12.5 billion and imports were merely US$6.9 billion only. Exports were concentrated mostly on meat, sugar, minerals, and cereals; respectively about 25 percent, 23 percent, 17 percent, and 13 percent of the total exports. The imports were essentially focused in oil resources (84 percent). Inward and outward FDI of Brazil and MENA countries are of little consequence. UAE investors in the hotel sector in Brazil did the most significant investment.*

According to Marcelo Nabih Sallum,[15] President of the Chamber of Commerce Brazil-Arab Countries, the exponential growth in trade between Brazil and the Arab countries is due mainly to the large potential market of MENA countries. Mr. Sallum mentioned that there are opportunities to improve bilateral relations not only in trade but also in tourism, financial services and investments, construction, and health.

## Russia and MENA

The cooperation between Russia and the MENA countries benefits from the Soviet legacy. During the 1950 to 1980s the Soviet Union assisted Arab nations in building several infrastructure projects, but that cooperation ceased and only started to pick up again in the 1990s and 2000s particularly after official visits of the Russian presidents to Algeria in 2006 and 2010.[16] According to Senkovich, Russia aims to reestablish cooperation with the traditional partner countries of Algeria, Lybia, Syria, and Iraq, as well as enter in the markets of the GCC monarchies' markets.

Trade between Russia and MENA was about US$14 billion in 2011 and was largely dominated by the Russian exports (90 percent of trade) of precious metals and stones, metal products and machines, transport

---

* Ibidem.

equipment, coal, and arms, as well as oil and petroleum products which are exported to non-oil producing countries in MENA.

In terms of investment, Arab nations are interested in Russian's technology expertise in higher value industries such as oil and gas production, petrochemicals, remote sensing, water demineralization, nuclear power, space, and Information Technology (IT).* On the flip side, Russia is interested in attracting investments from Arab resource-rich countries, however, Senkovich argues, Arabs perceive Russia as a high-risk market.† Yet, he adds, both inward and outward investments between Russia and MENA seem to be moving too slowly allegedly due to competition from Western countries and China.

### India and MENA

The influence of India and China in the MENA region is growing rapidly and is expected to become critical for the development of the three regions. Two recent studies have examined the recent economic integration of MENA region with India and China (Al Masah Capital Management Limited, 2010; Pigato 2009).

The MENA countries have been major trading partners in meeting India's energy needs, particularly Saudi Arabia (the largest oil supplier to India), as well India's export markets, namely UAE (the largest external MENA market for India). In 2009–10 total trade between India and MENA countries was US$116.9 billion but two thirds of this (US$83.9 billion) was trade only with the GCC, as depicted in Figure 10.21.

According to Al Masah Capital,[17] the MENA region can benefit further from India's expertise in services, namely IT related industries, science and technology, and education. To boost economic ties in the MENA region India has been in talks with GCC countries to establish a free trade agreement and is now pushing for a quick conclusion of the negotiation process.

The investments between India and MENA are essentially anchored in Saudi Arabia. Since mid-2000 more than 100 Indian companies have established joint ventures in Saudi Arabia and half of these have reciprocated and established joint ventures in India.‡ Incorporating Al Masah Capital's report in 2006–07, more than 82 new licenses were granted to

---

* Ibidem.
† Ibidem.
‡ Ibidem.

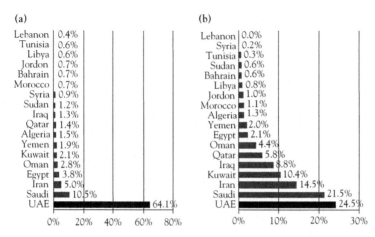

*Figure 10.21  India's exports and imports to and from MENA countries, percent share, 2009–2010*

Source: Department of commerce, India

Indian companies in order to establish business in Saudi Arabia. These are expected to be valued at roughly US$467 billion in Saudi Arabia, mostly in service industries.

Regarding MENA's FDI in India, the GCC countries are the major investors in India. For example, Saudi investment in India, from 1991 to 2004, was US$228 billion, mostly from the industrial sector, (e.g., chemicals, machinery, cement, metallurgy, paper manufacture), as well as in the computer software sector. In just the second and third quarters of 2010, UAE invested US$1,792 billion in India and an additional US$326.6 billion in Oman.*

In terms of future cooperation, Al Masah Capital points out that 4.5 million Indians already live and work in the Gulf region in a range of jobs from unskilled to professional and highly skilled labors; meaning the human capital from India can be a suitable complement to MENA's countries that lack qualified workers. It is suggested that MENA's oil resources combined with India's technology and human capital may provide the opportunity to create new ventures and cooperation, particularly in four sectors: real estate development, energy, petrochemicals, and transport infrastructure.

To conclude, it is worth noting that despite political risks in the MENA region, India is expected to become its main trading partner by 2013–15

---

* Ibidem.

(HSBC Bank, 2013). The rich MENA countries, particularly Turkey, Saudi Arabia, and Egypt are likely to be the main drivers of India's exports.

### China and MENA

China and India's spectacular economic rise over the last two decades has accelerated their trade with Africa, Latin America, and MENA. Their demands for oil, gas, and other natural resources have been forging new relationships with MENA countries based not only on energy but also on trade, investment, and political ties. Indeed, Dubai has become the new Silk Road—the intersection where people, capital, and ideas meet—and Beijing, Shanghai, Hong Kong, Mumbai, Riyadh, and Cairo are the new centers.

The future may well bring new opportunities and faster growth to MENA countries, but the challenges are formidable. For MENA oil-producing countries, faster growth in China and India will increase revenues from oil and the difficult choices associated with their management. For the labor abundant, non-oil producing countries, competition with China and India will spotlight the need for policy measures to increase productivity. This may require broader institutional changes seen in China and India—and thus may take time. But the horizon for creating much needed employment is shorter, suggesting the importance of a pragmatic reform agenda that can accelerate productivity, trade, and investment in the region.

Trade between China and MENA has increased significantly in recent years. In 2009, China became the largest exporter to Middle East countries with a two-way trade value of US$107 billion,* Saudi Arabia and UAE are the two major trading partners of China in the MENA region, with the former being the major exporter to China and the latter the main importer from China, as depicted in Figure 10.22.

Bilateral trade between[†] Saudi Arabia and China rose to US$41.8 billion in 2008 and is estimated to reach US$60 billion by 2015 based mostly on oil exports to China. Trade between China and UAE has centered mostly on exports of low-cost Chinese goods into UAE and base materials and related materials from UAE to China.

---

\* Ibidem.
[†] Ibidem.

(a)                                              (b)

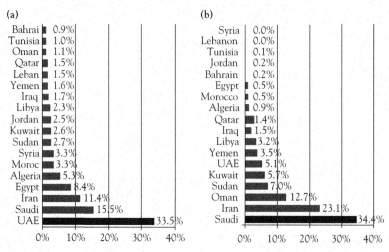

*Figure 10.22 China's exports to MENA (left) and China's import from MENA (right), percent share, Jan–Oct 2008*

Source: Ministry of foreign Trade, People's republic of China

A report focusing on the link between MENA and China (Arabia Monitor, 2012) indicates that there are growing trading synergies between the two regions not only in the traditional oil and resources sectors but also in agriculture and industry. With the decline of exports to Europe, MENA's food exporters are expected to capitalize on China's increasing food demand. The same research indicates that Chinese industrial conglomerates (particularly in the automobile industry) also are expected to invest directly in MENA countries in order to gain faster access to the markets in the region. While China's FDI in the region represents just 1.5 percent of its total investment outflow, in terms of MENA's FDI it represents 3.5 percent of the total inflow. Thus the effects of Chinese integration are likely to create significant impact.

## South Africa and MENA

For centuries, trade has been integral to most countries that constitute the MENA region. As momentum in global business shifts toward greater intra-emerging markets, or "south-south" trade and investment, the MENA economies are well positioned to benefit. But how far and fast the MENA region integrate into these new economic relationships will depend on how executives from other emerging markets view it, and how such perspectives may differ from those of their peers in the developed world. Hence, it is important to understand a few historical facts regarding the MENA region to better understand its impact on global trade.

Historical Perspectives

At the beginning of the 1990s, just before the end of Apartheid, South Africa had diplomatic relations with no country in the Middle East except Israel, another country with limited ties to nations in its own region until the end of the Cold War.* Before Israel's recognition as a nation in 1948, the same year that Apartheid became official government policy, South Africa had established diplomatic relations with Egypt. Formal relations with Lebanon and Iran came later. Egypt had become a prominent support of African liberation organizations following the establishment of the Arab nationalist regime of Gamal Abdel Nasser in 1956 that lasted until the early 1960s.

According to Michael Bishku, on an essay published at the Middle East Policy Council Journal,[18] in Lebanon's situation, trading relations continued until the mid-1970s, at which time they were formally severed due to pressure from the Arab League states. As for Iran, the Islamic Revolution brought a definitive end to relations with the Apartheid government. Naturally, Jewish and Lebanese ethnic populations in South Africa are factored in, with regard to Israel and Lebanon. As for Egypt, it was the most important African country aside from South Africa and one of only a few independent African states until the late 1950s, the others being Ethiopia and Liberia.

In addition, South Africans were militarily involved in Egypt during WWII as part of British Commonwealth forces fighting the Germans. During that war, Reza Shah Pahlavi, ruler of Iran from the 1920s, was sent into exile on Mauritius—but later moved to South Africa, where he died

---

* It should be noted, however, that Israel had great success in developing relations with independent African states beginning with the decolonization of Ghana in 1957, but due to expanding Arab influence in Africa, especially around the time of the Yom Kippur/Ramadan War of 1973, Israel was drawn closer to white-ruled South Africa, another so-called Pariah state; these ties also included controversial military cooperation.

in 1944—by the British, who accused him of German sympathies; his son and successor, Muhammad Reza Pahlavi, who faced a Soviet threat to his rule following WWII, viewed South Africa as a bulwark against the spread of communism and, like Israel, an important market for Iranian oil. The shah was a rival of Nasser, who looked toward the Soviet Union for military support during the mid-1950s, when Soviet leader Nikita Khrushchev began supporting Third World liberation movements. Diplomatic relations between South Africa and the Soviet Union were severed during his time.

## Perspectives on Investments Inflow and Trade

According to a survey conducted by Lewis, Sen, and Tabary for the Economist Intelligence Unit[19] in July 2011, there are striking differences in the way respondents from different regions of the world perceive the MENA region as a place of doing business. Of course, there are similarities too. According to the survey, most multinational companies plan to expand significantly in the region, especially in the Gulf States. And most cite concerns over political risk, bureaucratic red tape and, in particular, a perceived lack of transparency in the region. However, there are major differences in the way that executives from different regions view the prospects for democracy in the Middle East and the likely implications for their own businesses. The culture and norms of respondents' home markets also seem to influence their attitudes toward such factors such as volatility in the business environment, corruption, and diversity.

Lewis, Sen, and Tabary* argue that the Middle East region will benefit strongly from accelerating "south-south" business, particularly with increasing trade between emerging markets. While executives from all regions expect the Middle East to feature more prominently in their global business plans over the next five years, it is among Latin American firms, followed by those from Asia-Pacific and North America, where this trend is most pronounced.

Businesses' views on the potential impact of the *Arab Spring* on trade and investment are divided. While investors broadly welcome the outbreak of pro-democracy movements across the Middle East, the upheavals of the Arab Spring create short-term political risk that can dent business confidence. Almost one-half of all respondents of the Economist

---

* Ibidem, pg. 3–4.

Intelligence Unit survey report* agree that the current unrest in the region is likely to have an adverse effect on their business in the near future.

The UAE is the most favored destination in the Middle East for business expansions and trade, with expansion plans centered on the wealthy Gulf States, probably reflecting the beneficial impact of high oil prices on the economic outlook for these countries. The Gulf States also are favored due to the perception that political risk is lower than in other countries in the region. The UAE is by far the most popular investment and trading location, cited by 63 percent of respondents overall. Latin American executives also showed strong interest in Egypt and Morocco. Emerging-market firms are more likely to focus activities on less saturated markets and sectors.

Latin American firms are less worried about the impact of political turmoil on business in the Middle East than any other region in the world. According to Lewis, Sen, and Tabary survey[†] 55 percent of total respondents from Latin America say that the political upheaval seen recently in the region (2013) is unlikely to affect business adversely in the medium to long term, compared with 43 percent of respondents from both North America and Asia-Pacific. This could reflect the fact that many Latin American countries have come through their own transitions from authoritarian or military rule to democracy in the past 25 years. Nevertheless, a majority of investors, unsure how to handle rapid change, say that if forced to choose, they would prefer stability over democracy.

Corruption is less of a concern for emerging-market firms than it is for businesses from developed markets. Corruption is a relatively minor concern for emerging-market investors in the Middle East, especially among Asian and Latin American companies. However, for European and North American firms, corruption is cited as having a major impact on operations, possibly reflecting tighter anti-corruption legislation, such as the Foreign Corrupt Practice Act (FCPA), in their home markets.

Cultural factors also present major concerns for emerging-market businesses. A significant minority of the Economist's's[‡] survey respondents from all regions adheres to the view that businesses and workers may face discrimination on the basis of gender, race, or nationality in the Middle

---

* Ibidem, pg. 3–4.
[†] Ibidem, pg 5–6.
[‡] Ibidem, pg. 3–4.

East. Attitudes toward women and ethnic minorities significantly deter economic development of the region. Almost half of Latin American businesses believe that the business culture of the Middle East is more suitable for corporations from other emerging markets than for corporations from advanced economies. Some emerging-market investors also expressed concern that their goods, services, or employees are not treated on par with those from Western countries.*

The burgeoning youth population that is demanding political change in the Middle East is also valued as an economic resource. Demographics are seen at least as important as oil and gas resources when it comes to driving opportunities for business in the Middle East. Nearly 50 percent of all Economist's survey† respondents expect business opportunities to emerge from the growth of a new middle class, while 41 percent cite the growing youth population as a source of opportunity. Respondents from Europe are particularly likely to value the region's demographics, probably reflecting concerns about slowing population growth, aging populations, and market saturation in their home markets. Fifty-two percent of European respondents cite the growth of young population as a source of opportunity, compared with just 33 percent who cite commodities.

The gradual shift toward emerging markets reflects policy decisions by Middle Eastern governments, including the region's major oil exporters, who are well aware that their future top customers are located in Asia, and not in the G-7 group. Indeed, when the current Saudi ruler, King Abdullah bin Abdel-Aziz Al Saud, came to the throne, his first overseas trip was to Beijing, not to the United States or UK. For a brief period in 2009, China imported more oil from Saudi Arabia than the United States—something that may become a permanent reality in the near future assuming Chinese oil consumption grows and the United States continues its policy of reducing its reliance on Middle East oil. Moreover, some of the region's authoritarian rulers have been particularly attracted to the so-called *China model*: focusing on economic development but not on political reform. In contrast to the United States or Europe, China does not seek commitments on human rights in order to sign trade deals. While China's approach to trade may appeal to authoritarian regimes in

---

* Ibidem.
† Ibidem.

the Middle East, this year's Arab Spring of popular uprisings in favor of greater democracy is likely to force governments in the region to reconsider their foreign and trade policies.

South Africa has expressed keen interest in expanding its trade relations with the MENA bloc. In late November 2013, the South African Department of Trade and Industry (DTI) lead a business delegation to the Middle East, one of South Africa's important trade zones, with the objective of enhancing trade and investment relations in that region. According to the news outlet allAfrica,[20] DTI's outward trading mission to Saudi Arabia and Kuwait was aimed at building the commitments made by the DTI to expose South African companies to the Middle East market and to deepen bilateral trade and investment relations between these countries.

DTI's Minister, Rob Davies, argues that the Middle East is an important trade zone for South Africa, holding great potential for South Africa as an export market, and serving as a potential source of FDI, as he sees the Middle East as one of the world's fastest growing markets for manufactured products and services.* Indeed, Saudi Arabia is South Africa's largest trading partner and second largest export destination in the Gulf region. In 2012 alone, total bilateral trade between the two countries amounted to R61.7 billion rand. Kuwait is one of South Africa's major trading partners, and is the sixth largest export destination in the Middle East, with a total bilateral trade between the two countries amounted to R246 million rand in 2012.

Turkey also has a role to play in South African DTI's trade mission, as its Deputy Minister, Elizabeth Thabethe, has been focusing on an outward selling and investment mission to that country. According to Thabethe both South Africa and Turkey are featured in one another's top 40 lists of imports and export trade partners. The two countries are regional powerhouses in their respective regions. South Africa's exports to Turkey have been steadily increasing to an extent that the trade deficit in favor of Turkey has been significantly reduced.

Currently, South Africa conducts trade with MENA in various industrial sectors including agro-processing, manufacturing machinery and equipment, and capital equipment. Turkey has targeted the following sectors for the mission: energy, mining, infrastructure, information and communication technology, capital equipment and engineering, and textiles.

---

* Ibidem.

In concluding this section, it is worth mentioning that, according to Cashin, Mohaddes and Raissi,[21] the MENA countries are more sensitive to macroeconomic developments in China than to shocks in the EU or the United States According to McKinsey Consulting,[22] trade flows between China and the GCC are expected to rise to between US$350 and US$500 billion by the year 2020. This supports the idea that the interconnectedness between China and MENA region will be a significant force shaping the world economic environment.

## Rising Together?

In March 2013, the fifth BRICS summit was held in Durban, South Africa. The heads of these governments acknowledged the need to operationalize the recommendations received by the think tanks of their countries. There is a need to accelerate from talk into action. One idea shared during the meetings was the possibility of the BRICS countries to create a new development bank, one mandated to assist developing nations (south-south development). Deen[23] mentioned that one area of intervention of this bank could be to assist some MENA countries, specifically Egypt, who is seen as having significant influence in the Arab world.*

Certainly, companies around the globe recognize the long-term economic potential of the Arab world. Trade between Middle East countries and others, particularly those from emerging markets, has been increasing for years, and is likely to grow further as part of a broader trend of greater economic exchange between non-OECD countries. Political authoritarianism and instability have forced many investors to think twice about their plans in the short term, although many emerging-market firms appear less worried about volatile operating conditions. A significant minority of executives in all regions (except the Middle East itself) believes that local attitudes toward women and ethnic minorities would hold back the region's economic development. Nevertheless, the current upheavals of the Arab Spring are giving hope to investors from all regions that despite obvious short-term difficulties inherent in political transition, a more transparent business environment will emerge eventually.

---

* Ibidem.

## Why do MENA Countries Attract less FDI than Other Emerging Countries?

While concerns about corruption, infrastructure, and political uncertainty will remain worrisome in the medium term, the opportunities deriving from a young and growing population are all too evident, and our survey shows that investors from all regions are planning major expansion into the MENA region. Firms from other emerging markets are increasingly seeking opportunities outside the oil and gas industry, in the less-developed sectors and countries across the region. Latin American firms are leveraging their expertise in fostering innovation in agriculture. Others are finding a niche in providing goods and services by competing on price or quality.

For companies from industrialized countries and emerging markets alike, significant challenges remain in doing business and attracting FDI in the Middle East. But the region is changing in visible ways, as made clear from the Arab Spring, and in ways that are more imperceptible, as in the recalibration of policies and attitudes toward business. The region today represents opportunities that businesses around the world are keen to grasp. Given the trends in global trade and investment, it is more than likely that the attractiveness of the opportunities will outweigh the risks over time.

According to Daniele and Marani,[24] however, the underperformance of MENA countries to attract FDI is due to several major factors, namely: the small size of local markets and lack of real economic integration; changes in international competition for FDI; slow institutional and trade reforms; and political and macroeconomic instability. However, to overcome these obstacles MENA countries need to improve their governance systems that, according to various indicators, display poor performance, as depicted in Figure 10.23.

The MENA region encompasses countries with diverse wealth concentrations and resource levels, widely divergent economic structures and trajectories ranging from wealthy Gulf monarchies to poor countries such as Yemen.[25] As Cammett* pointed out the development of MENA countries is shaped not only by economic and institutional factors but also by the culture and history of these countries. While most of the explanations regarding development in MENA countries are valid there is still no clear understanding of what are the most important factors, and more

---

* Ibidem.

| | Voice accountability | Political stability | Government effectiveness | Regulatory quality | Rule of law | Control corruption |
|---|---|---|---|---|---|---|
| Algeria | 160 | 192 | 133 | 173 | 152 | 124 |
| Egypt | 166 | 157 | 107 | 154 | 97 | 105 |
| Israel | 85 | 177 | 41 | 62 | 55 | 49 |
| Jordan | 149 | 116 | 79 | 95 | 84 | 70 |
| Lebanon | 155 | 161 | 121 | 142 | 117 | 127 |
| Libya | 203 | 112 | 157 | 197 | 145 | 175 |
| Morocco | 142 | 126 | 92 | 120 | 101 | 93 |
| Syria | 201 | 151 | 153 | 187 | 122 | 153 |
| Tunisia | 171 | 101 | 64 | 118 | 89 | 78 |
| Turkey | 123 | 144 | 89 | 110 | 96 | 106 |

*Figure 10.23 MENA governance indicators*

Notes: Rank on 209 countries and territories. Year 2004.
Sources: Calculation on Kaufmann, Kraay, and Mastruzzi (2005), & Daniele and Marani, (2006)

importantly of how political and economic institutions in MENA region will reproduce and change in the future. The future presents opportunities for both the MENA and BRICS countries to cooperate further but not without uncertainties and risks.

### Opportunities in the MENA Region

Growth and trade in the MENA region is constrained by several factors. On the one hand growth is hindered by difficulties in access to finance, labor skill disparities and shortages, and electricity constraints.[26] On the other hand underperformance in MENA's trade is constrained by logistics and transport limitations and inefficiencies in custom clearance processes.[27] Despite such huge challenges, O'Sullivan and colleagues[28] noted that there are some clear opportunities in the MENA region to consider, and which the BRICS countries should be aware of when developing relations with MENA. The opportunities are as follows:

- The young population as a market and labor force. As the average age in the MENA countries is just 25 years, well below other emerging regions, there will soon be a larger labor force and consequently a rise in consumption levels. However, for this opportunity to materialize governments need to develop institutional frameworks that promote essential social needs, namely education, employment, health, and housing. Renewable energies, including solar sources in all MENA countries, hydropower (Egypt, Iran, Iraq, and Syria) and wind (along the Red Sea and Morocco's Atlantic coast). The International Energy Agency forecasts that by 2035 the use of renewables for electricity generation could reach 33 percent and FDI reach US$400 billion provided that adequate policies and institutions are implemented.

- The tourism sector already represents a large industry in some MENA countries and provides significant sources of employment and exports. MENA countries have traditionally targeted tourists from European and Gulf markets, however with increased purchasing power of people in emerging countries MENA can expand into new tourism markets.

- Agro-industries in MENA countries with sufficient water resources also offer significant growth potential. Such countries include Iraq, Lebanon, Morocco, Egypt, and Syria. The opportunities will exist in both domestic and emerging markets essentially due to demographic trends and economic growth. Internally, the demographic trend in the MENA region and its subsequent expected consumption (as described earlier), there will be higher demand for food products. The same phenomenon can already be seen in other emerging countries, such as China. One particular benefit of the agro-industries is that it will open up business opportunities and create employment in related industries upstream (farming) and downstream (handling, packaging, processing, transporting, and marketing).

- And of course there will be a plethora of opportunities in the energy sector. The resource-rich countries of the MENA region account for nearly 60 percent of the world's oil reserves and 45 percent of the natural gas reserves. This sector will continue to attract investments, technology, and know-how.

# The U.S. Changes Direction in the Middle East

By M.K. Bhadrakumar*

The politics of the Middle East are undergoing a period of great turbulence emanating from changes in direction of the regional policies pursued by the United States. When the ship makes a turnaround, it has to be over an arc, and it is now possible to discern the reset of the compass.

This is primarily being felt in the Obama administration's rethink on the Syrian conflict and its decision to constructively engage with Iran. Neither is an afterthought, but rather they took time to mature.

To take Syria first, Leslie Gelb, President Emeritus at the Council on Foreign Relations in New York needs no introduction as an influential voice in the U.S. foreign policy establishment. His views on the Syrian conflict will always merit attention—especially when aired through the Voice of America (VOA).

Gelb made four key points on Syria in an exclusive interview with the VOA. First, the specter that haunts all the parties inside Syria as well as the United States' friends and allies who neighbor Syria—Iraq, Turkey, Jordan, Israel—is the rise of the *jihadi*. Second, the elimination of the *jihadis* will take time because they are seasoned fighters and it is best achieved through cooperation between the Syrian regime and the moderate rebels. The basis of such cooperation could be through a "power-sharing arrangement, mainly along federal lines," as stated by Gelb. Third, there is urgency to lay the basis of cooperation between the regime and the moderate rebels—that is, as argued by Gelb, "how they could compromise and live together." Or else, Geneva 2 may not prove productive. And fourth, the United States is according to Gelb, "beginning to change direction" as it has "finally figured out... that the only way to stop this

---

* Mr. Bhadrakumar is a former career diplomat in the Indian Foreign Service whom devoted much of his three-decade long career to the Pakistan, Afghanistan and Iran desks in the Ministry of External Affairs and in assignments on the territory of the former Soviet Union. After leaving the diplomatic service, he took to writing and contributing to The Asia Times, The Hindu, and Deccan Herald. I, Dr. Goncalves, appreciate his valuable contribution to this chapter. Mr. Bhadrakumar lives in New Delhi, India.

fighting is to work something out between the moderate rebels and the Alawites.*

For example, the United States has stopped saying that Syria's president, Assad, must go. That used to be the hallmark of U.S. policy. The United States no longer says that. The U.S. administration says only he has lost legitimacy, and that it wants him and his government to participate in negotiations. So that's changed. Also changed is the notion that the United States can simply help the rebels, as it finally realized that it does not exactly know who these rebels are and what they can do. After all, they have never gotten fully organized. And there's a big gap, it seems, between the rebels the United States deals with and that council [Syrian National Coalition] in Turkey and the good rebels fighting in the field.

Indeed, it is palpable that the United States is currently supportive of the series of diplomatic initiatives Moscow has been taking during early fall 2013 in a renewed push for a Syrian peace conference. The Russian Deputy Foreign Minister Mikhail Bogdanov met the Syrian National Coalition (SNC) representatives in Istanbul during that time. The SNC also had come under American pressure to accept Russia's invitation to go to Moscow to discuss the peace conference.

Equally, there has been a sea change in the United States-Iran standoff. The probability that the ongoing negotiation of the P5+1† is high and Iran may produce an interim nuclear deal. Contrary to the widely held

---

* Today, Alawites represent 12 percent of the Syrian population and are a significant minority in Turkey and northern Lebanon. The Alawites, also known as Alawis are a prominent mystical religious group centered in Syria who follow a branch of the Twelver school of Shia Islam (the largest branch of Shi'a Islam), but with syncretistic elements. Alawites revere Ali (Ali ibn Abi Talib), and the name "Alawi" means followers of Ali. The sect is believed to have been founded by Ibn Nusayr during the 8th century. For this reason, Alawites are sometimes called "Nusayris," though this term has come to have derogatory connotations in the modern era.

† The P5+1 is a group of six world powers, which in 2006 joined the diplomatic efforts with Iran with regard to its nuclear program. The term refers to the P5 or five permanent members of the UN Security Council, namely United States, Russia, China, United Kingdom, and France, plus Germany. P5+1 is often referred to as the E3+3 (or E3/EU+3) by European countries.

view that the Obama administration's push to reach an interim agreement with Iran would be torpedoed on Capitol Hill, the Democratic leadership in the U.S. Senate, in particular the heads of the Armed Services Committee, Carl Levin, and Intelligence Committee, Dianne Feinstein, have concurred that this would be a bad time to impose new sanctions against Iran when negotiations are under way.

The former U.S. national security advisors Zbigniew Brzezinski and Brent Scowcroft have written a letter to the Senate Majority Leader Harry Reid strongly pleading, "If more sanctions are enacted now, as these unprecedented negotiations are just getting started, this would reconfirm Iranians' belief that the United States is not prepared to make any agreement with the current government of Iran. We call on all Americans and the U.S. Congress to stand firmly with the President in the difficult but historic negotiations with Iran."[29]

Indeed, Gelb himself is on record that a short-term deal "would lead to the Mideast equivalent of ending the Cold War with the Soviet Union … [and] could reduce, even sharply, the biggest threat to regional peace, an Iranian nuclear bomb, and open pathways to taming dangerous conflicts in Syria, Iraq, and Afghanistan."*

Therefore, there is cautious optimism that an agreement can be finalized. The leaders of Russia, China, and UK have had telephone conversations with Iranian President Hassan Rouhani. After a fall 2013 meeting President Obama, Secretary of State John Kerry, and National Security Advisor Susan Rice called with key U.S. senators, the White House issued the following statement, "We have the opportunity to halt the progress of the Iranian (nuclear) program and roll it back in key respects, while testing whether a comprehensive resolution can be achieved."[30] It warned that if there is not an initial agreement, Iran will continue making progress on increasing enrichment capacity, growing its stockpiles of enriched uranium, installing new centrifuges, and developing a plutonium reactor in the city of Arak.

Meanwhile, Iran's surprise announcement that relinquishing its insistence that the world powers should acknowledge explicitly its right to enrich uranium deftly sidesteps a potentially tendentious aspect of the dispute and shifts the emphasis to practical steps that can be agreed on the interim.

---

* Ibidem.

Of course, it is not going to be a cakewalk for the Obama administration and a showdown is still very much possible between the White House and Congress regarding Iran. The conflict in Syria is not so much a contentious (and emotive) issue for the U.S. political establishment as the situation around Iran is, but everything converges ultimately on how the Obama administration will handle U.S. foreign policy in the Middle East for remainder of his presidency.

What makes this a high stakes contestation is that this is both a real time fight as well as a struggle over long-term issues. Let's not forget, relations between the Obama administration and the Israeli government led by Prime Minister Benjamin Netanyahu have entered uncharted waters and the latter has launched a full-scale attack on the entire trajectory of Obama's Middle East policies. Compounding matters further, Israel's concerns are not exclusively its own, but are shared by other U.S. key allies in the region, especially Saudi Arabia.

Due to a combination of circumstances, including the searing experience in Iraq, crisis of the U.S. economy, and the U.S. public's lack of support for war, all against the backdrop of a rebalance in Asia, Washington wants to reduce its military "footprint" in the Middle East; whereas, U.S. alliances in the region tried to pressure the Obama Administration into launching new wars against Syria and Iran. In his United Nations General Assembly speech in September 2013, President Obama virtually admitted U.S. helplessness in modulating the Arab Spring and spelled out that Washington's core concerns in the Middle East would narrow down to four areas: protect allies from external aggression, ensure the free flow of oil, prevent proliferation of weapons of mass destruction, and counter the Al-Qaeda threat.

Conceivably, the United States appears to be distancing itself from its entangled alliances so as to avoid being cajoled into conflicts from its closest regional allies. In a manner of speaking, the Obama Administration is seeking an optimal regional policy to suit U.S. interests rather than Israeli or Saudi interests. This is not tantamount to a "strategic retreat" from the region and it does not necessarily mean that U.S. interventionism is gone forever. It means simply that Washington's actions will be guided by a range of U.S. interests rather than succumbing to Israeli demands or Saudi Arabia's regional ambitions. If this reset is carried to its logical conclusion, the balance of forces in the Middle East will be transformed beyond recognition.

# CHAPTER 11

# Entering an Emerging Market

## Overview

Entering an emerging market is not easy. In our experience in teaching this topic, consulting for several multinational corporations around the world, and being a practitioner ourselves, we find that emerging markets are tough to enter. Government interference, backward infrastructure, and a lack of skilled workers require a lot of patience, perseverance, and specialized assistance. Opportunities in the emerging markets come with their own set of challenges. For instance, often lack of education of the workforce translates into thwarted growth being curbed lack of a skilled workforce. Other challenges that arise are legal frameworks with regard to trade policies, which may be absent or underdeveloped, or tendencies for political paternalism or blatant interferences, which we see in India and Latin America.

Compare the above to the advanced economies, which, despite the fact that growth has been flat to negative since 2008, continues to supersede emerging markets. When looking at the EU, the 27-member countries allow for labor mobility and a free flow of goods without tariff or nontariff restrictions. Furthermore, the workers in many EU countries are highly educated and have conferred great reputations for their economies. "German engineering" is well known around the world for its high level of quality, the same cannot be said for Indian or Russian engineering.

India has been making progress in opening its economy, but its political response to a much-needed foreign investment is troubling. Large foreign retailers such as IKEA are willing to employ thousands of Indians, but politicians continue to fret about mom-and-pop stores and other small businesses that may be displaced. In 2012, politicians forbade IKEA from selling half its product line in India. In 2012, the deputy chief minister for Punjab went as far as to declare that there was no need for foreign-owned discount retail chains because there are already a multitude of stores selling cheap goods.[1]

Foreign investors become confused and frustrated with these types of patriarchal decisions such as these. Although many nations have transitioned from autocratic rule to democracies with free markets, some continue to dabble in market interference. Take Argentina as an example, where President Cristina Fernández de Kirchner, to prevent a run on the peso by Argentines, has put strict currency controls in place. It is not wonder that in an annual World Bank study titled *Doing Business* (2013), New Zealand, Singapore, and Hong Kong ranked first, second, and third place respectively in protecting investors, while Argentina ranks 98.[2]

Emerging markets such as India and China have huge and growing populations and thus demand rapid growth rate if they are to make any headway in social development. If India's economic growth falls below six percent the nation would be in crisis, whereas in most advanced economies, such as the United States, if the economy grew at that rate it would risk overheating.

India can barely keep up with educating its rising populations. It needs as many as 1,000 new universities and 35,000 new colleges if it is to achieve its stated goal of raising postsecondary enrollment from 12 percent today to 30 percent by 2020. Meanwhile, Mexico is turning out more engineers and engineering technicians a year than Germany, and it must scramble to ensure they all get jobs. To fail would be to spawn social unrest.

Another key factor when considering entering emerging markets is the distance between emerging markets, which can hamper trade. One study found that a 10 percent increase in distance between north-to-north traders reduces trade by 10 percent; the same distance between south-to-south traders reduces trade by 17 percent.[3]

An improved policy would make an important difference in resolving such problems but emerging market have yet to demonstrate serious desires for true bilateral cooperation. Although the ASEAN nations have a trade agreement, it has yet to yield much economic improvement, as the bloc has yet to turn their loose organization into a trading block, even though economic integration has been touted as a central pillar.

Public administration in emerging markets has much to be desired. The 2013' *Doing Business*[4] study by the World Bank ranks Brazil, Russia,

India, China, and South Africa (BRICS) as 116th, 92nd, 134th, 96th, and 41th respectively out of 189 countries.

Infrastructure remains a significant problem in most emerging markets. China continues to invest heavily in roads, railways and ports, but elsewhere the progress is weak. India has called for US$1 trillion in infrastructure modernization but it lacks the funds to do so independently and its politicians remain suspicious of external sources of capital. The situation is no different in Latin America, in fact, it is arguably worse, as 80 percent of Latin Americans live in cities, compared to fewer than half of Asians. The need for modern urban infrastructure is urgent. Brazil, for instance, wants to improve its infrastructure, which is a bottleneck for the outflow of many of its export products, but it is moving glacially. It has been so slow that Sao Paulo's underground rapid transit system covers only one-tenth of the distance of the one in Seoul, South Korea.*

Does all this mean that foreign investors should avoid trading with or investing in emerging markets? On the contrary, however, any organized program of opening up to emerging markets must include specialized expertise, on-the-ground knowledge, local partnerships, and, most of all, patience.

## Why Multinationals Fail in Emerging Markets

Pacek and Thorniley[5] identified an exhaustive range of factors contributing to the failure of companies from advanced economies into emerging markets. These factors may be divided into external and internal factors and almost all are related to strategic and leadership issues:

- Leaders fail to consider emerging markets as an integral part of strategy and acknowledge that such markets need to be approached with a distinct set of criteria for judging progress and success.
- Top leaders fail to commit sufficient resources to get businesses established and growing in emerging markets, or acknowledge that it is never a short-term affair.
- Companies fail to appoint a head manager for emerging markets and often assign this responsibility to an international manager who is responsible for markets in both developed

---

\* Ibidem.

and emerging countries. The problem with this is that operational approaches are distinct in each of these markets.

- Companies fail to understand that business is driven by heads of regions and business units rather than by heads of functional areas. While the former have a focus and appreciation for the emerging markets, the latter tend also to be interested in developed markets.

- Companies do not acknowledge that emerging markets operate under distinct business models and structures, and often merely transfer practices tested in developed markets without considering adaptation.

- The board members of many companies have limited diversity in terms of culture and ethnic background and do not develop sufficient appreciation for the peculiarities of emerging markets.

- Multinationals underestimate the potential and often early competition from smaller international and domestic companies, thus never accepting that they may be destined as a follower in emerging markets.

- Economic and political crisis also exist in emerging markets and have a significant impact on business performance. Top managers need to understand this, be prepared to adapt, and introduce new tactics rather than changing strategy, which despite having short-term success, tend to be the wrong approach in the long-term.

- Companies get alarmed by short-term slippages and cut costs to attain favorable temporary results, yet this is likely to have a structural impact on strategy implementation and long term results.

- Companies set unrealistic targets to achieve, which leave managers with limited maneuvering space and short-lived careers.

- Companies fail to recognize that entering the market early is fundamental in establishing networks, developing brands, and learning the larger context from which it will operate.

- Senior leaders fail to recognize that developing a network of reliable contacts often requires establishing friendships with locals, which requires time and visibility in emerging markets.

- Companies fail to empower regional and country managers and delegate decision-making power to local managers.
- Foreign companies fail to recognize that emerging markets are more price-sensitive and often stick to their pricing structures instead of adapting to local sensitivities.
- International firms fail to recognize that their product portfolio is not tailored to the lower and middle segments of emergent markets and do not develop innovations that are context-oriented.
- Foreign companies underestimate the competition from local companies in emergent markets, which gradually move from up from lower to upper segments. Local companies under-stand better than anyone about local markets, sometimes employ dubious practices, and often have the support of local governments.
- One of the largest obstacles that foreign companies face may be the unwillingness to change long-standing business practices.
- Another challenge is to appoint senior managers who are not familiar with the local market, culture, and language in emerging countries.
- Multinationals that focus too much on the larger emerging markets, such as BRIC, may neglect smaller markets and miss better-suited opportunities.
- The fact that demand is volatile and unpredictable in emer-gent markets may discourage multinationals, which often expect reliable market information.

The failure factors are numerous and diverse but as Pacek and Thorniley noted it all boils down to a lack of adequate market entry preparation. Preparation requires companies to continuously research the external environment and know how to use internal resources to take advantage of opportunities. Hence, a preliminary audit that focuses on external and internal factors is essential. The external factors may be examined by posing questions concerning the market, the political envi-ronment, the economic environment, and the business environment, as depicted in Table 11.1.

*Table 11.1  External Factors and Sample Questions*

| Understanding the market | |
|---|---|
| Market potential | • How large and wealthy is the market?<br>• Is there unsatisfied demand for the product/service? |
| Understanding local consumers/ customers | • Who are the consumers/ customers? What are their characteristics?<br>• How do consumers make their decisions? |
| Reaching the consumer/ customer | • How difficult/easy is it to reach potential consumers/customers?<br>• How do competitors and noncompetitors reach their customers? |
| Competition | • Which competitors are already operating in the market?<br>• How strong are these competitors? |
| Lessons learned by noncompetitors | • What do noncompetitors say about the business environment in the country?<br>• What have been the largest obstacles to successful operations? |
| Local culture | • What aspects of local culture are relevant to running a successful local business? |
| **Understanding the political and economic environment** | |
| Economic outlook | • How sustainable is economic growth?<br>• What is driving economic growth? |
| Political outlook | • What is the level of political risk and how will or might affect the business? |
| Government policies | • Does the government allow a level playing filed?<br>• Is the government in the hands of local lobbies? |
| **Understanding the business environment** | |
| Finance | • Is it possible to finance operations locally?<br>• What access do customers/consumers have to finance? |
| Labor market | • What are the wage/salary rates for the employees who will be needed?<br>• What are the most effective ways of recruiting local employees? |
| Taxation | • What are the current levels of taxation?<br>• What is the outlook for tax incentives? |
| Legal environment | • How effective and efficient is the local judiciary?<br>• Is there any hope that the legal system will improve? |
| Bureaucratic obstacles to business | • What are the most common bureaucratic obstacles for business?<br>• How easy or difficult it is to set up business in the country? |
| Crime and corruption | • Is crime a problem for business?<br>• What is the level of corruption? |
| Infrastructure | • What is the quality of local transport infrastructure?<br>• And telecommunications? |

*Table 11.1  (Continued)*

| Understanding the business environment | |
|---|---|
| Foreign trade environment | • Is the country a WTO member?<br>• Does it belong to any trading blocs or regional free-trade areas? |
| Cost of building a business and brand | • How expensive is it to build a brand?<br>• How much time will it take to do what is necessary to get the business off the ground? |

*Table 11.2  Internal Factors and Sample Questions*

| Resources | • How much time and money will be required?<br>• Is the CEO committed to support business development and provide necessary resources? And the senior managers?<br>• What human resources are needed? |
|---|---|
| Products | • Is the product portfolio right for the market?<br>• Will investment be available for developing new products? |
| Organization | • Will existing internal processes and operational practices help or hinder what is planned?<br>• What existing capabilities can be drawn? |
| Risks | • Can the risks that have been identified be managed?<br>• How would entry be financed? |

By the same token, the internal factors must inquire about resources, products, organization, and risks, as depicted in Table 11.2.

Having done a preliminary external and internal audit, managers need to prepare a business proposal describing what to do, how to do it, by when, and resources required. Business must then ask themselves whether there are similar or better opportunities available in other emerging markets. How then, can we compare the potential of different emerging markets?

## Ranking Emerging Markets

According to the GlobalEdge[6] team at the International Business Center (IBC) at The Eli Broad Graduate School of Management, Michigan State University, there are three main reasons why emerging markets are attractive. They are target markets, manufacturing bases, and sourcing destinations.

As target markets they present a growing middle class with substantial demand for consumer products and services. They are also excellent targets for electronics, automobiles, and health care services. The textile (machinery) industry in India is huge, oil and gas exploration plays a vital role in Russia, agriculture is a major sector in China, and airplanes are almost everywhere.

As manufacturing bases they present advantages such as low-wages, high quality labor for manufacturing, and assembly operations. South Africa is a key source for industrial diamonds; Thailand has become an important manufacturing location for Japanese MNEs such as Sony, Sharp, and Mitsubishi; Malaysia and Taiwan are home to manufacturing of semiconductors by MNEs such as Motorola, Intel, and Philips; and in Mexico and China we find platforms for consumer electronics and auto assembly.

As sourcing destinations the emerging markets also are using their advantages to attract MNEs. MNEs have established call centers in Eastern Europe, India, and the Philippines; Dell and IBM outsource certain technological functions to knowledge workers in India; Brazil is a leading raw material supplier namely in oil and agriculture.

The Emerging Market Potential Index (EMPI) was based on Cavusgil[7] indexing approach and developed by the GlobalEdge team to assess the market potential of Emerging Markets. As shown in Table 11.3, EMPI is based on eight dimensions: market size, market growth rate, market intensity, market consumption capacity, commercial infrastructure, economic freedom, market receptivity, and country risk. Each dimension is measured using various indicators and are weighed in determining the overall index. The result is a score on a scale from 1 to 100.

Table 11.3's, based on Cavugil, Kiyak, and Yeniyurt[8] indicator is useful in that it provides the relative position of each country but is lacking analysis as it does not provide what the data actually mean, nor what managers can do with this data.

### From Indicators to Institutions

It is common wisdom that size and growth potential are the two best criteria to select an emerging market. Not so for Khanna and Palepu[9] who argue that

Table 11.3 Market potential index (PMI for emerging markets, 2013)

| Overall rank | Country | Market size | Market growth rate | Market intensity | Market cans capacity | Comm infrast | Economic freedom | Market receipt | Country risk | Overall score |
|---|---|---|---|---|---|---|---|---|---|---|
| 1 | Singapore | 1 | 86 | 74 | 66 | 80 | 83 | 97 | 100 | 62 |
| 2 | Hong Kong | 1 | 44 | 100 | 58 | 100 | 90 | 100 | 92 | 61 |
| 3 | China | 100 | 100 | 1 | 70 | 39 | 8 | 4 | 54 | 56 |
| 4 | South Korea | 9 | 40 | 56 | 100 | 87 | 82 | 18 | 65 | 49 |
| 5 | Israel | 1 | 39 | 65 | 79 | 70 | 78 | 22 | 66 | 43 |
| 6 | Czech Republic | 1 | 11 | 45 | 95 | 88 | 88 | 16 | 71 | 43 |
| 7 | Poland | 3 | 33 | 55 | 82 | 72 | 81 | 8 | 63 | 41 |
| 8 | Turkey | 6 | 73 | 65 | 79 | 52 | 53 | 5 | 49 | 41 |
| 9 | India | 37 | 74 | 28 | 78 | 22 | 52 | 3 | 42 | 41 |
| 10 | Chile | 1 | 40 | 48 | 35 | 60 | 100 | 15 | 79 | 38 |
| 11 | Hungary | 1 | 1 | 58 | 88 | 77 | 78 | 20 | 37 | 37 |
| 12 | Malaysia | 3 | 60 | 29 | 58 | 63 | 52 | 21 | 61 | 37 |
| 13 | Russia | 13 | 45 | 36 | 68 | 73 | 17 | 4 | 43 | 36 |
| 14 | Peru | 2 | 76 | 40 | 56 | 40 | 70 | 6 | 50 | 35 |
| 15 | Mexico | 9 | 31 | 53 | 49 | 47 | 63 | 21 | 53 | 35 |
| 16 | Indonesia | 10 | 68 | 28 | 77 | 32 | 54 | 3 | 39 | 34 |
| 17 | Brazil | 18 | 36 | 42 | 37 | 56 | 60 | 1 | 55 | 34 |
| 18 | Argentina | 4 | 68 | 49 | 67 | 60 | 45 | 4 | 11 | 33 |
| 19 | Saudi Arabia | 4 | 68 | 15 | 0 | 56 | 15 | 14 | 67 | 32 |
| 20 | Thailand | 3 | 19 | 31 | 66 | 47 | 49 | 17 | 48 | 30 |
| 21 | Egypt | 4 | 33 | 58 | 83 | 47 | 27 | 4 | 10 | 30 |
| 22 | Colombia | 3 | 44 | 42 | 31 | 45 | 62 | 4 | 52 | 29 |
| 23 | Philippines | 4 | 24 | 52 | 58 | 31 | 51 | 5 | 37 | 28 |
| 24 | Pakistan | 5 | 37 | 66 | 83 | 1 | 32 | 1 | 1 | 25 |
| 25 | Venezuela | 3 | 40 | 36 | 67 | 44 | 1 | 8 | 10 | 24 |
| 26 | South Africa | 5 | 29 | 40 | 1 | 25 | 66 | 5 | 50 | 22 |

lack of institutions, such as distribution systems, credit cards systems, or data research firms, is the primary factor to consider when entering into an emerging market. For them, the fact that emerging markets have poor institutions, thus, inefficient business operations, present the best business opportunities for companies operating in such dynamic markets. However, the ways businesses enter into emerging markets is different, and are contingent upon variations presented by the institutions and the abilities of the firms.

Khanna and Palepu point out that the use of composite indexes to assess the potential of emerging markets, as executives often do, has limited use because these indicators do not capture the soft infrastructures and institutions. These composite indexes are useful in ranking market potential of countries when and only these countries have similar institutional environments. When soft infrastructures differ we must then look at the institutional context in each market. In fact when comparing the composite indexes of the BRICS countries we find that they are similar in terms of competitiveness, governance, and corruption. Yet the key success factors for companies in the BRICS differ significantly from country to country. Take for example the retail chain industry.

In China and Russia retail chain operators, both multinationals and local companies, converge in urban and semi-urban areas. In contrast, in Brazil very few multinational retail chains are located in urban centers, and in India we find even fewer international retail chains due to government restrictions that until 2005 did not allow foreign direct investment in this industry. Thus, when looking at the economic indicators of the BRICS countries we find that increased consumption provides opportunities for retail operators.

### Best Opportunities Fill in Institutional Voids

From an institutional view the market is a transactional place embedded in information and property rights, and emerging markets are a place where one or both of these features are underdeveloped.* Most definitions of emerging markets are descriptive based on poverty and growth indicators. In contrast a structural definition as proposed by Khanna and

---

* Ibidem.

Palepu points to issues that are problematic therefore allowing an immediate identification of solutions. Moreover, a structural definition allows us not only to understand commonalities among emerging markets but also to understand what differentiates each of these markets. Finally, a structural approach provides a more precise understanding of the market dynamics that genuinely differentiates emerging markets from advanced economies.

To illustrate, let us contrast the equity capital markets of South Korea and Chile. According to the IFC definition, Korea is not an emerging market because it is an OECD member, however when we look at its equity capital market we notice that until recently it was not functioning well, in other words it has an institutional void. Chile on the other hand is considered an emerging market in Latin America but has an efficient capital market, thus no institutional void appears in this sector. However, Chile has institutional voids in other markets such as the products market.

Strategy formulation in emerging markets must begin with a map of institutional voids. What works in the headquarters of a multinational company does not per se work in new locations with different institutional environments. The most common mistake companies do when entering emerging markets is to overestimate the importance of past experience. This common error reflects a recency bias, or when a person assumes that recent successful experiences may be transferred to other places. A manager incorrectly may assume that the way people are motivated in one country would be the same in the new country (context). It may be assumed that everyone likes to be appreciated, but the way of expressing appreciation depends on the institutional environment. Khanna points out that the human element is the cornerstone of operating in new contexts. Ultimately, human beings, who provide a mix of history, culture, and interactions, create institutions.

In short, based on Khanna and Palepu's institutional approach to emerging markets it is necessary to answer several questions. Which institutions are working and missing? Which parts of our business model (in the home country) would be affected by these voids? How can we build competitive advantage based on our ability to navigate institutional voids?

How can we profit from the structural reality of emerging markets by identifying opportunities to fill voids, serving as market intermediaries?

## Strategies for Emerging Markets

The work of Khanna and Palepu indicate that there are four generic strategic choices for companies operating in emerging markets:

- Replicate or adapt?
- Compete alone or collaborate?
- Accept or attempt to change market context?
- Enter, wait, or exit?

Emerging markets attract two competing types of firms, the developed market-based multinationals and the emerging market-based companies. Both bring different advantages to fill institutional voids. Multinational enterprises (MNEs) bring brands, capital talent, and resources, whereas local companies contribute with local contacts and context knowledge. Because they have different strengths and resources, foreign and domestic firms will compete differently and must develop strategies accordingly.

Table 11.4 summarizes the strategies and options for both multinational firms and local companies.

An example of how companies fill institutional voids is provided by Anand P. Arkalgud (2011).[10] Road infrastructure in India is still underdeveloped in terms of quality and connectivity. Traditionally Tata Motors has been the dominant player in the auto industry but when it started to receive competition from Volvo in the truck segment and by Japanese auto makers in the car segment Tata responded. It created a mini-truck that not only provided more capacity and safety than the two and three-wheeled pollutant vehicles used to access market areas, but also an environmentally sound vehicle, one that could easily maneuver U-turns in such narrow streets.

Another case in India involved Coca Cola, who discovered that their beverages were being sold "warm." Coca Cola realized that it needed a solution to sell its product "chilled." The reason for the warm bottles was

*Table 11.4  Responding to institutional voids*

| Strategic choice | Options for multinationals from developed countries | Options for emerging market-based companies |
|---|---|---|
| Replicate or adapt? | • Replicate business model, exploiting relative advantage of global brand, credibility, know-how, talent, finance, and other factor inputs.<br>• Adapt business models, products, or organizations to institutional voids. | • Copy business model from developed countries.<br>• Exploit local knowledge, capabilities, and ability to navigate institutional voids to build tailored business models. |
| Compete alone or collaborate? | • Compete alone.<br>• Acquire capabilities to navigate institutional voids through local partnerships or JVs. | • Compete alone.<br>• Acquire capabilities from developed markets through partnerships or JVs with multinational companies to bypass institutional voids. |
| Accept or attempt to change market context? | • Take market context as given.<br>• Fill institutional voids in service of own business. | • Take market context as given.<br>• Fill institutional voids in service of own business. |
| Enter, wait, or exit? | • Enter or stay in market spite of institutional voids.<br>• Emphasize opportunities elsewhere. | • Build business in home market in spite of institutional voids.<br>• Exit home market early in corporate history if capabilities unrewarded at home. |

*Source*: Khanna and Palepu (2010)

electricity supplies in these remote locations was unstable especially in summer periods. Thus the company developed a solar-powered cooler and partnered with a local refrigeration company.

Tarun Khanna and Krishna Palepu propose the following five contexts as a framework in assessing the institutional environment of any country. The five contexts include the markets needed to acquire input (product, labor, and capital), and markets needed to sell output. This is referred to as the products and services market. In addition to these three dimensions the framework includes a broader sociopolitical context defined by political and social systems and degrees of openness. When applying the framework managers need to ask a set of questions in each dimension. An example of these questions is indicated in Table 11.5.

*Table 11.5 Framework to assess institutional voids*

| Institutional dimension | Questions |
|---|---|
| Product markets | 1. Can companies easily obtain reliable data on customer tastes and purchase behaviors? Are there cultural barriers to market research? Do world-class market research firms operate in the country? |
| | 2. Can consumers easily obtain unbiased information on the quality of the goods and services they want to buy? Are there independent consumer organizations and publications that provide such information? |
| | 3. Can companies access raw materials and components of good quality? Is there a deep network of suppliers? Are there firms that assess suppliers' quality and reliability? Can companies enforce contracts with suppliers? |
| | 4. How strong are the logistics and transportation infrastructures? Have global logistics companies set up local operations? |
| | 5. Do large retail chains exist in the country? If so, do they cover the entire country or only the major cities? Do they reach all consumers or only wealthy ones? |
| | 6. Are there other types of distribution channels, such as direct-to-consumer channels and discount retail channels that deliver products to customers? |
| | 7. Is it difficult for multinationals to collect receivables from local retailers? |
| | 8. Do consumers use credit cards, or does cash dominate transactions? Can consumers get credit to make purchases? Are data on customer creditworthiness available? |
| | 9. What recourse do consumers have against false claims by companies or defective products and services? |
| | 10. How do companies deliver after-sales service to consumers? Is it possible to set up a nationwide service network? Are third-party service providers reliable? |
| | 11. Are consumers willing to try new products and services? Do they trust goods from local companies? How about from foreign companies? |
| | 12. What kind of product-related environmental and safety regulations are in place? How do the authorities enforce those regulations? |
| Labor markets | 1. How strong is the country's education infrastructure, especially for technical and management training? Does it have a good elementary and secondary education system as well? |
| | 2. Do people study and do business in English or in another international language, or do they mainly speak a local language? |
| | 3. Are data available to help sort out the quality of the country's educational institutions? |

*Table 11.5 (Continued)*

| Institutional dimension | Questions |
|---|---|
| Labor markets | 4. Can employees move easily from one company to another? Does the local culture support that movement? Do recruitment agencies facilitate executive mobility? |
| | 5. What are the major post recruitment-training needs of the people that multinationals hire locally? |
| | 6. Is pay for performance a standard practice? How much weight do executives give seniority, as opposed to merit, in making promotion decisions? |
| | 7. Would a company be able to enforce employment contracts with senior executives? Could it protect itself against executives who leave the firm and then compete against it? Could it stop employees from stealing trade secrets and intellectual property? |
| | 8. Does the local culture accept foreign managers? Do the laws allow a firm to transfer locally hired people to another country? Do managers want to stay or leave the nation? |
| | 9. How are the rights of workers protected? How strong are the country's trade unions? Do they defend workers' interests or only advance a political agenda? |
| | 10. Can companies use stock options and stock-based compensation schemes to motivate employees? |
| | 11. Do the laws and regulations limit a firm's ability to restructure, downsize, or shut down? |
| | 12. If a company were to adopt its local rivals' or suppliers' business practices, such as the use of child labor, would that tarnish its image overseas? |
| Capital markets | 1. How effective are the country's banks, insurance companies, and mutual funds at collecting savings and channeling them into investments? |
| | 2. Are financial institutions managed well? Is their decision making transparent? Do noneconomic considerations, such as family ties, influence their investment decisions? |
| | 3. Can companies raise large amounts of equity capital in the stock market? Is there a market for corporate debt? |
| | 4. Does a venture capital industry exist? If so, does it allow individuals with good ideas to raise funds? |
| | 5. How reliable are sources of information on company performance? Do the accounting standards and disclosure regulations permit investors and creditors to monitor company management? |
| | 6. Do independent financial analysts, rating agencies, and the media offer unbiased information on companies? |
| | 7. How effective are corporate governance norms and standards at protecting shareholder interests? |
| | 8. Are corporate boards independent and empowered, and do they have independent directors? |
| | 9. Are regulators effective at monitoring the banking industry and stock markets? |

*(Continued)*

*Table 11.5 Framework to assess institutional voids (continued)*

| Institutional dimension | Questions |
| --- | --- |
| Capital markets | 10. How well do the courts deal with fraud?<br>11. Do the laws permit companies to engage in hostile takeovers? Can shareholders organize themselves to remove entrenched managers through proxy fights?<br>12. Is there an orderly bankruptcy process that balances the interests of owners, creditors, and other stakeholders? |
| Political and social system | 1. To whom are the country's politicians accountable? Are there strong political groups that oppose the ruling party? Do elections take place regularly?<br>2. Are the roles of the legislative, executive, and judiciary clearly defined? What is the distribution of power between the central, state, and city governments?<br>3. Does the government go beyond regulating business to interfering in it or running companies?<br>4. Do the laws articulate and protect private property rights?<br>5. What is the quality of the country's bureaucrats? What are bureaucrats' incentives and career trajectories?<br>6. Is the judiciary independent? Do the courts adjudicate disputes and enforce contracts in a timely and impartial manner? How effective are the quasi-judicial regulatory institutions that set and enforce rules for business activities?<br>7. Do religious, linguistic, regional, and ethnic groups coexist peacefully, or are there tensions between them?<br>8. How vibrant and independent is the media? Are newspapers and magazines neutral, or do they represent sectarian interests?<br>9. Are nongovernmental organizations, civil rights groups, and environmental groups active in the country?<br>10. Do people tolerate corruption in business and government?<br>11. What role do family ties play in business?<br>12. Can strangers be trusted to honor a contract in the country? |
| Openness | 1. Are the country's government, media, and people receptive to foreign investment? Do citizens trust companies and individuals from some parts of the world more than others?<br>2. What restrictions does the government place on foreign investment? Are those restrictions in place to facilitate the growth of domestic companies, to protect state monopolies, or because people are suspicious of multinationals?<br>3. Can a company make greenfield investments and acquire local companies, or can it only break into the market by entering into joint ventures? Will that company be free to choose partners based purely on economic considerations?<br>4. Does the country allow the presence of foreign intermediaries such as market research and advertising firms, retailers, media |

*Table 11.5  (Continued)*

| Institutional dimension | Questions |
|---|---|
| Openness | companies, banks, insurance companies, venture capital firms, auditing firms, management consulting firms, and educational institutions?<br>5. How long does it take to start a new venture in the country? How cumbersome are the government's procedures for permitting the launch of a wholly foreign-owned business?<br>6. Are there restrictions on portfolio investments by overseas companies or on dividend repatriation by multinationals?<br>7. Does the market drive exchange rates, or does the government control them? If it's the latter, does the government try to maintain a stable exchange rate, or does it try to favor domestic products over imports by propping up the local currency?<br>8. What would be the impact of tariffs on a company's capital goods and raw materials imports? How would import duties affect that company's ability to manufacture its products locally versus exporting them from home?<br>9. Can a company set up its business anywhere in the country? If the government restricts the company's location choices, are its motives political, or is it inspired by a logical regional development strategy?<br>10. Has the country signed free-trade agreements with other nations? If so, do those agreements favor investments by companies from some parts of the world over others?<br>11. Does the government allow foreign executives to enter and leave the country freely? How difficult is it to get work permits for managers and engineers?<br>12. Does the country allow its citizens to travel abroad freely? Can ideas flow into the country unrestricted? Are people permitted to debate and accept those ideas? |

# Cases[11]

A series of recent case studies of Western companies operating in emerging markets illustrates the diversity and complexity of marketing issues faced in areas such as socio-cultural dynamics, market orientation, brand strategies, product development, market entry, communications, and social media (Mutum, Roy, and Kipnis, 2014). Even though most cases in Mutum et al's (2014) research have lessons that are relevant for this chapter, we specifically draw on a selected few cases directly related to market entry.

Principles:

- Speed up new product development for firms aiming to increase export involvement
- Pressure for business responsiveness demands adaptation capabilities to the local environment
- Diverse range of marketing strategies

## Case: Kraft—Cadbury in India

In 2010 the United States based Kraft Foods, Inc. acquired Cadbury, a UK-based confectionary maker. Cadbury was founded in 1824 and as of 2009 it held a 10 percent share of the global market for chocolate, gums, and candy industry. It had a strong presence in emerging markets where it held a dominant position in relation to other major competitors. One particular market where Cadbury had a well-established presence for over 60 years is India. One reason why Kraft Foods acquired Cadbury was precisely to access to emerging markets, namely India and China, where Kraft's presence was marginal. Prior to acquiring Cadbury, Kraft did not have any meaningful presence in India, and currently it is entering India's packaged food market with new innovative products and packages. For example the Kraft's Oreos brand has been repackaged using Cadbury's banner and is being funneled through Cadbury's network of mom-and-pop stores.

## Case: McDonalds in India

McDonalds entered India in 1996 and by 2011 it had opened 211 restaurants in tier 1 and tier 2 cities across the country. In a country where people are biased toward their own food habit and cultures, one might expect foreign food retailing companies to face challenges upon entering India. However, while this was hitherto the scenario, it has changed recently with the new lifestyles and food consumption patterns in India, namely due to increased disposable income of middle and upper classes. McDonalds took advantage of these opportunities by adapting the menu to Indian tastes and offering home delivery.

# Conclusion

Entry mode[12] is determined by product, market, and organizational factors. In regards to products, companies need to know whether the nature and range of the product, along with available marketing strategies will require any adaptation. If so, they should consider a partner in that emerging market. Usually a higher level of control and resource commitment in the foreign market is required for new or wider product offerings as well as higher levels of adaptation. When taking into account market factors managers need to consider physical distance and experience, as well as identify appropriate marketing strategies and distribution channels, and priorities in revenues, costs, and profits.

Organizationally, major concerns are communication with foreign operations and control of overseas activities. One particular concern in foreign markets is the control of assets. Firms will prefer to internalize activities where there is a higher chance of opportunism by the partners in the emerging market.

# CHAPTER 12

# The Importance of Market Research and Business Intelligence

## Overview

In recent years, the global economy has undergone transformational changes. Countries, which benefitted from industrialization and emerged as advanced economies, are experiencing a slowdown and their financial markets are under considerable stress. On the other hand, after many *lost decades*, a few other countries, now pegged as emerging economies, have started making remarkable progress on the GDP growth front. While some emerging countries in Asia, such as Korea and Taiwan, have made economic progress by latching onto the growth wave unleashed by the electronic, information, by the electronic, information, communication technology industry, others have made progress by expanding their trade[1] with developed countries.

In the midst of these changes, the global economy also have experienced some major crises and resets, such as the Asian Financial Crisis, the U.S. housing bubble, followed by the global financial crisis, and the European sovereign debt crisis, with some of the above happening in quick succession. Due to these economic and financial crises, the real economy and financial markets suffered, people lost jobs, and growth slackened. As discussed in earlier chapters, while most advanced economies continue to struggle to recover from these developments, emerging economies have emerged more resilient;[2] either they recovered more quickly[3] or managed to avoid being hurt as much. Following the global financial crisis, some analysts even thought that the emerging economies could decouple and chart their own growth paths. However, later developments, such as the worsening of current account deficits for some emerging countries, such as India, a strengthening of the BRIC countries' currencies resulting from U.S. qualitative easing (QE) programs, and their subsequent drastic weakening from the expected gradual withdrawal of QE, have clearly established that we are truly living in a flat and interconnected world. We believe these developments have reinforced the view that in the emerging new economic order both advanced and emerging countries possess complementary roles to play in achieving sustainable economic progress, and that they need to collaborate to stabilize the global financial system.

Gaining a better understanding of the global and country specific economic development dynamics is important both for developing growth strategies and for creating a more stable financial system. Collecting relevant data at the global and country levels and analyzing them to arrive at actionable information aids us in the progress of gaining a necessary understanding. Converting the actionable information into strategic decisions and implementation plans coupled with regular feedback analysis and corrections would require analysis that is specific to the concerned stakeholder. Our world is an economically interconnected one, where many forces are at play and constantly changing. This requires efficient data gathering, analysis, and generation of actionable information. The stakeholders may include business corporations, nation states, economic development and research organizations, and investors.

Several global organizations, such as the World Bank, the IMF, the OECD, and leading consulting firms, such as McKinsey and PricewaterhouseCoopers, publish numerous research and survey reports that provide data and other qualitative information about the economy, trade, and related topics relating to developed and emerging countries. In addition, various agencies release, at regular intervals, information relating to the comparative positions of various countries by metrics, such as the global competitiveness index, global innovation index, ease of doing business, nominal GDP, GDP growth rate, per capita income, export and import trade, demography, current account deficit, and others. While stakeholders have access to these metrics that provide macro data, they also require information and analysis specific to their needs. This is in fact one of our fortes at Marcus Goncalves Consulting Group (MGCG)*, as such

---

* www.mgcgusa.com

specific and nuanced international market research needs would require custom market research and further business intelligence analysis in order to refine the macro data and thus generate actionable information, which supports the decision-making and related processes.

While the need for a research and analysis based approach is well underway and open discussions are taking place in numerous multilateral forums, the same is not true about reforms in the global financial system. We believe the global financial system is still very much the prerogative of the few developed economies, especially the United States, with the dollar as the world's de facto currency, and continues to wield too much power. Regretfully, necessary informed discussions among monetary and other policy makers do not take place transparently. The growing disconnect between the financial economy and the underlying real economy is a source of serious concern that deserves the urgent attention of policy makers, if a total collapse at some future date is to be averted. Presently, policy makers are in a quandary and seem quite content with putting out one crisis after the other.

True success of market research depends first on an unambiguous definition of the purpose of the exercise, accuracy of the research, timeliness of the data, and proper selection of the firm to carry out the market research and deep collaboration (i.e., partnership) between the involved parties or stakeholders.

## Modern Global Economic Evolution and Industrialization

Industrialization, which started around 1780 in Europe and North America, changed the pace of the global economic evolution. While technological inventions and breakthroughs spurred growth of the manufacturing industry, trade among countries, and economic activities. The global economic expansion resulted in the emergence of not only industrial centers of excellence and consumer demand centers, but also created markets for a broad portfolio of industrial products and goods that cater to basic needs and aspirational desires. Industrialization led to demand creation and fulfillment, increased consumption and investment, economic activity, and wealth creation. It set in motion a virtuous cycle of economic expansion resulting in job creation in manufacturing industries and growth of institutions and support services, such as banking, finance, insurance, and transportation, that either center around industrialization or are offshoots.

Industrialization was an inflection point in human history, which forever transformed our lives. Inventions and technological developments, such as the steam engine and the creation of railroads, development of the internal combustion engine, growth of the automotive industry, rapid expansion of information, and communication technology have all profited from what began as an invention of vacuum tubes and have revolutionized mass transportation, personal mobility, personal and mass communication, and information processing and computing. Such developments have created livelihoods and opportunities outside the traditional vocations, initially in manufacturing and subsequently in service and financial sectors. This occurred first in Europe, the birthplace of industrialization, and thereafter, in North America. As industrialization progressed, some of these countries emerged as advanced economies of the modern era and became the home of large engineering and business conglomerates spanning manufacturing, infrastructure, health care, transportation, and banking.

Industrialization created a new wave of aspirational wants among people and the disposable incomes in their pockets empowered them to indulge in discretionary spending. This led to a virtuous cycle of demand creation and fulfillment, increased consumption and investment, and wealth creation, starting in the real economy and after in the financial economy. Bain & Company's report "A world awash in money" points out that while the rate of growth of world output of goods and services has seen an extended slowdown over recent decades, global financial assets have expanded at a rapid pace.[4]

## Economic Growth Spreads to Asia

After incubating for decades in Europe and North America, industrialization spread to Japan and later to some other countries in East Asia, such as South Korea and Taiwan. While technological inventions and breakthroughs was the bedrock of economic growth in countries where industrialization took root, Japan took it to the next level though the path of productivity improvements by focusing on production processes, seen notably in automotive and electronic industries. Other countries in Asia, such as Singapore, South Korea, and Taiwan also latched onto the electronic and information technology industries' growth momentum to emerge as high-income economies during the latter half of the 20th century. Later, the opening up of China's economy and its integration into the global economy paved the way for it to emerge as the world's factory.

The emerging economies' development spurred consumption demand outside the advanced markets for a wide range of manufactured industrial products. Manufacturing moved away from a monolithic structure to become collaborative entities; each entity focused on what it does best at locations nearby to consumption centers.

Typical examples of collaborative and deconstructed manufacturing are the electronic and information technology industries, which largely contributed to the growth of Asian countries, such as South Korea and Taiwan. Large conglomerates dominate this industry. While integrated device manufacturers, such as Intel and Samsung design, make, and sell their chips, fabless* manufacturers such as Qualcomm and AMD only design and sell chips by outsourcing manufacturing to foundry companies. While Sony and LG Electronics are among the leading suppliers of consumer electronic goods, Lenovo and HP are top suppliers of personal computers. These companies then buy embedded devices from vendors such as Texas Instruments, and they in turn depend on companies such as Wipro and HCL Technologies to develop embedded software.

Companies such as Microsoft and SAP dominate the software market. Many of these companies and their affiliates have facilities in geographically dispersed locations. The expansion of the electronics industry, of which information and communication technology is comprised, not only helped countries in Asia to prosper but also resulted in increasing intra-regional and inter-regional trade. In the Working Paper,[5] "Fragmentation and East Asia's Information Technology Trade" published in 2004, the authors Carl Bonham, Byron Gangnes, and Ari Van Assche argued, "Over the past two decades, international production fragmentation by

---

* Without silicon wafer manufacturing facilities.

U.S. and Japanese IT firms has gradually turned developing East Asia into a global manufacturing base for IT products." On one hand, this provided further impetus for the economic growth across countries in Asia, especially in ASEAN countries, and on the other to the consolidation of globalization trends. Countries and companies that successfully align their growth strategies with global trends reap the benefits.

## New Economic Order and Financial System Vulnerabilities

When economic growth began to spread across countries in East and South East Asia, by mid-1990s the Japanese economy began to show signs of slowdown, driven by various factors including U.S. pressure. Later, loss of trade due to the emergence of China as a low cost manufacturer and demographic influence on the country's labor further accentuated the situation. In addition, Japan also experienced an asset price bubble resulting in plunging stock and asset prices. Since then, Japan has not been successful in reviving its growth, and in 2010 the country ceded its moniker as the world' second largest economy to China. It may be safe to hypothesize that Japan's protracted slowdown is among the first indicator of two developments; one, the emergence of a new economic order in the shaping of which emerging markets would play a significant role and two, the vulnerability of the global financial system.

Figure 12.1 show how the Chinese economy has overtaken the advanced economies of France, UK, Germany, and Japan, and how the Japanese economy remained stagnant for well over a decade while China was expanding.

Due to increased economic development in emerging countries the world is witnessing the emergence of a massive middleclass population with significant disposable incomes and a robust appetite for aspirational wants, such as automobiles and consumer durables. If their demands are to be satisfied, these countries need a robust manufacturing industry, which many lack. Typically, emerging countries continue to struggle in overcoming the initial mover advantage that advanced countries continue to enjoy in the industrial sector. A few are in a position to grasp the technology, have acquired negotiating power due to their recent achievement of economic growth, and have become attractive to would be global investors.

(a)

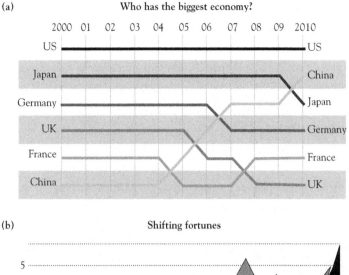

(b)

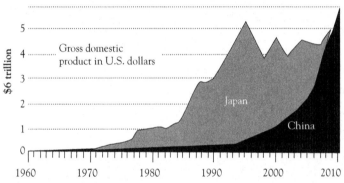

*Figure 12.1  China's economy has overtaken France, UK, Germany, and Japan, the advanced economies*

*Sources:* The World Bank, IMF

The importance of the manufacturing industry in spurring growth in emerging countries cannot be overstated. A McKinsey report[6] "Manufacturing the growth: The next era of global growth" says very aptly "… manufacturing remains critically important to both the developing and the advanced world. In the former, it continues to provide a pathway from subsistence agriculture to rising incomes and living standards. In the latter, it remains a vital source of innovation and competitiveness, making outsized contributions to research and development, exports, and productivity growth." It is important to add that sustainable growth is possible *only when* all other industries work together in supporting the framework, including the service industry, banking and finance, law, and a national policy on taxation and trade. As economic prosperity expands, the aspirational demand for services increases and the service industry expands. In their book,[7] "Beyond Economic Growth," authors Tatyana P. Soubbotina with Katherine A. Sheram, underscore this thought; "As incomes continue to rise, people's needs become less 'material' and they begin to demand more services—in health, education, entertainment, and many other areas."

Resulting from the spread of industrialization and wealth creation, we are witnessing the emergence of new economic order in which emerging countries would play an important role. The formal recognition by the G-7 countries, discussed in earlier chapters, verifies that close integration of their economies with emerging countries, and effective collaboration with them, is necessary to sustain the long-term global economic growth strategies, and led to the creation of G-20.

Despite the exclusion of some large economies, G-20 acts as an excellent platform to deliberate and decide on mutually beneficial economic growth and financial strategies. Of course, advanced and emerging countries have other platforms, such as trade agreements and groupings like Transatlantic Trade and Investment Partnership (TTIP) and ASEAN in which to achieve national and regional economic objectives.

G-20's deliberations include, apart from economic growth and globalization issues, matters relating to the international financial system. The U.S. subprime mortgage crisis in 2008, the banking crisis in Ireland, and the European sovereign debt crisis, which began in 2009, have brought to the fore the weaknesses in the financial system. Figure 12.2 illustrates the global capital pyramid and the magnitude of its impact on global GDP growth.

As depicted in Figure 12.2, with the current financial assets at nearly 10 times the value of the global output of all goods and services,[8] the relationship between the financial economy and the underlying real economy has become unformulated and unstable. The financial assets, subjected to speculative forces, keep expanding. While getting divorced from the real economy of the common people, who constitute the majority, the expanding financial economy is beginning to affect them profoundly. It accentuates the normal business growth and downturn cycles, creates asset

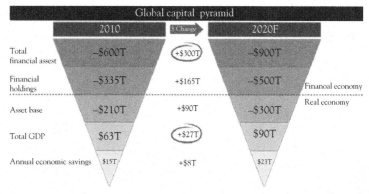

**Figure 12.2 A $27 trillion growth in global GDP will support a $300 trillion increase in total financial assets by 2020**

*Source*: IMF, OECD, Bain

bubbles, and leads to currency fluctuations. Resulting from the financial economy's growing disconnect with the real economy it has reached a decisive point which calls for the financial market participants and other policy makers to initiate corrective measures.

While discussions relating to the role of emerging countries in ensuring sustainable global economic growth and global trade continue to make progress, discussions on the appropriate steps for ensuring the stability of the financial system have not. In order to move forward, stakeholders must make serious efforts to address the core issues instead of short-term fixes.

### Need for Market Research and Business Intelligence to Succeed

Numerous global organizations, such as World Bank, the OECD, and leading consulting firms such as McKinsey and Boston Consulting, develop research and survey reports that provide data and qualitative information about the global economy, industry, and topics relating to advanced and emerging countries. In addition, various agencies release at regular intervals information relating the comparative position of countries by metrics, such as ease of doing business, global competitiveness index, nominal GDP, GDP growth rate, per capita income, export and import trade, demography, current account deficit, and global innovation index.

Stakeholders, such as the business corporations, nation states, consultants and analyst firms, institutional and private equity investors, and economic development and research organizations interested in global economic development and in ensuring the future stability of the financial system, need not only macro level data and basic information, but they need it in granular detail. With the help of analytics and business intelligence tools they can generate actionable information that help them make informed investment decisions. Business intelligence tools also could help them to perform what-if analysis under changing economic scenarios.

Succeeding in business, formulating a country's growth strategies, making the right investment decisions, developing and introducing the right product, and advising clients about business transformation are complex and require real time information gathering and analysis with powerful algorithms.

Qualitative and quantitative information gathering or market research, both primary and secondary, is required to identify market needs, opportunities, and threats, to make informed decisions. It is the minimum required to maximize the probability of success and minimizes risks. The type of information required would depend on the stakeholder's specific needs. For example, an automotive company from a developed country, interested in establishing its business presence in an emerging country, might like the research for information, such as the country's demand projection, growth prospects, competitors profile, import policy and tariffs, acceptable price points, buying pattern, and business nuances. Its initial interest may be to shortlist few countries out of list of probable countries that have business potential and a high probability of success.

In order to select the country or countries, the company would invariably need information, such as the country's market size, GDP, and per capita income growth rates, demography, import–export trade, currency rate, economic, and political stability. The required information is customized to the stakeholder's needs and the information gathered is country and timeframe specific. After deciding upon the country in which to expand, the company may shift its focus to select potential partners, necessitating operational, financial, and legalese requiring extensive detailed data gathering and information analysis. After establishing a presence, the company might like to have research about brand acceptance, customer satisfaction, its market share, and prospects of launching a new product into the market. On the other hand, a developed country's automotive industry association, wanting to estimate the business potential for its members might require more broad based market research to gather information, such as current status of the industry, demand patterns and growth potential for compact cars, trucks, sport utility vehicles, and sedans in selected countries.

If, instead of the automotive company, a consumer durable manufacturer from a developed country wanted to explore the feasibility of entering an emerging market, the research requirements would be very different. Typically, a consumer durable manufacturer would be offering a broad portfolio of products ranging from simple generic models to feature-rich high-end products. Therefore, the company may need information that would facilitate decision making on matters relating to sales channels, which products to offer initially, branding strategy, distribution logistics, and best location of the company's production facility.

On the other hand, if a developing country wants to draw up the country's industrial roadmap, it would probably start by researching the country's developmental needs and priorities, its industry's capacity to absorb the technology, and skill availability.

The need for research-based data and information gathering and the use of business intelligence and analytics to analyze and generate actionable information to track the efficacy of the actions is that much greater in a world on the threshold of entering a new economic order. The lingering perception is that organizations and institutions operating in the realm of a real economy more often resort to a research and analytical-based approach in comparison to those belonging to the financial economic fraternity.

The capture of accurate qualitative and quantitative information is important. Stakeholders must also clearly define upfront the purpose of the exercise, as that will decide the research methodology and the information to be gathered and analyzed. They must be clear in stipulating what data and information they need, why they need it, and how they intend to use it. The answers to these questions would determine the type, either primary or secondary, and in the case of primary, the questionnaire design, mode of data and information collection, and the responsible agency. In the case of secondary research, the sources, its time relevance, and reliability would be important. Market research requires that it be both systematic and objective to serve the intended purpose. Prior to analyzing the data and information, it is necessary to validate it.

Selecting and appointing the firm to carry out the market research plays a crucial role in a project's success. This process involves evaluating the past performance of the market research firm and whether it has the necessary resources, such as the required field staff, domain knowledge, and expertise. It is important for the stakeholder commissioning the market research to be completely involved during each phase of the market research, such as formulating the questionnaire, the data, and information gathering methodology.

# CHAPTER 13

# Coping with Political and Economic Risks

## Overview

We hope we have adequately conveyed that diversification in global trading benefits international business investments, especially in emerging markets, which have become a prominent feature of the financial globalization sweeping the world over the last decade. Investing in emerging markets, however, exposes companies and investors to political environments that are not typically present in advanced economies.

Over the past two decades, we have witnessed Russian default on its debt to foreigners in 1998, the Mexican peso crisis in 1994, and the Asian economic meltdown in 1997. While these risks are usually well known to major banks and multinational companies, and assessment techniques in these domains are relatively well developed, they tend not to be appropriate in assessing the geopolitical aspects associated with cross country correlations.

Political risks for FDI are affected when difficult to anticipate discontinuities resulting from political change occur in the international business environment. Some example include the potential restrictions on the transfer of funds, products, technology and people, uncertainty about policies, regulations, governmental administrative procedures, and risks on control of capital such as discrimination against foreign firms, expropriation, forced local shareholding, and so on. Wars, revolutions, social upheavals, strikes, economic growth, inflation and exchange rates should also be figured into the political and economic risk assessment, as these instances can negatively impact local investments as well as FDI.

## Recent Political Unrests

Conducting business internationally, therefore, may offer many opportunities, but not without risks, especially political ones. There have been a myriad of events occurring around the world in the past three years, particularly among emerging economies, more notably the MENA region, as depicted in Figure 13.1. For instance, a revolutionary wave of demonstrations and protests, riots, and civil wars in the Arab world began in early December 2010. Its effects are still lingering. As of November 2013, rulers from this region have been forced from power, as in Tunisia,[1] which took down the country's long-time dictator, Zine El Abidine Ben Ali. At the time, many were looking to it as a turning point for the Arab world, and rampant speculation about what it could mean for other countries toiling under Islamic dictatorships.

Although the Arab Spring began in Tunisia, the decisive moment that changed the Arab region forever was the downfall of Egyptian President Hosni Mubarak, who ensconced in power since 1980. Similar to Tunisia, mass protests started in late January of 2011 and by early February Mubarak was forced to resign after the military refused to intervene against the masses occupying Tahrir Square in Cairo. Deep divisions

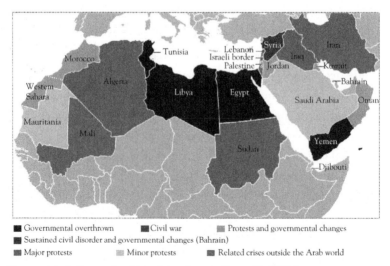

*Figure 13.1 Several political conflicts affected MENA economies in the past three years*

emerged over the new political system as Islamists from the Freedom and Justice Party (FJP) won the parliamentary and presidential election in 2011/12 souring relations with secular parties that continued protests for deeper political change. The Egyptian military remains the single most powerful political player, and much of the old regime remains in place. The economy has been in decline since the start of unrest.[2]

By the time Mubarak resigned, large portions of the Middle East were already in turmoil. Soon after Mubarak's resignation, in February 2011, protests against Col. Muammar al-Qaddafi's regime in Libya started, escalating into the first civil war caused by the Arab Spring. NATO[3] forces had to intervene in March 2011 against Qaddafi's army, helping the opposition rebel movement to capture most of the country by August 2011. In October 2011 Qaddafi was killed, but the rebels' coup was short-lived, as various rebel militias effectively partitioned the country among them, leaving a weak central government that continues to struggle to exert its authority and provide basic services to its citizens. Most of the oil production has returned on stream, but political violence remains endemic, and religious extremism has been on the rise*

From Libya, the Arab Spring blew toward Yemen. Bolstered by events in Tunisia, anti-government protesters of all political parties started pouring onto the streets in mid-January 2011. Hundreds of people died in clashes as pro-government forces organized rival rallies, and the army began to disintegrate into two political camps. As a result, the Yemeni leader, Ali Abdullah Saleh, became the fourth victim of the Arab Spring. Amidst all this turmoil, Al Qaeda in Yemen began to seize territory in the south of the country. Had it not been for Saudi Arabia's facilitation of a political settlement Yemen would have fallen victim to an all-out civil war. President Saleh signed the transition deal on November 23, 2011, agreeing to step aside for a transitional government led by the Vice-President Abd al-Rab Mansur al-Hadi. However, little progress toward a stabile democratic order has been made and regular Al Qaeda attacks, separatism in the south, tribal disputes, and a collapsing economy, all stall this nascent transition.[4]

---

* North Atlantic Treaty Organization, an international organization composed of the Unites States, Canada, UK, and a number of European countries for purposes of collective security.

Many Arab Spring demonstrations have been met with violent responses from authorities, as well as from pro-government militias and counter-demonstrators. These attacks have been answered with violence from protestors in some cases. A major slogan of the demonstrators in the Arab world has been *Ash-sha`b yurid isqat an-nizam* ("the people want to bring down the regime").[5] Hence, at the same time Tunisia, Egypt, and Libya were dealing with the consequences of the Arab Spring, civil uprisings were also breaking out in Bahrain and Syria, while several major protests continued to erupt in Algeria, Iraq, Jordan, Kuwait, Morocco, and Sudan.

Protests in Bahrain began on February 2012, just days after Mubarak's resignation. Bahrain has always had a long history of tension between the ruling Sunni royal family, and the majority Shiite population demanding greater political and economic rights. The Arab Spring acted as a catalyst, reenergizing the largely Shiite protest movement, driving tens of thousands to the streets defying fire from security forces. The Bahraini royal family was saved by a military intervention of neighboring countries led by Saudi Arabia. A political solution, however, was not reached and the crackdown failed to suppress the protest movement. As of early fall 2013, protests, clashes with security forces, and arrests of opposition activists continue in that country with no solution in sight.[6]

Syria, a multi-religious country allied with Iran, ruled by a repressive republican regime, and amid a pivotal geo-political position was next. The major protests began in March 2011 in provincial towns at first, but gradually spreading to all major urban areas. The regime's brutality provoked an armed response from the opposition, and by mid-2011 army defectors began organizing in the Free Syrian Army. Consequently, by the end of 2011, Syria slid into an obstinate civil war, which is still ongoing today, with most of the Alawite* religious minority siding with President Bashar al-Assad, and most of the Sunni majority supporting the rebels. Both camps have outside backers. Russia supports the regime, while Saudi Arabia supports the rebels with neither side able to break the deadlock.[7]

On February 20, 2011, the Arab Spring engulfed Morocco, when thousands of protesters gathered in the capital city, Rabat demanding

---

* Member of a Shiite Muslim group living mainly in Syria.

greater social justice and limits to King Mohammed VI's power. The king responded by offering constitutional amendments ceding some of his powers, and by calling a fresh parliamentary election controlled less by the royal court than in previous elections. This, together with fresh state funds to help low-income families, diminished the appeal of the protest movement, with many Moroccans content with the king's program of gradual reform. Rallies demanding a genuine constitutional monarchy continue, but have so far failed to mobilize the masses as it did in Tunisia and Egypt.[8]

Demonstrations in Jordan gained momentum in late January 2011, as Islamists, leftist groups, and youth activists protested against living conditions and corruption. Parallel to Morocco, most Jordanians wanted to reform, rather than abolish the monarchy, giving King Abdullah II the breathing space his republican counterparts in other Arab countries didn't have. Consequently, the king managed to ease the Arab Spring by making superficial changes to the political system and reorganizing the government. Fear of chaos similar to Syria did the rest. To date, the economy, however, is still performing poorly and none of the key issues have been addressed, which may prompt protesters' demands to grow more radical over time.[9]

Algerian protests, which started in late December 2010, were inspired by similar protests across the MENA region. Causes included unemployment, the lack of housing, food-price inflation, corruption, restrictions on freedom of speech, and poor living conditions. While localized protests were already commonplace in previous years, extending into December 2010, an unprecedented wave of simultaneous protests and riots, sparked by a sudden rise in staple food prices, erupted all over the country beginning in January 2011. These protests were suppressed by government swiftly lowering food prices, but were followed by a wave of self-immolations, most of which occurred in front of government buildings. Despite being illegal to do so without government permission, opposition parties, unions, and human rights groups began holding weekly demonstrations. The government's reaction was a swift repression of these demonstrations.[10]

The 2011 Iraqi protests came in the wake of the Tunisian and Egyptian revolutions. The protests have resulted in at least 45 deaths, including at least 29 on the *Day of Rage*, which took place on February

25, 2011. Several of the protests in March 2011, however, were against the Saudi-led intervention in Bahrain.[11] Protests also took place in Iraqi Kurdistan, an autonomous Kurdish region in Iraq's north that lasted for 62 consecutive days. More recently, on December 21, 2012, a group raided Sunni Finance Minister Rafi al-Issawi's home and resulted in the arrest of 10 of his bodyguards.[12] Beginning in Fallujah, the protests have since spread throughout Sunni Arab parts of Iraq, and have even gained support from non-Sunni Iraqi politicians, such as Muqtada al-Sadr. Pro-Maliki protests have taken place throughout southern Iraq, where there is a Shia Arab majority. In April 2013, sectarian violence escalated after the 2013 Hawija clashes.[13]

Kuwaiti protests took place in 2011–2012, also calling for government reforms. On November 28, 2011, the government of Kuwait resigned in response to the protests, making Kuwait one of several countries affected by the Arab Spring to experience major governmental changes due to unrest.[14]

As part of the Arab Spring, protests in Sudan began in January 2011 with a regional protest movement. Unlike other Arab countries, however, popular uprisings in Sudan succeeded in toppling the government prior to the Arab Spring, in both 1964 and 1985. Demonstrations were less common throughout the summer of 2011, during which time South Sudan seceded from Sudan. It resumed in force in June 2012 shortly after the government passed its much criticized austerity plan.[15]

There have been other minor protests, which broke out in Mauritania, Oman, Saudi Arabia, Djibouti, and West Sahara. In Mauritania,[16] the protests were largely peaceful, demanding President Mohamed Ould Abdel Aziz to institute political, economic, and legal reforms. The common themes of these protests included slavery, which officially is illegal in Mauritania, but is widespread in the country,[17] and other human rights abuse the opposition had accused the government of perpetrating. These protests started in January 2011 and continued well into 2012. In Oman,[18] demonstrations were demanding salary increases, increased job creation, and fighting corruption. The sultan's responses included dismissal of one third of his government cabinet.[19] In Saudi Arabia,[20] the protests started with a self-immolation in Samtah and demonstration in the streets of Jeddah in late January 2011. It was then followed by protests against anti-Shia discrimination in February and early March of the same year in Qatif, Hofuf, al-Awamiyah, and Riyadh. In Djibouti,[21] the protests, which showed a clear support of the Arab Spring, ended quickly after mass arrests and exclusion of international observers. Lastly, in Western Sahara,[22] the protests were a reaction to the failure of police to prevent anti-Sahrawi looting in the city of Dakhla, Western Sahara, and mushroomed into protests across the territory. They were related to the Gdeim Izik protest camp in Western Sahara, established the previous fall, which had resulted in violence between Sahrawi activists and Moroccan security forces and supporters.

Still, there were other related events outside of the region. In April 2011, also known among protesters as the Ahvaz *Day of Rage*, protests occurred in Iranian Khuzestan by the Arab minority. These violent protests erupted on April 15, 2011[23] marking the anniversary of the 2005 Ahvaz unrest. These protests lasted for four days and resulted in about a dozen protesters killed and many more wounded and arrested. Israel also experienced its share of political conflicts with border clashes in May 2011,[24] to commemorate what the Palestinians observe as *Nakba Day*. During the demonstrations, various groups of people attempted to approach or breach Israel's borders from the Palestinian-controlled territory, Lebanon, Syria, Egypt, and Jordan.

## Assessing Political Risks

As barriers to international trade easel, the dynamic global marketplace continues to attract investors who are eager to capitalize on opportunities they see in emerging markets around the world. Compared to a quarter century ago, these markets enjoy greater stability and are experiencing steady growth. However, these emerging markets remain vulnerable to a host of forces known as political risk that are largely beyond the control of investors. Among these risk factors are currency instability, corruption, weak government institutions, unreformed financial systems, patchy legal and regulatory regimes, and restrictive labor markets.

Assessment techniques for political risk are as wide-ranging as the sources that generate it. Traditional methods for assessing political risk range from the comparative techniques of rating and mapping systems,

| Score legend<br>5 = excellent<br>3 = acceptable<br>1 = poor | Political stability | Worker skill, supply | Culture compatibility | Infrastructure | Government support | Product-to-market advantage |
|---|---|---|---|---|---|---|
| Singapore | 5 | 4 | 4 | 4 | 4 | 3 |
| India | 3 | 4 | 3 | 3 | 3 | 3 |
| Ireland | 5 | 4 | 5 | 5 | 5 | 5 |

*Figure 13.2  Sample of a country profiling assessment matrix*

as depicted in Figure 13.2, to the analytical techniques of special reports, dynamic segmentation, expert systems, and determination to the econometric techniques of model building and discriminant and logit analysis.* These techniques are very useful for identifying and analyzing individual sources of political risk but aren't sophisticated enough to handle cross relationships or correlations well. They also are not accurate measurements of levels of loss generated by the risks being analyzed. Hence, it is difficult to evaluate country profiling and analysis into a practical decision making tool.

In Dr. Goncalves' lectures at Nichols College, when analyzing the inter-dynamics of advanced economies and emerging markets, two approaches are used for incorporating political risk in the capital budgeting process for foreign direct investments. The first approach involves an ad hoc adjustment of the discount rate to account for losses due to political risk, while the second approach involves an ad hoc adjustment of the project's expected future cash flows and expected return on investment (ROI).

No company, domestic or international, large or small, can conduct business abroad without considering the influence of the political environment in which it will operate. One of the most undeniable and crucial

---

* Logit analysis is a statistical technique used by marketers to assess the scope of customer acceptance of a product, particularly a new product. It attempts to determine the intensity or magnitude of customers' purchase intentions and translates that into a measure of actual buying behavior.

realities of international business is that both host and home governments are integral partners. A government controls and restricts a company's activities by encouraging and offering support or by discouraging and restricting its activities contingent upon the whim of the government.

International law recognizes the sovereign right of a nation to grant or withhold permission to do business at the privileges of the government. In addition, international law recognizes the sovereign right of a nation to grant or withhold permission to do business within its political boundaries and to control where its citizens conduct business.

In the context of international law, a sovereign state is independent and free from all external control; enjoys full legal equality with other states; governs its own territory; selects its own political, economic, and social systems; and has the power to enter into agreements with other nations. Sovereignty refers to both the powers exercised by a state in relation to other countries and the supreme powers exercised over its own members. A state outlines and decides the requirements for citizenship, defines geographical boundaries, and controls trade and the movement of people and goods across its borders.

Nations can and do abridge specific aspects of their sovereign rights in order to coexist with other nations. The European Union, UN, NAFTA, NATO, and WTO represent examples of nations voluntarily agreeing to succumb some of their sovereign rights in order to participate with member nations for a common, mutually beneficial goal. However, U.S. involvement in international political affiliations is surprisingly low. For example, the WTO is considered by some as the biggest threat, thus far to national sovereignty. Adherence to the WTO inevitably means loss to some degree of national sovereignty because member nations have pledged to abide by international covenants and arbitration procedures. Sovereignty was one of the primary issues at the core of a kerfuffle between the United States and the EU over Europe's refusal to lower tariffs and quotas on bananas. Critics of the free trade agreements with both South Korea and Peru claim America's sacrifice of sovereignty goes too far.

Figure 13.3 provides a sampling of countries electing other options including authoritarianism, theocracy, dictatorship, and communism, which are taking different approach. Troubling is the apparent regression of some countries toward autocracy and away from democracy, such as

| Country | Government type |
|---|---|
| Afghanistan | Islamic republic |
| Belarus | Republic in name, though in fact a dictatorship |
| Bosnia and Herzegovina | Emerging federal democratic republic |
| Burma (Myanmar) | Military junta |
| Canada | Confederation with parliamentary democracy |
| China | Communist state |
| Congo, Democratic Republic of the | Dictatorship, presumably undergoing a transition to representative government |
| Cuba | Communist state |
| Iran | Theocratic republic |
| Libya | Jamahiriya (a state of the masses) in theory, governed by the populace through local councils; in fact a military dictatorship |
| North Korea | Communist state, one-man dictatorship |
| Saudi Arabia | Monarchy |
| Somalia | No permanent national government; transitional, parliamentary federal government |
| Sudan | Authoritarian regime—ruling military junta |
| United Kingdom | Constitutional monarchy |
| United States | Constitutional federal republic |
| Uzbekistan | Republic; authoritarian presidential rule, with little power outside the executive branch |
| Vietnam | Communist state |

*Figure 13.3  A sampling of government types*

Nigeria, Kenya, Bangladesh, Venezuela, Georgia, and Kyrgyzstan. It is transparent for all to witness the world's greatest experiment in political and economic change—the race between Russian reforms and Chinese gradualism as communism is left further behind in both countries.

Economic and cultural nationalism, which exists to some degree within all countries, is another important risk factor when assessing the international business environment. Nationalism can best be described as an intense feeling of national pride and unity. One of the economic nationalism's central aims is the preservation of economic autonomy whereby residents identify their interests with that preservation of the sovereignty. Hence, national interests and security become far more important than international business relations.

Generally, the more a country feels threatened by some outside force or a decline in domestic economy is evident, the more nationalistic it becomes in protecting itself against intrusions. By the late 1980s, militant nationalism had subsided. Today, the foreign investor, once feared as a dominant tyrant threatening economic development, is often sought after as a source of needed capital investment. Nationalism vacillates as conditions and attitudes change, and foreign companies welcomed today may be harassed tomorrow.

It is important for international business professionals not to confuse nationalism, whose animosity is directed generally toward all foreign countries, with a widespread fear directed at a particular country. Toyota committed this mistake in the United States during the late 1980s and early 1990s. At the time Americans considered the economic threat from Japan greater than the military threat from the Soviet Union. So when Toyota spent millions on an advertising campaign showing Toyotas being made by Americans in a plant in Kentucky, it exacerbated the fear that the Japanese were "colonizing" the United States. The same sentiments ring true with China, who some believe, is colonizing the United States.[25]

The United States is not immune to these same types of directed negativity. The rift between France and the United States over the Iraq–U.S. war led to hard feelings on both sides and an American backlash against French wine, French cheese, and even products Americans thought were French. French's mustard felt compelled to issue a press release stating that it was an American company founded by an American named French. Thus, it is quite clear that no nation-state, however secure, will tolerate penetration by a foreign company into its market and economy if it perceives a social, cultural, economic, or political threat to its well-being.

Various types of political risks should be considered before investing in foreign markets, for both advanced and emerging economies. The most severe political risk is confiscation, that is, the seizing of a company's assets without payment. The two most notable recent confiscations of U.S. property occurred when Fidel Castro became the leader in Cuba and later when the Shah of Iran was overthrown. Confiscation was most prevalent in the 1950s and 1960s, when many underdeveloped countries saw confiscation, albeit ineffective, as a means of economic growth.

Less drastic, but still severe, is expropriation, when the government seizes an investment but some reimbursement for the assets is made. Often the expropriated investment is nationalized, that is, it becomes a government-run entity. An example is Bolivia, where the president, Ivo Morales, confiscated Red Eletrica, a utility company from Spain.

**Operational risk**
Countries, September 2008 (September 2007 score, if different)

| Least risky | | Most risky | |
|---|---|---|---|
| Rank | Score* | Rank | Score |
| 1 Switzerland | 8 (7) | 150 Iraq | 84 (88) |
| 2 Denmark | 10 (8) | 149 Guinea | 80 (79) |
| Singapore | 10 | 148 Myanmar | 79 (78) |
| Sweden | 10 | 147 Zimbabwe | 78 (77) |
| 5 Finland | 12 (10) | 146 Turkmenistan | 77 |
| 6 Austria | 14 | Uzbekistan | 77 |
| Luxembourg | 14 | 144 Venezuela | 75 (74) |
| Norway | 14 | 143 Tajikistan | 71 (70) |
| 9 Netherlands | 15 (13) | 142 Eritrea | 70 (69) |
| Britain | 15 (12) | 141 Chad | 68 |
| 11 Canada | 16 (15) | Ecuador | 68 |
| Hong Kong | 16 | 139 Kenya | 66 |
| 13 France | 17 (16) | 138 Côte d'Ivoire | 65 |
| Germany | 17 (16) | Nigeria | 65 (67) |
| 15 Australia | 18 (16) | Sudan | 65 |
| Belgium | 18 | | |
| Malta | 18 (19) | | |

*Figure 13.4  Country ranking by political and operating risks*

Note: *Out of 100, with higher numbers indicating more risk.
Source: The Economist Intelligence Unit

A third type of risk is domestication. This occurs when host countries gradually induce the transfer of foreign investments to national control and ownership through a series of government decrees by mandating local ownership and greater national involvement in a company's management. Figure 13.4 provides a sample list of country rankings in terms of political risks when operating a business.

Even though expropriation and confiscation are waning, international companies are still confronted with a variety of economic risks that can occur with little warning. Restraints on business activity may be imposed under the banner of national security to protect an infant industry, to conserve scarce foreign exchange, to raise revenue, or to retaliate against unfair trade practices. Following are important and recurring reality of economic risks, and recurring of the international political environment, that few international companies can avoid:

- **Exchange control**—These stem from shortages of foreign exchange held by a country.
- **Import restrictions**—These are selective restrictions on the import of raw materials, machines, and spare parts; fairly common strategies to force foreign industry to purchase more supplies within the host country and thereby create markets for local industry.
- **Labor problems**—In many countries, labor unions have strong government support that they use effectively in obtaining special concessions from business. Layoffs may be forbidden, profits may have to be shared, and an extraordinary number of services may have to be provided.
- **Local-content laws**—In addition to restricting imports of essential supplies to force local purchase, countries often require a portion of any product sold within the country to have local content, that is, to contain locally made parts.
- **Price controls**—Essential products that command considerable public interest, such as pharmaceuticals, food, gasoline, and cars are often subjected to price controls. Such controls applied during inflationary periods can be used to control the cost of living. They also may be used to force foreign companies to sell equity to local interests. A side effect could be slowing or even halting capital investment.
- **Tax controls**—Taxes must be classified as a political risk when used as a means of controlling foreign investments. In such cases, they are raised without warning and in violation of formal agreements.

Boycotting is another risk, whereby one or a group of nations might impose it on another, using political sanctions, which effectively stop trade between the countries. The United States has come under criticism for its demand for continued sanctions against Cuba and its threats of future

sanctions against countries that violate human rights issues. History, however, indicates that sanctions are almost always unsuccessful in reaching
desired goals, particularly when other nations' traders ignore them.

International business professionals traveling to emerging markets or
even, to the so-called least develop countries (LDCs), must be aware of
any travel warnings related to political, health, or terrorism risks. The
U.S. Department of State (DOS) provides country specific information
for every country. For each country, there is information related to location of the U.S. embassy or consular offices in that country, whether a
visa is necessary, crime and security information, health and medical
conditions, drug penalties, and localized hot spots. This is an invaluable
resource when assessing country risks.

The DOS also issue *travel alerts* for short-term events important for
travelers when planning a trip abroad. Issuing a travel alert might include
an election season that is bound to have many strikes, demonstrations,
disturbances; a health alert like an outbreak of H1N1; or evidence of an
elevated risk of terrorist attacks. When these short-term events conclude,
the DOS cancels the alert.

*Travel warnings* are more important as the DOS issues them when
it wants travelers to consider carefully whether to enter into the country
at all. Reasons for issuing a travel warning might include an unstable
government, civil war, ongoing intense crime or violence, or frequent terrorist attacks. The U.S. government wants international travelers to know
the risks of traveling to these places and to strongly consider not going
at all. These travel warnings remain in place until the situation changes;
although some have been in effect for years. They are often issued when
long-term, protracted conditions lead the State Department to recommend Americans avoid or consider the risk of travel to that country.
A *travel warning** also is issued when the U.S. government's ability to
assist American citizens is constrained due to the closure of an embassy
or consulate, or because of a drawdown of its staff. As of fall 2013, the
countries listed in Figure 13.5 meet those criteria.

---

\* Such information changes often, so we advise you to check the website for
up-to-date information at http://travel.state.gov/travel/travel_1744.html, last
accessed on 10/10/2013.

Korea, Democratic People's Republic of 11/19/2013
Eritrea 11/18/2013
Central African Republic 11/14/2013
Egypt 06/16/2013
Congo, Democratic Republic of the 10/24/2013
Republic of South Sudan 10/22/2013
Sudan 10/11/2013
Burundi 10/11/2013
Colombia 10/11/2013
Chad 10/11/2013
Lebanon 10/09/2013
Syria 10/07/2013
Tunisia 10/04/2013
Kenya 09/27/2013
Pakistan 09/06/2013
Iraq 09/05/2013
Algeria 08/23/2013
Afghanistan 08/23/2013
Haiti 08/13/2013
El Salvador 08/09/2013
Yemen 08/06/2013
Saudi Arabia 07/25/2013
Mali 07/18/2013
Niger 07/15/2013
Mexico 07/12/2013
Philippines 07/05/2013
Somalia 06/21/2013
Israel, the West Bank and Gaza 06/19/2013
Honduras 06/17/2013
Libya 06/07/2013
Nigeria 06/03/2013
Iran 05/24/2013
Mauritania 05/21/2013
Cote d'Ivoire 05/16/2013

**Figure 13.5  List of countries in the U.S. Department of State travel-warning list as of fall 2013**

*Source*: U.S. Department of State

# Managing Political Risk

Elisabeth Boone, chartered property casualty underwriter (CPCU) and manager of political risk and credit at ACE Global Markets,[26] argues that very few companies actually have a formal approach to risk management when it comes to emerging markets. She indicates that although the great majority of companies she surveys and advises are aware that political risk management is important to their operations, just 49 percent of them integrate it formally into their investment process, while 41 percent take an informal approach to considering political risk as part of their investment process. This gap between awareness of political risk and formal action to manage it, Boone argues, is serious cause for concern given the fact that 79 percent of her survey respondents reported that their investments in emerging markets had increased over the past three years.

Not surprising, in the post-9/11 era is another survey finding that Boone deems noteworthy. She argues that there is "a perception that terrorism is a greater or at least an equal risk to U.S. assets as political risk, but if you look at the severity of what a confiscation would do to your balance sheet, I believe you'd want to consider political risk as an equal or greater threat in terms of lost investments."*

Indeed, as discussed earlier, in some emerging markets governments seize foreign assets wholesale. In other areas they go after entire sectors. According to Boone, "We're seeing that in mining, oil and gas, and telecommunications. So it's not that they get one of your facilities; they take the whole thing. If you couple that risk with the fact that you don't have an actual risk management process in place, the question becomes: What do you do if you're hit?"†

With emerging markets in every corner of the globe, some challenges for international business professionals and investors are bound to be specific to a particular country or political system. To answer the question of how to manage emerging market risk, you first have to define what is emerging market risk. Essentially, it's volatility and uncertainty. Again, according to Boone, if "you're in a place where there are unstable political, social, and economic conditions, are you able to clearly identify the risks? And if you have identified them, do you have a backup plan for how to respond to a crisis when it happens?"‡ Once you've made that investment you have to continue to monitor and manage the risk.

When considering emerging markets you must find ways to manage risks introduced by unstable and less predictable governments. International business professionals and investors may be faced with an uncertain

---

* Ididem.
† Ididem.
‡ Ididem.

legal environment, environmental and health care issues, volatile employment and labor relations, and the involvement of NGOs (nongovernmental organizations). It is important to consider reputational risk as well; being targeted by companies or countries for any reason.

There are a few great companies, such as ACE Global Markets,[27] that cover emerging market risks and focus on three areas: political insurance, trade credit, and trade credit insurance. First is political risk insurance, where they cover investments and trade by addressing confiscation of assets as well as interruption of trade in emerging markets due to political events. They also manage structured trade credit, short and medium term, and offer trade credit insurance.

# CHAPTER 14

# FCPA

## Dealing with Corruption and Crime

### Overview

For the last 20 years, we have witnessed rapid development in the effort to combat corruption under international law, as we now live in a world where, according to Transparency International,[1] and as illustrated in Figure 14.1, more than one in four people report having paid a bribe. International criminals and dishonest businessmen don't hesitate to make use of loose regulatory systems put in place by politicians in certain "safe haven" countries around the world to attract capital.

Currently two regional anti-corruption conventions are in force. The first convention was negotiated and adopted by the members of the Organization of American States (OAS),[2] while the second was adopted under the auspices of the OECD.* In addition, a number of international organizations are vigorously working on developing appropriate anti-corruption measures. These groups include several bodies within the UN, the EU, IBRD, also known as the World Bank Group (WB). Also involved are several nongovernmental organizations, such as Transparency International and the International Chamber of Commerce (ICC).

Figure 14.2 provides the perceived corruption levels by country and companies' propensity for bribery. The higher the score means fewer propensities to bribe.

---

* Convention on Combating Bribery of Foreign Public Officials in International Business Transactions, Done at Paris, Dec. 18, 1997, 37 I.L.M. The OECD Convention was signed on Nov. 21, 1997 by the twenty-six member countries of the Organization of Economic Co-operation and Development and by five nonmember countries: Argentina, Brazil, Bulgaria, Chile, and the Slovak Republic.

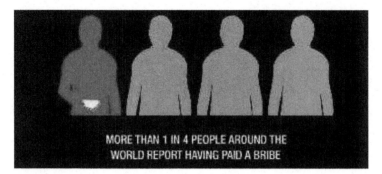

**Figure 14.1** *More than one in four people around the world report having paid a bribe*

Source: Transparency International

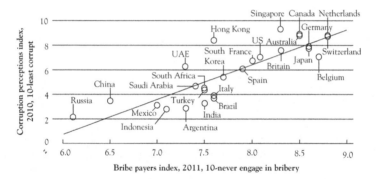

**Figure 14.2** *The perceived corruption levels by country and companies' propensity to bribe*

Source: Transparency International

When journalists with the Center for Investigative Journalism in Bucharest, Romania started investigating a gold mining operation in the village of Rosia Montana, in the heart of Transylvania, they didn't know they would soon be looking at a far wider web of corruption that linked commercial enterprises on five continents. The name of a company and the name of its founder led the journalists to Russian oligarchs, officials in Eastern European governments, former employees of well-known corporations, and even NATO* officials.

---

* NATO is an international organization composed of the United States, Canada, UK, and a number of European countries, established by the North Atlantic Treaty (1949) for purposes of collective security.

The tangled network of connections unraveled as journalists looked deeper and deeper at corporate records in over 20 countries. Company records exposed the connections between former Communist government officials and devious, western-based companies. They also revealed that big chunks of Eastern European economies are still handled by former employees of the Communist Secret Services.

In another example, a name on a corporate record in Bulgaria led to an investigation involving the Irish Republican Army's (IRA) money laundering through purchases of real estate on the shores of the Black Sea. A company record in Hungary led to one of the most powerful Russian organized crime bosses and his questionable interests in the natural gas industry.

When we consider these examples, and there are numerous news outlets around the world showcasing many more, we also must consider ways of responding to the challenges of dealing with international corruption and crime, not only as international business investors and professionals, but also as a responsible global society. Corruption not only disrupts businesses, but also generates social imbalances and poverty. The international response to corruption, therefore, raises many important questions:

Could global corruption and crime be a manifestation of oppression around the world?

- Is the anti-corruption movement a global outcry against the abuse of power?
- Is the pressure on trade competition around the globe promoting corruption?
- Is global corruption a result of globalization?
- Is the anti-corruption movement a consequence of a renewed sense of morality around the world?
- Should global corruption be a concern for international law?

While certainly provoked by these questions, this chapter does not pretend to give definitive answers. It seeks only to contribute to the understanding of the development of anti-corruption measures under the international law, since, according to the United Nations Interregional Crime and Justice Research Institute (UNICRI), corruption today is one of the main threats to global development and security.* Corruption and

---

* http://www.unicri.it/topics/organized_crime_corruption/

crime often is considered the negative side of globalization as international crime has been rapidly capitalizing on the expansion of global trade and broadening its range of activities. Several criminal groups, organized as multinational companies, are often seeking profits through the evaluation of countries' risks, benefits, and markets analysis.

## The Challenges of Combating Corruption Around the World

For entities fighting crime and corruption around the world, one of the main challenges, therefore, consists of preventing such groups from continuously adapting to the changes at local and international levels. It is important to disrupt the creation of intercontinental networks, prevent them from diversifying their activities, and taking advantage of the potential offered by globalization. These factors are the main obstacles for all entities around the world fighting organized crime. Furthermore, the lack of judicial and enforcement tools plays a strategic role in the growth of global criminal syndicates' management of trafficking drugs, arms, human beings, counterfeiting, and money laundering.

Under the veil of banking and commercial secrecy laws, huge amounts of money exchange hands in havens outside jurisdiction scrutiny of the source countries. Capital cycled through such dealings can be transformed into real estate, bonds, or other goods and then moved back into the country or to other global markets legitimately. Such transactions are looked closely at by international law enforcement because they raise suspicion of money laundering associated with organized crime and terrorism.

Although off-shore havens are usually associated with tropical islands somewhere in the Caribbean, in many instances countries such as Austria, Switzerland, or the United States have off-shorelike facilities that enable businesses and individuals to hide ownership and deter investigators from finding out who owns companies that are involved in crooked deals.

Organized crime figures would rather use *private foundations* (Privatstiftungs) in Austria, or companies in the state of Delaware in the United States, than companies in the British Virgin Islands (BVI), the Isle of Man, Aruba, or Liberia, known as safe havens that the media and law enforcement have associated as a places for money laundering. The mere mention of any of these places can mark a red flag on a transaction that is then monitored by international law enforcement.

All over the world, organized crime adopts all forms of corruption to infiltrate political, economic, and social levels. Although strong institutions, in particular government ones, are supposed to be impermeable to corruption, weak governance often coexists with corruption and a mutually causal connection exists between corruption and feeble governmental institutions and often ends up in a vicious cycle. Thus, well-known offshore havens are fighting to clean up their names and show that proper control mechanisms are in place. It should be mentioned that in most cases such jurisdictions are now used for tax purposes.

For instance, Liechtenstein, a European country of 35,000 people located in the Alps, was hit hard in the beginning of 2008 when data stolen by a former bank employee was sold to law enforcement agencies in many European countries. The data showed that wealthy citizens from many countries had used Liechtenstein's banks in tax evasion schemes. As a result of the leak, the German authorities who bought the disks managed to recover over US$150 million in back taxes within months of obtaining the data. The United States, Canada, Australia, and the EU countries are also in possession of the same data and they are independently pursuing their own investigations into tax evasions involving banking in the tiny country.

The scandal not only shook Liechtenstein's political relationships with other countries but spread to Switzerland and Luxembourg, two other European countries that have a record of bank secrecy and nontransparent financial transactions. The head of the Swiss Bankers' Association, Pierre Mirabaud, was so outraged by the fact that the stolen data ended up in German law enforcement's hands that he said in an interview with a Swiss TV station that the German investigators' methods reminded him of Gestapo practices, referring to the secret police of Nazi-era Germany. He later apologized for the unfortunate comparison. Just like Liechtenstein, Cyprus has been blamed many times for harboring money from organized crime groups and former communist officials from Eastern European countries.

The growing problem of offshore havens, corruption, and crime, and the damage they bring to the global economy, has been pointed out repeatedly in the context of the global financial crisis. The OECD together with French and German government leaders vowed to make the offshore industry *disappear*. They called the offshore areas the *black holes of global finance*.[3] The offshore company formation industry, however, is kept alive by scores of lawyers, incorporation agents, and solicitors. They advertise complex business schemes to maximize returns and minimize taxation.

Take for example the website http://www.off-shore.co.uk/faq/company-formation/ which explicitly presents potential customers with the possibility of hiding real ownership of a company behind a nominee shareholder or director. According to the site's frequently asked questions (FAQ) section, "A nominee shareholder or director is a third party who allows his/her name to be used in place of the real or beneficial owner and director of the company. The nominee is advised particularly in those jurisdictions where the names of the officers are part of a public record, open for anyone who cares to look can find out these identities. The name of the nominee will appear and ensure the privacy of the beneficial owner."

The primary role of such company formation schemes is to avoid paying taxes. However, some countries go to extremes when they try to hide the real beneficial owners. Panama and Liberia are among the countries that go to great lengths to preserve the anonymity of company owners. Under Panamanian law, an *S.A. corporation** can be owned by the physical holder of certificates or shares, with no recorded owner in any database or public registry. In fact, there is no public registry in Panama, so the government does not even know who owns shares in corporations. Shares can exchange hands at any time and the beneficial owners are impossible to trace through public records.

Discerning the ownership of companies trading around the world has become increasingly complex. A company in Belgrade, Serbia, could be owned by a firm in Rotterdam, the Netherlands, which could

---

* Designates a type of corporation in countries that mostly employ civil law. Depending on language, it means anonymous society, anonymous company, anonymous partnership, or Share Company, roughly equivalent to public limited company in common law jurisdictions.

in turn be owned by a private foundation in Austria that has Russian oligarchs as its beneficial owners. This is a common scheme. Investigative journalists in the Balkans have identified schemes as complicated as twenty layers of companies. Searches performed for names of such companies often lead to lawyers or designated shareholders. But this should not be seen as a dead or a fait accompli. Organized crime figures quite often rely on the same lawyers or the same formation agent when they establish new companies to limit the number of people aware of their moves. Once a lawyer or straw party is identified, searches of the lawyer's name can be performed on various databases. This could reveal dozens or hundreds of companies associated with the solicitor's name.

Therefore, as mentioned earlier in this chapter, corruption is a challenge not only for emerging markets but also for advanced economies. In the United States, as a result of the U.S. Securities and Exchange Commission (SEC) investigations in the mid-1970s, over 400 U.S. companies admitted making questionable or illegal payments in excess of $300 million dollars to foreign government officials, politicians, and political parties. The abuses ran the gamut from bribery of high foreign officials to securing some type of favorable action by a foreign government to so-called facilitating payments that were made to ensure that government functionaries discharged certain ministerial or clerical duties.

One major example is the aerospace company Lockheed bribery scandals, in which its officials paid foreign officials to favor their company's products.[4] Another example is the *Bananagate* scandal in which Chiquita™ Brands bribed the president of Honduras to lower taxes.[5]

Congress enacted the FCPA, which is discussed in more detail later in this chapter, to bring a halt to the bribery of foreign officials and to restore public confidence in the integrity of the American business system. The Act was signed into law by President Jimmy Carter on December 19, 1977, and amended in 1998 by the International Anti-Bribery Act of 1998, that was designed to implement the anti-bribery conventions of the OECD. The FCPA makes it a crime for any American citizen and business to bribe foreign public officials for business purposes. It also imposes certain accounting standards on public U.S. companies.

## Corruption Generates Poverty

Being poor not only means falling below a certain income line. Poverty is a multi-dimensional phenomenon that is often characterized by a series of different factors, including access to essential services (health, education, sanitation, and so on.), basic civil rights, empowerment, and human development.[6] Corruption undermines these development pillars, an individual's human rights, and the legal frameworks intended to protect them. In countries where governments can pass policies and budgets without consultation or accountability for their actions, undue influence, unequal development, and poverty result.[7] People become disempowered (politically, economically, and socially) and, in the process, further impoverished.

In a corrupt environment, wealth is captured, income inequality is increased, and a state's governing capacity is reduced, particularly when it comes to attending to the needs of the poor. For citizens, these outcomes create a scenario that leaves the poor trapped and development stalled, often forcing the poor to rely on bribes and other illegal payments in order to access basic services. Multiple and destructive forces take roots in corrupt country: increased corruption, reduced sustainable growth, and slower rates of poverty reduction.* As warned by the World Bank, corruption is "the greatest obstacle to reducing poverty."[†] This growing socio-economic inequality causes the loss of confidence in public institutions. Social instability and violence increase because of growing inequality, poverty, and abject mistrust of political leaders and institutions.

When it comes to income inequality, even Alan Greenspan is worried about this troubling trend. As argued by Chrystia Freeland, a Canadian international finance reporter at Thompson Reuters, in her book *Plutocrats*,[8] there has always been a gap between rich and poor in every country around the globe, but recently what it means to be rich has changed

---

* For more information on this theme, see Paolo Mauro, "Corruption and Growth," Quarterly Journal of Economics, 110, 681–712 (1995); Sanjeev Gupta, Hamid Davoodi and Rosa Alonso Terme, "Does Corruption Affect Income Equality and Poverty?" IMF Working Paper 98/76 (Washington, DC: IMF, 1998); Paolo Mauro, "The Effects of Corruption on Growth and Public Expenditure." Corruption: Concepts and Context, 3rd Edition, Arnold J. Heidenheimer and Michael Johnston, Editors, Transaction Publishers, 2002, New Brunswick, NJ.
† www.worldbank.org/anticorruption. Last accessed on 10/10/2012.

dramatically. Forget the one percent as is commonly believed; Plutocrats prove that it is the wealthiest 0.1 percent who are outpacing the rest of us at breakneck speed. Most of these new fortunes are not inherited; they are amassed by perceptive businesspeople that see themselves as deserving victors in a cutthroat competitive world. In her book, Freeland exposes the consequences of concentrating the world's wealth into fewer and fewer hands.

The question Freeland raises is whether the gap between the superrich and the rest is the product of impersonal market forces or political machinations. She draws parallels between current inequality and the Gilded Age of the late 1800s, when the top 1 percent of the U.S. population held one-third of the national income. Globalization and the technological revolutions are the major factors behind what she sees as new and overlapping Gilded Ages: the second for the United States, the first for emerging markets. Drawing on interviews with economists and the elite themselves, Freeland chronicles hand wringing over the direction of the global economy by these 0.1 percent plutocrats around the world. As she laments, the feedback loop between money, politics, and ideas is both cause and consequence of the rise of the super-elite.

Corruption, therefore, often accompanies centralization of power, when leaders are not accountable to those they serve. More directly, corruption inhibits development when leaders help themselves to money that would otherwise be used for development projects. Corruption, both in government and business, places a heavy cost on society. Businesses should enact, publicize, and follow codes of conduct banning corruption on the part of their staff and directors. Citizens must demand greater transparency on the part of both government and the corporate sector and create reform movements where needed.

Corruption on the part of governments, the private sector, and citizens affect development initiatives at their core root by skewing decision-making, budgeting, and implementation processes. When these actors abuse their entrusted power for private gain, corruption denies the participation of citizens and diverts public resources into private hands. The poor find themselves at the losing end of this corruption chain—without state support and the services they demand. The issue of corruption is also very much inter-related with other issues. On a global level, the economic system that has shaped the current form of globalization in the past decades requires further scrutiny for it also has created conditions whereby corruption can flourish and exacerbate the conditions of people around the world who already have little say about their own destiny.

Corruption is both a major cause and a result of poverty around the world. It occurs at all levels of society, from local and national governments, civil society, judiciary functions, large and small businesses, military, and other services and so on. Corruption, nonetheless, affects the poorest the most, whether in rich or poor nations.

It is difficult to measure or compare, however, the impact of corruption on poverty against the effects of inequalities that are structured into law, such as unequal trade agreements, structural adjustment policies, free trade agreements, and so on. The reality is that corruption and crime generate a lot of poverty around the world, especially among the LDC. A list of the top 50 is depicted in Figure 14.3.

To identify corruption is not difficult, but it is harder to see the layers it can have, especially under the more formal, even legal forms of *corruption*. It is easy to assume that these formal forms are not even an issue because they are often part of the laws and institutions that govern

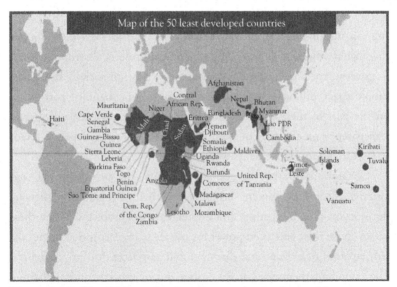

*Figure 14.3 The 50 least developed countries in the world*

Source: UNCTAD

national and international communities of which many of us are accustomed to. If a president of an emerging country gets paid a bribe and as a result taxes are reduced to benefit certain corporations or even markets, what do we, the general public, know?

Corruption promotes, and often determines, the misuse of governments' resources by diverting them from sectors of vital importance such as health, education, and development. Hence, the people who have the most needs, the poor people, are the ones deprived of economic growth and development opportunities, which in turn causes significant income inequalities and lack of social mobility. Corruption also siphons off goods and money intended to alleviate poverty. These leakages compromise a country's economic growth, investment levels, poverty reduction efforts, and other development-related advances.

At the same time, petty corruption saps the resources of poor people by forcing them to offer bribes in exchange for access to basic goods and services—many of which may be free by law, such as health care and education. With few other choices, poor people may resort to corruption as a survival strategy to overcome the exclusion faced when trying to go to school, get a job, buy a house, vote, or simply participate in their societies. Consequently, the cost of public services rises to the point where economically deprived people can no longer afford them. As the poor become poorer, corruption feeds poverty and inequality.

Combating poverty and corruption, therefore, means addressing and overcoming the barriers that stand in the way of citizen engagement and a state's accountability. While most emerging economies claim that the equal participation and rights of citizens exist, in reality they rarely apply to the poor. Hence, to be effective, pro-poor anti-corruption strategies must look more closely at the larger context that limits opportunities for poor citizens to participate in political, economic, and social processes.

### The Importance of Political Participation and Accountability

Corruption in the political sphere attracts growing attention in more and more countries. The demand for accountability of political leaders and the transparency of political parties has begun to trigger reform in those areas. Private businesses also have become a focus of anti-corruption reform. Besides being the object of state oversight, this sector has started its own initiatives to curb corruption.

Linking the rights of marginalized communities and individuals to seek government's accountability is a fundamental first step for developing a pro-poor anti-corruption strategy. Citizens giving their governments the power to act on their behalf shape a country's policies. Corruption by public and private sector officials taints this process, distorts constitutions and institutions, and results in poverty and unequal development. Strengthening political accountability would result in policies that ensure that the poor are seen not as victims but rather as stakeholders in the fight against corruption. For now, a consensus on how to strengthen these elements into action remains elusive within development cooperation circles.[9]

Notwithstanding the large differences in the problems prevalent in various countries and the existing remedies, it is satisfying to see efforts to prevent corruption target similar areas across the region. Most countries that have endorsed the OECD's Anti-Corruption Action Plan, for example, attribute an important role to administrative reforms. Hence, the various strategies to prevent corruption address integrity, effective procedures, and transparent rules.

The integrity and competence of public officials are fundamental prerequisites for a reliable and efficient public administration. Many countries in the OECD region have subsequently adopted measures that aim to ensure integrity in the hiring and promoting of staff, provide adequate remuneration, and set and implement clear rules of conduct.

Past and current efforts to reduce poverty suggests that corruption has been a constant obstacle for countries, particularly emerging economies, trying to bring about the political, economic and social changes desired for their development. Across different country contexts, corruption has been a cause and consequence of poverty. At the same time, as depicted in Figure 14.4, corruption is a by-product of poverty. The poorest countries in the world, already marginalized, tend to suffer a double level of exclusion in countries where corruption characterizes the rules of the game. Interestingly enough, oil-producing countries also make the list.

| Rank | Country | Score |
|------|---------|-------|
| 175 | Somalia | 8 |
| 175 | North Korea | 8 |
| 175 | Afghanistan | 8 |
| 174 | Sudan | 11 |
| 173 | South Sudan | 14 |
| 172 | Libya | 15 |
| 171 | Iraq | 16 |
| 168 | Turkmenistan | 17 |
| 168 | Syria | 17 |
| 168 | Uzbekistan | 17 |
| 167 | Yemen | 18 |
| 163 | Equatorial Guinea | 19 |
| 163 | Chad | 19 |
| 163 | Haiti | 19 |
| 163 | Guinea Bissau | 19 |
| 160 | Cambodia | 20 |
| 160 | Eritrea | 20 |
| 160 | Venezuela | 20 |

*Figure 14.4  The most corrupt countries in the world*

Source: Business Insider

## The Foreign Corrupt Practice Act

The FCPA of 1977 is a U.S. federal law known primarily for two of its main provisions. One that addresses accounting transparency requirements under the Securities Exchange Act of 1934, and the other concerning bribery of foreign officials.* It was enacted in the surge of public morality following the Watergate Scandal and in response to a U.S. congressional investigation uncovering widespread bribery among domestic companies operating overseas.

The FCPA applies to any person who has a certain degree of connection to the United States and engages in foreign corrupt practices.

---

* U.S. Department of Justice page on the FCPA, including a layperson's guide. Download a free copy of it at http://www.justice.gov/criminal/fraud/fcpa/guide. pdf.

As argued by Alexandro Posadas,[10] of Duke University, the Act governs not only payments to foreign officials, candidates, and parties, but also any other recipient if part of the bribe is ultimately attributable to a foreign official, candidate, or party. These payments are not restricted to monetary forms and may include anything of value.*

The meaning of foreign official, however, is broad. For example, an owner of a bank who is also the minister of finance is considered a foreign official according to the U.S. government. Doctors at government-owned or managed hospitals are also considered to be foreign officials under the FCPA, as is anyone working for a government-owned or managed institution or enterprise. Employees of international organizations such as the United Nations are also considered to be foreign officials under the FCPA.

Individuals subject to the FCPA include any U.S. or foreign corporation that has a class of securities registered (public trade companies), or that is required to file reports under the Securities and Exchange (SEC) Act of 1934. The SEC actually has increased the level of FCPA action, as shown in Figure 14.5, from 17 cases in 2007 to 20 cases in 2011.

The U.S. Department of Justice (DOJ), as depicted in Figure 14.6, has ramped up enforcement of the FCPA against individuals. In 2005, less than five individuals were prosecuted, but by 2010 more than 22 individuals were charged with violation. As an example, the former U.S. representative William J. Jefferson, democrat of Louisiana, was charged

---

* Ibidem.

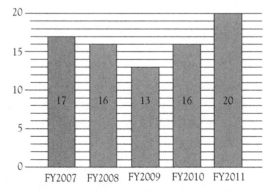

*Figure 14.5* **FCPA** *actions brought by the* **SEC**

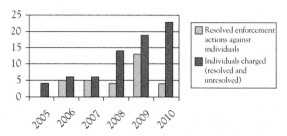

*Figure 14.6 Increase in DOJ enforcement of FCPA against individuals*

*Note:* 2010 statistics through April 1, 2010.

with violating the FCPA for bribing African governments for business interests.[11]

The FCPA also requires companies whose securities are listed in the United States to meet its accounting provisions.* These accounting provisions, which were designed to operate in tandem with the anti-bribery provisions of the FCPA, require corporations covered by the provisions to maintain records that accurately and fairly reflect the transactions of the corporation and to devise and maintain an adequate system of internal accounting controls. An increasing number of corporations are taking additional steps to protect their reputation and reduce exposure by employing the services of due diligence companies. Identifying government-owned companies in an effort to identify easily overlooked government officials is rapidly becoming a critical component of more advanced anti-corruption programs.

Regarding payments to foreign officials, the act draws a distinction between bribery and facilitation or *grease payments*, which may be permissible under the FCPA but may still violate local laws. The primary distinction is that grease payments are made to an official to expedite his performance of the duties he is already bound to perform. Payments to foreign officials may be legal under the FCPA if the payments are permitted under the written laws of the host country. Certain payments or reimbursements relating to product promotion also may be permitted under the FCPA.

---

* See FCPA Act See 15 U.S.C. § 78m.

## FCPA Violations

Recent changes to the U.S. FCPA now allow individuals to potentially collect millions of dollars by reporting corruption in U.S. companies or any company traded on U.S. exchanges. If a person knows of any improper payments, offers, or gifts made by a company to obtain an advantage in a business in the United States or abroad they are encouraged to report it. There are several law firms in the United States set up to assist whistleblowers in reporting their suspicions. There is no materiality to this act, making it illegal to offer anything of value as a bribe, including cash or noncash items. The government focuses on the intent of the bribery rather than on the amount.

Becoming a FCPA whistleblower may entitle the individual to receive substantial compensation, potentially millions of dollars. New changes in U.S. laws now allow individuals reporting FCPA violations to receive full protection from retaliation and collect up to 30 percent of the fines that the government collects. The U.S. government can fine companies up to US$2 million for each violation of the law. Thus for each payment made and each false record there may be a fine levied even if the payments are nominal. In 2010 the U.S. government collected over $1.5 billion in FCPA fines.

In addition, the Travel Act, enacted into law in 1961, forbids the use of travel and communications means to commit state or federal crimes. Ostensibly, it has been used to prosecute domestic crimes, such as the Racketeer Influenced and Corrupt Organizations Act* (RICO) and gambling violations committed either by individuals or groups of persons.

As depicted in Figure 14.7, some notable examples of FCPA violations include but are not limited to multinational corporations such as

---

* Commonly referred to as the RICO Act, this is a U.S. federal law that provides for extended criminal penalties and a civil cause of action for acts performed as part of an ongoing criminal organization. The RICO Act focuses specifically on racketeering, and it allows the leaders of a syndicate to be tried for the crimes which they ordered others to do or assisted them, closing a perceived loophole that allowed someone who told a man to, for example, murder, to be exempt from the trial because he did not actually commit the crime personally.

**Eight of the 10 largest settlements for violations of the Foreign Corrupt Practices Act occurred in 2010**

| S. no | Penalty (in $ mil.) | Company | Company's headquarters | Year penalty was assessed |
|---|---|---|---|---|
| 1 | $800 | Siemens | Germany | 2008 |
| 2 | $579 | KBR/Halliburtort | United States | 2009 |
| 3 | $400 | BAE Systems | United Kingdom | 2010 |
| 4 | $365 | ENI S.p.A/Snampro-getti Netherlands B.V. | Italy/Holland | 2010 |
| 5 | $338 | Technip S.A. | France | 2010 |
| 6 | $185 | Daimler AG | Germany | 2010 |
| 7 | $137 | Alcatel-Lucent | France | 2010 |
| 8 | $82 | Panalpina | Switzerland | 2010 |
| 9 | $58 | ABB Ltd. | Switzerland | 2010 |
| 10 | $56 | Pride International | United States | 2010 |

*Figure 14.7  FCPA enforcement: Billion-dollar fines and jail time*

Source: Hogan Lovells

Walmart, BAE Systems, Baker Hughes, Daimler AG, Halliburton, KBR, Lucent Technologies, Monsanto, Siemens, Titan™ Corporation, Triton Energy Limited, Avon Products, and Invision Technologies.

In April of 2012 an article in The New York Times reported that a former executive of Walmart de Mexico alleged in September 2005 that Walmart's Mexican subsidiary had paid bribes to officials throughout Mexico in order to obtain construction permits. Investigators of Walmart actually found credible evidence that Mexican and American laws had been broken, which prompted Walmart executives in the United States to *hush-up* the allegations.[12]

Another article in Bloomberg argued Wal-Mart's "probe of possible bribery in Mexico may prompt executive departures and steep U.S. government fines if it reveals senior managers knew about the payments and didn't take strong enough action, corporate governance experts said."[13] Eduardo Bohorquez, the director of Transparencia Mexicana, a "watchdog" group in Mexico, urged the Mexican government to investigate the allegations.[14] Wal-Mart and the U.S. Chamber of Commerce had participated in a campaign to amend FCPA, where, according to proponents, the changes would clarify the law, while according to opponents, the changes would weaken the law.[15]

In 2008, Siemens AG paid a $450 million fine for violating the FCPA. This was one of the largest penalties ever collected by the DOJ for an FCPA case.[16] The U.S. Justice Department and the SEC currently are investigating whether Hewlett Packard Company executives paid $10.9 million in bribery money between 2004 and 2006 to the Prosecutor General of Russia "to win a €35 million euros (US$47.86 million dollars) contract to supply computer equipment throughout Russia."[17]

In July 2011, the DOJ opened an inquiry into the News International phone hacking scandal that brought down News of the World, the recently closed UK tabloid newspaper. In cooperation with the Serious Fraud Office in the UK, the DOJ is examining whether News Corporation violated the FCPA by bribing British police officers.[18]

In 2012, Japanese firm Marubeni Corporation paid a criminal penalty of US$54.6 million for FCPA violations when acting as an agent of the TKSJ joint venture, which comprised of Technip S.A., Snamprogetti Netherlands B.V., Kellogg Brown & Root Inc. (KBR), and JGC Corporation. Between 1995 and 2004, the joint venture won four contracts in Nigeria worth more than US$6 billion, as a direct result of having paid US$51 million to Marubeni for the purpose of bribing Nigerian government officials.[19]

In March 2012, Biomet Inc. a Warsaw, Indiana company paid a criminal fine of US$17.3 million in its settlement with the DOJ, and US$5.5 million in disgorgement of profits and prejudgment interest to the SEC.[20] Biomet had bribed doctors at government hospitals in Argentina, Brazil, and China from 2000 to 2008. It paid out more than US$1.5 million and disguised the payments as commissions, royalties, consulting fees, and scientific incentives.

Johnson & Johnson also paid US$70 million in 2011 to settle criminal and civil FCPA charges for bribes to public sector doctors in Greece. Its subsidiary DePuy Inc. was charged in a criminal complaint with conspiracy and violations of the FCPA. A former DePuy executive in the UK, Robert John Dougall, was jailed for a year after he pleaded guilty in a London court to making £4.5 million pounds (US$7.36 million) in corrupt payments to Greek medical professionals.*

Other settlements for FCPA violations in 2012 include Smith & Nephew,[21] who paid US$22.2 million to the DOJ and SEC, and BizJet International Sales and Support Inc.,[22] who paid US$11.8 million to the DOJ for bribery of foreign government officials. Both companies entered into a deferred prosecution agreement.

## FCPA Criticism

While the FCPA has the unquestionably noble goal of eliminating corruption and holding U.S. concerns to a high standard of morality, it has come under recent criticism for the substantial and, some would say, anti-competitive, costs that it imposes. In December 2011, the New York City Bar Association's Committee on International Business Transactions issued a report critical of the FCPA, and, perhaps more significantly, its enforcement. [23]

The report noted that the FCPA imposes substantial compliance costs on companies subject to its jurisdiction—costs that their foreign competitors may not face. It also lamented the seemingly unchecked prosecutorial power to obtain huge settlements in FCPA cases, as the consequences of an FCPA indictment are potentially fatal to a company, and, as a result, most companies are willing to settle for large sums—regardless of whether they believe the allegations are valid. Indeed, as the report notes, in April 2011, each of the eight top fines for FCPA "violations" exceeded $100 million.

The report expressed concern that the U.S. DOJ is both prosecutor and judge in the FCPA context and that some U.S. companies have ceased foreign operations in the face of FCPA uncertainty. To that end, the report makes a number of recommendations to reign in the FCPA, such as adding a "willfulness" requirement before imposing liability on corporations, which currently can be criminally liable without having knowledge of the wrongful conduct, to ensure that only those companies that intend to violate the law are subject to the harsh fines, as well as a provision limiting a company's successor liability for the premerger FCPA violations of a company that it acquired.

---

* Ibidem.

In an article titled *State Hypocrisy on Anti-Bribery Laws*, Stephan Kinsella* argues that the duplicity of

> FCPA is blinding, as it makes it okay for the state to bribe (and extort and coerce) private business by means of threats, subsidies, tax breaks, and protectionist legislation, and okay for businesses to bribe elected officials (campaign contributions), and okay for the U.S. administration to bribe foreign governments, and okay for U.S. companies to be forced to pay bribes in the form of taxes, that are less than the amount of bribes they would have to pay to foreign officials, but not okay for U.S. companies to bribe foreign officials—even if this is customary and essential to "doing business" in that country, despite the fact this puts American businesses at a competitive disadvantage with companies from other countries that do not prohibit such bribery.

As Lew Rockwell,[†] former congressional chief of staff to U.S. senator Ron Paul, noted in his article *Extortion, Private and Public: The Case of Chiquita Banana*,[24]

> Paying bribevs and being subject to this kind of extortion is just part of what it takes to do business in many countries. This might sound awful, but the truth is that such payments are often less than the companies would be paying to the tax man in the U.S., which runs a similar kind of extortion scam but with legal cover.[‡]

In Rockwell's opinion, American businesses are howling at the competitive disadvantage this Act imposes on them. Instead of repealing the FCPA Act, Rockwell argues the United States is using its legislative

---

* Kinsella is an American intellectual property lawyer and libertarian legal theorist. His legal works have been published by Oceana Publications, which was acquired in 2005 by Oxford University Press and West/Thomson Reuters

† Mr. Rockwell was also the former editorial assistant to Ludwig von Mises institute. He is the founder and chairman of the Mises Institute, and the executor for the estate of Murray N. Rothbard, and editor of LewRockwell.com.

‡ Ibidem.

imperialism to force other countries to adopt similar laws, while twisting the arms of other countries in a number of areas, including intellectual property, antitrust law, central banking policies, oil & gas ownership by the state, environmental standards, labor standards, tax levels and policy, and so on. It did this mainly by pushing the OECD Anti-Bribery Convention, now ratified by 38 states, which are required by the Convention to implement FCPA style laws nationally. The UK has confirmed by creating the UK Bribery Act.[25]

It is important to note that the FCPA does not contain a private right of action. Hence, only the government can enforce the Act. But, private complainants have steadily found creative ways to use FCPA violations as predicated acts in private causes of action. These private actions are often opportunistic in that they usually commence after a government investigation has become public, and they use admissions and settlements in the government context to further their own cause of action.

For example, in 2010, Innospec Inc. pleaded guilty to violating the FCPA by bribing officials in Iraq and Indonesia to ensure sales of its product in those areas. It agreed to pay $14.1 million dollars in penalties and to retain an independent compliance monitor for three years to oversee the imposition of an anti-corruption compliance protocol. On the same day, it also settled a civil complaint with the U.S. SEC requiring it to disgorge $11.2 million in profits.[26]

After Innospec pleaded guilty, its competitor, NewMarket Corp., brought claims against it for antitrust violations.[27] NewMarket claimed that Innospec paid bribes to the Iraqi and Indonesian governments so that those governments would favor Innospec's product, would not transition to NewMarket's product, and would therefore maintain Innospec's monopoly in those markets. Pointedly, NewMarket's principal financial officer, David Fiorenza, said that it was only after reading about the plea that he learned about Innospec's actions,[28] which would eventually form the basis of NewMarket's complaint. This case ultimately settled in October 2011 when Innospec agreed to pay NewMarket $45 million.[29]

The lack of a compliance defense, as shown in Innospec's case, is particularly problematic in the successor liability context, as a company does not have any defense under the FCPA for the corrupt actions of an acquired company. This is true even if the acquiring company adhered to its compliance program by conducting a rigorous due diligence investigation, but ultimately failing to uncover corrupt acts.

In light of government's resistance to amend the FCPA and the pace of recent FCPA enforcement, the addition of a corporate willfulness requirement or a compliance program defense is unlikely in the short term. Nor can one expect to see the elimination of successor liability. With this legal environment, companies should focus on effectively implementing a compliance program, while actively looking for opportunities to ensure that other companies (particularly competitors) are not able to reap the benefits of illegal acts.

## Preventing Corruption and Crime through Software and Web-Based Analysis

With the rapid development of the Web, cross border investigative processes are literally assaulted and overwhelmed by huge quantities of data. To process and understand these data, due diligence personnel and investigators must make use of software and Web tools. To chart and track potential criminal enterprises, one can use software applications such as Mindjet[30] or IBM's I2.[31]

While Mindjet is more generic for brainstorming data, I2 provides intelligence analysis, law enforcement, and fraud investigation solutions, delivering flexible capabilities that help combat crime, terrorism, and fraudulent activity. Jay Liebowitz's book on information analysis, *Strategic Intelligence: Business Intelligence, Competitive Intelligence, and Knowledge Management*,[32] describes I2's use in cases of major investigations on prescription-drug-diversion fraud and other scenarios. I2, Pajek,* UCInet† and similar software are ultimate tools for cross-border investigative tasks and will provide new value to the due diligence process when trading abroad.

---

* Pajek, a Slovene word for Spider, is a program for analysis and visualization of large networks. It is freely available, for noncommercial use, at its download page at http://pajek.imfm.si/doku.php?id=download.
† UCINET is a software for analyzing social network data.

*Figure 14.8  The European business registry database unifies
registries of commerce from several European countries*

Source: EBR

The European Business Registry (EBR) database[33] is another very efficient tool for due diligence process in attempting to prevent an investor
in dealing with a corrupt organization abroad. The database, depicted
in Figure 14.8, has unified data contained in registries of commerce in
Austria, Belgium, Denmark, Estonia, Finland, France, Germany, Greece,
Ireland, Italy, Jersey, Latvia, Netherlands, Norway, Serbia, Spain, Sweden,
Ukraine, and UK. Name-based searches are possible. Prices differ from
country to country and are mentioned with each search.

Another excellent software application is Lexis-Nexis,[34] as depicted
in Figure 14.9. It requires subscription and payment. Lexis-Nexis is a
compilation of databases and offers access to media reports, company
registrars in many countries, court cases, financial markets information,
people's searches, and many others. One useful tool inside Lexis-Nexis
is the access to the Dun and Bradstreet companies' database, which covers the whole world. Usually companies involved in imports-exports are
listed in this database.

The United States has a wealth of databases, which can be used to
track down suspicious corporations. A useful web portal is the National
Association of Secretaries of State (NASS) at http://www.nass.org. You
will need to register with the portal, free of charge, in order to have access
to the registrar of companies of 50 states plus the District of Columbia.

Another good resource is the Global Legal Information Network
(GLIN), at http://www.glin.gov, which is a public database of laws,
regulations, judicial decisions, and other complementary legal sources
contributed by governmental agencies and international organizations.

*Figure 14.9  The LexisNexis database offers access to media reports, company registrars in many countries, court cases, financial markets information, people's searches and many others*

You can find in it data on Paraguay-based companies, published by official publications such as the *Gaceta Oficial de la Republica del Paraguay*.

There are many other resources to assist an investor or organization in conducting a sound due diligence regarding a foreign company. These listed here are just a few of the many resources available, which are beyond the scope of this chapter and book.

## Conclusion

The support of international agencies in curbing corruption indicates heightened awareness in the public sector and growing concern on the part of governments to put in place structures and programs dealing with this formidable problem. The increasing concern about the dangers of corruption among the emerging markets, often by multinational corporations from advanced economies, and the need for urgent action must be matched by a similar sense of urgency in the G-7 and G-20 summits. In the final analysis, the political will to empower and support those whose task it is to discover, investigate, reveal, and punish corporations in the public sector will be the major determinant of success. Support from these summits could assist in that regard.

In our opinion, the international business community should work more closely with law enforcement to detect patterns and methods of organized crime, since so many crimes fund terrorism. More detailed analysis of the operation of illicit activities around the world would help advance an understanding of wide spread corruption, crime, and terrorist financing. Corruption overseas, which is so often linked to facilitating organized crime and terrorism, should be elevated to a U.S. national security concern with an operational focus. A joint task force composed of analysts from the Federal Bureau of Investigation (FBI), Department of Homeland Security (DHS), the Central Intelligence Agency (CIA), as well as Interpol, should be formed to create an integrated system for data collection and analysis. A broader view of today's terrorist and criminal groups is needed, given that their methods and their motives are often shared.

# CHAPTER 15

# Coping with the Global and Emerging Market Crisis

## Overview

After years of robust global economic growth, the implosion in advanced economy financial centers quickly began to negatively affect emerging market economies. Financial markets froze in the aftermath of the Lehman bankruptcy in September 2008 and the emerging markets faced an externally driven collapse in trade and pronounced financial volatility, magnified by deleveraging by banks worldwide further aggravated the situation. As a result, growth of the global economy fell six percent from its pre-crisis peak to its trough in 2009, the largest straight fall in global growth in the post-war era.

The global crisis had a pronounced but diverse impact on emerging markets. Overall, real output in these countries fell almost four percent between the third quarter of 2008 and the first quarter of 2009, which was the most intense period of the crisis. This average performance, however, masked considerable variation across emerging economies. While real output contracted 11 percent during that period, the worst affected quarter for emerging markets, this was true mostly in emerging Europe only, as output rose one percent during the same period in other less affected emerging market regions, such as with the BRICS.

Emerging markets are still being confronted with two major factors as a result of the global financial crisis, as depicted in Figure 15.1, which include a sudden halt of FDI driven by a massive global deleveraging, mostly from advanced economies, and a huge collapse in export demand associated with the global slump. Although some emerging markets were already predisposed for a homegrown crisis following unsustainable credit booms or fiscal policies, and face large debt overhangs, the majority were not expecting the downturn and have been absorbing the hit from the unwelcome vantage point of surprise.

(a)    Net Private Capital Flows (In percent of GDP)

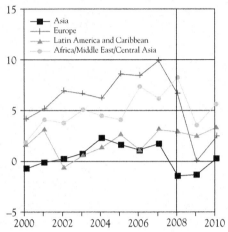

(b)  Exports of Goods and Services (In percent of GDP)

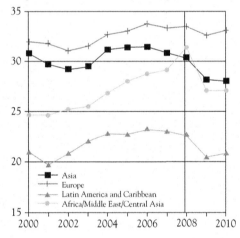

*Figure 15.1  Impact of world economic crisis on emerging markets*

Source: IMF[1]

# Advanced Economies Challenges

To make matters worse for emerging markets, advanced economies (G-7) are in a much worse economic situation. The G-7 and industrialized economies are struggling with debt and slow growth, which continue to impair its ability to trade and invest with emerging markets. Although these countries represent about 50 percent of world GDP, which totals around

$30 trillion, these countries also have a total debt of US$140 trillion, a remarkable 440 percent of their GDP. In 1998, total debt of the G-7 was US$70 trillion, and their GDP was US$30 trillion. Since then, total debt in these advanced economies has doubled between 1998 and 2012, from US$70 trillion to US$140 trillion dollars, and GDP has risen only by US$10 trillion.

In the eurozone, recent economic indicators support the idea that the common-currency area will return to moderate growth by 2014. The road to recovery, however, remains fraught with uncertainties, as the strictly economic issues are far more severe. It has been impossible to summon the necessary political will to take the needed steps until and only when the euro economy teeters on the brink of collapse. At each stage, when the markets crack the whip loudly enough, governments respond. But at each stage, the price of the necessary fix rises. Steps that could have resolved the crisis at one point are inadequate months later. At the time of these writings, the euro crisis continues to drag on without any concrete exit strategy. Greece is still a member of EU, along with Spain, Portugal, Italy, and France with varying degrees of threat. Germany continues to insist that the euro will survive while resisting bold steps to make it so.

Meanwhile, the relative international inactivity, especially during 2012, was partly due to an unusually large number of leadership changes, especially in East Asia. Most major countries, such as Russia, China, North Korea, South Korea, and Japan have witnessed changes of governments and heads of state. While political changes can be breathtakingly swift in the current global landscape, resolving or finding answers to complex economic challenges take time. During this slow economic recovery process, advanced economies have incurred US$70 trillion additional debt to produce US$10 trillion of additional GDP.

In other words, the world's richest economies are coping with a market crisis where it needs US$7 of debt to produce US$1 of GDP. Furthermore, for every one percent increase in the borrowing interest rate in its debt, the G-7 adds a staggering $1.4 trillion in debt, undeniably a massive amount of debt. Consider the fact that US$1.4 trillion is only slightly less than the entire GDP of Canada. Should interest rates increase by 10 percent, these countries will be looking at an increase in interest expense that equals the entire GDP of the United States.

Some economic sources, policymakers, and particularly the media have been suggesting that the G-7 economies, predominantly the euro-zone, are slowly recovering, mainly in the UK. What that country is experiencing, however, in our view, is an expansion of nominal GDP. This is not equivalent to real economic growth, as GDP reflects money and credit being injected into the economy. People incorrectly assume this to be the same. Instead of economic recovery, GDP is reflecting money leaving financial markets, particularly bonds, for less interest-rate sensitive havens, which may benefit emerging markets, but has the effect of a double-edge sword. Globally, bonds represent invested capital of over US$150 trillion, or more than twice the global GDP. Therefore, even marginal amounts released by rising bond yields can be financially destabilizing, and the effect on GDP growth could be significant.

It is our belief that the mistake of confusing economic progress, a better description of what global markets desire, with GDP is about to show its ugly side, pressuring interest rates to rise early and dragged up by rising bond yields. Take the United States for example, where personal credit in the form of car and student loans has been growing exponentially. The U.S. debt crisis is going up by at least US$1 trillion every year. In addition, the U.S. Federal Reserve continues to expand its balance sheet by another US$1 trillion each year, which means the U.S. government is currently printing US$2 trillion per year. At this pace, unless policymakers change course, we believe the country, and the world economy, will enter a more significant deterioration beginning in 2014. Under such scenario, which we hope won't happen, the United States could be forced to borrow even more, and the Federal Reserve's balance sheet would need to expand by several trillions of dollars.

Eventually it might be much more impactful than that, as in addition to the trillions of dollars of debt, the dollar likely will continue to fall, interest rates will rise, and a hyperinflationary economy starts. Meanwhile, prolonged negotiations in the United States, the largest economy and buyer in the world, regarding the country's debt ceiling have increased uncertainty over its economic growth, and that in turn is contributing further to dampening of the global economic growth.

The implosion of the U.S. debt will be extremely unpleasant for the world, particularly for those emerging markets that still rely on U.S.

imports, as well as those trading with other advanced economies invested in the United States. The authors, with sober judgment and concern, anticipate a very difficult time for advanced economies and emerging markets that may extend from 2014 through 2018 and beyond. They believe it will take a very long time for this debt, accumulated by the G-7 countries, to unwind and for the growth to recover.

It is critical, therefore, that emerging economies develop a credible exit strategy. IMF-like fund may be a good start for BRICS and other similar blocks such as ASEAN, MENA, and CIVETS trading with it, but monetary policy in these emerging countries should not be loosened too quickly, as a rapid reversal would just exacerbate the global *currency wars*\* already at play and damage credibility for these countries.

The same holds true for fiscal policy interventions, where the stimulus should not be withdrawn too soon and not without a credible exit strategy that places government finances on long-term sustainable footing and helps contain the costs of financing the short-term stimulus. Such an exit strategy would bestow the benefit of strengthening investor confidence and facilitating the resumption of FDI inflows during the recovery phase.

The problem facing G-7 central planners is that a predominantly financial community that has the money to invest in capital assets, such as housing, automobiles, and other luxury items, drives the GDP whimsy. The vast majority of economic stakeholders comprising of pensioners, low-wage workers living from payday to payday, and the unemployed are simply disadvantaged as prices, already often beyond their reach, become even more unaffordable. It is a misfortune encapsulated in the concept of the Pareto Principal, otherwise known as the 80/20 rule. The substantial majority will be badly squeezed by rising prices generated by the spending of the few. Global markets are blithely assuming that advanced economies' central banks are in control of events!

Unfortunately, the authors believe central banks are not even in control of their own governments' profligacy, and they are losing their control over markets, as the tapering episode shows. In the authors' view, the destructive error of rescuing both the banking system and government finances by heedless currency inflation is in the process of becoming more

---

\* Paraphrasing James Richards in his book Currency Wars: The Making of the Next Global Crisis, Portfolio Trade, 2012.

apparent. Unless this policy is reversed, the world risks a rerun of the collapse of the German mark witnessed in 1923. The printing of money will not positively contribute to long-term economic revival.

The central banks' policies have caused debt to expand exponentially. This has greatly enhanced the economic power of the wealthy, and given the masses the illusion that they are better off, when all they have is a massive debt that can never be repaid. If we just look at the richest one percent in the United States, they have an average of 20 percent debt compared to 80 percent assets. But the masses, 80 percent of the people, have in comparison 90 percent vis-à-vis assets. This, of course, does not include government debt, which is also the people's debt.

For decades, the United States and Europe have been the two centers of global governance. They have, on one hand the ability and experience in international problem solving and, on the other, both the energy and the will to act. All these are assets only when centers of global governance deploy them successfully. Once their model fails, the world will look elsewhere for leadership. At least in the foreseeable future, it will not find any substitutes. Hence, we argue that in the coming years, the United States and China will have to separate rhetoric and fear of the other from actual changes in global policy.

For instance, Stephen Ambrose[2] already had pointed such foreign policy issues in his book *Rise to Globalism*. The author, while seeming to have a serious distaste for the U.S. Presidents Reagan and Johnson, believes Carter was an ideological senseless President that ended up doing the exact opposite of everything he stood for. While holding President Kennedy as naive and being led/misled by the people around him, the author seems to have the most admiration for Nixon, not as a person, but as a president. He felt Nixon's administration was probably most up to the task of running a super-power.

For instance, a simmering conflict in the East China Sea will have to be managed through and beyond Japan's elections. The United States will have to undo the damage wrought by its announced "Pivot to Asia." The underlying message is that the United States is planning to increase its military presence in the region for the purpose of containing China and forcing Asian countries to choose between allying themselves with one or the other great power. It will take much time to convince China that the actual intent of the United States was, and is, to rebalance its attention from the Middle East toward East Asia, given that the United States has always attempted to exercise its power in Asian with diverse economic, political, and security interests there.

## Emerging and Frontier Market Challenges and Opportunities

As discussed throughout this book, emerging markets have been on an inexorable rise over the past decade. During that period, the BRICS powered the high growth rate in emerging market economies, volatility notwithstanding. The rally, however, has started to trickle down in recent years, and came to a screeching halt in 2013, mainly due to fears of U.S. Federal Reserve tapering the stimulus and the slowdown of the Chinese economy.

It is important to note, however, that emerging markets entered the global crisis with varying economic maturity levels and conditions, and thus they are being impacted by the global financial crisis in diverse degrees. Some were already dealing with the beginnings of their own internal economic crisis associated with the end of unsustainable credit booms or fiscal policies, which left in their wake high levels of debt caused mainly by unhedged foreign currency exchange, which will probably require restructuring and perhaps write-offs. Other emerging countries were just caught up in the crash.

A number of emerging economies had to turn to the IMF for financial support. Increases in lending resources, as well as reforms to the lending framework, enabled the IMF to quickly react to global developments and put in place 24 arrangements, many with exceptional access, including the recently introduced Flexible Credit Line.* Other

---

* The Flexible Credit Line (FCL) was designed to meet the increased demand for crisis-prevention and crisis-mitigation lending for countries with very strong policy frameworks and track records in economic performance. To date, three countries, Poland, Mexico and Colombia, have accessed the FCL: due in part to the favorable market reaction, none of the three countries have so far drawn on FCL resources. http://www.imf.org/external/np/exr/facts/fcl.htm

countries, many of them highlighted by Jim O'Neil in 2005, dubbed the Next 11, are poised to embark on rapid growth. Many of these countries have matured, improved their economic and trading policies, strengthened their institutions, achieved greater global credibility, and, in many cases, hoarded substantial war chests of foreign exchange reserves.

Progress, however, has not been across the board, with monetary and fiscal policies, FDI flow imbalances, and stock vulnerabilities, varying widely across these emerging economies. Emerging markets are not in "crisis," in fact, their growth outpaces that of the United States, Europe, and Japan. But there are many other emerging markets—such as the "frontier" states—that are performing very well economically and deserve attention.

Despite the slowdown of leading emerging markets, these breed of countries, often referred to as "frontier" markets due to their small, unpopular, and illiquid economies, are prone for fast growth as well. Although these countries have not yet joined the global investment community, they have already joined the global economic community.

Following is a list of the main frontier and emerging market countries, sorted alphabetically and by GDP growth forecasts over the next five years, based on our own research and careful observations of economic data, political stability, and infrastructure challenges. Keep in mind that some measures in certain countries are mere estimates as real data may be lacking, and these estimates may vary considerably depending on our sources and timing. Progress has not been across the board, as monetary and fiscal policies, imbalances in foreign direct investment, and stock vulnerabilities vary widely. This situation is aggravated by the fact that the media tend to emphasize news of conflicts, violence, drought, flood, and human suffering in frontier markets, shifting public opinion against them. Behaviors such as that of Robert Mugabe, president of Zimbabwe, who allowed inflation to reach an absurd 231,000,000 percent in 2008 is an example of news that fosters a general prejudice. But each country should be judged on its own merits.

## *Highlights of Some Frontier Markets*

There are significant opportunities in frontier markets, especially considering their solid capital bases, young labor pool, and improving productivity, particularly in Africa, where the sub-Saharan region will eventually overtake China and India. It's plausible to assume that Africa's economy will grow from $2 trillion to $29 trillion by 2050, greater than the current economic output of both the United States and the eurozone. But we must consider the frontier market's deepening economic ties to China, which makes it vulnerable to a slowing Chinese economy. Also, frontier markets are not without risks, as local politics are complex, and there are still several pockets of corruption and instability. Further, liquidity is scarce, transaction costs can be steep, and currency risk is real. There's also the risk of nationalization of industries.

### Bangladesh

Bangladesh is a country the size of the state of Iowa in the United States, and situated in the northeastern corner of the Indian subcontinent and bordered by India and Burma. Although geographically small, in reality, Bangladesh is a moderate, secular, and democratic country with a population of 160 million, making it the seventh most populous country in the world; notably it is more populous than Russia. Bangladesh is a big potential market for foreign investors, with a growing garment industry that supports steady export-led economic growth. The country is densely populated, with a rapidly developing market-based economy. Bangladesh is a major exporter of textiles and seafood, with the United States as its largest trading partner. Financial markets are still in their infancy, and thus present a major challenge for growth.

Bangladesh will soon attain lower-middle income status of over $1,036 GDP per capita, thanks to consistent annual GDP average growth of six percent since the 1990s. Much of this growth continues to be driven by the US$20 billion garment industry, second only to China, and continued remittance inflows, topping US$16 billion in 2013. In 2012, Bangladesh's GDP reached US$123 billion, complemented by sound fiscal policy and low inflation, which measured less than 10 percent in 2012.

Bangladesh offers promising opportunities for investment, especially in the energy, pharmaceutical, and information technology sectors as well as in labor-intensive industries. The government of Bangladesh actively seeks foreign investment, particularly in energy and infrastructure projects, and offers a range of investment incentives under its industrial policy and export-oriented growth strategy, with few formal distinctions between foreign and domestic private investors. Bangladesh has among the lowest wage rates in the world, which has fueled an expanding industrial base led by its ready-made garment industry. The country is well positioned to expand on its success in ready-made garments, diversification of its exports, and moving up the value chain.

## Egypt

As discussed in earlier chapters, Egypt has being politically unstable as a result of the Arab Spring that spread through the Middle East. This political uncertainty has caused massive damage to the economy. Egypt, the third largest economy in Africa, however remains an important emerging market in the region, and the substantial revenues from the Suez Canal, which it controls, makes it even more significant.

Furthermore, Egypt's ability to withstand the financial burden of the revolution, for now at least, was helped by the remarkable growth it posted until December 2011. A financial reform program that began in 2003 had also helped create a well-capitalized and well-managed banking system. For Egypt's economy to revitalize, however, much will depend on how the political process evolves over the coming months. Private-sector investment, which is important for meeting the job creation needs of the country, is currently on hold.

## Indonesia

Indonesia is the fourth-largest country in the world by population. Not only it is a G-20 economy, but also the country has a significant and growing middle class with a society that is transitioning to a democracy. The country has relatively low inflation and government debt, and is rich in natural resources including oil, gas, metals, and minerals. Recently, with the fall of its currency, the rupiah, exports received a boost.

While advanced economies were slowing down and many emerging countries were experiencing slowdowns and *exported*\* financial crisis, Indonesia with a large domestic market and less reliance on international trade, grew through the global financial crisis. Domestic demand constituted the bulk of output in Indonesia, about 90 percent of real GDP in 2007.

Many other emerging markets that also either grew through the crisis or experienced relatively small adverse impact had large domestic markets, such as in China, Egypt, and India. Indonesia also benefited from increased spending associated with national elections in 2009. Hence, Indonesia is recovering faster than many other emerging countries, in part due to a well-timed stimulus. From the first through the last quarters of 2009, output grew 4.5 percent, well above the emerging market's average of three percent for the same period. Fiscal stimulus was a step ahead of the curve. As the global economic crisis struck, the government topped up the existing fiscal loosening with cash transfers and other social spending to protect the poor and support domestic demand. The monetary policy response and liquidity management by Bank Indonesia also supported the recovery.

## Iran

Although one of the largest oil exporters in the world, Iran's economy is unique as 30 percent of the government, spending goes to religious organizations, which is a major challenge for achieving sustainable growth. The other challenges include administrative controls and widespread corruption and these outweigh positive factors such as a younger, better-educated population, and rapid industrialization. Yet another challenge is the constant risk of economic sanctions and military conflicts. As long as Iran remains committed to supporting terrorism and its nuclear weapons program, any foreign direct investment opportunity will continue to remain unrealistic.

---

\* Exported financial crisis from advanced economies, and devaluation of those currencies caused inflation in these countries due to hot money inflows.

The United States and EU sanctions targeting Iran's oil exports have hit the country harder than earlier measures, as these financial sanctions have seriously disrupted Iran's trade, for which government authorities were ill prepared. As of fall 2013, Iran was still trying to figure out how to cope with a currency crisis and higher inflation.

Since sanctions were imposed, the rial has fallen to record lows against the U.S. dollar with some reports suggesting it had lost more than 80 percent of its value. The sanctions have slashed Iran's oil exports to around one million barrels a day (b/d). As tensions have increased over Iran's controversial nuclear program, with the United States leading a campaign to undermine the country's economy for coercing the leadership to rescind its policies, the authorities in Tehran have become more secretive over economic data.

## Nigeria

As the largest African nation by population, Nigeria is projected to experience high GDP growth rate in the next few years and perhaps for the next several decades. Oil and agriculture account for more than 50 percent of the country's GDP, while petroleum products account for 95 percent of exports. The industrial and the service sectors also are growing. This economic growth potential spurs significant FDI initiatives, mostly from China, the United States, and India. The challenge, however, is with its legal framework and financial markets regulations, which leave much to be desired.

## Pakistan

As another frontier market, we believe Pakistan has potential for growth based on its growing population and middle class, rapid urbanization and industrialization, and ongoing, albeit slow, economic reforms. Pakistan has experienced significant growth for several decades. From 1952 until 2013, Pakistan's GDP growth rate has averaged 4.9 percent, reaching an all-time high of 10.2 percent in June of 1954 and a record low of -1.8 percent in June of 1952. Since 2005 the GDP has been growing at an average of five percent a year, although such growth is not enough to keep up with its fast population growth. Its GDP expanded 3.59 percent from 2012 to 2013.[3] According to the World Bank,[4] the Pakistani government has made substantial economic reforms since 2000, and medium-term prospects for job creation and poverty reduction are at their best in nearly a decade.

Pakistan's hard currency reserves have grown rapidly. Improved fiscal management, greater transparency, and other governance reforms have led to upgrading of Pakistan's credit rating. Together with the prevailing lower global interest rates, these factors have enabled Pakistan to prepay, refinance, and reschedule its debts to its advantage. Despite the country's current account surplus and increased exports in recent years, Pakistan still has a large merchandise-trade deficit. The budget deficit in fiscal year 1996–97 was 6.4 percent of GDP. The budget deficit in fiscal year 2013–14 is expected to be around four percent of GDP.

In the late 1990s Pakistan received roughly US$2.5 billion per year in loan/grant assistance from international financial institutions such as the IMF, the World Bank, and the Asian Development Bank (ADB).[5] Increasingly, however, the composition of assistance to Pakistan shifted away from grants toward loans repayable in foreign exchange. All new U.S. economic assistance to Pakistan was suspended after October 1990, and additional sanctions were imposed after Pakistan's May 1998 nuclear weapons tests. President George W. Bush lifted the sanctions after Pakistani President Musharraf allied Pakistan with the United States in its war on terror. Having improved its finances, the government refused further IMF assistance, and consequently ended the IMF program.[6]

Despite such positive GDP growth, Pakistan is still one of the poorest and least developed countries in Asia, with a growing semi-industrialized economy that relies on manufacturing, agriculture, and remittances. To make things worse, political instability, widespread corruption, and lack of law enforcement hamper private investment and foreign aid.

Ahmed Rashid, an investigative journalist with the Daily Telegraph in Lahore,* exposes many facets of Pakistan's political instability in his book titled *Pakistan on the Brink*,[7] where he argues that the bets the U.S. administration has made on trusting Pakistan to support its war efforts

---

* Lahore is the capital of the Pakistani province of Punjab and the second largest and metropolitan city in Pakistan.

in destroying Al Qaeda were not working. Pakistani Taliban, for instance, while pursuing terrorism within Pakistan, has killed more than 1,000 traditional tribal leaders friendly to the Pakistan State, and views the state as an enemy due to its tacit support to U.S. drone attacks. The Taliban's aim, according to Rashid, was, and still is, to establish an Islamic caliphate* ignoring political borders.[8]

Pakistan's political framework, Rashid contends, continues to be dominated by its army. Hence, civil government is weak, corrupt, and powerless. Apart from the ruling Pakistan Peoples Party[†] (PPP) there is no other national party, as all other parties are either ethnic or regional, making democracy difficult in a society where the 60 percent Punjab population dominates civil service and the army; others feel underprivileged. Pakistan's political elite has failed to create a national identity that unifies the country. The army's anti-India security paradigm has filled the void to define national identity making the army the most important component of the country.

According to the Asian Development Bank[9] (ADB), the new government that took office in June 2013, however, quickly signaled restoring economic sustainability and rapid growth as high priorities for its five-year term. It emphasized focus on the energy crisis, boosting investment and trade, upgrading infrastructure, and ceding most economic functions to the private sector. To address low foreign exchange reserves, fiscal and external imbalances, and low growth, the government agreed on a wide ranging economic reform program with the IMF, supported by a three-year loan worth US$6.7 billion.

The program aims to eliminate power subsidies in fiscal consolidation that include strengthening the country's notorious weak revenue base and ending the drain from debt-producing public enterprises. Other structural reforms hope to strengthen the financial system and improve the business climate. ADB[‡] contends that fiscal consolidation would

---

* A caliphate is an Islamic state led by a supreme religious as well as political leader known as a caliph (meaning literally a successor, i.e., a successor to Islamic prophet Muhammad) and all the Prophets of Islam.

[†] Pakistan People's Party is a center-left, progressive, and social democratic political party in Pakistan.

[‡] Ibidem.

limit GDP growth in 2014 to three percent. The current account deficit forecast remains at 0.8 percent of GDP, as the foreign reserve position strengthens. The monetary program is likely to limit average inflation to 8.0 percent for 2014.

## Philippines

The Philippines has shown strong economic progress in the past few years, as shown in Figure 15.2, posting the highest GDP growth rates in Asia during the first two consecutive quarters in 2013. The country weathered the global economic crises very well owed to significant progress made in recent years on fiscal consolidation and financial sector reforms, which contributed to a marked turnaround in investor sentiment, fostering significant FDI inflows.

The government used this opportunity of increased FDI inflows to build reserve buffers while keeping exchange rate flexible. Hence, the Philippines entered the global financial crisis on the back of significant improvements in external exposures, which afforded them a smaller output.

The challenges, as a newly industrialized country, are that the Philippines is still an economy with a large agricultural sector, although services

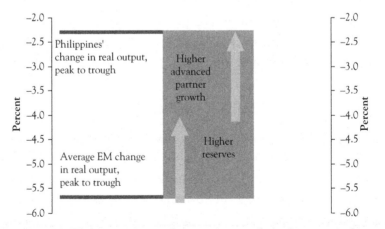

*Figure 15.2 Philippines' contributions to growth performance relative to average emerging market growth*[10]

Source: Haver; Bloomberg; IMF

are beginning to dominate the economy. Much of the industrial sector is based on processing and assembly operations in the manufacturing of electronics and other high-tech components, usually from foreign multinational corporations. As with many emerging markets, the United States remains Philippines largest trading partner.

## Turkey

Turkey's economy, much like the Philippines, has been growing at a fast pace, and for much of the same reasons. Rapid industrialization coupled with steady economic reforms has made Turkey an attractive emerging market. In 2013, however, Turkish economy suffered with civil unrest in the summer and the U.S. taper talk. Turkey's economy remains prone for FDI inflows, but it draws its strength from the country's political stability, unique geographical location on the border of Europe and Asia, market maturity, and economic growth potential.

## Vietnam

While agriculture still accounts for 20 percent of Vietnam's GDP (rice and coffee remain the most important crops), its industry and service sectors continue to grow. The major challenge is still its authoritarian regime, which causes its economy to be split between state planned and free market sections. In addition, its economy is still volatile, despite much progress, due to relatively high inflation, lack of transparency in government policy, and a dearth of large enterprises.

# MENA Challenges

The Middle East continues to be consumed with the political upheavals of the Arab Awakening: Islamists moving from the familiar role of opposition to the far harder job of governing, religious movements being transformed into political parties, the struggle to organize secular parties, the writing of constitutions, and the holding of elections. In the coming years, it seems likely that sectarian strife will become the defining thread of events across the region.

Through decades of otherwise ineffective rule, the Middle East's dictators did manage to keep divisions between Sunnis and Shia under control. The enforced peace first unraveled in Iraq, where the American invasion triggered a sectarian civil war. The political agreements imposed under the U.S. occupation began to unravel after the departure of American forces, and Iraq today looks like a country about to splinter into Kurdish pieces, late into separate Shia and Sunni pieces, in par, due to Iranian Shia influence.

Iran's mullahs are also playing a major role in Syria, where minority Shia rulers are fighting for existence in a largely Sunni country. Christians, Kurds, and others are also fighting together and extricating from their countrymen. Sunni and Shia governments across the region ship arms and money to like-minded groups, choosing sides in this second sectarian civil war. Only miles from Damascus, Lebanon—always a sectarian tinderbox—tries desperately to hold on to its fragile peace.

In Bahrain, uprisings, brutally repressed by a Sunni government in a Shia-majority country, are also along sectarian lines. When it comes to foreign affairs, poorly chosen words can do lasting damage. The "Pivot to Asia" was one such example; the other was the "Arab Spring," which led many to expect that the upheavals in the Middle East would lead to swift change and resolution. Unlike the end of Soviet rule in Eastern Europe, these are genuine internal revolutions that will take decades to play out.

The challenge for advanced economies, especially the United States and EU, is to develop the necessary strategic tolerance to distinguish between inevitable ups and downs and long-term trends while helping new governments deliver the economic progress they will need for political survival. We believe Egypt's extraordinarily complex political evolution will continue to play out for the next few years. Overall, events there have been encouraging—the discipline of governing has exerted a moderating influence on the Muslim Brotherhood, the military has relinquished a desire to rule, the country has stuck by its agreement with Israel, and political violence is the exception, not the rule.

In Libya, the government will continue to struggle to take back a government's rightful monopoly on the use of force for internal security from well-armed militias, helped by its oil revenues but hampered terribly by the country's complete lack of functional institutions after forty years of Qaddafi's personal rule. Governments in countries where unrest is still below the surface—Jordan, Kuwait, the Gulf emirates, and Morocco—will continue to stall, hoping that the greater legitimacy they enjoy as monarchies will enable them to avoid major protests and, therefore, retain power. Syria, Iraq, and Iran are where fundamental change is most likely in the year ahead.

As of fall 2013, much is in flux in Israel. Prime Minister Benjamin Netanyahu will have to reevaluate his options in light of the outcome of the U.S. election and public opposition to war. Though his political opposition is weak, elections scheduled for January could force adjustments in Israeli policy.

## Other Emerging Market Challenges

The major challenges in the Latin American region are the deterioration of its global economic outlook. We expect regional GDP to expand three percent in 2014, as there has been a negative trend in growth prospects for Argentina, Chile, Uruguay, and Venezuela, although growth prospects for Bolivia and Ecuador are positive. Brazil and Mexico will likely grow at a 2.7 percent, which we believe to be a rebound trend from the nearly uninterrupted negative trend downward that began in June 2012.

The deterioration of some BRICS economies, particularly Russia and India also has contributed to the slowdown of global growth. Within Latin America, we believe Brazil and Mexico will experience growth starting in 2014. In the late summer of 2013 Brazil's economy grew 0.1 percent over the previous month, from a decline of 0.3 percent in July.

Mexico is the second-largest economy in Latin America, following Brazil. The country, which has been on the U.S. FDI radar for some time, is a G-20 member and democracy. Its geographical location and the NAFTA agreement make the United States its largest trading partner. Mexico's low inflation and unemployment add to the economy's promise.

Mexico has been engendering much confidence with both policy reforms and the country's inherent strategic advantages. It is easy to forget just how sizable the economy is. At fourteenth in the world, ahead of South Korea, Mexico enjoys a balanced government budget, a steadily growing population, a dramatically reduced deficit, and relatively high

| Rank | Name | Industry | Foreign assets |
|------|------|----------|----------------|
| 1 | Cemex | Non-metallic minerals | 40,334 |
| 2 | America Movil | Telecommunications | 23,610 |
| 3 | Carso Global Telecom | Telecommunications | 11,768 |
| 4 | Grupo FEMSA | Beverages | 3,508 |
| 5 | Grupo ALFA | Diversified | 3,439 |
| 6 | Grupo México | Mining | 2,850 |
| 7 | PEMEX | Oil & gas | 2,090 |
| 8 | Gruma | Food products | 1,986 |
| 9 | Grupo BIMBO | Food products | 1,850 |
| 10 | Grupo Televisa | Television, motion pictures, radio & telecommunications | 1,614 |
| 11 | Cementos de Chihuahua | Non-metallic minerals | 952 |
| 12 | Industrias CH | Steel & metal products | 790 |
| 13 | Mexichem | Chemicals & petrochemicals | 730 |

*Figure 15.3 Ranking of Mexican multinational companies, as of 2008*

Source: Columbia University

interest rates. The country boasts many large multinational companies, as depicted in Figure 15.3;[11] many of them listed in the U.S. stock exchanges.

The Mexican economy also is expected to grow, although in this case it is providing mixed signals. The external sector continues to show healthy developments as Mexican exports grew solidly in early fall of 2013. Nonetheless, the manufacturing indicator fell in October 2013 after three consecutive months of improvement. The index is again below the 50-point threshold, which separates expansion from contraction in the manufacturing sector.

While the Mexican government's push for economic reforms promises to boost economic growth in the medium- to long-term, short-term economic headwinds persist amid uncertainty in the U.S. economy, sluggish domestic demand, and a negative weather-related impact. We believe Mexico is prone to grow 3.5 percent in 2014. Against a backdrop of contained inflationary pressures and sluggish domestic demand, central banks across Latin America must decide whether to lower or maintain interest rates in order to support economic growth. We expect Mexico's central bank to cut interest rates, but not so in Brazil, as the country's central bank is still involved in a tightening cycle.

Led by a collapse in domestic demand, Russia experienced a sharper-than-expected contraction in output during the global economic crisis causing the output to fall sharply by about 11 percent of GDP from its peak. Compared to many other emerging economies, Russia had much lower external vulnerabilities when the crisis started, but the country suffered one of the largest output downfalls in the emerging markets. Oil prices were an important factor in the collapse of Russia's outputs.

As oil prices collapsed in the midst of the global recession, trading partners revised their outlook for the economy and the ruble, causing domestic demand to plunge due to the immediate change in policies by trading partners. At the same time, capital outflows, banks' increased risk aversion, and an associated credit crunch exacerbated the collapse. High oil prices also may have masked inefficiencies in un-restructured sectors.

In addition, a pre-crisis credit boom fueled in part by a rigid exchange rate regime helps explain the eventual impact of the crisis. Through 2007, Russia was growing at seven percent per year on average, driven by high oil prices, expanding domestic demand, and a credit boom. As a result, by the time of the crisis, some corporations and banks had become increasingly reliant on short-term capital flows.

As the crisis unfolded, Russia spent more than $200 billion of its reserves, the equivalent of about 13 percent of its 2008 GDP in an attempt to temper the pressure on the ruble, but eventually the government appeared to given up and allowed for a significant fall in the exchange rate. This was one of the largest declines amongst emerging markets.

Russia's high reserves provided some space for corporates and banks to adjust to a revised global outlook with lower oil prices, and this helped Russia to avoid the crisis from spinning out of control completely. Nevertheless, this had its own costs. Some market participants were able to benefit from speculating on the eventual devaluation, and some of the problem banks will eventually need intermediation to support the recovery.

| Impact of the crisis | | |
|---|---|---|
| | Emerging markets | Advanced economies |
| Output collapse[1] | | |
| Median | –4.9 | –4.5 |
| 25th percentile | –8.4 | –6.6 |
| 75th percentile | –2.0 | –2.9 |
| Stock market collapse[1] | | |
| Median | –57.1 | –55.4 |
| 25th percentile | –72.0 | –64.1 |
| 75th percentile | –45.2 | 49.0 |
| Rise in sovereign spreads[2] | | |
| Median | 462 | 465 |
| 25th percentile | 287 | . . . |
| 75th percentile | 772 | . . . |

[1]Measured as percent change from peak to trough.
[2]Measured as increase in basis points from trough to peak. For AEs, table reports rise in spreads on U.S. corporates rated BBB.

**Figure 15.4  The impact of the global financial crisis on advanced economies and emerging markets**

Sources: Haver; Bloomberg; IMF[*]

# Conclusion

This chapter ends where it began. Even though the global crisis started in the financial markets of advanced economies, emerging markets suffered a heavy toll. The median emerging market economy suffered about as large a decline in output as the median advanced economy, but the impact was more varied in emerging markets, as depicted in Figure 15.4. Several emerging markets were impacted more than the worst hit advanced economies, while other emerging markets continued to grow throughout the crisis period. While on average emerging markets experienced significant decline in stock markets and as wide span as advanced economies, there was considerable cross-country variability.

Countries with higher precrisis vulnerabilities and trade and financial linkages with the global economy, in particular the advanced economies, were more impacted by the crisis. Countries that experienced a decline in

---

[*] Ibidem.

vulnerabilities before the crisis came out well ahead of others. One of the factors that lowered precrisis exposure was higher international reserve in relation to short-term external financing needs. Nevertheless, additional reserves were less useful at limiting output collapse at very high levels of reserves.

In our view, no foreign policy issue, in 2014 and beyond, will matter as much for the global economic, political, and ultimately security conditions as the ability or the willingness of the United States and EU to deal decisively with their economic crises. If the United States can find an exit strategy for its "fiscal cliff," the resolution of the acute economic uncertainty would unleash private sector investment, spark an economic recovery, and enhance the country's pivotal international role.

Advanced economies have responded to the crisis through unprecedented monetary and fiscal easing. As for the emerging markets, those in the midst of a homegrown capital account crisis may have to orient their policies toward restoring confidence in the currency, with little scope for easing in either dimension without exacerbating capital outflows. Emerging markets with credible inflation targeting frameworks should have considerable scope for monetary policy easing without compromising their inflation outlooks.

Likewise, the collapsing external demand and weakening domestic economic activity would, in general, call for fiscal easing to support demand, provided debt sustainability is not a concern and financing is available. Given a targeted level of aggregate demand/inflation, a more expansionary monetary policy can compensate for a less expansionary fiscal policy—though both may be relatively ineffective if domestic credit markets are frozen. Substituting for monetary easing by fiscal expansion can be constrained by debt sustainability concerns, because both relatively higher interest rates and fiscal spending will exacerbate debt dynamics.

There is no one-size-fits-all prescription, and the appropriate policy mix depends on the particular circumstances in each country, including a number of trade-offs described next in detail. For Europe, the world's largest economic entity and a critical leader of a liberal and peaceful world order, the challenge continues to be to summon sustained economic discipline and political will.

Progress has been made. Governments have firmly convinced themselves, if not the markets, that they will do whatever it takes to save the euro. Thanks largely to the efforts of two Italians—Mario Monti, the economist appointed interim prime minister to put Italy's house in order, and Mario Draghi, the new head of the European Central Bank—concrete steps have been taken that show a rescue is possible. But painful structural reforms will have to be endured for many years—a tall order for any one democracy, let alone for many sharing each other's pain. In effect, the euro crisis morphed in 2012 from a life-threatening emergency to a chronic disease that will be with us for years to come. The challenge for 2013[4] is to maintain the harsh treatment, avoid setbacks (in France, especially), and continue to inch toward restored growth.

For emerging markets, recovery was underway in most of the nations by late 2009, with considerable variation across countries. On average,

| Recovery from the Crisis (averages, percent) | | |
|---|---|---|
| | GDP growth, 2009Q4/2009Q1 | Industrial production growth[1] |
| | (1) | (2) |
| All EMs | 3.1 | 10.8 |
| By exchange rate regime | | |
| Fixed exchange rate regimes | 0.2 | −1.6 |
| Flexible exchange rate regimes | 3.9 | 14.0 |
| By region | | |
| Asia | 6.4 | 26.7 |
| Europe | 1.2 | 4.3 |
| MCD | 4.8 | 10.9 |
| Western hemisphere | 3.1 | 9.7 |

[1]From each country's trough to Dec. 2009.

**Figure 15.5 Emerging markets recovery from the global financial crisis**

Sources: Haver; IMF AREAR; IMF.[*]

---

[*] Ibidem.

real GDP expanded three percent in emerging markets during the last three quarters of 2009, but as in the impact of the crisis, this masks considerable cross-country variation. For instance, countries not pegging to the dollar, or other advanced economy currency, recovered much faster than those that were pegged. Across emerging market regions, as depicted in Figure 15.5, the recovery was most pronounced in Asia, particularly in the ASEAN bloc, and least in emerging Europe.

# About the Authors

**Marcus Goncalves, EdD** is an international management consultant with more than 25 years of experience in the United States, Latin America, Europe, Middle East, and Asia. Mr. Goncalves is the former CTO of Virtual Access Networks, which under his leadership was awarded the *Best Enterprise Product* at Comdex Fall 2001, leading to the acquisition of the company by Symantec. He holds a master's degree in Computer Information Systems and a doctorate in Educational Leadership from Boston University. He has more than 45 books published in the United States, many translated into Portuguese, German, Chinese, Korean, Japanese, and Spanish. He's often invited to speak on international business, global trade, international management, and organizational development subjects worldwide. Marcus has been lecturing at Boston University and Brandeis University for the past 11 years. He has also been a visiting professor and graduate research adviser/examiner at Saint Joseph University, in Macao, China for the past three years. He is an Associate Professor of Management, and the International Business Program Chair at Nichols College, in Dudley, MA Dr. Goncalves can be contacted via e-mail at marcus.goncalves@nichols.edu or at marcusg@mgcgusa.com.

**José Alves, PhD** is an Associate Professor of Management at the Faculty of Business, Government, and Social Work of the University of Saint Joseph, Macau. He holds a PhD in Business Administration from the University of Massachusetts Amherst. He currently is based in Macau, China, but has lived in Europe and the United States. His major research interests include leadership and management in international contexts, namely in Asia and China. His research has been published in journals and conference proceedings, such as the *Journal of Managerial Psychology, Human Resources Management Review*, and *International Journal of Leadership Studies*. He has also presented at various conferences, including the Academy of Management, Iberoamerican Academy of Management, International Association for Chinese Management Research, and

Academy of Human Resource Development. He is an entrepreneur and advisor to European companies intending to enter into Asia and China. Dr. Alves can be contacted via email at jose.alves@usj.edu.mo.

**Ambassador Carlos Frota, PhD** is a Portuguese career diplomat who retired recently from the Portuguese diplomatic career, after 33 years of uninterrupted service in consulates and embassies in Europe, Africa, and Asia. He served as Consul-General in Bordeaux (France) and as the first Consul-General of Portugal to Macau SAR after the handover of Macau by Portugal to China in 1999. In 2002, Dr Carlos Frota was appointed ambassador to Seoul. In 2004 he presented credentials in Pyongyang as ambassador nonresident. After three years in Lisbon as Deputy Director General for Political Affairs, he moved to Jakarta where he represented his country in Indonesia, in ASEAN as permanent representative and in the Philippines and Brunei as ambassador nonresident. Ambassador Frota traveled extensively in Southeast Asia when he was accredited to ASEAN, following closely the social and economic developments of the 10 member states. He now teaches International Relations as senior lecturer and research fellow at the University of Saint Joseph in Macau, China. He also writes a daily column in a Macau newspaper—*Jornal Tribuna de Macau*—on international issues. He participates weekly in a radio program commenting on the main international topics of the week. Ambassador Frota can be contacted via email at carlos.frota@ymail.com.

**Harry Xia, DBA** is an Assistant Professor of Finance at the Faculty of Business, Government & Social Work of the University of Saint Joseph (USJ) in Macau, China. He had held key management positions in finance and marketing for multinational corporations in the United States and Asia Pacific for almost 20 years before joining USJ, and still serves as an active business consultant and advisor to companies in China and its surrounding areas. His major research interests include corporate finance, international business, and corporate governance. His research has been published in journals and conference proceedings, such as the International Review of Business Research Papers, and presented in the Asian Business Research Conference and Academy of International Business Annual Meeting. He holds a Doctor of Business Administration from the Hong Kong Polytechnic University and a Master of Hospitality Management from the University of Houston in Texas.

**Rajabahadur V. Arcot, MSc Physics** is an Independent Industry Analyst/Columnist and Business Consultant with around 40 years of senior managerial experience. He has held C-level executive positions in leading companies, such as Honeywell, Thermax, Bells Controls an affiliate of Foxboro/Invensys, Electronics Corporation of India Limited, and Instrumentation Limited. Until recently, he was responsible for ARC Advisory Group's business operations in India. He has authored and reviewed numerous market research and industry trend reports, white papers, and case studies, widely traveled, transacted business with numerous leading Indian and Fortune 500 transnational companies. He has been a regular contributor to Industry and Industry Association Publications and speaker at numerous conferences and events in India and abroad. Presently, as an Independent Industry Analyst/Columnist and Business Consultant, he focuses on providing consultancy services and writes reports, articles, case studies, and white papers on critical infrastructure industry control systems cyber security, sustainable manufacturing, Industry 4.0 trends, renewable energy and distributed generation, and professional and skill competency development. He is a postgraduate from the University of Mysore and holds MSc degree in physics. Rajabahadur can be contacted at rajabahadurav@gmail.com.

# Advance Quotes for
# *Advanced Economies and Emerging Markets*

"This book provides a clear to-the-point review of the current status between advanced economies and emerging markets, the economic and political factors as well as the local conditions in general in the emerging countries. I found it very interesting and highly recommend it to anyone with a global footprint."

*—Robert Moore Bernardos, European Program Manager,*
*Atradius, Amsterdam, Netherlands*

"As a multinational American businessman currently living and working as an investment banker in Turkey, I firsthand experience the unique opportunities and the challenges in the emerging economies of CNETS or MINT countries, which include Turkey. *Advanced Economies and Emerging Markets* reiterates my belief in the importance of rising economic giants from the perspectives of their demographics, workforce, growth in GNP and individual income, increase in public and personal spending versus risks represented in the of level of corruption, political stability, and vulnerability to effects of global economic crises."

*—Semih Arslanoglu, Managing Director, mSolve Partners,*
*Istanbul, Turkey*

"This book is a must read for everyone who wants to understand not only the opportunities but also the risks involved when entering emerging markets. The book provides an in-depth economic and political analysis of the MENA, BRICS, ASEAN, and CIVETS regions and the authors link it all together in such a way that you get best foundation for understanding the complexity of the global political and economic landscape."

*—Dr. Finn Majlergaard, Managing Partner,*
*Gugin, Copenhagen, Denmark*

"Entrepreneurs who want to explore the emerging markets will stand a better chance of success if they read this book. University students in the fields of business and international relations will learn something very useful about the real world from this book. Strategic planners and analysts of multinationals will need this book in their libraries so that they can refer to it over the years. Full of interesting insights and practical ideas."

*—Vincent Yang, PhD, Professor and Personal Chair*
*of International Law Advisor to the Rector for Academic*
*Council and Quality Assurance, Saint Joseph University, Macau, China*

"A comprehensive and complete view of the current state of the world economy order; this book presents the reader a clear macro-view before diving into country-specific analysis. Professor Goncalves' new book offers precious contribution to existing economic and financial outlook, highlighting the ongoing currency war and the importance of governmental policies, which are impacting every risk dimensions. It is an easy and interesting read for any global investor. A person who is seeking to diversify her portfolio risks should read this book before making any investment decisions."

*—Bo Young Lin, Private Investor,*
*Character Alternative Investment, Zürich, Switzerland*

"All readers will find much to stimulate their thinking in this book. Its breadth and scope and the variety of data explored will provoke both thought and reflection. Currently, in this dynamic global business environment, knowledge of country-specific factors is vital for effective decision-making. Specifically, information about political situations and prevailing economic conditions are important when making both strategic and tactical business decisions. Market Research and Business Intelligence are useful for both Emerging Markets that are new to a country or market as well as Advanced Economies that stay in step with the changing scenarios. Often, MENA are overlooked when discussing business and global markets, however, they continue to play an increasing role in the development of current and future trends. A closer look at these topic areas opens the door for development and innovation and resulting implications."

*—Elena Fraile Renedo, Business Intelligence Consultant,*
*Nexium, XMadrid, Spain*

"Not being an expert in the 'dismal science,' I often find economic discussions of growth, development and competition between countries and regions somewhat confusing. *Advanced Economies and Emerging Markets* by Goncalves, Alves, Frota, Xi, and Arcot approaches these issues systematically but using layman's terms to consider the interplay between advanced and emerging economies. I am familiar with the situation in Asia, and I find what they have to say about the region has merit and brings some interesting perspectives to the table. Much of what they say also resonates with my own experiences of entering emerging markets. On the whole, this is an interesting and informative book that can help readers get a well-rounded understanding of an important topic."

*—Richard Whitfield PhD, President, East-West Institute for*
*Advanced Studies, Macau, China*

"This is a well-done, extensive compendium of up-to-date facts and analysis that help us to understand and hopefully measure the risks and rewards of doing business in the world's emerging markets. Professor Goncalves' research and experience is a chief source of information coupled with his intelligent and level-headed real-world judgment on the existing global economy and where world-power policies will lead us. If you are an investor, a business professional, a student, or just want to better understand the global issues as they are now and where they might be headed, then you must read this book."

*—Vic Marcus Muschiano, CEO, Vortex Advisory Group*
*—A Global Consultancy, Boston, MA, USA*

"A comprehensive account detailing contemporary issues pertinent to global economics and international trade. An invaluable reference book for students, professionals, entrepreneurs, and politicians."

*—Osei Owusu-Agyeman, CEO, Agyeman Projects*
*and Investments, Accra, Ghana*

"I am proud to endorse this quality contribution to the world of international business and global economics. I was particularly interested in the authors' revelations about the complex world of tomorrow. As an academic with degrees in Economics and Leadership, and as a businessperson with over a half-century of global business experience, this is a must-read for all who realize that tomorrow's success will result from today's in-depth understanding of the world in which we live.  Make haste, tomorrow's world started about five minutes ago."

*—Professor Richard Hilliard, Associate Professor*
*of Management, Emeritus, Nichols College, Dudley, MA, USA*

"Most of times analyze emerging markets put anyone in a myriad of data that no one risk analyses method can solve. Despite the importance of data gathering, a clear knowledge on the recent evolution of those economies and their relation with central ones can show answers that otherwise only the expertise forged after long years could bring. This is the main feature that this book provides to the readers: understand the main aspects and its evolution after years that forged the actual situation, and the permanent crises that may be opportunities to those who understand it."

*—Alvim Borges, PhD, professor at Federal University of Brazil (UFES)*
*and business consultant, Vitoria ES, Brazil*

# Notes

## Chapter 1

1. Axworthy, T. (2010).
2. CNN (2009).
3. www.g20.org, (last accessed in 10/03/2013).
4. IMF (2013).
5. http://www.businessinsider.com/largest-economies-world-gdp-2013–6#ixzz2gl0iUYEo
6. China The People's Daily (2011).
7. Bremmer, Ian (2013).
8. Bremmer, Ian (2013). pg 3.
9. Bremmer, Ian (2013). pg VIII.
10. Bremmer, Ian (2013). pg 5.
11. Orgaz, L., Molina, L. & Carrasco, C. (2011).
12. Project leader, Joseph Francois, research accessed on 10/06/2013 - http://trade.ec.europa.eu/doclib/docs/2013/march/tradoc_150737.pdf
13. Reinhart, Carmen M. & M. Belen Sbrancia (2011).
14. McKinnon, Ronald I. (1973).
15. Reinhart, C.M. & Kirkegaard, J.F. (2012).
16. Rickards, J. (2011).

## Chapter 2

1. http://www.imf.org/external/np/exr/glossary/index.asp, (last accessed on 10/29/2013).
2. Forbes (2000).
3. Forbes (2007).
4. Wilson, D. and R. Purushothaman (2003).
5. Poncet, S. (2006).
6. Hawksworth, J. (2008).
7. http://www.oecd.org/eco/outlook/2088912.pdf
8. http://www.oecd.org/eco/outlook/2088912.pdf
9. http://www.asean.org/asean/asean-member-states
10. Cheewatrakoolpong, K., Sabhasri, C., & Bunditwattanawong, N. (2013). IDBI, # 409.
11. http://investvine.com/aseans-gdp-to-double-by-2020/, (last accessed on 10/29/2013).

12. http://www.ihs.com/products/Global-Insight/industry-economic-report. aspx?ID=106594726
13. Durand, M.C., C. Madaschi & F. Terribile (1998). No. 195.
14. Krugman, P. (1996).
15. Kowitt, Beth (2009).
16. Reuters (2011).
17. According to article on South Africa Info titled "New era as South Africa joins BRICS." SouthAfrica.info, 06/19/2012.
18. Foroohar, R. (2009).
19. Investopedia (2008).
20. O'Neill, Jim (2011).
21. Foroohar, R. (2009).
22. Young, V. (2006).
23. Haub, Carl (2012).
24. Faulconbridge, G. (2008).
25. Mortished, Carl (2008).
26. Halpin, T. (2009).
27. http://www.sipa.columbia.edu/news_events/announcements/BRI-CLab04132011.html
28. Dresen, F.J. (2011).
29. The Economist magazine (2009).
30. The Economist magazine (2009).
31. O'Neill, Jim. (2005), No. 134.
32. According to the World Bank definition of MENA countries. http://web.worldbank.org/WBSITE/EXTERNAL/COUNTRIES/MENAEXT/0,,men uPK:247619~pagePK:146748~piPK:146812~theSitePK:256299,00.html . Last accessed on 11/01/2013.
33. http://www.worldbank.org/html/cgiar/newsletter/april97/8beltagy.html
34. Wiley Online Library (2013).
35. IMF Reports. (2013) Middle East and North Africa: Defining the Road Ahead, Regional Economic Outlook Update, Middle East and Central Asia Department.
36. Saseendran, Sajila (2013).
37. IMF Reports (2013).
38. http://www.imf.org/external/pubs/ft/weo/2013/01/ (last accessed on 11/02/2013).
39. QNB Group (2013).

# Chapter 3

1. Schwartz, Nelson (2013).
2. Blanchart, Olivier (2013).
3. Golf, E., Boccia, R., Fleming, J. (2012).

4. Golf, E., Boccia, R., Fleming, J. (2013).
5. OECD (2013). "Economic surveys and country surveillance: Economic Survey of Japan 2013."
6. http://www.indexmundi.com/g/g.aspx?v=66&c=ja&c=xx&l=en, (last accessed on 11/10/2013).
7. Matsui, Kathy (2012).
8. Wheatley, Alan (2013).
9. Taborda, Joana (2013).
10. Papademos, Lucas (2006).
11. Freeman, R. (2006).
12. Pain, N., I. Koske & M. Sollie (2006).
13. IMF Report (2006). "Globalization and inflation."
14. O'Neill, Jim. (2012). pg. 125.
15. http://www.businessinsider.com/july-pmi-global-roundup-2012-8#ixzz2l1PH9OmV, (last accessed on 11/15/2013).
16. http://www.happyplanetindex.org, (last accessed on 11/10/2013).

# Chapter 4

1. Wagstyl, S. (2013).
2. The Economist's Writers (2013).
3. Amadeo, Kimberly (2013).
4. Canuto, Otaviano (2010).
5. Canuto, Otaviano, and Marcelo Giugale, eds. (2010).
6. Portes, Richard (2010).
7. Brahmbhatt, Milan (2010).
8. Rodrik, Dani (2009).
9. IMF (2010a).
10. Brahmbhatt, Milan (2010).
11. Svensson, Lars E.O. (2008).
12. Jahan, Sarwat (2012).
13. Economists Staff Writers (2013).
14. Qatar National Bank (2013).
15. Hood, Michael (2013).
16. The Economist's Writers (2012). The rise of state capitalism.
17. Williams, Raymond (1983).
18. Johnson, Allan G. (2000). p. 306.
19. Bukharin, N. (1972). p. 158.
20. Schmidt, Vivien (2003).
21. The Economist's Writers (2012). And the winner is....
22. The Economist's Writers (2012). Pros and Cons: Mixed Bags.
23. Bremmer, Ian (2009).

24. Das, Satyajit (2013).
25. The Economist's Writers (2013). The gated globe.
26. The Economist's Writers (2013). When giants slow down.

# Chapter 5

1. Rickards, J. (2011).
2. Economists Staff Writers (2013). http://www.economist.com/blogs/graph-icdetail/2013/11/european-economy-guide.
3. http://www.tradingeconomics.com, (last accessed on 09/12/2013).
4. Guerrera, Francesco. (2013).
5. http://mises.org/daily/6043/Value-in-Devaluation
6. The Telegraph Staff Writers. (2013).

# Chapter 6

1. http://blogs.cfainstitute.org/investor/2013/01/15/rebalancing-global-trade-there-is-no-quick-fix/, (last accessed on 11/29/2013).
2. http://www.investopedia.com/terms/g/great-recession.asp, (last accessed on 11/30/2013).
3. Caballero, Ricardo. (2009).
4. Pettis, Michael. (2013).
5. http://carnegieendowment.org/2010/09/16/global-rebalancing-mirage/3eop, (last accessed on 11/30/2013).

# Chapter 7

1. O'Neill, Jim (2001). Building Better Global Economic BRICs.
2. Garcia-Herrero, Alicia (2012).
3. IMF (2013). World Economic Outlook, April 2013.
4. Marquand, Robert (2011).
5. IMF (2013). Transitions and Tensions.
6. Hawksworth, John and Dan Chan (2013).
7. IMF (2013).
8. Schwab, Klaus (2013).
9. https://www.cia.gov/library/publications/the-world-factbook/geos/rs.html.
10. World Bank (2012) World Development Indicators Database.
11. Schwab, Klaus (2013).
12. Nilekani, Nandan (2008).
13. Mookerji, Nivedita (2013).
14. Schwab, Klaus (2013).
15. Amin, M. (2009).

16. Schwab, Klaus (2013).
17. Rai, V. and W. Simon (2008). p. xi
18. http://www.weforum.org/pdf/Global_Competitiveness_Reports/Reports/gcr_2007/gcr2007_rankings.pdf, (last accessed on 02/02/2012).
19. Blanke, Jennifer (2013).
20. Rai, V. and W. Simon (2008).
21. O'Neill, Jim. (2005). How solid are the BRICS.
22. https://www.cia.gov/library/publications/the-world-factbook/geos/ch.html.
23. Schwab, Klaus (2013).
24. https://www.cia.gov/library/publications/the-world-factbook/geos/rs.html.
25. http://www.tradingeconomics.com/south-africa/gdp-growth, (last accessed on 10/20/2013).
26. Schwab, Klaus (2013).
27. Evans-Pritchard, Ambrose (2013).
28. Cartas, Jose (2010).
29. Business Standard Of India Staff Writers (2011).
30. Clinton, Hillary (2011).
31. Zoffer, Joshua (2012).
32. The International News of Pakistan Staff Writers (2012).
33. The RT Staff Writers (2013).

# Chapter 8

1. https://globalconnections.hsbc.com/us/en
2. http://blogs.lesechos.fr/echosmarkets/vous-aimez-les-bric-vous-allez-a5662.html
3. http://wealthyopinions.blogspot.com/2011/03/bric-countries-vs-civets-countries.html
4. Stern, Melanie (2012).
5. Hutchinson, Martin (2010).
6. Embassy of Colombia in Washington D.C. (2013).
7. Central Intelligence Agency (2013). The World Factbook.
8. Grewal, Kevin (2010).
9. The World Bank Staff Writers (2013). "Doing Business: Ease of Doing Business in Colombia."
10. Markey, Patrick (2010).
11. The Economists Staff Writers. (2012). Gushers and guns.
12. Colombo, Jesse (2013).
13. American Chamber of Commerce, International Affairs, (2013).
14. Hayton, Bill (2006).
15. Voice of Vietnam, http://english.vov.vn/Economy/Vietnam-Retailers-Association-to-be-set-up/22869.vov, (last accessed on 11/03/2013).

16. Khaithu (2012).
17. The World Bank Staff Writers (2013). "An Update on Vietnam's Recent Economic Development July 2013: Key Findings." 17. http://www.worldbank.org/en/news/feature/2013/07/12/taking-stock-july-2013-an-update-on-vietnams-recent-economic-development-key-findings, (last accessed on 11/05/2013).
18. The Economist's Writers (2013). "It's the politics, stupid."
19. Ghanem, Hafez & Salman Shaikh (2013).
20. The World Bank (2013)."World Development Indicators Database"
21. Werr, Patrick (2013).
22. Geromel, Ricardo (2013).
23. The World Bank (2012) "World Development Indicators Database."
24. OECD (2013). Economic Outlook: Analysis and Forecast.
25. IMF (2013). "Transitions and Tensions."
26. IMF (2013) Survey, "Economic Health Check."
27. OECD (2013). "Economic surveys and country surveillance."
28. The Fox News Staff Writers (2013).
29. Blanke, Jennifer (2013).
30. http://www.transparency.org/country
31. http://www.theriskradar.com/tag/corruption/
32. Kowalczyk-Hoyer, Barbara and Susan Côté-Freeman (2013).
33. http://www.justice.gov/criminal/fraud/fcpa/
34. http://www.grant-thornton.co.uk/

# Chapter 9

1. Qiang, Hou (2013).
2. ASEAN.org
3. http://www.tradingeconomics.com/brunei/inflation-cpi, (last accessed on November 2, 2013).
4. http://www.quandl.com/economics/brunei-all-economic-indicators
5. Shahminan, Fitri (2013).
6. http://www.state.gov/r/pa/ei/bgn/2700.htm, (last accessed on 09/12/2013).
7. The Oxford Business Group's Staff Writers (2013).
8. http://www.tradingeconomics.com/brunei/imports, (last accessed on November 2, 2013).
9. Chheang, Vannarith (2008).
10. Wallace, Julia (2013).
11. Heng, Dyna (2011).
12. Gronholt-Pedersen, Jacob (2012).
13. Ministry of Economy and Finance of Cambodia (2013) Council for the development of Cambodia (CDC), Economic Trends, http://www.cambo-

diainvestment.gov.kh/investment-enviroment/economic-trend.html,    (last accessed on 11/04/2013).

14. Weggel, Oskar (2006).
15. Jeong Chun Hai @Ibrahim, & Nor Fadzlina Nawi (2007).
16. OECD; ASEAN Secretariat: CIA Faxback (2014).
17. Department of Statistics Singapore (2011).

# Chapter 10

1. World Bank Staff Writers (2007). "Job Creation in an Era of High Growth."
2. Roudi, Farzaneh (2001).
3. Cammett, M. (2013).
4. IMF Staff Writers (2013). "Economic Growth Moderates Across Middle East."
5. "Two, Three, Many Middle Easts: A Region's Economic Prospects," April 29, 2013, http://www.milkeninstitute.org/events/gcprogram.taf?function= detail&eventid=gc13&EvID=3959, (last accessed on 12/20/2013).
6. World Bank Staff Writers (2013). "Tourism in the Arab World can mean more than Sun, Sand and Beaches."
7. O'Sullivan, A., M.E. Rey, and M.J. Galvez, M. J. (2011). http://archive. transparency.org/regional_pages/africa_middle_east/middle_east_and_ north_africa_mena, (last accessed 01/03/2014).
8. http://siteresources.worldbank.org/INTMNAREGTOPPOVRED/ Resources/MNA_Gender_EN_Final.pdf, (last accessed 01/03/2014).
9. O'Sullivan, A., M.E. Rey, and M.J. Galvez, M. J. (2011). http://www.wefo- rum.org/reports/arab-world-competitiveness-report-2011-2012, last accessed on 01/02/2014.
10. Ahmed, Masood (2010).
11. O'Sullivan, A., Rey, M. E., & Galvez, M. J. (2011). http://www.weforum. org/reports/arab-world-competitiveness-report-2011-2012, last accessed on 01/02/2014
12. Pigato, M. (2009).
13. Ernst & Young, & Oxford Economics (2011).
14. Montibeler, E.E., & Gallego, E.S. (2012).
15. Sallum, M.N. (2013).
16. Senkovich, V. (2013)
17. Al Masah Capital Management Limited (2010).
18. Bishku, Michael B. (2010). Fall 2010, Volume XVII, Number 3.
19. Lewis, P., Sen, A., & Tabary, Z. (2011).
20. Africa Staff Writers (2013). http://allafrica.com/stories/201311220292. html, (last accessed on 01/03/2013).

21. Cashin, P., Mohaddes, M.K. & Raissi, M.M. (2012). The Global Impact of the Systemic Economies and MENA Business Cycles (Working Paper No. 12–255). International Monetary Fund.

22. Al Masah Capital Management Limited (2010).

23. Deen, E.S. (2013).

24. Daniele, V. & Marani, U. (2006).

25. Cammett, M. (2013).

26. Bhattacharya, R. & Wolde, H. (2010a). Constraints on Growth in the MENA Region. IMF Working Papers, 1–21.

27. Bhattacharya, R. & Wolde, H. (2010b). Constraints on Trade in the MENA Region. IMF Working Papers, 1–18.

28. O'Sullivan, A., M.E. Rey, and M.J. Galvez, M. J. (2011). http://www.weforum.org/reports/arab-world-competitiveness-report-2011-2012, last accessed on 01/02/2014.

29. Lobe, Jim (2013).

30. Condon, Stephanie (2013).

# Chapter 11

1. Mitchell, Jared (2013).

2. The World Bank (2013), (last accessed on 09/22/2012).

3. Mitchell, Jared (2013).

4. The World Bank (2013), (last accessed on 09/22/2012).

5. Pacek, N. (2007).

6. http://globaledge.msu.edu/mpi

7. Cavusgil, S.Tamer (1997).

8. Cavusgil, S. Tamer (2004).

9. Khanna, Tarun (2010).

10. Arkalgud, Arnand Prasad (2011).

11. Mutum, Dilip S. (2014).

12. http://globaledge.msu.edu/reference-desk/online-course-modules/market-research-and-entry

# Chapter 12

1. http://en.wikipedia.org/wiki/Trade_and_development (last accessed on 12/03/2013).

2. Maxwell, John (2012).

3. Kose, M.A., (2012).

4. Bain & Company's Staff Analysts (2012).

5. Bonham, C. (2004).

6. Manyika, J. (2012).

7. Soubbotina, Tatyana P. (2004).

8. http://www.bain.com/publications/articles/a-world-awash-in-money.aspx (last accessed on 12/07/2013).

# Chapter 13

1. Al Jazeera Staff Writers (2011).

2. Peterson, S. (2011).

3. Spencer, R. (2011).

4. Bakri, N. & D. Goodman (2011).

5. Abulof, Uriel (2011).

6. Richter, Frederick (2011).

7. Koelbl, Susanne (2011).

8. Afrol News of Morocco Staff Writers (2011).

9. Al Jazeera Staff Writers (2011).

10. Associate Press Staff Writers (2011).

11. Al-Ansary, Khalid (2011).

12. Hauser, Christine (2013).

13. McCrummen, Stephanie (2011).

14. Middle East Online Staff Writers (2011).

15. Al Jazeera Staff Writers (2011).

16. Seyid, Seyid Ould (2011).

17. Corrigan, Terence (2007).

18. Vaidya, Sunil (2011).

19. Nath, Ravindra (2011).

20. BBC News Middle East Staff Writers (2011).

21. Manson, Katrina (2011).

22. Afrol News of Morocco Staff Writers (2011).

23. Human Rights Watch Staff Writers (2012).

24. Donnison, Jon (2011).

25. Snyder, Michael (2012).

26. Boone, E. (2007).

27. www.aceglobalmarkets.com

# Chapter 14

1. Transparency International Secretariat (2013).

2. Organization of American States: Inter-American Convention Against Corruption (1996).

3. Radu, Paul C. (2008).
4. Rich, Ben R. & Janos, Leo. (1994).
5. "Banana tax raised." Facts on File World News Digest. May 3, 1975.
6. Amartya Sen (1999).
7. Moore, M. (2005).
8. Freeland, Chrystia (2012).
9. OECD (2007).
10. Posadas, Alejandro (2000).
11. Stout, David (2009).
12. Barstow, David (2012).
13. Welch, D. (2012).
14. Garcia-Palafox, Galia (2012).
15. Hamburger, T. (2012).
16. http://www.foreign-corrupt-practices-act.org/foreign-corrupt-practices-act-news/5-siemens-ag-pays-450-million-to-settle-fcpa-bribery-charges.html, (last accessed August 12, 2013).
17. Crawford, David, Searcey & Dionne (2010).
18. BBC News Staff Writers (2011).
19. U.S. Department of Justice (2012).
20. The FCPA Blog (2012).
21. Smith & Nephew (2012).
22. Barrera, Dobbyn (2012).
23. New York City Bar Association (2011).
24. http://archive.lewrockwell.com/rockwell/case-of-chiquita-banana185.html, (last accessed on December 14, 2013).
25. http://www.legislation.gov.uk/ukpga/2010/23/contents
26. Department of Justice (2010).
27. Department of Justice (2011).
28. Dooley, Emily (2010).
29. Carton, Bruce (2011).
30. www.mindjet.com
31. http://www-01.ibm.com/software/info/i2software/
32. Auerbach Publications (2006).
33. http://www.ebr.org
34. http://www.lexisnexis.com/risk/

# Chapter 15

1. Ghosh A.R. (2009).
2. Ambrose, S. (2011).
3. http://www.tradingeconomics.com/pakistan/gdp-growth, (last accessed on 03/23/2012).

4. World Bank, (2012), (last accessed 11/10/2012).

5. Cheema, F. (2004).

6. Hoti, Ikram (2004).

7. Rashid, Ahmed (2012), p. 87.

8. Rashid, Ahmed (2012), p. 87.

9. Asian Development Bank (2013).

10. Moghadam, Reza (2010).

11. Vale Columbia Center on Sustainable International Investment (2009).

# References

Abulof, Uriel. 2011. "What Is the Arab Third Estate?" *Huffington Post*, http://www.huffingtonpost.com/uriel-abulof/what-is-the-arab-third-es_b_832628.html, (last accessed on 11/12/2013).

Afrol News of Morocco Staff Writers. 2011. "Morocco King on holiday as people consider revolt," *Afrol News*, http://www.afrol.com/articles/37175, (last accessed 11/01/2013).

Afrol News Staff Writers. 2011. "New clashes in occupied Western Sahara," *Afrol News*, http://www.afrol.com/articles/37450, (last accessed 10/25/2013).

Ahmed, Masood. 2010. "Trade Competitiveness and Growth MENA," *World Economic Forum's Arab World Competitiveness Review*, http://www.imf.org/external/np/vc/2010/103010.htm, (last accessed 01/03/2014).

Akhtar, S.I., Bolle, M.J., & Nelson, R.M. 2013. "U.S. Trade and Investment in the Middle East and North Africa: Overview and Issues for Congress," *Congress Research Service*. http://fpc.state.gov/documents/organization/206138.pdf, (last accessed 02/18/2014).

Al Jazeera Staff Writers. 2011. "Sudan police clash with protesters," *Al Jazeera*, http://www.aljazeera.com/news/africa/2011/01/2011130131451294670.html, (last accessed on 09/12/2013).

Al Jazeera Staff Writers. 2011. "Tunisia's Ben Ali flees amid unrest," *Al Jazeera*, http://www.aljazeera.com/news/africa/2011/01/20111153616298850.html, (last accessed on 11/15/2013).

Al Masah Capital Management Limited. 2010. "China and India's Growing Influence in the MENA Region: Their Legacy and Future Footprint." http://s3.amazonaws.com/zanran_storage/ae.zawya.com/ContentPages/142996358.pdf, (last accessed on 01/03/2014).

Al-Ansary, Khalid. 2011. "Iraq's Sadr followers march against Bahrain crackdown," *Reuters*, http://www.reuters.com/article/2011/03/16/us-bahrain-iraq-idUSTRE72F4U220110316, (last accessed on 11/12/2013).

Aljazeera Staff Writers. 2011. "Thousands protest in Jordan," *Al Jazeera*, http://www.aljazeera.com/news/middleeast/2011/01/2011128125157509196.html, (last accessed on 10/25/2013).

Amadeo, K. 2013. "What Is a Currency War?" http://useconomy.about.com/od/tradepolicy/g/Currency-Wars.htm, (last accessed 01/23/2014).

Amartya Sen. 1999. *Development as Freedom*. Oxford, United Kingdom: Oxford University Press, 1999.

Ambrose, S. and Brinkley, D. (2011) Rise to Globalism, Penguin Group, New York City, NY.

American Chamber of Commerce, International Affairs. 2013. "ASEAN Business Outlook Survey," *Singapore Business Federation*, http://www. amcham.org.sg/wp-content/uploads/2013/08/2014ABOS.pdf, (last accessed on 10/24/2013).

Amin, M. 2009. "Labor Regulation and Employment in India's Retail Stores," *Journal of Comparative Economics* 37 (1): 47–61.

Arabia Monitor. 2012. "Shifting Sands, Shifting Trade: Building a New Silk Route," *Middle East and North Africa Outlook Q4 2012*. http://arabiaholding.com/ arabiamonitor/index.php?option=com_k2&view=item&id=170:arabia-monitor-autumn-conference-shifting-sands-shifting-trade-building-a-new-silk-route&Itemid=697&lang=en, (last accessed on 12/19/2013).

Arkalgud, A.P. 2011. "Filling "institutional voids" in emerging markets," *Forbes*. http://www.forbes.com/sites/infosys/2011/09/20/filling-institutional-voids-in-emerging-markets/

Asian Development Bank. 2013. "Asian Development Outlook 2013 Update," *ADB*. Manila, http://www.adb.org/countries/pakistan/economy, (last accessed 12/20/2013).

Associate Press Staff Writers. 2011. "Algeria protest draws thousands," *CBC News World/Associate Press*. http://www.cbc.ca/news/world/algeria-protest-draws-thousands-1.1065078, (last accessed on 11/02/2013).

Axworthy, T. 2010. *Who gets to rule the world?* Canada: Macleans. 1 July 2010.

Bain & Company's Staff Analysts. 2012. "A world awash in money," *Bain & Company*. http://www.bain.com/publications/articles/a-world-awash-in-money. aspx, (last accessed on 12/07/2013).

Bakri, N. and D. Goodman. 2011. "Thousands in Yemen Protest against the Government," *The New York Times*. http://www.nytimes.com/2011/01/28/ world/middleeast/28yemen.html?_r=0, (last accessed on 11/11/2013).

Barrera, C., and T. Dobbyn. 2012. "U.S. says BizJet settles foreign bribery charges," *Reuters*. http://www.reuters.com/article/2012/03/14/us-mexico-lufthansa-idUSBRE82D1H220120314, (last accessed on 10/28/2013).

Barstow, David. 2012. "Vast Mexican Bribery Case Hushed Up by Wal-Mart After High-Level Struggle," *The New York Times*. http://www.nytimes. com/2012/04/22/business/at-wal-mart-in-mexico-a-bribe-inquiry-silenced. html?_r=0, (last accessed on 05/13/2012).

BBC News Middle East Staff Writers. 2011. "Man dies after setting himself on fire in Saudi Arabia," *BBC News*. http://www.bbc.co.uk/news/world-middle-east-12260465, (last accessed on 11/04/2013).

BBC News Staff Writers. 2011. "News Corp shares hit two-year low on hacking arrest," *BBC World News*. http://www.bbc.co.uk/news/business-14181119, (last accessed on 02/04/2012).

Bhattacharya, R., and H. Wolde. 2010a. "Constraints on Growth in the MENA Region," *IMF Working Papers*, 1–21.

Bhattacharya, R., and H. Wolde. 2010b. "Constraints on Trade in the MENA Region," *IMF Working Papers*, 1–18.

Bishku, Michael B. 2010. "South Africa and the Middle East," *Journal Essay Middle East Policy Council*. Fall 2010, Volume XVII, Number 3.

Blanchart, Olivier. 2013. "Advanced Economies Strengthening, Emerging Market Economies Weakening," *iMFDirect*. http://blog-imfdirect.imf.org/2013/10/08/advanced-economies-strengthening-emerging-market-economies-weakening/, (last accessed on 10/15/2013).

Blanke, Jennifer. 2013. "The Global Competitiveness Report 2013–2014," *World Economic Forum*. http://www.weforum.org/issues/global-competitiveness, (last accessed in 11/24/2013).

Bonham, C., B. Gangnes, and A.V. Assche. 2004. "Fragmentation and East Asia's Information Technology Trade," *Department of Economics at the University of Hawaii at Manoa, and University of California at Davis*. Working Paper No. 04.09. http://www.economics.hawaii.edu/research/workingpapers/WP_04–9.pdf, (last accessed on 12/01/2013).

Boone, Elisabeth. 2007. "Political Risk in Emerging Markets," *The Rough Notes Company, Inc.* http://www.roughnotes.com/rnmagazine/2007/october07/10p060.htm, (last accessed 11/11/2013).

Brahmbhatt, M., O. Canuto, and S. Ghosh. 2010. "Currency Wars Yesterday and Today." *Economic Premise*, 43.

Bremmer, Ian. 2009. *State capitalism and the crisis*. Eurasia Group.

Bremmer, Ian. 2013. *Every Nation for Itself: Winners and Losers in a G-zero World*. Portfolio/Penguin, New York City, NY.

Bukharin, N. 1972. *Imperialism and World Economy*. London: Merlin.

Business Standard of India Staff Writers. 2011. "BRICS is passé, time now for 3G:Citi," *Business Standard*. New Delhi, India. http://www.business-standard.com/india/news/brics-is-passe-time-now-for-percent5C3gpercent5C-citi/126725/on, (last accessed on 11/01/2013).

Caballero, Ricardo. 2009. "Sudden Financial Arrest." *10ᵗʰ Jacques Polak Annual Research Conference*. http://www.imf.org/external/np/res/seminars/2009/arc/pdf/caballero.pdf, (last accessed on 11/30/2013).

Cammett, M. 2013. "Development and Underdevelopment in the Middle East and North Africa." In Carol Lancaster and Nicolas van de Walle (eds.), *Handbook of the Politics of Development*. New York: Oxford University Press, 2013 (Forthcoming). Available at SSRN: http://ssrn.com/abstract=2349387, (last accessed on 12/20/2013).

Canuto, O. 2010. "Toward a Switchover of Locomotives in the Global Economy." *Economic Premise*, 33.

Canuto, O., and M. Giugale (Eds.). 2010. *The day after tomorrow—A handbook on the future of economic policy in the developing world*. Washington, DC: World Bank.

Cartas, Jose. 2010. "Dollarization Declines in Latin America, Finance and Development," March 2010, Volume 47, No. 1. http://www.imf.org/external/pubs/ft/fandd/2010/03/pdf/spot.pdf, (last accessed on 11/05/2013).

Carton, Bruce. 2011. "Company Allegedly Bumped Out of Contract by Rival's Corruption Recovers $45 Million in Civil Settlement," *Compliance Week*, (Oct. 5, 2011), http://www.complianceweek.com/company-allegedly-bumped-out-of-contract-by-rivalscorruption-  recovers-45-million-in-civil-settlement/article/213666/, (last accessed on 12/10/2013).

Cashin, P., M.K. Mohaddes, and M.M. Raissi. 2012. "The Global Impact of the Systemic Economies and MENA," *Business Cycles* (Working Paper No. 12–255). International Monetary Fund.

Cavusgil, S. Tamer. 1997. "Measuring The Potential of Emerging Markets: An Indexing Approach," *Business Horizons*. January-February 1997, Vol. 40 Number 1, 87–91.

Cavusgil, S. Tamer, Tunga Kiyak, and Sengun Yeniyurt. 2004. "Complementary Approaches to Preliminary Foreign Market Opportunity Assessment: Country Clustering and Country Ranking," *Industrial Marketing Management*, October 2004, Volume 33, Issue 7, 607–617.

Central Intelligence Agency. 2013. "The World Factbook," https://www.cia.gov/library/publications/the-world-factbook/, (last accessed on 09/23/13).

Cheema, Faisal. 2004. "Macroeconomic Stability of Pakistan: The Role of the IMF and World Bank (1997–2003)," *Programme in Arms Control, Disarmament, and International Security (ACDIS)*. University of Illinois at Urbana-Champaign. http://acdis.illinois.edu/assets/docs/250/MacroeconomicStabilityofPakistanTheRoleoftheIMFand WorldBank19972003.pdf, (last accessed on 12/14/2013).

Cheewatrakoolpong, K., C. Sabhasri, and N. Bunditwattanawong. 2013. "Impact of the ASEAN Economic Community on ASEAN Production Networks," *IDBI*, #409. http://www.adbi.org/files/2013.02.21.wp409.impact.asean.production.networks.pdf, (last accessed on 03/12/2013).

Chheang, Vannarith. 2008. "The Political Economy of Tourism in Cambodia," *Asia Pacific Journal of Tourism Research* 13 (3): 281–297. Retrieved 9 February 2013.

China The People's Daily. 2011. "Asia to play bigger role on world stage, G20: ADB report." *The People's Daily*. April 26, 2011. http://english.people.com.cn/90001/90778/98506/7361425.html, (last accessed on 10/1/2013).

Clinton, Hillary. 2011. "America's Pacific Century," *Foreign Policy*. http://www.foreignpolicy.com/articles/2011/10/11/americas_pacific_century, (last accessed on 11/12/2012).

CNN. 2009. "Officials: G-20 to supplant G-8 as international economic council." *CNN.*, http://edition.cnn.com/2009/US/09/24/us.g.twenty.summit/, (last accessed 10/3/2013).

Colombo, Jesse. 2013. "Why The Worst Is Yet To Come For Indonesia's Epic Bubble Economy," *Forbes*. http://www.forbes.com/sites/jessecolombo/2013/10/03/why-the-worst-is-yet-to-come-for-indonesias-epic-bubble-economy/2/, (last accessed on 10/05/2013).

Condon, Stephanie. 2013. "Obama appeals to senators to hold off on more Iran sanctions," *CBSNews*. http://www.cbsnews.com/news/obama-appeals-to-senators-to-hold-off-on-more-iran-sanctions/, (last accessed on 12/19/2013).

Corrigan, Terence. 2007 "Mauritania: Country Made Slavery Illegal last Month," *The East African Standard*. http://www.saiia.org.za/opinion-analysis/mauritania-made-slavery-illegal-last-month, (last accessed on 11/10/2013).

Crawford, David and Dionne Searcey. 2010. "U.S. Joins H-P Bribery Investigation." *The Wall Street Journal*. http://online.wsj.com/news/articles/SB10001424052702304628704575186151115576646, (last accessed on 12/28/2012).

Daniele, V., and U.Marani. 2006. "Do institutions matter for FDI? A comparative analysis for the MENA countries." *University Library*, Munich, Germany.

Das, Satyajit. 2013. "The new economic nationalism," *ABC Australia*. http://www.abc.net.au/news/2013–09-30/das-the-new-economic-nationalism/4988690, (last accessed on 12/12/2013).

Deen, Ebrahim Shabbir. 2013. "BRICS & Egypt: An Opportunity to Begin Creating an Alternative Economic System." *Al Jazeera Center for Studies*. http://studies.aljazeera.net/en/reports/2013/06/20136474134190632.htm, (last accessed on 12/19/2013).

Department of Justice. (2010) "Innospec Inc. Pleads Guilty to FCPA Charges and Defrauding United Nations; Admits to Violating the U.S. Embargo Against Cuba." http://www.justice.gov/opa/pr/2010/March/10-crm-278.html, (last accessed on 12/10/2013).23.

Department of Justice. (2011) "Innospec Inc. Pleads Guilty to FCPA Charges and Defrauding United Nations; Admits to Violating the U.S. Embargo Against Cuba." Second Amended Complaint 1, Newmarket Corp. v. Innospec Inc., No. 3:10-cv-00503 (E.D.Va. Jan. 27, 2011) (ECF No. 41).

Dilip S. Mutum, Sanjit Kumar Roy, and Eva Kipnis (eds). 2014. *Marketing Cases from Emerging Markets*. New York: Springer.

Dooley, Emily C. 2010. "Richmond firm claims in suit that competitor paid kickbacks to Iraqis," *Richmond Times- Dispatch*. B-03.

Donnison, Jon. 2011. "Palestinians emboldened by Arab Spring," *Ramallah: BBC News*. http://www.bbc.co.uk/news/world-middle-east-13417788, (last accessed on 11/16/2013).

Dresen, F.J. 2011. "BRICS: Shaping the New Global Architecture," *Woodrow Wilson International Center for Scholars*. http://www.wilsoncenter.org/publication/brics-shaping-the-new-global-architecture, (last accessed on 4/5/2012).

Durand, M., C. Madaschi, and F. Terribile. 1998. "Trends in OECD countries' international competitiveness: the influence of emerging market economies," *OECD Economics Department Working Paper, No. 195.*

Economists Staff Writers. 2010. "BRICS and BICIS." *The Economist.* http:// www.economist.com/blogs/theworldin2010/2009/11/acronyms_4,    (last accessed on 11/9/2012).

Economists Staff Writers. 2012. "And the winner is…." *The Economist.* http:// www.economist.com/node/21542926, (last accessed on 12/13/2013).

Economists Staff Writers. 2012. "Pros and Cons: Mixed Bags," *The Economist.* http://www.economist.com/node/21542929, (last accessed on 12/13/2013).

Economists Staff Writers. 2012. "The rise of state capitalism," *The Economist.* http://www.economist.com/node/21543160, (last accessed on 12/13/2013).

Economists Staff Writers. 2013. "Taking Europe's pulse," *The Economist.* http:// www.economist.com/blogs/graphicdetail/2013/11/european-economy-guide, (last accessed on 12/13/2013).

Economists Staff Writers. 2013. "When giants slow down," *The Economist.* http://www.economist.com/news/briefing/21582257-most-dramatic-and-disruptive-period-emerging-market-growth-world-has-ever-seen,    (last accessed on 12/13/2013).

Economists Staff Writers. 2013. "It's the politics, stupid," *The Economist.* http:// www.economist.com/news/leaders/21574495-economy-faces-collapse-broader-based-government-needed-take-tough-decisions-its, (last accessed on 11/12/2013).

Economists Staff Writers. 2013. "The gated globe," *The Economist.* http:// www.economist.com/news/special-report/21587384-forward-march-globalisation-has-paused-financial-crisis-giving-way,    (last    accessed    on 11/12/2013).

Economists Staff Writers. 2013. "The perils of falling inflation," *The Economist.* http://www.economist.com/news/leaders/21589424-both-america-and-europe-central-bankers-should-be-pushing-prices-upwards-perils-falling, (last accessed on 11/12/2013).

Economists Staff Writers. 2012. "Gushers and guns," *The Economist.* http://www. economist.com/node/21550304, (last accessed on 12/11/2013).

Embassy of Colombia in Washington D.C. 2013. *About Colombia.* http://www. colombiaemb.org/overview, (last accessed on 10/30/2–13).

Ernst & Young, & Oxford Economics. 2011. *Trading Places: The Emergence of New Patterns of International Trade. Growing Beyond Series.* Ernst Young & Oxford Economics.

Evans-Pritchard, Ambrose. 2013. "IMF sours on BRICs and doubts eurozone recovery claims," *The Telegraph.* http://www.telegraph.co.uk/finance/financialcrisis/10365206/IMF-sours-on-BRICs-and-doubts-eurozone-recovery-claims.html, (last accessed on 11/08/2013).

Faulconbridge, G. 2008. "BRICs helped by Western finance crisis: Goldman," *Reuters*. http://www.reuters.com/article/2008/06/08/us-russia-forum-bric-idUSL071126420080608, (last accessed on 07/12/2012).

Forbes. 2000. "Global 2000." http://www.forbes.com/lists/2007/18/biz_07forbes2000_The-Global-2000_Rank.html.

Forbes. 2007. "Forbes' billionaire's." http://www.forbes.com/lists/2007/10/07billionaires_The-Worlds-Billionaires_Rank.html.

Foroohar, R. 2009. "BRICs Overtake G7 By 2027," *Newsweek*. http://www.newsweek.com/brics-overtake-g7–2027-76001, (last accessed on 04/12/2009).

Fox News Staff Writers. 2013. "IMF issues warning on South African economy," *Fox News*. http://www.foxnews.com/world/2013/10/01/imf-issues-warning-on-south-african-economy/, (last accessed in 10/24/2013).

Freeland, Chrystia. 2012. *Plutocrats: The rise of the new global super-rich and the fall of everyone else*. New York City, NY: Penguin Press.

Freeman, R. 2006. "The Great Doubling: The Challenge of the New Global Labor Market," *European Central Bank*. http://eml.berkeley.edu/~webfac/eichengreen/e183_sp07/great_doub.pdf, (last accessed on 11/02/2013).

Garcia-Herrero, Alicia. 2012. "BBVA EAGLES Emerging and Growth-Leading Economies," *BBVA Research*. http://www.bbvaresearch.com/KETD/fbin/mult/120215_BBVAEAGLES_Annual_Report_tcm348–288784.pdf?ts=1642012, (last accessed in 11/01/2013).

Garcia-Palafox, Galia. 2012. "Walmart Bribery Allegations: Watchdog Group Says Mexican Government Should Investigate Claims Of Vast Bribery Campaign," *Huffington Post*. http://www.huffingtonpost.com/2012/04/22/walmart-bribery-allegations-watchdog-urges-probe_n_1444488.html, (last accessed on 04/23/2012).

Geromel, Ricardo. 2013. "Forbes Top 10 Billionaire Cities - Moscow Beats New York Again," *Forbes*. http://www.forbes.com/sites/ricardogeromel/2013/03/14/forbes-top-10-billionaire-cities-moscow-beats-new-york-again/, (last accessed on 10/30/2013).

Ghanem, Hafez and Salman Shaikh. 2013. "On the Brink: Preventing Economic Collapse and Promoting Inclusive Growth in Egypt and Tunisia," *Brookings*. http://www.brookings.edu/research/papers/2013/11/economic-recovery-tunisia-egypt-shaikh-ghanem, (last accessed on 12/12/2013).

Ghosh A.R., M. Chamon, C. Crowe, J.I. Kim, and J.D. Ostry. 2009. "Coping with the Crisis: Policy Options for Emerging Market Countries," *International Monetary Fund*. http://www.imf.org/external/pubs/ft/spn/2009/spn0908.pdf, (last accessed 12/12/2013).

GlobalEdge. 2013. "Market potential index (MPI) for emerging markets – 2013," *Michigan State University*, International Business Center. Retrieved from http://globaledge.msu.edu/blog/post/1492/2013-emerging-market-outlook

Golf, E., R. Boccia, and J. Fleming. 2012. "Federal Spending per Household Is Skyrocketing, Federal Budget in Pictures," *The Heritage Foundation.* http://www.heritage.org/federalbudget/federal-spending-per-household, (last accessed on 01/23/2013).

Golf, E., R. Boccia, and J. Fleming. 2013. "2013 Index of Economic Freedom," *The Heritage Foundation.* http://www.heritage.org/index/ranking, (last accessed on 01/23/2013).

Grewal, Kevin. 2010. "CIVETS: The next gateway to growth," *Daily Markets.* http://www.dailymarkets.com/stock/2010/08/24/civets-the-next-gateway-to-growth/, (last accessed on 02/13/2011).

Gronholt-Pedersen, Jacob. 2012. "Cambodia Aims for Offshore Production Next Year." *The Wall Street Journal.* http://online.wsj.com/news/articles/SB100008 7239639044350720457802002371164072, (last accessed on 02/11/2013).

Guerrera, Francesco. 2013. "Currency War Has Started." *The Wall Street Journal.* http://online.wsj.com/news/articles/SB100014241278873247610045782 83684195892250, (last accessed on 12/13/2013).

Halpin, Tony. 2009. "Brazil, Russia, India and China form bloc to challenge U.S. dominance," *The Times.* http://www.timesonline.co.uk/tol/news/world/us_and_americas/article6514737.ece, (last accessed on 23/03/2011).

Hamburger, T., B. Dennis, and J.L. Yang. 2012. "Wal-Mart took part in lobbying campaign to amend anti-bribery law," *The Washington Post.* http://www.washingtonpost.com/business/economy/wal-mart-took-part-in-lobbying-campaign-to-amend-anti-bribery-law/2012/04/24/gIQAyZcdfT_story_1.html, (last accessed on 11/19/2012).

Haub, Carl. 2012. "The BRIC Countries," *Population Reference Bureau.* http://www.prb.org/Publications/Articles/2012/brazil-russia-india-china.aspx, (last accessed on 12/05/2012).

Hauser, Christine. 2013. "Iraq: Maliki Demands That Protesters Stand Down," *The New York Times.* http://www.nytimes.com/2013/01/03/world/middleeast/iraq-maliki-demands-that-protesters-stand-down.html?_r=1&, (last accessed on 02/16/2013).

Hawksworth, J. 2011. "The world in 2005: How big will the major emerging market economies get and how can the OECD compete," *Price Waterhouse Coopers.* http://www.pwc.com/en_GX/gx/psrc/pdf/world_in_2050_carbon_emissions_psrc.pdf, (last accessed on 01/02/2011).

Hawksworth, John and Dan Chan. 2013. "World in 2050: The BRICS and Beyond: Prospects, Challenges, and Opportunities," *PWC Economics.* http://www.pwc.com/en_GX/gx/world-2050/assets/pwc-world-in-2050-report-january-2013.pdf, (last accessed on 03/12/2013).

Hayton, Bill. 2006. "Vietnam: ¿comunista o consumista?," *BBC Mundo*, Hanoi. http://news.bbc.co.uk/hi/spanish/business/newsid_5308000/5308298.stm, (last accessed on 07/22/2012).

Heng, Dyna. 2011. "Managing Cambodia's economic fragility," *CamproPost.* http://campropost.org/2011/07/15/managing-cambodia-s-economic-fragility.html, (last accessed on 10/10/2013).

Hood, Michael. 2013. "The Stubborn Inflation in Emerging Markets," *Institutional Investors.* http://www.institutionalinvestor.com/gmtl/3279243/The-Stubborn-Inflation-in-Emerging-Markets.html, (last accessed on 11/15/2013).

Hoti, Ikram. 2004. "Pakistan ends ties with IMF tomorrow," *PakistaniDefence.com.* http://forum.pakistanidefence.com/index.php?showtopic=36120, (last accessed 10/12/2013).

HSBC Bank. 2013. "India Trade Forecast Report - HSBC Global Connections," *HSBC Global Connections Report.* India. https://globalconnections.hsbc.com/global/en/tools-data/trade-forecasts/in, (last accessed on 12/19/2013).

Human Rights Watch Staff Writers. 2012. "Iran: Arrest Sweeps Target Arab Minority," *Human Rights Watch.* http://www.refworld.org/docid/4f34de412.html, (last accessed 11/03/2013).

Hutchinson, Martin. 2010. "The CIVETS: Windfall Wealth From the 'New' BRIC Economies," *European Business Review.* http://www.europeanbusinessreview.eu/page.asp?pid=829, (last accessed on 11/02/2013).

IMF Report. 2006. "Globalization and inflation," *World Economic Outlook.* Washington D.C. http://www.imf.org/external/pubs/ft/weo/2006/01/pdf/weo0406.pdf, (last accessed on 11/08/2013).

IMF Report. 2010a. Global Financial Stability Report. April. http://www.imf.org/External/Pubs/FT/GFSR/2010/01/index.htm (last accessed on 01/02/2014).

IMF Reports. 2013. :Middle East and North Africa: Defining the Road Ahead, Regional Economic Outlook Update," *Middle East and Central Asia Department.* http://www.imf.org/external/pubs/ft/reo/2013/mcd/eng/pdf/mcdreo0513.pdf, (last accessed on 11/02/1013).

IMF Report. 2013. "Economic Growth Moderates Across Middle East," *IMF Survey Magazine.* http://www.imf.org/external/pubs/ft/survey/so/2013/car052113a.htm, (last accessed on 01/03/2014).

IMF Report. 2013. *World Economic Outlook.* http://www.imf.org/external/pubs/ft/weo/2013/01/weodata/index.aspx, (last accessed on 04/12/2013).

IMF Report. 2013. "South Africa Searches for Faster Growth, More Jobs," *IMF Survey Magazine.* http://www.imf.org/external/pubs/ft/survey/so/2013/car080713a.htm, (last accessed on 11/05/2013).

IMF Report. 2013. "Transitions and tensions," *World Economic Outlook.* http://www.imf.org/external/pubs/ft/weo/2013/02/, (last accessed on 11/02/2013).

International News of Pakistan Staff Writers. 2012. "Asia Nations to Double Currency Swap Deal," *Pakistan.* http://www.thenews.com.pk/Todays-News-3–98519-Briefs, (last accessed on 11/05/2013).

Jahan, S. 2012. "Inflation Targeting: Holding the Line," *IMF.* Washington DC.

Jeong Chun Hai @Ibrahim, and Nor Fadzlina Nawi. 2007. *Principles of Public Administration: An Introduction.* Kuala Lumpur: Karisma Publications.

Johnson, A.G. 2000. *The Blackwell Dictionary of Sociology.* Oxford: Blackwell Publishing.

Khaithu. 2012. "Traditional Market in Vietnam: a Social and Economic Angle," 10/15/2012. http://khaithu.wordpress.com/2012/10/15/traditional-market-in-vn-a-social-and-economic-angle/, (last accessed on 11/01/2013).

Khanna, T., and K.G. Palepu. 2010. *Winning in emerging markets: A roadmap for strategy and execution.* Boston, MA: Harvard Business School Publishing.

Koelbl, Susanne. 2011. "It Will Not Stop: Syrian Uprising Continues Despite Crackdown," *Der Spiegel.* http://www.spiegel.de/international/world/it-will-not-stop-syrian-uprising-continues-despite-crackdown-a-753517.html, (last accessed on 11/10/2013).

Kose, M.A., P. Loungani, and M.E. Terrones. 2012. "Tracking the Global Recovery," *IMF Finance and Development Magazine.* Vol. 49, No. 2.

Kowalczyk-Hoyer, Barbara and Susan Côté-Freeman. 2013. "Transparency in corporate reporting: Assessing emerging market multinationals," *Transparency International.* http://transparency.org/whatwedo/pub/transparency_in_corporate_reporting_assessing_emerging_market_multinational, (last accessed on 11/02/2013).

Lewis, P., A. Sen, and Z. Tabary. 2011. "New routes to the Middle East: Perspectives on inward investment and trade," *Economist Intelligence Unit.* https://www.business.hsbc.co.uk/1/PA_esf-ca-app-content/content/pdfs/en/new_routes_to_middle_east.pdf, (last accessed on 01/03/2014).

Lobe, Jim. 2013. "Scowcroft, Brzezinski Urge Iran Accord," *Lobe Log: Foreign Policy.* http://www.lobelog.com/scowcroft-brzezinski-urge-iran-accord/, (last accessed on 12/16/2013).

Manson, Katrina. 2011. "Pro-democracy protests reach Djibouti," *Financial Times.* http://www.ft.com/intl/cms/s/0/001f94f6–3d18–11e0-bbff-00144feabdc0.html?siteedition=intl, (last accessed 10/25/2013).

Manyika, J., et al. 2012. "Manufacturing the future: The next era of global growth and innovation," *McKinsey Global Institute,* http://www.mckinsey.com/insights/manufacturing/the_future_of_manufacturing, (last accessed on 12/01/2013).

Markey, Patrick. 2010. "Colombia's Santos takes office with strong mandate," *Reuters.com.* http://www.reuters.com/article/2010/08/07/us-colombia-santos-idUSTRE6760DD20100807, (last accessed on 10/30/2012).

Marquand, Robert. 2011. "Amid BRICS' rise and 'Arab Spring', a new global order forms," *Christian Science Monitor.* http://www.csmonitor.com/World/Global-Issues/2011/1018/Amid-BRICS-rise-and-Arab-Spring-a-new-global-order-forms, (last accessed 01/02/2013).

Matsui, Kathy. 2012. "A View from Japan," *Goldman Sachs*. http://www.youtube.com/watch?v=bfkqe4vLdFY, (last accessed on 11/10/2013).

Maxwell, John. 2012. "Beyond the BRICS: How to succeed in emerging markets (by really trying)," *PWC*. http://www.pwc.com/us/en/view/issue-15/succeed-emerging-markets.jhtml, (last accessed on 11/27/2013).

McCrummen, Stephanie. 2011. "13 killed in Iraq's 'Day of Rage' protests," *The Washington Post*. http://www.washingtonpost.com/wp-dyn/content/article/2011/02/24/AR2011022403117.html, (last accessed on 06/12/2011).

McKinnon, Ronald I. 1973. *Money and Capital in Economic Development*. Washington, DC: Brookings Institution Press.

Middle East Online Staff Writers. 2011. "Kuwaiti stateless protest for third day," *Middle East Online*. http://www.middle-east-online.com/english/?id=44476, (last accessed 10/25/2013).

Ministry of Economy and Finance of Cambodia. 2013. "Council for the development of Cambodia (CDC)," *Economic Trends*. http://www.cambodiainvestment.gov.kh/investment-enviroment/economic-trend.html, (last accessed on 11/04/2013).

Mitchell, Jared. 2013. "Why Emerging Markets are tough to enter," *HSBC Global Connections*. https://globalconnections.hsbc.com/canada/en/articles/why-emerging-markets-are-tough-enter, (last accessed on 12/16/2013).

Moghadam, Reza. 2010. "How Did Emerging Markets Cope in the Crisis?, the Strategy, Policy, and Review Department, in consultation with other IMF departments," *IMF*. http://www.imf.org/external/np/pp/eng/2010/061510.pdf, (last accessed on 11/15/2013).

Montibeler, E. E., and E.S. Gallego. 2012. "Relaciones Bilaterales Entre Brasil y Liga Árabe: Un Análisis a Partir de la Teoría de la Internacionalización de la Producción y de la Diversificación Comercial." *Observatorio de la Economía Latinoamericana*, (163).

Mookerji, Nivedita. 2013. "Walmart continues to bide its time over Bharti investment," *Business Standard*. http://www.business-standard.com/article/companies/walmart-continues-to-bide-its-time-over-bharti-investment-113081600670_1.html, (last accessed on 12/15/2013).

Moore, M. 2005. "Signposts to More Effective States: Responding to Governance Challenges in Developing Countries," *Institute of Developing Studies, The Centre for the Future State, UK*, http://www2.ids.ac.uk/gdr/cfs/pdfs/SignpoststoMoreEffectiveStates.pdf, (last accessed on 12/10/2013).

Mortished, Carl. 2008. "Russia shows its political clout by hosting BRIC summit". *The Times*. http://www.thetimes.co.uk/tto/business/markets/russia/article2143017.ece, (last accessed on 05/12/2012).

Mutum, D.P., S.K. Roy, and E. Kipnis (Eds.). 2014. *Marketing cases from emerging markets*. New York, NY: Springer.

Nath, Ravindra. 2011. "Qaboos fires 10 ministers," *Khaleej Times*, Muscat, UAE. http://www.khaleejtimes.com/displayarticle.asp?xfile=data/middleeast/2011/March/middleeast_March140.xml&section=middleeast&col=, (last accessed on 10/12/2013).

New York City Bar Association. (2011) "The FCPA and its Impact on International Business Transactions — Should Anything be Done to Minimize the Consequences of the U.S.'s Unique Position on Combating Offshore Corruption?", *New York City Bar Association*. http://www2.nycbar.org/pdf/report/uploads/FCPAImpactonInternationalBusinessTransactions.pdf, (last accessed on 12/18/2013).

Nilekani, Nandan. 2008. *Imagining India: the Idea of a Renewed Nation.* New York City, NY: Penguin Group.

O'Neill, Jim. 2001. "Building Better Global Economic BRICs," *Global Economics Paper No. 66,* Goldman Sachs. http://www.goldmansachs.com/our-thinking/archive/archive-pdfs/build-better-brics.pdf, (last accessed 12/17/2011).

O'Neill, Jim. 2005. "How solid are the BRICS," *Goldman Sachs' Global Economics Paper No. 134.* http://www.goldmansachs.com/our-thinking/archive/archive-pdfs/how-solid.pdf, (last accessed on 11.14.2012).

O'Neill, J. 2011. *The Growth Map: Economic Opportunity in the BRICs and Beyond.* Penguin Group.

O'Sullivan, A., M.E. Rey, and M.J. Galvez. 2011. "Opportunities and Challenges in the MENA Region." *The Arab world competitiveness report, 2011–2012, World Economic Forum.* http://www.weforum.org/reports/arab-world-competitiveness-report-2011–2012, (last accessed on 01/02/2014).

Organization of American States: Inter-American Convention Against Corruption, Mar. 29, 1996, 35 I.L.M. 724. http://www.unicri.it/topics/organized_crime_corruption/.

OECD. 2007. Overview by the DAC Chair, In Development Co-operation Report. Vol. 8(1), chapter 1 (Paris, France: OECD, 2007).

Organization for Economic Co-operation and Development. 2013. "Economic surveys and country surveillance: Economic Survey of Japan 2013," *OECD.* http://www.oecd.org/eco/surveys/economic-survey-japan.htm, (last accessed on 11/05/2013).

Organization for Economic Co-operation and Development. 2013. "Economic outlook: analysis and forecast: Turkey Economic forecast summary, May 2014," *OECD,* http://www.oecd.org/eco/outlook/turkey-economic-forecast-summary.htm, (last accessed on 11/04/2013).

Organization for Economic Co-operation and Development. 2013. "Economic surveys and country surveillance: Economic Survey of South Africa 2013," *OECD,* http://www.oecd.org/eco/surveys/economic-survey-south-africa.htm, (last accessed on 11/05/2103).

Orgaz, L., L. Molina and C. Carrasco. 2011. "In El Creciente Peso de las Economias Emergentes en la Economia y Gobernanza Mundiales, Los Paises BRIC", *Documentos Ocasionales numero 1101*, Banco de Espana, Eurosistema. http://www.bde.es/f/webbde/SES/Secciones/Publicaciones/PublicacionesSeriadas/DocumentosOcasionales/11/Fich/do1101.pdf, (last accessed on 12/12/12).

Oxford Business Group's Staff Writers. 2013. "Brunei Darussalam looks to its labs for growth," *Brunei Darussalam*, http://www.oxfordbusinessgroup.com/economic_updates/brunei-darussalam-looks-its-labs-growth, (last accessed on 11/02/2013).

Pacek, N. and D. Thorniley. 2007. *Emerging Markets: Lessons for business and the outlook for different markets (2nd edition)*. London: The Economist and Profile Books.

Pain, N., I. Koske and M. Sollie. 2006. "Globalization and inflation in the OECD Economies," *Economics Department Working Paper No. 524*, OECD, Paris. http://www.oecd.org/eco/42503918.pdf, (last retrieved on 11/12/2013).

Papademos, Lucas. 2006. "Globalization, inflation, imbalances and monetary policy," *Bank for International Settlement*, St. Louis, U.S., http://www.bis.org/review/r060607d.pdf, (last accessed on 11/09/2013).

Peterson, S. 2011. "Egypt's revolution redefines what's possible in the Arab world," *The Christian Science Monitor*, http://www.csmonitor.com/layout/set/r14/World/Middle-East/2011/0211/Egypt-s-revolution-redefines-what-s-possible-in-the-Arab-world, (last accessed on 11/10/2013).

Pettis, Michael. 2013. *The Great Rebalancing: Trade, Conflict, and the Perilous Road Ahead for the World Economy*, Princeton University Press.

Pigato, Miria. 2009. *Strengthening China's and India's Trade and Investment Ties to the Middle East and North Africa*. Washington DC: The World Bank.

Portes, R. 2010. *Currency Wars and the Emerging-Market Countries. VoxEU*, http://www.voxeu.org/article/currency-wars-and-emerging-markets, (last accessed 04/15/2013 )

Posadas, Alejandro. 2000. "Combating Corruption Under International Law," *Duke University Journal of Comparative and International Law*, pages 345–414, http://scholarship.law.duke.edu/djcil/vol10/iss2/4, (last accessed 12/02/2013).

Qatar National Bank (QNB Group). 2013. "Economic and International Affairs." http://www.qnb.com.qa/cs/Satellite/QNBQatar/en_QA/AboutQNB/CorporateSocialResponsibility/enEconomicandInternationalAffairs, (last accessed 11/02/2013).

Qatar National Bank (QNB Group). 2013. "US, eurozone deflation calls for 'expansionary policy'." http://www.gulf-times.com/business/191/details/374694/us,-eurozone-deflation-calls-for-'expansionary-policy,' (last accessed 01/12/2014).

Qiang, Hou. 2013. "ASEAN businesses see integration as opportunity, not threat: survey," *The English News*, Xinhua, China, http://news.xinhuanet.com/english/business/2013–12/11/c_132960344.htm, (last accessed on 12/11/2013).

Radu, Paul C. 2008. "The Investigative Journalist Handbook," *International Center for Journalist*, https://reportingproject.net/occrp/index.php/en/cc-resource-center/handbook/191-the-investigative-journalist-handbook, (last accessed on 09/08/2012).

Rai, V. and W. Simon. 2008. *Think India*. New York, NY.: Penguin Group,

Rashid, Ahmed, (2012) *Pakistan on the Brink: The Future of America, Pakistan, and Afghanistan*. New York, NY: Viking/Penguin Group.

Reinhart, C.M. and M.B. Sbrancia. 2011. "The Liquidation of Government Debt", *NBER Working Paper 16893*. http://www.nber.org/papers/w16893, (last retrieved 03/02/12).

Reinhart, C.M. and J.F. Kirkegaard. 2012. "Financial Repression: Then and Now," *Vox*, http://www.voxeu.org/article/financial-repression-then-and-now, (last accessed on 04/23/12).

Rich, Ben R. and Leo Janos. 1994. *Skunk Works: A Personal Memoir of My Years at Lockheed*. New York: Little Brown & Co., 1994, p. 10.

Richter, Frederick. .2011. "Protester killed in Bahrain *Day of Rage*," *Reuters,* http://uk.reuters.com/article/2011/02/14/uk-bahrain-protests-idUKTRE71D1G520110214, (last accessed on 11/02/2013).

Rickards, J. 2011. *Currency Wars: The Making of the Next Global Crisis*, Penguin/Portfolio Group.

Rodrik, D. 2009. *Growth after the Crisis*. Cambridge, MA.: Harvard Kennedy School.

Roudi, Farzaneh. 2001. "Population Trends and Challenges in the MENA," *PRB*. http://www.prb.org/Publications/Reports/2001/PopulationTrendsand ChallengesintheMiddleEastandNorthAfrica.aspx, (last accessed 12/20/2013).

RT Staff Writers. 2013. "BRICS agree to capitalize development bank at $100bn," *RT,* http://rt.com/business/russia-brics-bank-g20-468/, (last accessed on 11/06/2013).

Sallum, M.N. 2013. "Potencial a explorar é enorme." *Agência de Notícias Brasil-Árabe*. http://www.anba.com.br/, (last accessed 01/03/2014).

Schmidt, V. 2003. "French Capitalism Transformed; yet still a Third Variety of Capitalism." *Economy and Society*, 32(4). http://www.vedegylet.hu/fejkrit/szvggyujt/schmidt_frenchCapitalism.pdf

Schwab, Klaus. 2013. "The Global Competitiveness Report 2012–2013," *World Economic Forum*, http://www3.weforum.org/docs/WEF_Global CompetitivenessReport_2012–13.pdf, (last accessed on 08/12/2013).

Schwartz, Nelson. 2013. "Growth Gain Blurs Signs of Weakness in Economy," *New York Times*, http://www.nytimes.com/2013/11/08/business/economy/us-economy-grows-at-2–8-rate-in-third-quarter.html?_r=0, (last Accessed on 11/10/2013).

Saseendran, Sajila. 2013. "Shaikh Mohammed inaugurates solar power park phase-1," *Khaleej Times* 10/23/2013. http://www.khaleejtimes.com/kt-article-display-

Senkovich, V. 2013. "The Arab World's Potential Importance to Russia's Economy." *Russian International Affairs Council.* http://russiancouncil.ru/en/inner/?id_4=1548#top, (last accessed 01/03/2014).

Seyid, Seyid Ould. 2011. "Mauritania police crush protest – doctors announce strike," *Radio Netherlands Worldwide,* Africa Desk, Mauritania. http://www.rnw.nl/africa/article/mauritania-police-crush-protest-doctors-announce-strike, (last retrieved 12/12/2012).

Shahminan, Fitri. 2013. "Brunei economy to grow 2.4pc in next four years," *Dawn.com*, http://www.dawn.com/news/1048280/brunei-economy-to-grow-24pc-in-next-four-years, (last accessed on 10/10/2013).

Smith & Nephew Corporate. 2012. "Smith & Nephew reaches settlement with US Government," *Smith & Nephew*, http://www.smith-nephew.com/news-and-media/news/smith-and-nephew-reaches-settlement-with-us-gover/, (last accessed on 12/12/2013).

Snyder, Michael. 2012. "45 Signs That China Is Colonizing America," *End of The American Dream*, http://endoftheamericandream.com/archives/45-signs-that-china-is-colonizing-america, (last accessed on 09/08/2013).

Soubbotina, Tatyana P. and Katherine A. Sheram. 2004. *Beyond Economic Growth: An Introduction to Sustainable Development*, World Bank, 2nd edition.

Spencer, R., 2011. "Libya: civil war breaks out as Gaddafi mounts rearguard fight," *The Telegraph*, http://www.telegraph.co.uk/news/worldnews/africaandindianocean/libya/8344034/Libya-civil-war-breaks-out-as-Gaddafi-mounts-rearguard-fight.html, (last accessed on 11/12/2013).

Stern, Melanie. 2012. "International Trade: CIVETS Economies," *Financial Director Newspaper*, London, UK. http://www.financialdirector.co.uk/financial-director/feature/2169190/international-trade-civets-economies, (last accessed on 11/03/2013).

Stout, David. 2009. "Ex-Rep. Jefferson Convicted in Bribery Scheme," *The New York Times*. p. A14. http://www.nytimes.com/2009/08/06/us/06jefferson.html, (last accessed on 06/14/2013).

Svensson, L.E.O. 2008. "Inflation Targeting," in S.N. Durlauf & L.E. Blume (Eds.), *The New Palgrave Dictionary of Economics, 2nd edition*. Palgrave Macmillan.

Taborda, Joana. 2013. "Death of the Dollar 2014: Euro Area GDP Growth Rate," *Trading Economics*, http://www.tradingeconomics.com/euro-area/gdp-growth, (last accessed on 12/15/2013).

Tarun Khanna and Krishna G. Palepu. 2010. *Winning in Emerging Markets: A Roadmap for Strategy and Execution*. Boston: Harvard Business School Publishing.

Telegraph Staff Writers. 2013. "Next chief Lord Wolfson launches £250,000 prize to solve housing crisis." *The Telegraph*, http://www.telegraph.co.uk/finance/newsbysector/constructionandproperty/10448303/Next-chief-Lord-Wolfson-launches-250000-prize-to-solve-housing-crisis.html, (last accessed on 12/11/2013).

The FCPA Blog. 2012, "Biomet Pays $22.8 Million To Settle Bribe Charges," *The FCPA Blog*, http://www.fcpablog.com/blog/2012/3/26/biomet-pays-228-million-to-settle-bribe-charges.html#, (last accessed on 09/09/2012).

Transparency International Secretariat. 2013. "Media Advisory: Major Exporters still lag in enforcing rules against foreign bribery," *Transparency International*, http://www.transparency.org/news/pressrelease/bribe_paying_still_very_high_worldwide_but_people_ready_to_fight_back, (last accessed on 12/14/2013).

U.S. Department of Justice. 2012. "Marubeni Corporation Resolves Foreign Corrupt Practices Act Investigation and Agrees to Pay a $54.6 Million Criminal Penalty," *U.S. Department of Justice*, http://www.justice.gov/opa/pr/2012/January/12-crm-060.html, (last accessed on 07/02/2013).

Vaidya, Sunil. 2011. "One dead, dozens injured as Oman protest turns ugly," *Gulf News*, Oman, http://gulfnews.com/news/gulf/oman/one-dead-dozen-injured-as-oman-protest-turns-ugly-1.768789, (last accessed on 11/01/2013).

Vale Columbia Center on Sustainable International Investment. 2009. "First ranking survey of Mexican multinationals finds grey diversity of industries," *Columbia Law School*, http://www.vcc.columbia.edu/files/vale/documents/EMGP-Mexico-Report-Final-09Dec09.pdf, (last accessed on 11/30/2013).

Wagstyl, S. 2013. "Eurasia: emerging markets are world's 'top risk' for 2013," *Financial Times*, http://blogs.ft.com/beyond-brics/2013/01/07/eurasia-emerging-markets-are-worlds-top-risk-for-2013/#axzz2nkpeGUB7, (last accessed on 12/17/2013).

Weggel, Oskar. 2006. "Cambodia in 2005: Year of Reassurance." *Asian Survey* 46 (1): 158.

Welch, D., and T. Weidlich. 2012. "Wal-Mart Bribery Probe May Exposes Retailer to U.S. Fines," *Bloomberg*, http://www.bloomberg.com/news/2012-04-23/wal-mart-bribery-probe-may-exposes-retailer-to-u-s-fines.html, (last accessed on 04/23/2012).

Werr, Patrick. 2013. "Egypt's economy to miss government growth forecasts: Reuters poll," *Reuters* Cairo, Egypt, http://www.reuters.com/article/2013/10/01/us-economy-egypt-poll-idUSBRE99012O20131001., (last accessed on 10/30/2013).

Wheatley, Alan. 2013. "Emerging markets thrive as eurozone suffers," *The International News,* http://www.thenews.com.pk/Todays-News-3–167386-Emerging-markets-thrive-as-eurozone-suffers, (last accessed on 11/10/2013).

Wiley Online Library. 2013. "Shlomit, Tourre, and Planton," http://onlinelibrary.wiley.com/doi/10.1029/2003GL017862/abstract, (last accessed on 11/01/2013).

Williams, R. 1983. *Capitalism (Revised Edition).* Oxford: Oxford University Press.

Wilson, D. and R. Purushothaman. 2003. "Dreaming with BRICs: The Path to 2050," *Global Economics Paper No. 99*, Goldman Sachs,, http://www.goldmansachs.com/our-thinking/archive/archive-pdfs/brics-dream.pdf, (last accessed on 04/05/11).

World Bank Staff Writers. 2012. "Doing Business 2014: Ease of Doing Business in Pakistan," *The World Bank.* http://www.doingbusiness.org/data/exploreeconomies/pakistan, (last accessed 11/10/2012).

World Bank Staff Writers. 2012. "World Development Indicators Database. Gross Domestic Product 2011," *The World Bank*, http://data.worldbank.org/data-catalog/world-development-indicators, (last accessed on 09/22/2012).

World Bank Staff Writers. 2013. "Doing Business: Measuring Business Regulations," *The World Bank*, http://www.doingbusiness.org/rankings, (last accessed on 09/22/2012).

World Bank Staff Writers. 2013. "An Update on Vietnam's Recent Economic Development July 2013: Key Findings," *The World Bank*, http://www.worldbank.org/en/news/feature/2013/07/12/taking-stock-july-2013-an-update-on-vietnams-recent-economic-development-key-findings, (last accessed on 11/05/2013).

World Bank Staff Writers. 2013. "Doing Business: Ease of Doing Business in Colombia," *The World Bank*, http://www.doingbusiness.org/data/exploreeconomies/colombia/, (last accessed in 06/12/2013).

World Bank Staff Writers. 2013. "Tourism in the Arab World can mean more than Sun, Sand and Beaches," *The World Bank*, http://www.worldbank.org/en/news/feature/2013/02/11/tourism-in-the-arab-world-can-mean-more-than-sun-sand-and-beaches, (last accessed 01/03/2014).

World Bank. 2008. *Middle East and North Africa Region 2007 economic developments and prospects: job creation in an era of high growth.* Washington, DC: World Bank. http://documents.worldbank.org/curated/en/2008/06/9520526/middleeast-north-africa-region-2007-economic-developments-prospects-job-creation-era-high-growth, (last accessed 04/12/2013).

Young, V. 2006. "Macquarie launches Australia's first BRIC funds," *InvestorDaily*, http://www.investordaily.com.au/25542-macquarie-launches-australias-first-bric-funds, (last accessed on 05/23/2007).

Zoffer, Joshua. 2012. "Future of Dollar Hegemony," *The Harvard International Review*, http://hir.harvard.edu/crafting-the-city/future-of-dollar-hegemony, (last accessed on 10/12/2012).

# Index

## OTHER TITLES FROM THE ECONOMICS COLLECTION

Philip Romero, The University of Oregon and Jeffrey Edwards,
North Carolina A&T State University, Editors

- *Managerial Economics: Concepts and Principles* by Donald Stengel
- *Your Macroeconomic Edge: Investing Strategies for the Post-Recession World* by Philip J. Romero
- *Working with Economic Indicators: Interpretation and Sources* by Donald Stengel
- *Innovative Pricing Strategies to Increase Profits* by Daniel Marburger
- *Regression for Economics* by Shahdad Naghshpour
- *Statistics for Economics* by Shahdad Naghshpour
- *How Strong Is Your Firm's Competitive Advantage?* by Daniel Marburger
- *A Primer on Microeconomics* by Thomas Beveridge
- *Game Theory: Anticipating Reactions for Winning Actions* by Mark L. Burkey
- *A Primer on Macroeconomics* by Thomas Beveridge
- *Economic Decision Making Using Cost Data: A Guide for Managers* by Daniel Marburger
- *The Fundamentals of Money and Financial Systems* by Shahdad Naghshpour
- *International Economics: Understanding the Forces of Globalization for Managers* by Paul Torelli
- *The Economics of Crime* by Zagros Madjd-Sadjadi
- *Money and Banking: An Intermediate Market-Based Approach* by William D. Gerdes
- *Basel III Liquidity Regulation and Its Implications* by Mark A. Petersen and Janine Mukuddem-Petersen
- *Saving American Manufacturing: The Fight for Jobs, Opportunity, and National Security* by William R. Killingsworth

# Announcing the Business Expert Press Digital Library

*Concise E-books Business Students Need
for Classroom and Research*

This book can also be purchased in an e-book collection by your library as
- a one-time purchase,
- that is owned forever,
- allows for simultaneous readers,
- has no restrictions on printing, and
- can be downloaded as PDFs from within the library community.

Our digital library collections are a great solution to beat the rising cost of textbooks. E-books can be loaded into their course management systems or onto students' e-book readers.

The **Business Expert Press** digital libraries are very affordable, with no obligation to buy in future years. For more information, please visit **www.businessexpertpress.com/librarians**. To set up a trial in the United States, please email **sales@businessexpertpress.com**.

CPSIA information can be obtained at www.ICGtesting.com
Printed in the USA
BVOW09*0257231214

380581BV00002B/2/P